JUDGING BUSH

STUDIES IN THE MODERN PRESIDENCY

A series edited by Shirley Anne Warshaw

Stanford University Press is pleased to announce *Studies in the Modern Presidency*, an innovative new book series that brings together established and emerging voices in modern presidential scholarship, from the Nixon administration to the present. We are interested in publishing leading work that charts new territory and frames the intellectual debate on the modern presidency.

Scholarship is emerging on presidential rhetoric, executive-legislative relations, executive privilege, domestic and foreign policy, signing statements, and so on. We seek to publish outstanding research and analysis that reach beyond conventional approaches to provide both scholars and students with insightful investigations into presidential politics and power.

This new series will feature short and incisive books that do not shy away from controversy. Our aim is for them to be widely read.

JUDGING BUSH

EDITED BY

Robert Maranto, Tom Lansford,
and Jeremy Johnson

Stanford University Press
Stanford, California

Stanford University Press
Stanford, California

Printed in the United States of America on acid-free, archival-quality paper

Library of Congress Cataloging-in-Publication Data

Judging Bush / edited by Robert Maranto, Tom Lansford, and Jeremy Johnson.
    p. cm.--(Studies in the modern presidency)
  Includes bibliographical references and index.
  ISBN 978-0-8047-6088-1 (cloth : alk. paper)--ISBN 978-0-8047-6089-8 (pbk. : alk.
paper)
    1. Bush, George W. (George Walker), 1946- 2. Presidents--United States--Evaluation.
3. Political leadership--United States--Evaluation. 4. United States--Politics and
government--2001-2009. 5. United States--Foreign relations--2001-2009. I. Maranto,
Robert, 1958- II. Lansford, Tom. III. Johnson, Jeremy, 1974-
  E902.J825 2009
  973.931092--dc22   2009024654

Designed by Bruce Lundquist
Typeset at Stanford University Press in 10/15 Sabon

Contents

CONTENTS

Contributors

ROBERT MARANTO is the 21st Century Chair in Leadership in the Department of Education Reform at the University of Arkansas in Fayetteville. Maranto's research interests include education reform, the presidency, and civil service reform. With others, he has produced numerous scholarly works, including *Beyond a Government of Strangers: How Career Executives and Political Appointees Can Turn Conflict to Cooperation* (Lexington, 2005), *The Second Term of George W. Bush* (Palgrave Macmillan, 2006), *A Guide to Charter Schools* (Rowman & Littlefield Education, 2006), and *The Politically Correct University* (AEI, 2009).

TOM LANSFORD is academic dean of the Gulf Coast campus and professor of political science, international development and international affairs at the University of Southern Mississippi. He is a member of the governing board of the National Social Science Association and the author or coauthor of numerous books, including *All for One: Terrorism, NATO and the United States* (Ashgate, 2002), *A Bitter Harvest: U.S. Foreign Policy and Afghanistan* (Ashgate, 2003), and *Strategic Preemption: US Foreign Policy and the Second War in Iraq* (Ashgate, 2004), and coeditor of *George W. Bush: The President at Midterm* (SUNY Press, 2004) and *The Second Term of George W. Bush* (Palgrave Macmillan, 2006).

JEREMY JOHNSON is currently a doctoral candidate in political science at Brown University in Providence, Rhode Island. His research interests include American political development, the U.S. presidency, public policy, and the welfare state. His dissertation is entitled *The Republican Welfare State*. He has contributed to several scholarly journals and books, such as *White House Studies*, the *International Journal of Public Administration*, and *The Second Term of George W. Bush: Prospects and Perils* (Palgrave Macmillan, 2006).

LARA M. BROWN has been assistant professor of political science at Villanova University since August 2007. Before returning to academia and teaching at California State University, Channel Islands, in 2005, she worked as an education policy and public affairs consultant. Brown also served in President William J. Clinton's administration as the coordinator for corporate outreach at the U.S. Department of Education in Washington, D.C. Her research interests include presidential aspirants, political parties, congressional incumbents, and national elections. She has published articles in the *Journal of Political Marketing, Presidential Studies Quarterly,* and *Congress and the Presidency* (forthcoming).

DAVID B. COHEN is an associate professor of political science and fellow in the Ray C. Bliss Institute of Applied Politics at the University of Akron. His research on executive politics and other topics has been published in a number of scholarly journals and book chapters. He is coeditor of *American National Security and Civil Liberties in an Era of Terrorism* (Palgrave Macmillan, 2004) and *The Final Arbiter: The Consequences of Bush v. Gore for Law and Politics* (SUNY Press, 2005). His primary areas of research and teaching interest are the American presidency, particularly White House organization, Congress, and U.S. homeland security policy.

JEFFREY E. COHEN is professor of political science at Fordham University and visiting senior research scholar, Center for the Study of Democratic Politics, Woodrow Wilson School of Public and International Affairs, Princeton University (2008–2009). He is author or editor of numerous books, including *The Presidency in an Era of 24-Hour News* (Princeton University Press, 2008), *Public Opinion in State Politics,* editor (Stanford University Press, 2006), and *Presidential Responsiveness and Public Policy Making: The Public and the Policies That Presidents Make* (University of Michigan Press, 1997). The latter won the 1998 Richard E. Neustadt Award from the Presidency Research Group of the American Political Science Association.

LAURA CONLEY is a graduate of Wesleyan University with a degree in government and a certificate in international relations. She is currently a special assistant for national security and international policy at the

Center for American Progress, where she researches defense and military affairs. Prior to joining the center, she worked as a presidential campaign field organizer in Iowa. She has published in the *Baltimore Sun*, the *Boston Globe*, and *Innovations: Technology, Governance, Globalization*. Conley previously completed internships with the Center of Concern and the office of Senator Russ Feingold. She studied European politics in Copenhagen, Denmark.

JACK COVARRUBIAS is an assistant professor of political science, international development and international affairs at the University of Southern Mississippi. He is also a member of the governing board of the National Social Science Association. He has published several works in the field of security studies and American foreign policy, most recently including a coauthored book, *To Protect and Defend: U.S. Homeland Security Policy* (Ashgate, 2006), and an edited volume, *Strategic Interests in the Middle East: Opposition or Support for U.S. Foreign Policy* (Ashgate, 2007). He is also coeditor of the forthcoming volume *America's War on Terror: A Reader*, second edition (Ashgate, 2009).

JOHN J. DIIULIO JR. is the Frederic Fox Leadership Professor of Politics, Religion, and Civil Society at the University of Pennsylvania. He has directed public policy research centers at Princeton University, the Brookings Institution, the Manhattan Institute, and Public/Private Ventures. In 2001, he served as assistant to President George W. Bush and first director of the White House Office of Faith-Based and Community Initiatives. He is author or coauthor of books, including *Godly Republic: A Centrist Blueprint for America's Faith-Based Future* (University of California Press, 2007) and *Fine Print: The Contract with America, Devolution, and the Administrative Realities of American Federalism* (Brookings Institution Press, 1995), with Donald F. Kettl.

WILLIAM A. GALSTON holds the Ezra Zilkha Chair in Governance Studies at the Brookings Institution and is College Park Professor at the University of Maryland. He is a former policy advisor to President Clinton and presidential candidates, as well as an expert on domestic policy, political campaigns, and elections. His current research focuses on designing a new social contract and the implications of political polarization. He has authored numerous books and articles in political theory, American politics, and public policy, including *The Practice of Liberal Pluralism* (Cambridge University Press, 2005) and *Public Matters: Essays on Politics, Policy and Religion* (Rowman & Littlefield, 2005).

FREDERICK M. HESS is director of education policy studies at the American Enterprise Institute (AEI) and executive editor of *Education Next*. His many books include *When Research Matters* (Harvard Education Press, 2008), *No Remedy Left Behind* (AEI, 2007), *No Child Left Behind: A Primer* (Peter Lang, 2006), *Revolution at the Margins* (Brookings Institution Press, 2002), and *Spinning Wheels* (Brookings Institution Press, 1998). He holds an M.Ed. in teaching and curriculum and an M.A. and Ph.D. in government from Harvard University. Prior to joining AEI, Hess taught high school in Louisiana and was a professor of education and politics at the University of Virginia.

KAREN M. HULT is professor of political science at Virginia Polytechnic Institute and State University. Her primary research interests are the U.S. executive, organization theory and institutional design, and social science methodologies. She is the author or coauthor of numerous works, including *Empowering the White House: Governance Under Nixon, Ford and Carter* (University Press of Kansas, 2004), *Governing the White House: From Hoover Through LBJ* (University Press of Kansas, 1995), and *Governing Public Organizations* (Brooks/Cole, 1990). She is a past president of the American Political Science Association's Presidency Research Group, on the editorial boards of *Congress and the Presidency* and *Rhetoric and Public Affairs*, and book review editor of *Presidential Studies Quarterly*.

LORI A. JOHNSON is an assistant professor in the Department of Political Science at Mercer University in Macon, Georgia. She has published works on comparative regulation and court rule-making. In addition, she has coauthored a chapter on the federal courts and the George W. Bush administration in *The Second Term of George W. Bush* (Palgrave Macmillan, 2006). She won the American Political Science Association's Corwin Award for her dissertation on policy making for the federal courts, which she is currently revising for publication. She obtained her Ph.D.

from the University of California, Berkeley, in 2003 and a J.D. from the University of Virginia in 1989.

ROBERT G. KAUFMAN is professor of public policy at the Pepperdine School of Public Policy. He specializes in American foreign policy, national security, international relations, and various aspects of American politics. Kaufman received his J.D. from Georgetown University Law School and his Ph.D. from Columbia University. He has written numerous works, including *In Defense of the Bush Doctrine* (University Press of Kentucky, 2008), *Arms Control During the Pre-Nuclear Era* (Columbia University Press, 1990), and *Henry M. Jackson: A Life in Politics* (University of Washington Press, 2000), which received the Emil and Katherine Sick Award for the best book on the history of the Pacific Northwest.

ANNE M. KHADEMIAN is associate professor with Virginia Tech's Center for Public Administration and Policy, Alexandria Center. She received her Ph.D. in political science from Washington University in St. Louis and was a research fellow at the Brookings Institution. She is the author of *The SEC and Capital Market Regulation: The Politics of Expertise* (University of Pittsburgh Press, 1992), *Checking on Banks: Autonomy and Accountability in Three Federal Agencies* (Brookings Institution Press, 1996), and *Working with Culture: The Way the Job Gets Done in Public Programs* (CQ Press, 2002), and coauthor of *The Enduring Debate: Classic and Contemporary Readings in American Politics* (Norton, 2000), as well as author of numerous articles in public policy and public management.

LAWRENCE J. KORB is senior fellow at the Center for American Progress and senior advisor to the Center for Defense Information. Before that, he was a senior fellow and director of national security studies at the Council on Foreign Relations. From July 1998 to October 2002, he was council vice president, director of studies, and holder of the Maurice Greenberg Chair. Korb was assistant secretary of defense (manpower, reserve affairs, installations and logistics) from 1981 through 1985. His publications include *A New National Security Strategy in an Age of Terrorists, Tyrants, and Weapons of Mass Destruction: Three Options Presented as Presidential Speeches* (Council on Foreign Relations Press, 2003).

PATRICK J. MCGUINN is an assistant professor of political science at Drew University. His research interests are in national politics and institutions, education and social welfare policy, American political development, federalism, and the policy-making process. His first book, *No Child Left Behind and the Transformation of Federal Education Policy, 1965–2005* (University Press of Kansas, 2006), was honored as a Choice Outstanding Academic Title. McGuinn also has written several peer-reviewed publications, including "The Policy Landscape of Educational Entrepreneurship," in *Educational Entrepreneurship: Realities, Challenges, and Possibilities*, edited by Frederick Hess (Harvard Education Press, 2006).

MICHAEL P. MORELAND is assistant professor of law at Villanova University. Before joining the Villanova faculty, he was associate director for domestic policy at the White House, where he was responsible for coordinating policy development on a range of legal issues, including immigration, crime, civil rights, and tort reform. He has published and spoken on tort law, law and religion, and bioethics. Moreland's publications include "Subsidiarity, Localism and School Finance," *Journal of Catholic Social Thought* 369(2) (2005), and "Jacques Maritain, Thomism, and the Liberal-Communitarian Debate," in *The Failure of Modernism: The Cartesian Legacy and Contemporary Pluralism*, edited by Brendan Sweetman (American Maritain Association, 1999).

COSTAS PANAGOPOULOS is assistant professor of political science and director of the Center for Electoral Politics and the master's program in elections and campaign management at Fordham University. His academic research focuses on American politics, with an emphasis on campaigns and elections, voting behavior, public opinion and Congress, and has been published in the *American Journal of Political Science, Public Opinion Quarterly, Presidential Studies Quarterly, Electoral Studies,* and *PS: Political Science and Politics*. He is editor of *Rewiring Politics: Presidential Nominating Conventions in the Media Age* (Louisiana State University Press, 2007) and coauthor of *All Roads Lead to Congress: The $300 Billion Fight over Highway Funding* (CQ Press, 2007).

JAMES P. PFIFFNER is currently professor in the School of Public Policy at George Mason University and has occupied a number of academic and professional positions. He has written or edited twelve books on the presidency and American national government, including *The Strategic Presidency: Hitting the Ground Running*, second edition (University Press of Kansas, 1996), *The Modern Presidency*, fourth edition (Wadsworth, 2004), *The Character Factor: How We Judge Our Presidents* (Texas A&M University Press, 2004), and *Power Play: The Bush Administration and the Constitution* (Brookings Institution Press, 2008), as well as *Understanding the Presidency*, coedited with Roger H. Davidson (HarperCollins, 1997).

RICHARD E. REDDING is professor of law at Chapman University Law School. He has produced numerous scholarly works, including *Juvenile Delinquency: Assessment, Prevention, and Intervention* (Oxford University Press, 2005) and *The Politically Correct University* (AEI, 2009). Redding was professor of law at Villanova University, research professor of psychology at Drexel University, and director of the J.D./Ph.D. program in law and psychology at Villanova and Drexel Universities. He was also assistant professor and associate director of the Institute of Law, Psychiatry, and Public Policy at the University of Virginia School of Law, teaching on a range of subject areas.

NEIL REEDY holds a bachelor's degree in both history and political science and a master's degree in political science from Villanova University, where he authored the paper "Judging the Presidency: Foreign Policy as the Dominant Criteria." He has also contributed articles to a political website and has publications in the journal *Intelligence and National Security* (forthcoming) and a coauthored chapter, "The Evolution of Homeland Security and the War on Terror," in *America's War on Terror: A Reader*, second edition (Ashgate, 2009). He is currently an intelligence analyst for the U.S. government and lives in Falls Church, Virginia.

ANDREW RUDALEVIGE is the Walter Beach '56 Distinguished Chair in Political Science at Dickinson College in Carlisle, Pennsylvania. He is the author, coauthor, or editor of several books, including *The George W. Bush Legacy* (CQ Press, 2007), *The New Imperial Presidency: Renewing Presidential Power After Watergate* (University of Michigan Press, 2005), and *Managing the President's Program* (Princeton University Press,

2002). The latter won the Richard E. Neustadt Award as that year's best book on the presidency. In addition, Rudalevige has produced a number of scholarly journal articles, including "The Structure of Leadership: Presidents, Hierarchies, and Information Flow," *Presidential Studies Quarterly* 35 (June 2005).

CHARLES E. WALCOTT is professor of political science at Virginia Polytechnic Institute and State University. His research interests are political organizations and the institution of the U.S. presidency. He has written, co-written, or edited five books with Karen M. Hult, including *Empowering the White House: Governance Under Nixon, Ford and Carter* (University Press of Kansas, 2004), *Governing the White House: From Hoover Through LBJ* (University Press of Kansas, 1995), and *Governing Public Organizations* (Brooks/Cole, 1990). He also has produced or contributed to a number of scholarly essays. Walcott's articles have appeared in the *American Journal of Political Science*, *Congress and the Presidency*, *Polity*, *Presidential Studies Quarterly*, and other scholarly journals.

SHIRLEY ANNE WARSHAW is professor of political science at Gettysburg College, Gettysburg, Pennsylvania. She is the author of numerous books, including *The Clinton Years* (Checkmark, 2004), *The Keys to Power: Managing the Presidency*, second edition (Longman, 2005; 1st ed. 1999), *The Domestic Presidency: Decision Making in the White House* (Longman, 1996), *Powersharing: White House–Cabinet Relations in the Modern Presidency* (SUNY Press, 1996), *Reexamining the Eisenhower Presidency* (Greenwood, 1993), and *The Eisenhower Legacy* (Bartleby, 1991). She has recently written a book entitled *The Co-Presidency of Bush and Cheney* (Stanford University Press, 2009). Her research interests are concentrated on organizational decision structures for presidential decision making.

Preface: A Call for Modesty

THE GENESIS OF THIS BOOK came early in the second Bush term while I served in Villanova University's political science department, a productive and humane environment for teaching and research with wonderfully stimulating hallway conversations—as academia is meant to be but all too often is not. An outstanding graduate student, Neil Reedy, had insisted against the advice of Professor David Barrett and me not to write his thesis on presidential greatness. We warned Neil that most of the attempts to judge presidents are fuzzy to the point of incoherence. Lacking rigor, many such works serve merely to reinforce the predispositions of their authors, adding more heat than light. As Al Felzenberg (2008) points out in his insightful *The Leaders We Deserved (And a Few We Didn't): Rethinking the Presidential Rating Game*, in academia most of the arbiters of presidential greatness favor activist presidents who grow government, reflecting the left-of-center biases of modern social scientists and historians. The few right-of-center approaches are similarly "results oriented."

Eventually, Neil convinced me that despite the obstacles, both democracy and inquiry require that voters and scholars have *some* basis for judging presidents. In his thesis, Neil took from the best of the presidency literature to set forth reasonably coherent criteria for judgment. His provocative efforts led David Barrett, Tom Lansford, and former Villanova graduate student and Brown University doctoral candidate Jeremy Johnson to join me in discussions of how to make judging presidents more systematic, particularly in light of the controversial George W. Bush presidency. To do so, Tom, Jeremy, and I brought together nearly two dozen prominent scholars. This book is the result.

Of course, as Bush himself points out, historians still debate the presidency of the first GW, George Washington; so it requires some chutzpah for us to spring out of the box with evaluations of the forty-third presidency (Shenkman 2007). To this we have three responses. First, by employing the criteria set out in Neil Reedy and Jeremy Johnson's introductory chapter, we feel that this work is clearer and more systematic than most such analyses. Second, the quality of our contributing authors demands respect. Finally, we have purposely commissioned a diverse set of authors and encouraged them to interact with one another, to guard against the groupthink that so commonly occurs in both the White House and the ivory tower. The three editors themselves have very different political views, translating into somewhat different evaluations of the Bush presidency. In short, someone must be the first to attempt a systematic judgment of this presidency, and we are as well positioned as any.

Still, here at the end of the beginning, I wish to underscore the uncertain character of our enterprise. In particular, those who have not served in government should exercise modesty in judging those who have. Presidents and other policymakers work in highly unstable and unpredictable environments. Those of us in the ivory tower, like all citizens, can and should judge our leaders—that is key to democracy—but we should not entertain illusions that we could do better than they. Similarly, we must not practice faith-based social science, and so must remain tentative in our judgments. Bound by our own biases and the limited information of our own time, our evaluations of President Bush must be regarded as among the first words on this topic, not the last. Like good leadership, good scholarship requires humility. I learned this the hard way: I initially judged President Reagan a failure in office. Only later, after serving in government, did I come to view the old actor as the greatest president of my lifetime.

Finally, like all of us, presidents do best when forced to make accommodations with others, thereby broadening those to whom they are bound. The Bush presidency seemingly shows the wisdom of the framers in designing divided government. Arguably, Presidents Reagan, Clinton, and both Bushes were most effective and least prone to overreach with grand plans when the other party controlled at least one branch of Congress. At this, James Madison would smile.

ROBERT MARANTO
FAYETTEVILLE, ARKANSAS
JANUARY 2009

REFERENCES

Felzenberg, Alvin S. 2008. *The Leaders We Deserved (And a Few We Didn't): Rethinking the Presidential Rating Game.* New York: Basic Books.

Shenkman, Rick. 2007. "George Bush's Misplaced Hope That Historians Will Rank Him Higher than His Contemporaries." *History News Network*, January 1. http://hnn.us/articles/33283.html (Accessed January 3, 2009).

Acknowledgments

MANY PEOPLE helped bring this project to fruition. While teaching at Villanova, Robert Maranto had the good fortune to work with remarkable colleagues and students, who helped with this project in ways large and small, particularly David Barrett, Jason O'Brien, Bob Langran, Diane Mozzone, Markus Kreuzer, Catherine Warrick, and Catherine Wilson. He also received support from a great team of academic administrators, including Jack Johannes, Father Kail Ellis, Tom Smith, Milton Coles, and Lowell Gustafson. His new colleagues at the University of Arkansas were no less supportive, with particular kudos to Dirk van Raemdonck, who kept both the trains and authors running on time. In addition, Andrew Dowdle of the political science department provided useful advice along the way. Reed Greenwood, Heidi Stambuck, and Jay Greene were among the many administrators who gave help rather than hindrance. Professor Maranto also wishes to thank John Brown III of the Wingate Foundation for the material backing for projects such as this. Finally, Maranto's wife, April, was an endless source of ideas, while the Maranto family king and queen, Tony and Maya, provided joyful distraction.

As always, Tom Lansford would like to thank Gina, Ella, and Kate for their inspiration and love, and Dean Denise von Herrmann of the University of Southern Mississippi for her material and administrative support.

Jeremy Johnson wishes to thank his loving and ever supportive family, parents William and Jeanette Johnson and siblings Lynette, Jeffrey, Lysbeth, and Jason.

Finally, all three editors wish to thank Stacy Wagner and Jessica Walsh of Stanford University Press, our two anonymous reviewers, and the contributing authors for helping make this book on time, under budget, and, we hope, of significant scholarly merit.

RM   TL   JJ

JUDGING BUSH

PART ONE

Introduction

President Bush in Comparative Perspective

CHAPTER I

Evaluating Presidents

NEIL REEDY AND JEREMY JOHNSON

EVALUATING PRESIDENTS is a notoriously hazardous and often sloppy enterprise. Establishing objective criteria to judge presidents removed from partisan preferences is an elusive goal for scholars, journalists, and the public. Yet such chief executives as Franklin Roosevelt, Abraham Lincoln, and George Washington consistently rank at the top of surveys by scholars, with Warren Harding, Franklin Pierce, and James Buchanan at the bottom. Perhaps the most common characteristic of high-ranking presidents is the energy of the executive in times of crisis: they did not fear testing the boundaries of presidential powers.[1] Conversely, less-regarded presidents failed to offer energetic leadership or bold policy proposals.

Perhaps taking this lesson to heart, George W. Bush, the nation's forty-third chief executive, determined to leave his mark on the nation and the presidency. Elected without a popular mandate in 2000, he still chose to govern assertively. Bush's presidency certainly did not lack crises to test his mettle. He faced in the early days the terrorist attacks of September 11, 2001, and ended his administration trying to quell one of the gravest economic and financial crises since the Great Depression. In the middle of his presidency, he had to both manage the reconstruction efforts in Iraq and account for his administration's response to Hurricane Katrina. It might be said that Bush was besieged with opportunities.

The presidency, in the words of Stephen Skowronek, works best as a "battering ram," demolishing old, enervated systems (1997, 27–28). It does not function as effectively in building new structures to replace the discarded models. A president needs to sense when the time is ripe for assertive leadership. Typically, greatness has been thrust on presidents because of the political times: a president cannot make himself "great" by virtue of willing it through activity.[2] This is a dilemma that Bush, like all his presidential counterparts, has had to negotiate. How adroitly and competently did Bush and his entourage govern during his eight years in office? Did he take advantage of the opportunity for powerful leadership? Did he imagine opportunities that were not really there? Or did he have the opportunity but fail to respond effectively?[3]

Bush aggressively pushed policy—from cutting taxes to education reform—since the opening days of his administration. Moreover, after terrorism moved to the forefront of the political agenda, he promoted a robust, indeed explosive, foreign agenda. Bush self-consciously modeled himself as an active president who "hit the ground running" (Pfiffner 1996; Kettl 2003), yet currently both the contemporary scholarly community and the public judge Bush a failure (McElvaine 2008). A smaller cohort of scholars staunchly defends Bush.[4]

Scholarly disagreement is matched by an unprecedented lack of public consensus. Diverging partisan assessments were apparent during Bush's contentious 2004 reelection campaign, when political scientist Gary Jacobson found that 90.5 percent of Republicans but only 15.2 percent of Democrats approved of Bush's handling of the job (Brownstein 2007, 16). Bush's popularity decreased further during his second term. Only a third of respondents approved of his performance in the three years after Hurricane Katrina, with the decline coming mainly from political independents. Republicans still had a favorable view of the president, usually in the 70 percent range (Connelly 2007). This "hyperpartisanship" makes it all the more difficult to dispassionately rank George W. Bush, a theme developed by Jeffrey E. Cohen and Costas Panagopoulos in this volume.

In this chapter, we attempt to sort the wheat from the chaff by reviewing how the scholarly literature has grappled with the proper criteria for judging presidents. The question of how to rank and evaluate presidents is not new. Arthur Schlesinger Sr. pioneered the presidential ranking genre in the November 1, 1948, issue of *Life* magazine. He assembled a team of fifty-five authorities on American history to categorize presidents into groupings of great, near great, average, below average, and failures.[5] Subsequent scholars, journalists, and writers have made a virtual cottage industry of emulating Schlesinger's methods (Murray and Blessing 1994,

16–17, 81; Schlesinger Jr. 1997; Ridings and McIver 1997, xi; C-SPAN 1999; Federalist Society–*Wall Street Journal* 2005).

Moving beyond somewhat arbitrary rankings, the political science literature on the presidency has attempted more-systematic assessments of presidents, a half dozen of which we will discuss. We categorize the literature evaluating presidents as centered on (1) foreign policy, (2) domestic policy, (3) political skills, (4) presidential opportunity level, (5) presidential character, and (6) political organization. We frame these criteria around the content of crises. Following our treatment of these, we will propose our own four criteria to judge the George W. Bush administration, an eight-year period certainly not short of defining moments.[6]

FOREIGN POLICY

It is common for a president to endure a tumultuous relationship with Congress regarding domestic policy. Historically, this squabbling largely disappears when the arena shifts to foreign affairs; hence the cliché that "party politics stops at the water's edge."[7] As long ago as the first half of the nineteenth century, Alexis de Tocqueville wrote that "it is chiefly in its foreign relations that the executive power of a nation finds occasion to exert its skill and its strength" (Tocqueville [1956] 2001, 80). This dynamic was captured by Aaron Wildavsky's "two presidencies," one limited in domestic power and the other granted vast latitude in foreign policy, power further accentuated in times of crisis (Wildavsky 1969).[8] Both Congress and the courts traditionally give the president wide discretion in foreign policy matters. Congress has sanctioned every significant military action undertaken by a president throughout history, usually by large bipartisan majorities. The president has the de facto prerogative to launch the nation into war—a legacy modern presidents have inherited from Harry Truman (Berger 1974). These developments over the course of American history are aptly encapsulated by the adage "deployment is destiny" (Reedy 2008).

Conduct of war also falls under the rubric of the president's discretion, in part due to the "rally around the flag" effect, which increases presidential popularity in wartime (Mueller 1973). Between the Cold War and the twenty-first-century War on Terror, the post–World War II era has seen nearly continual international crises. An enhanced foreign policy presidency has quite possibly increased presidential interest and influence in domestic activity. During Dwight Eisenhower's administration, the capital to build the nation's network of highways and to increase funding for education came in the name of national defense. Presidential interest in civil rights stemmed at least in part from concern about America's reputation overseas rather than concerns over domestic equity. Likewise, presidents since Nixon have emphasized the importance of energy independence. Global contingencies give the president a greater hand in determining domestic policy.

However, global entanglements are a two-sided coin. Popularity from military success is often fleeting (Mueller 1973), as George H.W. Bush found to his chagrin after the quick prosecution of the Gulf War in 1991, and as his son learned after a quick victory over the Taliban in Afghanistan. Perhaps even more daunting for a president is being commander in chief during a prolonged, unpopular war. Continued American fatalities without measurable progress can overshadow domestic successes. The Vietnam conflict doomed Lyndon Johnson's prospects of fully funding and implementing his "Great Society" and "War on Poverty." Similarly, George W. Bush's handling of the Iraq War cost him clout on Capitol Hill and in the opinion polls, which contributed to his failure to transform Social Security and to pass immigration reform. After Democrats took control of Congress in 2006, Bush became an early lame duck unable to pass significant legislation. This was a radical departure from his first-term stature, when he was at the nexus of major reforms in taxation, education policy, and Medicare, all the while galvanizing the nation for wars against Afghanistan and Iraq.

Clearly, the signature initiative of the Bush administration is the war in Iraq; indeed, if that war had been more successfully prosecuted (or avoided altogether), President Bush would have ended his term with much higher public standing, and likely would earn a positive judgment from history. To varying degrees, this is a theme of the first, fourth, and fifth parts of this volume.

DOMESTIC POLICY

Proponents of foreign policy–centered approaches to judging presidents sometimes suggest that domestic policies are largely irrelevant since they require congressional cooperation. For instance, Franklin Roosevelt and

Lyndon Johnson were successful in expanding the welfare state because these presidents had overwhelming Democratic majorities in Congress.

However, domestic achievements are possible even without large partisan majorities in Congress. For instance, the passage of several modern presidents' plans to reduce taxes occurred despite small or no majorities in Congress. Ronald Reagan managed this feat despite Democratic majorities in the House of Representatives. George W. Bush replayed this scenario several times by reducing taxes despite slim majorities in the House, and at times no majority in the Senate. He also revamped Medicare and added a prescription drug benefit on essentially Republican terms, with little Democratic support, by the slimmest of margins in Congress. Bill Clinton was able to pass a tax hike in 1993 for the purposes of deficit reduction, without any Republican support and only modest Democratic majorities in Congress. It seems possible for a president who operates adroitly with Congress to build lasting domestic achievements without recourse to foreign military interventions.

Winning elections frequently turns on domestic policy. In 1992, Bill Clinton rode economic anxiety to the White House by defeating a president who seemed unbeatable just a year before. Most legislation coming from Congress is domestic in nature; the president is forced, whether willing or not, to devote considerable resources to it (Light 1999, 7). As Donald Peppers (1975) argued, presidential decisions on economic matters, from import quotas to floating the dollar, can affect inflation, economic growth, and unemployment. He believed that domestic policy would become the main avenue for a president to leave his mark, despite sharing powers with Congress. If voters care primarily about domestic policy when choosing a president, so too should those who rank chief executives.[9]

For a Republican administration, the Bush presidency has pursued an active domestic agenda. The president forced through a series of controversial tax cuts, promoted and signed into law a major education bill, and presided over a major expansion and reorientation of Medicare by adding a prescription drug benefit. Bush aimed for even more revolutionary domestic achievements, hoping to introduce private accounts into Social Security. However, the aptly named third rail of politics proved too formidable for the president to refashion. The third part of the book is devoted to Bush's domestic legacy.

POLITICAL SKILLS

Other scholars stress not only policy but also political skills. We have already seen Pfiffner's advice about "hitting the ground running." Along with Pfiffner, scholars such as John P. Burke (2000) emphasize the role that management and organization play in a successful presidency.

Richard Neustadt's seminal *Presidential Power and the Modern Presidents* argues that the informal power to persuade is an indispensable talent necessary for a president to succeed. As Harry Truman once lamented, "I sit here all day trying to persuade people to do the things they ought to have sense enough to do without my persuading them. . . . That's all the powers of the President amount to" (Neustadt 1990, 10). Neustadt and Truman mainly were referring to persuading political elites. However, many see a president's ability to communicate to a mass audience as a prerequisite for accomplishment. Ronald Reagan's effectiveness is often attributed to his ability as a "Great Communicator." Franklin Roosevelt's "fireside chats" likewise helped mobilize support for his agenda. In the nineteenth century, presidents rarely made rhetorical appeals to the public. What Jeffrey Tulis (1987) calls the "rhetorical presidency" is essentially a twentieth-century phenomenon.[10] Theodore Roosevelt and Woodrow Wilson were two of the first presidents to employ public appearances to mobilize support for preferred policy. Yet scholars such as Tulis, George Edwards (2003), and Samuel Kernell (2007) raise questions as to the degree that "going public" actually helps presidents obtain results. George W. Bush's failed Social Security gambit is the latest in a long line of failed high-profile public campaigns for presidential initiatives stretching back to Woodrow Wilson's stumping for a League of Nations.

Other respected presidency literature emphasizes the limitations that presidents, no matter how deft, face in influencing outcomes. Two studies on presidential-congressional relations emphasize this point in different ways. Edwards (1989, 224) explains how presidential skill and leadership work only at the "margins." The president is a "facilitator," not a "director" of change. Even while FDR supposedly performed the executive function most effectively during the first one hundred days of his first term, the durable portions of the New Deal were not created. Social Security did not pass until 1935 and was the product, according to Edwards, of forces other than presidential leadership. Charles O. Jones (2005) concurs, emphasizing the particular limitations on the presidency as a component of a separated system. He warns of isolating the presidency from the Congress and the bureaucracy. Thus, a rich debate exists over how much choreographed management contributes to an effective presidency.

Bush's political skills are still debated. He ran an efficient electioneering team, winning narrowly twice. Arguably, his ability to govern improved over time; for instance, he seemed better able to competently manage the Iraq War in the last two years of his presidency. The great irony is that as Bush's adeptness in governing may have been on the upswing, his popularity took a nosedive, as public opinion seems to have been a lagging indicator in judging Bush's handling of the presidency.

PRESIDENTIAL OPPORTUNITY LEVELS

A vibrant political science literature underscores the role that external, or structural, factors play in creating successful presidents. Chief executives are not intrinsically able to govern capably because of their own stratagems: other forces play a decisive role in determining a president's legacy.

For instance, William Lammers and Michael Genovese (2000) follow a modified structural interpretation by categorizing modern presidents according to levels of opportunity to influence events. Franklin Roosevelt, Lyndon Johnson, and Ronald Reagan rate as the presidents with the highest opportunity, while Richard Nixon, Jimmy Carter, George H. W. Bush, and Bill Clinton had minimal opportunities—a matter apparently lamented by Clinton (Morris 1997, 305–8). External factors, such as crises and national mood, are the main contributing factors influencing whether a president can make major contributions. Presidents have the opportunity to outperform or underperform because of managerial competence or personality—but a low-opportunity president will never have the chance to perform that a high-opportunity president has.

A variant of this conceptual framework is suggested by Stephen Skowronek (1997, 2008). He theorizes that a president's place in political time helps to determine whether history will brand him a "great president." He posits that presidents must act within the constraints of recurring cycles or regimes. The founder of a regime, a "reconstitutive" president, has a strong

[handwritten margin note: Judgments Based on Chance]

9

chance to be remembered favorably. For instance, Franklin Roosevelt broke a string of laissez-faire Republican presidents and created the New Deal regime featuring a robust domestic agenda. Other presidents who formed new regimes include Thomas Jefferson, Andrew Jackson, Abraham Lincoln, and probably Ronald Reagan. The "worst" presidents govern at the end of enervated regimes. These "disjunction presidents" cannot address crises, because they are constrained by antiquated governing methodologies. Franklin Pierce, James Buchanan, Herbert Hoover, and probably Jimmy Carter are the "failures" unlucky enough to govern in unhappy times. Skowronek's structural explanation accords greatness because of political time and minimizes attributes of individual presidential decision making. External structures also explain a president's policy-making success for Jon Bond and Richard Fleisher (1990). They trace presidential success in passing legislation. Bond and Fleisher explicitly find that presidential success derived more from the partisan and ideological constitution of Congress rather than intrinsic presidential characteristics such as popularity or bargaining power. They thereby discount presidential skill. Those holding this perspective might even question the utility of judging presidents, or indeed the whole notion of "greatness."

In a somewhat different vein, Brandice Canes-Wrone argues that patterns of presidential behavior are often driven by external circumstances. The president is not usually a panderer to public opinion; however, he emphasizes positions that he believes the people will embrace, particularly where public support is needed to move Congress. All presidents will hold unpopular positions; however, this part of the president's agenda tends to be hidden from public view. According to Canes-Wrone, presidents pander to public opinion and endorse positions they do not believe in when election outcomes seemingly hang in the balance. Of course, the entire George W. Bush presidency has involved cliff-hanger elections, and Canes-Wrone opens her book with a scene of Bush pandering and reversing course on the creation of the Department of Homeland Security in 2002 (Canes-Wrone 2006, 1–3).

Did George W. Bush govern in a time of high opportunity? The terrorist attacks of September 11, 2001, certainly suggest that he had more opportunity than most of his predecessors. He also governed with a fairly pliant Congress during the first half dozen years of his administration. But did this lack of congressional oversight prove to be a boon or a curse? One aim of this volume is to offer tentative answers to this question, a matter addressed in part by Andrew Rudalevige's chapter.

PRESIDENTIAL CHARACTER

Character is another criterion used for judging presidents. Its proponents hold that exogenous forces, policy statements, and the like do not explain the essence of presidential behavior. The course of events shaping success or failure often rests on the personality traits of an executive. This approach derives from James David Barber (1985), who developed a model attempting to predict presidential behavior in office.[11]

More recently, James P. Pfiffner (2004) examines issues of presidential character in *The Character Factor: How We Judge America's Presidents.* Like most observers, he attributes the demise of the Nixon presidency to Nixon's paranoia, which resulted in the Watergate burglary and cover-up. However, Pfiffner believes that character is complex and works as a double-edged sword. For instance, Pfiffner sees both positive and negative aspects in the last two presidencies. Clinton's tenacity led him to push the aforementioned 1993 deficit-reduction act through Congress. He faced unanimous Republican opposition, and the bill disappointed many of his own supporters. On the other hand, a negative consequence of Clinton's character was the fallout from his tawdry affair with a White House intern, Monica Lewinsky. The resoluteness of Bush's character was on full display after the attacks of September 11, 2001, a matter praised by many, including Robert Kaufman, a contributor to this volume. Bush's resoluteness also seemingly remade the judiciary, as Lori Johnson and Michael Moreland point out. However, other contributors, including Robert Maranto and Richard Redding; James Pfiffner, Lawrence Korb, and Laura Conley; and William Galston see resoluteness as stubbornness in the face of new information, particularly regarding the Iraq War.

The study of presidential psychology is most fully developed in Stanley Renshon's (1996, 2004) studies of Clinton and George W. Bush. Renshon, while not claiming character to be the sole determinant of the effectiveness of presidential leadership, believes character to be a very significant variable in presidential behavior. While Renshon's study of Clinton was hailed as insightful and penetrating, his study of Bush has engendered more controversy, since he has judged that president "reflective and heroic"—a conclusion that strikes many as mistaken. This is a theme developed further in the chapter by Maranto and Redding.

POLITICAL ORGANIZATION

A final interpretative approach squarely addresses the cliché quality of presidential greatness. Marc Landy and Sidney Milkis argue that highly regarded presidents are all distant memories. Their thesis is that when political parties are weak—or presidents are not tied intricately to the party organization—opportunities to exhibit greatness reach a nadir. Landy and Milkis, following Young's lead, attribute the lack of great presidential leadership in the time between Jefferson and Jackson as at least partially due to the lack of party competition (Young 1966, 250–54; Landy and Milkis 2000, 9).[12] The fourth and fifth presidents, James Madison and James Monroe, were accomplished statesmen previous to their accession to the presidency, but their administrations faltered in part due to the lack of spirited party competition. Landy and Milkis (2000, 198) also claim that there have been no great presidents since Franklin Roosevelt, partly because Roosevelt changed the presidency from an institution defined as a partisan entity to one that served as the head of an "administrative state in the service of programmatic rights." Coupled with a prolonged Cold War, presidents had little opportunity to demonstrate greatness, with only two, Lyndon Johnson and Ronald Reagan, even making creditable attempts.[13] Bush may also have had notions of achieving greatness with the development of an ambitious agenda; yet, he too probably will fall short, according to Landy and Milkis's approach.

emphasis on competence

HOW TO JUDGE BUSH?

In sum, the literature on appropriate criteria for judging presidents has wildly divergent points of emphasis. Yet all emphasize *competence*. Synthesizing the previous literature, the volume editors propose to distinguish four types of competence: (1) strategic, (2) political, (3) tactical, and (4) moral.

Strategic competence refers to a president's long-term influence on

(durability?)[12]

the policy regime, which usually includes the articulation and successful implementation of a clear policy vision. George W. Bush worked to
build a clear policy vision in order to avoid the fates of Jimmy Carter and
George H.W. Bush, who both lacked a discerning strategic vision, which
arguably contributed to their reelection defeats. Yet measuring strategic
competence through domestic accomplishments is rather exceptional. Only
three modern presidents—Franklin Roosevelt, Lyndon Johnson, and Ronald Reagan—probably qualify as having domestic accomplishments that
vastly weigh into their permanent assessments. The clear policy visions set
forth by these three have helped establish them as larger-than-life figures in
political lore. More frequently, a president's foreign policy outweighs his
domestic agenda in long-term judgments. Thus, the prestige of presidents
such as James K. Polk, Woodrow Wilson, and Harry S Truman, who were
often unpopular in their own times, has generally risen over the years.
Richard Nixon's rapprochement with China helped reshape the landscape
of international politics, bolstering some evaluations of his presidency.
Final assessments of George W. Bush's presidency, which also witnessed
an active and controversial foreign policy, will probably be determined
from the outcomes of the two wars his administration has fought. It is
still a matter of contention whether Bush's Iraq War will be remembered
as another Vietnam, as suggested by Korb and Conley, or as the birth of
democracy in the Islamic Middle East, as Kaufman argues.[14]

   Political competence refers to a president's ability to reshape the political regime. Realignments, while often predicted, are quite rare. After
the 2004 election came rumblings that George W. Bush had successfully
realigned electoral politics (Harris 2004). Such predictions evaporated
after the 2006 midterm elections. It is more usual for presidents to subtly
retool their existing parties in new directions. For example, the Eisenhower administration reshaped Republican views of the state, while the
Clinton administration reshaped Democratic views of markets. The most
vaunted political reshuffling of the last forty years has been the so-called
regional Southern strategy, in which the formerly solidly Democratic states
of the old Confederacy realigned as Republican at the presidential level,
first for Nixon and then more consistently for Reagan and subsequent
GOP presidents. How lasting Bush's influence on the Republican Party

will be is also a matter of debate, though in this volume Lara Brown and William Galston argue that Bush has not helped his party.

Tactical competence refers to the president's ability to make rational decisions and the ability of his administration to carry out the basic duties of government. George H.W. Bush's execution of the First Gulf War and Clinton's ability to contain the Mexican peso crisis and East Asian financial crisis exemplify tactical competence. The tactical competence of the George W. Bush administration was called into question by its inadequate response to Hurricane Katrina, a theme of Anne Khademian's chapter, and inadequate planning for the Iraq War (Fortier and Ornstein 2007), a theme of Chapters 2, 3, 4, 13, and 15 of this book. Previous administrations also suffered deficits of tactical competence. Kennedy's failed Bay of Pigs operation in Cuba harmed administration prestige, although the president rebounded with his response in the Cuban Missile Crisis. The prolonged agony of the hostage crisis in Iran contributed to Carter's defeat in the 1980 election, as the president seemed unable to decisively resolve the situation. An administration that appears unable to govern competently from a tactical perspective risks losing support from all but its most ideologically committed supporters.

Moral competence refers to an administration's ability to avoid scandal but more notably to its trustworthiness. Without this characteristic, it becomes more difficult to build a reservoir of goodwill with elites or the public. Eisenhower, Ford, and Carter all at some level exhibited characteristics of moral competence. Nixon's Watergate scandal, Reagan's Iran-Contra debacle, and Clinton's Lewinsky affair were major examples of moral failings. Moral competence is a two-sided coin. It involves integrity at the policy and administrative levels as well as the personal probity of the president. Moral competence is a standard that changes with the times, since personal scandals that were overlooked in an earlier age are now exposed. While George W. Bush has avoided personal scandal, many scholars argue that the Bush administration has simply failed in the larger context. Others, however, stoutly defend the administration's integrity. The deep partisan divide in the country is probably most sharply reflected by the debate over this aspect of competence (Jacobson 2006). Within this volume, Shirley Anne Warshaw and James Pfiffner identify particular moral failings of the Bush administration, pointing out how unprecedented presidential signing statements have subverted the legislative process.

The authors of the following chapters endeavor to use all of the above-mentioned criteria in order to evaluate the presidency of George W. Bush. As Felzenberg (2008) advises, different criteria may have different relative values at different times in history, and to different observers. Accordingly, the authors hail from a wide variety of ideological and professional backgrounds. Experts review Bush's approaches to dealing with institutions and an assortment of domestic and foreign policies. The Afterword of the book offers two very different early assessments of the Bush presidency.

Presidents alone do not determine history.[15] Yet the president of the United States is probably the single-most influential person determining events. The president makes decisions of great consequence and serves as a symbol for America's interests. Thus, George W. Bush must be judged, as must all presidents, for both his accomplishments and his failures.

PLAN OF THE BOOK

This book is divided into five thematic parts. The first part aims to situate George W. Bush in context. Maranto and Redding, in "Bush's Brain (No, Not Karl Rove): How Bush's Psyche Shaped His Decision Making," view the president as an individual actor, largely responsible for making decisions. Warshaw then turns Maranto and Redding's thesis on its head with a chapter minimizing Bush's role in decision making. "The Cheneyization of the Bush Administration: Cheney Captures the Transition" argues for the importance of the vice president in setting the policy-making agenda. Her provocative thesis suggests that Vice President Cheney has exerted such influence over the administration and White House structure that Bush has carried out Cheney's agenda as much as his own. In "President Bush as Chief Executive," Pfiffner analyzes how the Bush administration used executive power to carry out its agenda, particularly in the post–9/11 world, and criticizes it on legal, moral, and pragmatic grounds.

The focus of the second part of *Judging Bush* is to survey how the Bush administration influenced the policy-making branches of the federal government. Before evaluating the Bush administration's influence over the levers of the government, Brown reviews Bush's ability to build the Republican Party in "Reactionary Ideologues and Uneasy Partisans: Bush and Realignment." Rudalevige then demonstrates, in "Diminishing Returns: George W. Bush and Congress, 2001–2008," how during his first six years Bush and his fellow legislators worked as a formidable policy-making machine while stifling dissent. The switch in party control in 2006 marked a return to the tensions inherent in divided government. The federal bureaucracy, while not envisioned by the framers, has burgeoned, becoming increasingly important to both policy making and administrative functions. In "Not Always According to Plan: Theory and Practice in the Bush White House," Hult, Walcott, and Cohen, evaluate the interaction of bureaucrats and political appointees. In "A Legal Revolution? The Bush Administration's Effect on the Judiciary and Civil Justice Reform," Johnson and Moreland tackle federal judicial appointments and attempt to reform the litigation regime, finding more success on the former than on the latter.

The third part of the book turns to how the Bush administration influenced domestic policy. Hess and McGuinn, in "George W. Bush's Education Legacy: The Two Faces of No Child Left Behind," evaluate how a bipartisan education bill has changed the politics and policy of American public education, most likely for the better. Cohen and Panagopoulos, on the other hand, in "The Politics of Economic Policy in a Polarized Era: The Case of George W. Bush," analyze how the deep recession that began in late 2007, followed by the financial crisis of the summer of 2008, will overshadow any economic accomplishment from earlier in the president's administration. While Bush succeeded during his first term in implementing his agenda in both education and fiscal policy, his second term was marked by failure. Most notably, Bush and the Department of Homeland Security failed to adequately respond to the devastation wreaked by Hurricane Katrina. In the final chapter of this part, "Hurricane Katrina and the Failure of Homeland Security," Khademian evaluates the organizational failures that contributed to Bush's lackluster second term.

For President Bush in particular, foreign policy was preeminent. The fourth part, "Crusade: The Bush Foreign Policies," presents two very different views of the Bush doctrine and its strategic implications for world politics. Kaufman, in "Is the Bush Doctrine Dead?" offers a spirited defense of Bush's war on terror, arguing that it is worthwhile over the long term. He suggests that Bush will be recognized as another Truman, whose standing rose over time. Korb and Conley, in "Forging an American Empire," take a more circumspect view of Bush's ambitions. In contrast to Kaufman, they sound a more cautious note about the growing presence of the United States overseas. In "Fighting Two Wars," Lansford and Covarrubias investigate how feasible it is for the United States to engage in both the Afghanistan and Iraq Wars at the same time.

Tying all these elements together in the fifth and final part, Galston, in "Between Journalism and History: Evaluating George W. Bush's Presidency," evaluates the Bush presidency at its close. He stacks Bush in comparison to other recent two-term presidents, particularly Ronald Reagan and Bill Clinton. He finds the Bush legacy troubling, both from a budgetary and moral level. Finally, DiIulio, who was associated with the early Bush administration and its faith-based initiative, gives a closing word in "Why Judging George W. Bush Is Never as Easy as It Seems."

NOTES

1. George Washington, the first president, is a partial exception to this rule. Some presidents, such as Lincoln, tested these limits with some foreboding but thought it necessary due to external exigencies.

2. Since all presidents so far have been men, the masculine pronoun is used in reference to presidents throughout this volume.

3. See also Schier (2009), who probes similar questions.

4. The band of scholars defending various aspects of the Bush presidency includes Elshtain (2003), Hanson (2004), Kaufman (2008), and Renshon (2004).

5. In this seminal ranking there were six "great" presidents: Abraham Lincoln, George Washington, Franklin Delano Roosevelt, Woodrow Wilson, Thomas Jefferson, and Andrew Jackson. The two presidents deemed "failures" were Ulysses S. Grant and Warren G. Harding.

6. The editors' criteria are similar to those developed by Felzenberg (2008) in his excellent book evaluating presidential ratings.

7. The adage is usually attributed to Senator Arthur Vandenberg (R-MI). The sentiment, however, predates the American founding by several hundred years (Minogue 1995).

8. Anthony King (1993) agrees with Wildavsky that presidents inherently influence foreign policy more than domestic policy. King points out that executives are more influential in Westminster or continental European models.

9. For contrary evidence that voters care about foreign policy, see Aldrich et al. (1989).

10. For a somewhat contrary view of the nineteenth-century presidency, see Ellis and Walker (2007).

11. For a critique of Barber, see the essays in George and George (1998).

12. According to these authors, popular national attachment flagged without invigorating reinforcement from political parties. These authors also insist that the period's sobriquet, "The Era of Good Feelings," is a misnomer. George Washington served as the only truly successful nonpartisan president, and they argue his presidency was a unique circumstance that could not be repeated.

13. Skowronek (1997) also theorizes that the recent political environment truncates the cyclical nature of American politics and suggests that transformative greatness is a thing of the past.

14. The weight of scholarly opinion, at present, is that the war will not bring forth a democratic transformation of the region. Indeed, even administration officials eventually seemed to agree (e.g., Agresto 2007).

15. Thomas Carlyle (1908) formulated in 1841 the premise that "great men" determine the outcome of history.

REFERENCES

Agresto, John. 2007. *Mugged by Reality: The Liberation of Iraq and the Failure of Good Intentions*. New York: Encounter Books.

Aldrich, John H., John L. Sullivan, and Eugene Borgida. 1989. "Foreign Policy and Voting in Presidential Elections: Are Candidates 'Waltzing Before a Blind Audience'?" *American Political Science Review* 83(1): 123–41.

Barber, James David. 1985. *The Presidential Character: How We Judge America's Presidents*. College Station: Texas A&M University Press.

Berger, Raoul. 1974. *Executive Privilege: A Constitutional Myth*. Cambridge, MA: Harvard University Press.

Bond, Jon R., and Richard Fleisher. 1990. *The President in the Legislative Arena*. Chicago: University of Chicago Press.

Brownstein, Ronald. 2007. *The Second Civil War: How Extreme Partisanship Has Paralyzed Washington and Polarized America*. New York: Penguin.

Burke, John P. 2000. *The Institutional Presidency: Organizing and Managing the White House from FDR to Clinton*. Baltimore: Johns Hopkins University Press.

C-SPAN. 1999. *C-SPAN Survey of Presidential Leadership*. http://www.americanpresidents.org/survey (Accessed April 26, 2008).

Canes-Wrone, Brandice. 2006. *Who Leads Whom? Presidents, Policy, and the Public*. Chicago: University of Chicago Press.

Carlyle, Thomas. 1908. *On Heroes, Hero Worship and the Heroic in History*. London: J. Dent & Sons.

Connelly, Marjorie. 2007. "New Bush, Iraq Poll Numbers." *The Caucus: New York Times Blog*, March 1. http://thecaucus.blogs.nytimes.com/2007/03/01/new-bush-iraqpollnumbers/ (Accessed April 25, 2008).

Edwards, George C. 1989. *At the Margins: Presidential Leadership of Congress*. New Haven, CT: Yale University Press.

———. 2003. *On Deaf Ears: The Limits of the Bully Pulpit*. New Haven, CT: Yale University Press.

Ellis, Richard J., and Alexis Walker. 2007. "Policy Speech in the Nineteenth Century Rhetorical Presidency: The Case of Zachary Taylor's 1849 Tour." *Presidential Studies Quarterly* 37(2): 248–69.

Elshtain, Jean Bethke. 2003. *Just War Against Terror: The Burdens of American Power in a Violent World.* New York: Basic Books.

Federalist Society–*Wall Street Journal.* 2005. "Presidential Leadership: The Rankings." September 12. http://www.opinionjournal.com (Accessed April 26, 2008).

Felzenberg, Alvin S. 2008. *The Leaders We Deserved (And a Few We Didn't): Rethinking the Presidential Rating Game.* New York: Basic Books.

Fortier, John C., and Norman J. Ornstein, eds. 2007. *Second-Term Blues: How George W. Bush Has Governed.* Washington, DC: Brookings Institution and American Enterprise Institute.

George, Alexander L., and Juliette L. George. 1998. *Presidential Personality and Performance.* Boulder, CO: Westview Press.

Hanson, Victor Davis. 2004. *Between War and Peace: Lessons from Afghanistan to Iraq.* New York: Random House.

Harris, John F. 2004. "Was Nov 2 Realignment—or a Tilt? Political Parties Look For Answers." *Washington Post,* November 28, p. A1.

Jacobson, Gary C. 2006. *A Divider, Not a Uniter: George W. Bush and the American Public.* New York: Pearson Longman.

Jones, Charles O. 2005. *The Presidency in a Separated System,* 2nd ed. Washington, DC: Brookings Institution.

Kaufman, Robert G. 2008. *In Defense of the Bush Doctrine.* Lexington: University Press of Kentucky.

Kernell, Samuel. 2007. *Going Public: New Strategies of Presidential Leadership,* 4th ed. Washington, DC: CQ Press.

Kettl, Donald F. 2003. *Team Bush: Leadership Lessons from the Bush White House.* New York: McGraw-Hill.

King, Anthony. 1993. "Foundations of Power." In *Researching the Presidency: Vital Questions, New Approaches,* ed. George C. Edwards III, John H. Kessel, and Bert A. Rockman. Pittsburgh, PA: University of Pittsburgh Press, 415–51.

Lammers, William W., and Michael A. Genovese. 2000. *The Presidency and Domestic Policy: Comparing Leadership Styles, FDR to Clinton.* Washington, DC: CQ Press.

Landy, Marc, and Sidney M. Milkis. 2000. *Presidential Greatness.* Lawrence: University Press of Kansas.

Light, Paul C. 1999. *The President's Agenda: Domestic Policy Choice from Kennedy to Clinton.* Baltimore: Johns Hopkins University Press.

McElvaine, Robert S. 2008. "HNN Poll: 61% of Historians Rate the Bush Presidency Worst." *History News Network,* April 1. http://hnn.us/articles/48916.html (Accessed April 26, 2008).

Minogue, Kenneth. 1995. *Politics.* New York: Oxford University Press.

Morris, Dick. 1997. *Behind the Oval Office.* New York: Random House.

Mueller, John E. 1973. *War, Presidents, and Public Opinion.* New York: John Wiley.

Murray, Robert K., and Tim H. Blessing. 1994. *Greatness in the White House,* 2nd ed. University Park: Pennsylvania State University Press.

Neustadt, Richard. 1990. *Presidential Power and the Modern Presidents: The Politics of Leadership from Roosevelt to Reagan.* New York: Free Press.

Peppers, Donald A. 1975. "'The Two Presidencies': Eight Years Later." In *Perspectives on the Presidency,* ed. Aaron Wildavsky. Boston: Little, Brown, 462–73.

Pfiffner, James P. 1996. *The Strategic Presidency: Hitting the Ground Running*, 2nd ed. Lawrence: University Press of Kansas.

———. 2004. *The Character Factor: How We Judge America's Presidents*. College Station: Texas A&M University Press.

Reedy, Neil. 2008. "Judging the Presidency: Foreign Policy as the Dominant Criteria." Master's thesis. Villanova University.

Renshon, Stanley A. 1996. *The Clinton Presidency and the Politics of Ambition*. New York: New York University Press.

———. 2004. *In His Father's Shadow: The Transformations of George W. Bush*. New York: Palgrave Macmillan.

Ridings, William J., Jr., and Stuart B. McIver. 1997. *Rating the Presidents*. Secaucus, NJ: Carol.

Schier, Steven S. 2009. *Panorama of a Presidency: How George W. Bush Acquired and Spent His Political Capital*. Armonk, NY: M. E. Sharpe.

Schlesinger, Arthur M. 1948. "Historians Rate U.S. Presidents." *Life* 25(18): 65–74.

Schlesinger, Arthur M., Jr. 1997. "Rating the Presidents: Washington to Clinton." *Political Science Quarterly* 112(2): 179–90.

Skowronek, Stephen. 1997. *The Politics Presidents Make: Leadership from John Adams to Bill Clinton*. Cambridge, MA: Harvard University Press.

———. 2008. *Presidential Leadership in Political Time*. Lawrence: University Press of Kansas.

Tocqueville, Alexis de. [1956] 2001. *Democracy in America*. Abridged and edited by Richard C. Heffner. New York: Signet.

Tulis, Jeffrey. 1987. *The Rhetorical Presidency*. Princeton, NJ: Princeton University Press.

Wildavsky, Aaron B., ed. 1969. *The Presidency*. Boston: Little, Brown.

Young, James Sterling. 1966. *The Washington Community, 1800–1828*. New York: Columbia University Press.

CHAPTER 2

Bush's Brain (No, Not Karl Rove)

How Bush's Psyche Shaped His Decision Making[1]

ROBERT MARANTO AND RICHARD E. REDDING

[handwritten: Bush = strategic competence but luck of tactical]

COMIC ROUTINES TO THE CONTRARY, there is nothing dumb about George W. Bush. At the same time, as other chapters in this volume suggest, President Bush has psychological characteristics which limited his competence as a "decider" (to use his term) and ultimately undermined the administration. Arguably, President Bush had strategic competence: a vision of where he wanted to push government, compatible with national needs. He thus could have become a president of achievement (Nelson 1993). However, the president seemingly lacked the tactical competence to hew to and implement his vision. President Bush had bad luck in Hurricane Katrina, and White House insiders believed that the Democratic opposition would attack no matter what the president did (Feaver 2008). Indeed, increased partisanship is a feature of modern American politics (Jacobs and Shapiro 2000). Yet Bush's personal psychology also played a key role in his presidential failures. We believe that George W. Bush's tendency to personalize policy making, his unwillingness to seriously entertain opposing views, his disdain for detail, his enthusiasm for new challenges, and his reluctance to admit error and change course led to both successes and failures. Ultimately, the very substantial failures in Iraq doomed George W. Bush's second term agenda and clouded his legacy. We will summarize the better work on George W. Bush's psyche, stressing that a leader's personality traits should not be judged good or bad; rather, personality traits that match some situations mismatch others. We will apply this with a brief discussion of President Bush's most notable success, education reform. Here, his prior experience and knowledge, ebullient salesmanship, and holding firm to ideas whose time had come led to

[handwritten margin note: bad luck or poor decisions?]

success. We will follow with a more substantial discussion of President Bush's singular failure, Iraq.

As discussed in Chapter 1, presidents have more power in foreign policy, which magnifies the impact of personality on policy. Further, as shown by Jervis (1976, 2008), national security policy involves highly uncertain information, calling for leaders to seek and integrate new information. Finally, all leaders learn from history; the particular histories of American education policy and relations with Iraq influenced the president and other policymakers in ways few have discussed. History and flawed intelligence—not leader personality—led to the American invasion of Iraq. Yet, if the decision to invade may have been rational, the implementation of invasion was not. This failure reflected key aspects of President Bush's personality.

INSIDE BUSH'S BRAIN

Biographies and "psychohistories" of George W. Bush began to appear shortly after he became governor of Texas in 1994. This literature uses biographical, psychoanalytic, or empirical perspectives to analyze Bush's cognitive abilities and functioning, personality, or emotional makeup. Bush has not submitted himself for a psychological examination, so all three approaches must rely on the same available source materials (interviews, statements, news accounts, biographies) and the opinions of experts. The familiar biographical approach compiles a history of Bush's life, providing psychological insights (for example, Renshon 2004; Weisberg 2008) but proffering neither a clinical nor empirical analysis of his psychological functioning.[2] The psychoanalytic approach (for example, Frank 2004) uses the analyst's clinical opinion derived from psychoanalytically oriented principles that are now considered largely outmoded. The scientific approach provides psychological profiles derived from empirical analyses of source materials and by soliciting experts to rate Bush on standardized, scientifically validated psychological measures. All three methods have their weaknesses, but in combination they have some descriptive power. For the most part, we will use the empirical findings from the scientific approach, occasionally supplemented by the other two, to assess Bush's tactical competence. We do not provide a comprehensive portrayal of Bush's psyche, a project far beyond our scope, but rather discuss those aspects

most relevant to decision making and leadership. We will discuss Bush's
intelligence, decision-making style, and basic personality.

IS BUSH INTELLIGENT?

[handwritten annotation: they use the SAT to decide if Bush is intelligent?]

We can estimate Bush's intelligence quotient (IQ) in several ways. First,
we use his college Scholastic Aptitude Test (SAT) score, since SAT scores
correlate well with IQ measures (Frey and Detterman 2004). Bush scored
a 1200 on the SAT (roughly equaling 1300 on today's renormed SAT),
placing him in the top 16 percent of all college applicants (Immelman
2001). Second, we can look to Simonton's (2006) recent study of presidential IQ. Simonton compiled personality descriptions of the presidents
based on biographical sources, removed identifying information from
the descriptions, and asked independent judges to rate each along three
hundred descriptors using the Gough Adjective Checklist. The data were
then statistically analyzed to identify key factors relating to psychological
functioning, identifying one factor called "intellectual brilliance" (which
included adjectives such as "curious," "wise," "insightful," "inventive,"
"wide interests," and so on). The intellectual brilliance scores were cross-
validated with other indices of presidential intelligence, such as recorded IQ
test scores available for some of the presidents and other research studies
that have assessed the personality trait "openness to experience," which is
correlated with intelligence. Using these varied data and measures, Simonton employed a statistical procedure to estimate the IQ of each president.
The best estimate placed Bush's IQ at 120–125, *in the top 10 percent of
the population and above the 115 average IQ for college graduates.*

Thus, President Bush has a superior IQ, about the same as the estimated IQ for Eisenhower and Ford. Yet, he is less intelligent than most
presidents, many of whom were brilliant. Among the forty-two other
presidents, four are tied with Bush and only six rank lower in intellectual
brilliance or IQ.

Given the considerable political and intellectual skills required to successfully run for the presidency along with the demands of the office itself—in which presidents must think quickly and routinely make decisions
based on complex information—it is not surprising that most of our presidents have been highly intelligent. Studies find IQ to be a strong, often the

single best, predictor of job performance and leadership across a variety of occupations. Intelligence does correlate with measures of presidential leadership and greatness, as judged by historians and political scientists (Simonton 2006).[3] Intelligence also is moderately correlated with measures of presidential charisma, creativity, and motivation to achieve (Simonton 2002). Based on his IQ alone, we should expect that Bush will be judged by history to rank about twenty-six out of our forty-two presidents in presidential greatness (Simonton 2006, 523).

WHAT KIND OF THINKER IS BUSH?

Critics charge that President Bush did not seek out information or opposing viewpoints; disdained complexity, nuances, and expert opinion; viewed policy issues in black-and-white terms based on his own preconceptions; and refused to rethink problems or change his views. The research largely bears out these popular perceptions. One line of research addresses "integrative complexity" (IC), the complexity of a leader's thinking. It is best characterized as a style of thinking rather than an intellectual ability, though it does correlate with intelligence (Thoemmes and Conway 2007). Those having low IC "can be described as engaging in 'black-or-white' thinking, all-or-nothing judgments, possessing a general inability or unwillingness to accept uncertainty and divergent viewpoints, and a desire for rapid closure" (Thoemmes and Conway 2007, 195). They "can only see things from one perspective—their own—and so no integration is necessary" (Simonton 2006, 522). Researchers assess IC by randomly compiling excerpts from a leader's interviews and speeches, removing identifying information from those excerpts, and then having trained coders rate each statement in the excerpts for integrative complexity, as assessed by a standardized coding scheme for measuring IC (see Baker-Brown et al. 1992).[4] Thoemmes and Conway (2007) employed this methodology to assess the integrative complexity of all the presidents. Bush's integrative complexity score was about average, virtually identical to Reagan's and only a bit lower than Clinton's. However, "complex presidents were . . . not significantly more likely to be considered 'great' presidents in the eyes of history . . . what makes a successful leader is not so much the mean level of complexity but rather the *match* between complexity level and situation" (Thoemmes and Conway 2007, 215).

24

Thus, a better key to successful leadership lies in thinking complexly at the right *times*, in the right *situations*, and with respect to the right *issues*. For example, President Reagan held a relatively simplistic view of the Soviet "evil empire," but showed the cognitive flexibility to change his views shortly after Gorbachev came to power, which itself was perhaps in part due to Reagan's own policies (Winik 1996).

In contrast to his hero, Ronald Reagan, Bush failed with respect to the signature foreign policy decision of his presidency—the decision to invade Iraq (Weisberg 2008)—a theme of several other chapters in this volume. Suedfeld and Leighton (2002) analyzed the statements and speeches made by Bush between 1999 to mid-October 2002 (the time of the attack on Afghanistan following 9/11), finding that his IC remained relatively low and stable throughout this time period, lower than that of every elected twentieth-century president from McKinley to Carter (see Tetlock 1981). Bush's IC score "is indicative of someone who discusses issues without taking alternative points of view into serious consideration . . . Bush's score does not change with the political conditions, unlike what usually holds for successful political and military leaders" (Simonton 2006, 522; see also Merskin, 2004). Simplistic thinking about policy goals, while beneficial in some situations, may "lead to the ignoring of crucial information or potentially successful decisions, to a misunderstanding of what one's people, allies and opponents are doing or thinking, and to rigid adherence to a failing plan" (Suedfeld and Leighton 2002, 587). Though none have studied the matter, we suspect that President Bush's IC on education issues, on which he had more preexisting knowledge, would be higher. Notably, Weisberg (2008) argues that Bush, Woodrow Wilson, and Jimmy Carter all suffered from low IC, and all failed on their signature initiatives. Berggren and Rae (2006) argue that for Bush and Carter, in particular, evangelical *faith* led to foreign policy ineffectiveness.

A third factor related both to integrative complexity and intelligence is the leader's openness to new ideas and experiences (see Simonton 2006), a trait psychologists call "openness to experience" as measured by the NEO ("neuroticism-extraversion-openness") Personality Inventory (or simply NEO). In Rubenzer and Faschingbauer's (2004) study, three expert raters read the available biographies of Bush and rated him on the

NEO scales. Bush scored a 0 (zero) out of a possible 100 for openness, the lowest of any president (see Simonton 2006, 516). This "suggests that his well-documented lack of doubt may be due to lack of introspection or inability to perceive things from a different perspective" (Rubenzer and Faschingbauer 2004, 303).

Finally, although there are no empirical studies on the issue, Bush's inattention to detail, superficial approach, and relatively poor academic performance relative to his intellect might be explained by attention deficit disorder (ADD) or attention deficit hyperactivity disorder (ADHD) (Elovitz 2004; Frank 2004). These learning disabilities are characterized by a difficulty in focusing attention or attending to detail and often by impulsivity.

WHAT IS BUSH'S PERSONALITY?

The leading personality theory (the "5–Factor Model") conceptualizes personality as consisting of five primary facets, as assessed by the NEO Personality Inventory: "neuroticism" (anxiety, hostility, depression, self-consciousness, impulsiveness, vulnerability to stress), "extraversion" (warmth, gregariousness, assertiveness, activity level, excitement seeking, positive emotion), "openness to experience" (openness to fantasy, aesthetics, feelings, actions, ideas, and values), "agreeableness" (trust, straightforwardness, altruism, compliance, modesty, tender-mindedness), and "conscientiousness" (competence, orderliness, dutifulness, achievement striving, self-discipline, deliberativeness). According to Rubenzer and Faschingbauer's (2004) study (described above), *Bush is highly extraverted but not very agreeable or conscientious; he is about average in neuroticism.* When compared with other presidents', his personality most closely resembles that of Jackson, Reagan, and Harding, and he is very unlike his father, President George H.W. Bush. Indeed, this dissimilarity to his father is a key theme in *The Bush Tragedy* (Weisberg 2008).

Immelman (2002) had expert raters judge Bush's personality using the Millon Inventory of Diagnostic Criteria, a widely used personality test. Raters identified Bush as fitting the "outgoing," "dominant (controlling)," and "dauntless" personality patterns, which together constitute a style given to unreflectiveness, superficiality, and impulsivity. Such individuals are "full of ideas, though tending to be a superficial thinker; likely to start many projects but inconsistent in following through, compensating with a natural salesperson's ability to persuade others to join in getting things done" (see Immelman 2002, 98). They have "the propensity for a superficial grasp of complex issues, a predisposition to be easily bored by routine (with the attendant risk of failing to keep [themselves] adequately informed), [and] an inclination to act impulsively without fully appreciating the implications of [their] decisions or the long-term consequences of [their] policy initiatives" (Immelman 2002, 102). Immelman's findings are validated by Weisberg (2008, 183–220), who describes the *six* distinct Bush foreign policy doctrines in the course of the administration.

COMPARING EMPIRICAL FINDINGS WITH BIOGRAPHIES

The empirical research findings confirm much of what we are told in available biographies, psychohistories, political commentaries, and insider accounts of the Bush presidency. In *The Price of Loyalty*, former Bush treasury secretary Paul O'Neill (2004) paints a portrait of Bush as a casual and unreflective decision maker who did not like to have his opinions challenged by advisors and who valued personal loyalty above all else. Bush's disdain for complexity is typified by his alleged remark that he "never suffered doubt" about whether to invade Iraq (Woodward 2004, 420). *Bush on the Couch*, Justin Frank's (2004) wide-ranging psychoanalytic treatment, also describes Bush's tendency toward simplistic, moralistic thinking.[5] Similarly, Elovitz's (2004) psychohistorical analysis describes how gregarious and interpersonally skilled Bush was as a youth—often wild and mischievous, though a leader and always part of the "cool crowd," disdainful of the intellectuals at the preparatory and Ivy League schools he attended. In "George W. Bush: Policy, Politics, and Personality," James Pfiffner (2004, 161) describes Bush as having "shown a preference for moral certainty over strategic calculation; a tendency for visceral reaction rather than reflection; a preference for clarity rather than complexity; a bias toward action rather than deliberation; and a preference for the personal over the structural or procedural." The latter explains Bush's remarkable loyalty toward subordinates who were themselves loyal, including cabinet members Alberto Gonzales, Donald

Rumsfeld, and Michael Chertoff, who should have been held accountable long before they were actually separated from the administration (or in Chertoff's case, not separated), as well as Bush's failed nomination of Harriet Miers to the Supreme Court, an impulsive, ill-considered decision based on personal friendship (Weisberg 2008, 15, 19, 170).

BUSH'S PSYCHE:

IMPLICATIONS FOR PRESIDENTIAL LEADERSHIP

In summary, *Bush is an extraverted, domineering, and somewhat adventurous and impulsive individual, lacking in conscientiousness, who is intelligent but relatively superficial and unreflective.* People with Bush's personality pattern are gregarious and warm, skilled at persuading and rallying others; they seek attention and approval from others; they are assertive, positive, and enthusiastic; they are confident when wielding power or directing others but not very accommodating of others' wishes; they tend to act impulsively and are relatively unreflective; they tend to be shallow, lacking in introspection and unwilling to grapple with emotional conflicts; and they may engage in risk-taking or sensation-seeking behavior (Rubenzer and Faschingbauer 2004).

Bush's psyche had both positive and negative potential consequences for his presidential leadership (see Immelman 2002; Rubenzer and Faschingbauer 2004). On the positive side, such leaders tend to be politically skilled, charismatic, energetic, and effective at rallying and shaping public opinion, and are effective managers and delegators of authority. On the negative side, they may be prone to poor and unreflective decision making, refuse to consider alternative or unpleasant points of view, over-rely on friendship and loyalty when making appointments, and be overly confident or cocky. Bush's tendency toward simplistic, superficial, preconceived thinking, reinforced by his particular religious views, leads him to view problems in all-or-none, moralistic terms. Frank (2004) and Elovitz (2004) argue that Bush is prone to psychological "splitting"—the emotional need to categorize people as either all good or all bad, and thus to personalize conflicts accordingly.

Yet, Bush is smarter than those who have "misunderestimated" him have supposed, and his extraverted personality supports his considerable political skills. He was elected governor of Texas and president of the United States, two accomplishments requiring considerable intelligence, discipline, and political skill. He is smart enough to serve as president though not as smart as most presidents. Yet, in governing, he has a cognitive and personality style prone to ill-informed, rigid, and unreflective decision making. Thus, Bush's psyche provides an outstanding skill set for *campaigning* and rallying public opinion for agreed-on goals but a poor one for *governing*, at least to the extent that governing requires well-considered decision making.

BUSH'S PSYCHE IN ACTION:

SUCCESS ON NO CHILD LEFT BEHIND

The greatest domestic achievement of the Bush administration was the No Child Left Behind (NCLB) Act, as detailed by Frederick Hess and Patrick McGuinn elsewhere in this volume. Applying the Skowronek scheme described in Chapter 1, in this area President Bush used the presidency as a battering ram to demolish an obsolete policy regime, a dauntless presidential action suiting his bold leadership style. This revolutionary law forces states to develop school standards and to test students to measure (and foster) academic growth. Schools and school districts must make progress toward an eventual goal of 100 percent proficiency for all groups of students, including minority, low income, and special needs students. Those failing to do so are labeled "needing improvement," and eventually may face sanctions.

Bush's interest in education reflected his own painful experiences as a poor transfer student in prep school after doing well in his West Texas public school (Bush 1999); his genuine "compassionate conservative" goal to improve education in order to foster class mobility (a theme of the Afterword in this volume); and his political need to win votes from contested constituencies, particularly minorities and women. Texas governor Bush immersed himself in education policy, crafting accountability programs that built on those of his Democratic predecessor. Indeed, Bush was more in synch ideologically with Texas' Democratic legislators than with its more conservative Republicans. Bush's education record earned plaudits from the press and from policy wonks, giving him the credentials to run for president.

In short, on education he had a high comfort level and felt comfortable working with Democrats.[6] Like the rest of us, politicians learn both from history and from their personal histories (Jervis 1976). Governor Bush's political and policy success in Texas education reform provided a model for President Bush as a national education reformer. Further, Bush had success embracing education *standards*. In contrast, his limited foray into school choice, a rapid expansion of charter schooling with insufficient attention to quality, had mixed results (Maranto and Coppeto 2004). Though Washington Democrats are far to the left of the Texas Democrats Bush knew, on education he and they had much in common. For years, Washington policymakers felt frustration as public schools received more resources without improving student achievement. By the 1990s, centrist and even some liberal Democrats were ready to implement accountability-based reforms; indeed, President Clinton's proposed Goals 2000 resembled NCLB but was weakened by Congress (McGuinn 2006; Rudalevige 2003).

The relative bipartisan consensus on education reform made it easy for President Bush to involve Democrats in policy making. Much of NCLB came from the New Democratic Progressive Policy Institute, and the original White House point person for NCLB was Democrat Sandy Kress. Bush himself spent considerable time negotiating the details with key Democratic Congress members, particularly Representative George Miller (D-CA) and Senator Ted Kennedy (D-MA) (McGuinn 2006; Rudalevige 2003). The bill's progress was completely unaffected when Republicans lost the Senate with the defection of Senator James Jeffords in May 2001. Of course, as Maranto and Coppeto write (2004, 116), "compromise is easy when you get your way." Bush gladly bargained away the school choice–related parts of NCLB he did not care about to gain the testing and accountability-based provisions he valued. President Bush had no need to show flexibility since he got what he wanted. He also had a high level of knowledge of and comfort with education policy, so he could work with opponents without feeling insecure.

Like any complex intergovernmental law, NCLB has not been perfectly implemented by America's fifty states and roughly fourteen thousand local school districts (Hess and Finn 2007; Maranto and Maranto 2004). Yet the Bush administration did show flexibility in the law's implementation, particularly since the president replaced Education secretary Rod Paige with the more politically savvy Margaret Spellings (McGuinn 2006, 167–87). Evidence suggests that the law has succeeded in pushing public schools to raise the academic achievement of traditionally low-performing students and reducing the test score gaps between whites and minorities (Casserly 2007).

In short, in Bush's preeminent domestic policy area, he found success not by compromise but by working with Democrats who shared his goal to fashion a policy whose time had come (Hochschild 2003; Maranto and Maranto 2004). Bush's knowledge of education and his ebullient personality combined to make him an effective salesman for policies that elites had already by and large accepted.

SMART ON SCHOOLS, DUMB AT WAR

Education policy involves Congress and state and local governments. In sharp contrast, as detailed in Chapter 1, presidents have unusual authority and power in foreign and defense policy, which magnifies the impact of leader personality. The normal structural advantages presidents hold in foreign policy were further magnified by the national state of emergency after 9/11, an urgency compounded by the shadowy anthrax attacks and Beltway sniper in the months thereafter (Weisberg 2008, 189). In the foreign policy crises, the president could operate as a unitary actor beyond congressional scrutiny.

The desire for cognitive consistency causes people to believe that unsuccessful policies reflect foolish or evil decision making; but life is more complicated than that (Jervis 1976). So it is with the decision to invade Iraq. Unlike some contributors to this volume, we believe that the decision to invade Iraq was defensible. Bush's failings came less in the decision to go to war than in the lack of a process for that decision, his unwillingness to impose planning for the occupation of Iraq, his inability to recognize severely flawed occupation policies, his inability to face and learn from intelligence failures, and, most importantly, in his inability until far too late to hold accountable the war's architects and set a more effective course under more effective personnel. These indefensible failures in part reflect President Bush's psyche.

HOW HISTORY LED TO INVASION

President Bush's critics argue that his administration "cherry-picked" intelligence to justify the decision to invade Iraq. Yet, the critics fail to consider how uncertainty and history shape decision making. As Jervis (1976) shows in his landmark *Perception and Misperception in International Politics*, foreign policy decision makers must act with relatively little information. To fill in the gaps, they impose models from history to make sense of complex or uncertain information, particularly regarding the intent of foreign leaders—the key variable in defense policy. For example, while hawks might see a failure to counter a potential adversary as resembling Neville Chamberlain's attempts to appease an expansionist Hitler, a dove might see military mobilization as akin to the risky arms buildups leading to World War I.

Regarding Iraq, several recent historical events shaped the views of President Bush, Vice President Cheney, Secretary of Defense Rumsfeld, Undersecretary of Defense Wolfowitz, and other key foreign policy decision makers. Dumbrell (2008), Winik (1996), and the first-person account of Undersecretary of Defense for Policy Douglas Feith (2008) show that President Reagan's successful efforts to end the Cold War with the collapse of Communism taught a generation of neoconservative thinkers that assertive foreign policies worked. Beneath this general worldview, specific events shaped perceptions of the Iraqi Baathist regime, as explained by Pollack (2002) as well as Feith (2008) and Diamond (2008):

Saddam Hussein's 1980 invasion of Iran, a nation far larger than Iraq, suggested a highly risk-acceptant and aggressive personality.

Hussein's invasion of Kuwait after his army was depleted by eight years of war with Iran likewise suggested a high level of risk acceptance, coupled with expansionist goals; shortly beforehand, the CIA had predicted that no invasion would occur.

Shortly after the invasion of Kuwait, the CIA vastly overestimated the difficulty of defeating the Iraqi forces.

In 1990–91, the CIA predicted that Iraq was at least five years from developing nuclear weapons and had few chemical weapons; inspections immediately after the war showed the regime to have much larger and more advanced weapons of mass destruction (WMD) programs than predicted.

In 1994, the United States and its allies thought that Iraqi WMD programs had been dismantled; key defectors showed that this was not the case.

On defecting in 1995, Iraqi intelligence chief Wafiq Al-Samarrai said that Hussein claimed to have learned his lesson from the First Gulf War: once inspections ended, he intended to reconstitute WMD programs so that he could invade and occupy Kuwaiti and Saudi oil fields and deter American countermeasures.[7]

Save in Kurdistan, in northern Iraq, the CIA had few or no intelligence assets inside Iraq through most of the period and thus could not accurately assess the disparate information received from defectors, refugees, signals intelligence, and foreign intelligence agencies. In the 1990s, the agency again and again was "caught by surprise with the discovery of some new secret about Iraq's weapons of mass destruction that had been deliberately concealed by Saddam's regime" (Diamond 2008, 11).

In short, the CIA had consistently underestimated the threat posed by the Iraqi regime while overestimating the difficulties of defeating that regime in battle. These failures led Washington policymakers generally to doubt CIA estimates regarding Iraq and to err in the opposite direction. Eventually, the CIA did the same. Indeed, Bush critic Paul R. Pillar (2008, 233), who questions the decision to invade Iraq, nonetheless admits that the administration was correct to point out that "its perception of Saddam's weapons capacities was shared by the Clinton administration, congressional Democrats, and most other Western governments and intelligence services." Further, Diamond (2008, 13) writes that

the Agency's embattled posture during the 9/11 Commission's investigation of its failure to uncover the 9/11 plot made it more politically risky for the CIA to raise skeptical questions about whether the threat posed by Iraq was as serious as the White House alleged. An agency lambasted for missing clues that might have unraveled the deadliest terror plot in history was now handed the mission of interpreting a threat based on abundant clues about deadly weapons in the hands of a murderous dictator.

In addition, as Douglas Feith (2008) explains in defending his boss, Donald Rumsfeld, after 9/11, the Bush administration had determined to act against likely enemies *before* they were in a position to strike. This particular "Bush doctrine" then had widespread support.

Moreover, Bush's invasion of Afghanistan succeeded. On a matter of great importance and on which nearly all Americans agreed, President Bush set a clear direction and made rational decisions to attack Afghanistan rather than Iraq (as Rumsfeld seemingly wanted) and to act quickly with small forces rather than develop a large buildup over time. Indeed, his decision making in the run-up to the Afghanistan invasion is given high marks by Bush appointee Feith (2008) and also by political scientist Donald Kettl (2003). In Afghanistan, Bush's dauntless decision making may have paid off. On the other hand, Herspring (2008) and Feith (2008) respectively document the raging political battles within the administration that pitted Defense secretary Rumsfeld against CIA director George Tenet, Secretary of State Colin Powell, and his own generals even during the Afghanistan campaign. If Bush was even aware of these conflicts, there is no evidence he used them creatively to gain information from and about subordinates, as a multiple advocacy model suggests (George 1980), or to improve teamwork and policy coordination, as an administrative presidency model counsels (Nathan 1983). Indeed, even insider Feith (2008, 272) admits "government coordination—lively debate leading to solid teamwork—was not achieved in the Bush administration," partly since the president did not engage sufficiently to impose a disciplined process on subordinates. Luckily, the failings of the Taliban regime were such that Bush's leadership failures did not endanger initial success in Afghanistan. Still, better presidential oversight might have killed or captured Osama bin Laden.

One final part of recent history merits discussion. As Feith (2008) writes, the CIA and State Department thought the 2001 invasion of Afghanistan would be far more difficult and require far more troops than Secretary Rumsfeld proposed. As Bush sympathizer Victor David Hanson

(2007) suggests, too-rapid success in Afghanistan caused hubris and attendant failure in Iraq.

In short, the decision to invade Iraq, while perhaps mistaken, was not
in and of itself irrational. Given the success of a very small force in Afghanistan, even the decision to invade Iraq with far smaller forces than
Pentagon generals proposed could be defended. Had Iraq had extant WMD
programs and had the occupation worked well, we might well be writing a
chapter about how George W. Bush's boldness, optimism, and enthusiastic
big-picture leadership remade the Middle East *in a good way.*

This was not to be. All too eager to invade, the president proved unwilling or unable to monitor the implementation of his decision. Here,
the president's decision-making failures are manifest, and they reflect not
modern history but Bush psychology. As yet, we have no definitive historical accounts of presidential decision making during the war, in the way
that we have for Vietnam, so we cannot discuss the process in detail. Still,
from Ricks (2007), Herspring (2008), Pillar (2008), Pfiffner (2008), and
Woodward (2004, 2008), failings include:

The president's failure to impose a "staffing" process to review options
for Iraq regarding whether to invade, the number of troops needed
for the invasion, and the proposed length of time and character of the
occupation.

The president's failure to inform key members of the administration such
as the secretary of state until months after the decision to go to war.

The president's failure to study Iraq; for example, he reportedly did
not know about the differences between Sunnis and Shiites.

The president's failure to seriously consider views by administration
insiders including General Eric Shinseki, General Tommy Franks, and
Colin Powell that the invasion force was too small to occupy Iraq.

The president's failure to consider the views of analysts outside the
administration, such as hawkish Clinton administration Iraq expert
Kenneth Pollack (2002), who argued that an invasion force smaller
than three hundred thousand troops could not maintain order, with
civil war the most likely outcome.

The president's failure to review occupation plans by the Pentagon and State Department to see if they were in harmony and could stand up to scrutiny.

The president's failure to reconsider occupation policy after widespread rioting and looting following the fall of Baghdad in April 2003.

The president's failure to demand that the military kill or capture Muqtada al-Sadr when he began to kill opponents in May 2003: this signaled that occupation forces had no monopoly on violence, leading to civil war.

The president's failure to either work with Iran on Iraq border security or else use sufficient force to secure the border.

The president's failure to question Ambassador L. Paul Bremer's decision to disband the Iraqi Army, which left thousands of well-armed Iraqis unemployed, jump-starting the insurgency.

The president's failure to explain to the U.S. public why the administration thought Iraq had WMDs, and why they in fact were not there. This increased elite and popular distrust of the administration.

The president's failure to fundamentally rethink the occupation policy through 2003, 2004, 2005, and 2006 as the Iraqi insurgency deepened and widened.

After the 2004 presidential election, President Bush kept Secretary of Defense Rumsfeld, the architect of failed Iraqi policies, while hastening the departure of Secretary of State Powell, who had questioned those policies.

Charitably, one might excuse failings during the 2004 presidential campaign, but not in 2003, in the months after the invasion, when the course of occupation could have been righted, or after the 2004 presidential campaign, when reelection was no longer a factor. In short, on countless occasions, President Bush failed to impose a decision-making process to gather information, failed to monitor policy to make midcourse corrections, failed to seriously question subordinates, and failed to grapple with policy failures widely reported in the media. These failures showed an inability to consider alternative points of view and new information, a tendency to base policy on personal relationships, and a shocking disdain for detail. Only after the Republicans lost Congress in the 2006 elections, forcing his hand, did the president recognize the Iraqi insurgency, replace Secretary Rumsfeld, and change strategy.

CONCLUSION:
THE PERILS OF DAUNTLESS DECISION MAKING

President Bush's bold, ebullient personality and bias for action helped bring together Democratic and Republican elites to fundamentally reform American public schools. This may be his greatest legacy. The president's boldness in Afghanistan seemingly succeeded, though his disdain for details limited the scope of that success. Finally, on the signature decision of his administration, President Bush's tendency to make quick decisions, reluctance to admit error, disdain for details and experts, inability to entertain dissenting opinions, and tendency to categorize opponents as enemies meant that his administration did not sufficiently plan the invasion of Iraq. Further, he failed to systematically review occupation policy even as countless voices both inside and outside of the administration urged such a review. Here, the president proved cognitively rigid, not heroically steadfast. Nor did he find the strength to fire subordinates who had failed and to promote less-favored subordinates who had in fact proved prescient. Unfortunately, it is these essentially psychological failures of decision and indecision for which President George W. Bush will be best remembered.

NOTES

1. We borrow part of the title from the well-known book by James Moore and Wayne Slater, *Bush's Brain: How Karl Rove Made George W. Bush Presidential*, which argued that presidential advisor Karl Rove was the real brains behind the election and presidency of George W. Bush, the forty-third president of the United States. We wish to thank April Gresham Maranto and Dirk C. van Raemdonck for their considerable assistance on this chapter. The usual caveats apply.

2. Also available is Bush's political autobiography, *A Charge to Keep*, published in 1999.

3. Statistical analyses of the ratings of presidential greatness provided by various experts indicate that they represent "a firm and unified consensus" that is highly reliable and remarkably consistent across raters having different demographic characteristics and political attitudes (Simonton 2002, 144; Simonton 2006).

4. Although there may be strategic political reasons for leaders to make statements reflecting less complexity than their own views, IC scores do predict a leader's actual policy choices and strategies (Suedfeld and Leighton 2002).

5. Frank draws many other rather controversial conclusions as well (see Satel 2004), namely, that Bush exhibits some relatively serious psychological symptoms, largely stemming from his stern maternal upbringing, competitive relationship with his father, and history of alcoholism—issues often noted by Bush biographers (see Elovitz 2004; Renshon 2004). In addition, Frank (and many others!) have suggested that Bush's decision to run for governor of Texas and president, and his decision to invade Iraq, were driven in part by his competitive need to live up to his father's expectations and desire to vindicate his father's legacy (see Elovitz 2004). See also Weisberg (2008) on this theme.

6. Indeed, Bush's comfort with education policy was such that in the third Bush-Kerry presidential debate on October 13, 2004, Bush turned a question on jobs into a fairly effective disquisition on NCLB. See Commission on Presidential Debates (2004).

7. See Pollack (2002, 266–67). It strikes us that while the media frequently report on how silly the Bush administration was to believe intelligence from unreliable sources like the famous "Curveball," few acknowledge more credible sources like Al-Samarrai.

REFERENCES

Baker-Brown, Gloria, Elizabeth J. Ballard, Susan Bluck, Brian deVries, Peter Suedfeld, and Philip E. Tetlock. 1992. "The Conceptual/Integrative Complexity Scoring Manual." In *Motivation and Personality: Handbook of Thematic Content Analysis*, ed. Charles P. Smith. Cambridge, UK: Cambridge University Press, 400–418.

Berggren, D. Jason, and Nicol C. Rae. 2006. "Jimmy Carter and George W. Bush: Faith, Foreign Policy, and an Evangelical Presidential Style." *Presidential Studies Quarterly* 36(4) (December): 606–32.

Bush, George W. 1999. *A Charge to Keep*. New York: William Morrow.

Casserly, Michael. 2007. "America's Great City Schools: Moving in the Right Direction." In *No Remedy Left Behind*, ed. Frederick M. Hess and Chester E. Finn Jr. Washington, DC: American Enterprise Institute, 43–65.

Commission on Presidential Debates. 2004. "The Third Bush-Kerry Debate." *Commission on Presidential Debates—Voter Education—Debate Transcripts*, October 13. http://www.debates.org/pages/trans2004d.html (Accessed September 28, 2008).

Diamond, John. 2008. *The CIA and the Culture of Failure*. Stanford, CA: Stanford University Press.

Dumbrell, John. 2008. "The Neoconservative Roots of the War in Iraq." In *Intelligence and National Security Policymaking on Iraq: British and American Perspectives*, ed. James P. Pfiffner and Mark Phythian. College Station: Texas A&M University Press, 19–39.

Elovitz, Paul H. 2004. "A Comparative Psychohistorical Approach to Candidates: Bush and Kerry in the 2004 Election." *Journal of Psychohistory* 32(2): 109–42.

Feaver, Peter D. 2008. Comments during "Roundtable on Casualties, Public Opinion, and the Iraq War" at the 2008 Annual Meeting of the American Political Science Association.

Feith, Douglas J. 2008. *War and Decision: Inside the Pentagon at the Dawn of the War on Terrorism*. New York: HarperCollins.

Frank, Justin A. 2004. *Bush on the Couch: Inside the Mind of the President*. New York: HarperCollins.

Frey, Meredith C., and Douglas K. Detterman. 2004. "Scholastic Assessment or *g*? The Relationship Between the Scholastic Achievement Test and General Cognitive Ability." *Psychological Science* 15(6): 373–78.

George, Alexander L. 1980. *Presidential Decisionmaking in Foreign Policy: The Effective Use of Information and Advice.* Boulder, CO: Westview Press.

Hanson, Victor Davis. 2007. "Anatomy of Iraq: How Did We Get to This Baffling Scenario?" *National Review Online*, March 2. http://article.nationalreview.com/?q=MjdkOTA2Nm UxYzkwY2U4NzcyYTYwN2VhZDdmMTkxOWQ= (Accessed September 28, 2008).

Herspring, Dale R. 2008. *Rumsfeld's Wars.* Lawrence: University Press of Kansas.

Hess, Frederick M., and Chester E. Finn. 2007. *No Remedy Left Behind.* Washington, DC: American Enterprise Institute.

Hochschild, Jennifer. 2003. "Rethinking Accountability Politics." In *No Child Left Behind? The Politics and Practice of School Accountability*, ed. Paul E. Peterson and Martin R. West. Washington, DC: Brookings Institution, 116–29.

Immelman, Aubrey. 2001. "Bush Gets Bad Rap on Intelligence." *St. Cloud Times Online*, January 14. http://csbju.edu/USPP/Election/busho11401.htm (Accessed August 1, 2008).

———. 2002. "The Political Personality of U.S. President George W. Bush." In *Political Leadership for the New Century: Personality and Behavior Among American Leaders*, ed. Linda O. Valenty and Ofer Feldman. Westport, CT: Praeger, 81–103.

Jacobs, Lawrence R., and Robert Y. Shapiro. 2000. *Politicians Don't Pander: Political Manipulation and the Loss of Democratic Responsiveness.* Chicago: University of Chicago Press.

Jervis, Robert. 1976. *Perception and Misperception in International Politics.* Princeton, NJ: Princeton University Press.

———. 2008. "The Politics and Psychology of Intelligence and Intelligence Reform." In *Intelligence and National Security Policymaking on Iraq: British and American Perspectives*, ed. James P. Pfiffner and Mark Phythian. College Station: Texas A&M University Press, 162–71.

Kettl, Donald F. 2003. *Team Bush: Leadership Lessons from the Bush White House.* New York: McGraw-Hill.

Maranto, Robert, with Laura Coppeto. 2004. "The Politics Behind Bush's No Child Left Behind: Ideas, Elections, and Top-Down Education Reform." In *George W. Bush: Evaluating the President at Midterm*, ed. Bryan Hilliard, Tom Lansford, and Robert Watson. Albany: State University of New York Press, 105–20.

———, and April Maranto. 2004. "Can NCLB Increase Options for Low Income Students? Evidence from Across the States." In *Leaving No Child Left Behind? Options for Kids in Failing Schools*, ed. Frederick Hess and Chester E. Finn. New York: Palgrave Macmillan, 63–88.

McGuinn, Patrick J. 2006. *No Child Left Behind and the Transformation of Federal Education Policy, 1965–2005.* Lawrence: University Press of Kansas.

Merskin, Debra. 2004. "The Construction of Arabs as Enemies: Post-September 11 Discourse of George W. Bush." *Mass Communication & Society* 7(2): 157–75.

Moore, James, and Wayne Slater. 2004. *Bush's Brain: How Karl Rove Made George W. Bush Presidential.* Hoboken, NJ: John Wiley.

Nathan, Richard P. 1983. *The Administrative Presidency.* New York: John Wiley.

Nelson, Michael. 1993. "The Presidency: Clinton and the Cycle of Politics and Policy." In *The Elections of 1992*, ed. Michael Nelson. Washington, DC: CQ Press, 125–52.

O'Neill, Paul. 2004. *The Price of Loyalty: George W. Bush, the White House, and the Education of Paul O'Neill.* New York: Simon & Schuster.

Pfiffner, James P. 2004. "George W. Bush: Policy, Politics, and Personality." In *New Challenges for the American Presidency*, ed. George C. Edwards III and Phillip John Davies. New York: Longman, 161–81.

———. 2008. "Decisionmaking, Intelligence, and the Iraq War." In *Intelligence and National Security Policymaking on Iraq: British and American Perspectives*, ed. James Pfiffner and Mark Phythian. College Station: Texas A&M University Press, 213–32.

Pillar, Paul R. 2008. "Intelligence, Policy, and the War in Iraq." In *Intelligence and National Security Policymaking on Iraq: British and American Perspectives*, ed. James Pfiffner and Mark Phythian. College Station: Texas A&M University Press, 233–44.

Pollack, Kenneth M. 2002. *The Threatening Storm.* New York: Random House.

Renshon, Stanley Allen. 2004. *In His Father's Shadow: The Transformations of George W. Bush.* New York: Palgrave Macmillan.

Ricks, Thomas E. 2007. *Fiasco: The American Military Adventure in Iraq.* New York: Penguin Books.

Rubenzer, Steven J., and Thomas R. Faschingbauer. 2004. *Personality, Character, and Leadership in the White House: Psychologists Assess the Presidents.* Washington, DC: Potomac Books.

Rudalevige, Andrew. 2003. "No Child Left Behind: Forging a Congressional Compromise." In *No Child Left Behind? The Politics and Practice of School Accountability*, ed. Paul E. Peterson and Martin P. West. Washington, DC: Brookings Institution, 23–54.

Satel, Sally. 2004. "The Perils of Putting National Leaders on the Couch." *New York Times*, June 29, p. F5.

Simonton, Dean Keith. 2002. "Intelligence and Presidential Greatness: Equation Replication Using Updated IQ Estimates." In *Advances in Psychology Research*, Vol. 14, ed. Serge P. Shohov. Hauppauge, NY: Nova Science, 143–53.

———. 2006. "Presidential IQ, Openness, Intellectual Brilliance and Leadership: Estimates and Correlations for 42 U.S. Chief Executives." *Political Psychology* 27(4): 511–26.

Suedfeld, Peter, and Dana Charles Leighton. 2002. "Early Communications in the War Against Terrorism: An Integrative Complexity Analysis." *Political Psychology* 23(3): 585–99.

Tetlock, Philip E. 1981. "Pre- to Postelection Shifts in Presidential Rhetoric: Impression Management or Cognitive Adjustment?" *Journal of Personality and Social Psychology* 41(2): 207–12.

Thoemmes, Felix J., and Lucian Gideon Conway. 2007. "Integrative Complexity of 41 U.S. Presidents." *Political Psychology* 28(2): 193–226.

Weisberg, Jacob. 2008. *The Bush Tragedy.* New York: Random House.

Winik, Jay. 1996. *On the Brink.* New York: Simon & Schuster.

Woodward, Bob. 2004. *Plan of Attack.* New York: Simon & Schuster.

———. 2008. *The War Within.* New York: Simon & Schuster.

CHAPTER 3

The Cheneyization of the Bush Administration

Cheney Captures the Transition

SHIRLEY ANNE WARSHAW

AS WE EXAMINE THE LEGACY of the George W. Bush administration, nothing is more striking than the power that Vice President Dick Cheney wielded in both domestic and foreign policy. His influence spread not only across the policy continuum but also into the administrative actions of the presidency, particularly signing statements. Nearly every policy and administrative action that the White House initiated was affected by, if not directed by, Cheney.

To a large extent, the Bush administration was a co-presidency, in which a division of labor between the president and the vice president provided policy leadership. The co-presidency provided for Bush to move forward the key markers of the 2000 presidential campaign: tax reform, education reform, federally funded faith-based organizations, and policies that built a moral and civil society—to repeat a phrase he often used. The limited agenda that Bush built in the campaign was premised on his 1994 and 1998 gubernatorial campaigns, which had the same key markers.

Cheney managed a different portfolio, however, which included economic, environmental, energy, and national security policy. In addition, Cheney oversaw the creation of the President's Management Agenda in the Office of Management and Budget, which sought to transform the federal government from a civil service–based system into a contractor-based system, in which nearly half of all federal jobs would be outsourced.

Cheney's portfolio also included managing what he perceived as Congress's expanding challenges to presidential authority. His actions as the protector of presidential power led to frequent charges of an imperial presidency (Savage 2007). His positions on the unitary executive and the constitutional authority of the president in national security, all of which Bush endorsed, led to the most significant expansion of presidential authority since the Nixon administration (Goldsmith 2007).

While the influence of Cheney across the administration is an important discussion, this chapter will address only a small part of that discussion, focusing on the tools that Cheney employed at the outset of the administration to build the co-presidency. These consisted of controlling the transition and of crafting a single executive office during the transition, with the vice president's staff integrated into White House policy making. His ability to shape leadership across the administration and his access to information were central to his influence in the Oval Office. While the story of the co-presidency is a complex one, nothing is more important to Cheney's rise to power in the Bush administration than the control he exerted during the transition over appointments and the integration of his staff with Bush's staff, creating "full transparency," as the administration called it, between the two offices.

The appointments that Cheney made during the transition led to a business-friendly administration. Decisions made by Cheney appointments often included pro-business regulatory changes, such as drilling for oil and gas on federal lands, logging on federal lands without the necessity of an environmental impact statement, changing standards for industrial emissions, and using risk-benefit analyses that favored economic benefits over health benefits (Gellman 2008). Agency budgets for regulatory enforcement were slashed, leaving staffs struggling to manage minimal regulatory oversight. Agencies such as the Consumer Product Safety Commission, whose Cheney-appointed director was a former gas and oil lawyer from Texas, slashed staff from their enforcement division, which eventually led to a wave of product failures, such as the lead-based toys imported from China.

National security policy, in which Cheney eventually had equally significant influence, saw his footprints in the decision to topple Saddam Hussein in Iraq. This was a position Cheney put on the table at the first National Security Council meeting after the inauguration, months before the terrorist attacks of September 11, 2001. Decisions involving interrogation policy, warrantless surveillance, and rights of prisoners of war were framed in his office. The legal team which he appointed, in Alberto

Gonzales's office and in the Justice Department's Office of Legal Counsel, provided the legal cover for his decisions (Goldsmith 2007). Similarly, the expansive interpretation of presidential powers in terms of both the unitary executive and constitutional war powers emerged in his office.

Cheney was the single-most influential member of the Bush administration, using the transition to staff the key offices across the administration that would move forward his business-oriented agenda and support his positions in national security policy. Yet, Cheney's rise to power was facilitated not only by his control over the appointment process but also by the divisions within the White House staff. Karl Rove and Karen Hughes led the Texas-dominated political faction whose primary goal was ensuring George W. Bush's reelection in 2004; Michael Gerson and Peter Wehner led the religious conservatives, whose goal was to protect the evangelical base and the agenda that they pursued; John Bridgeland and John DiIulio pursued the administration's moderate social policies; and Condoleezza Rice oversaw the National Security Council staff (Bridgeland 2007; DiIulio 2005–2007; Gerson 2007; Hughes 2004; Wehner 2007). Andy Card, who assembled this disparate group, managed a compartmentalized staff with a narrow agenda. The combination of the narrow agenda (focused on tax cuts, education, and faith-based initiatives) and the compartmentalized staff of the Bush White House opened the door for Cheney to address his extensive policy and administrative goals.

The research for this chapter, which addresses only the transition, is part of a larger study that I conducted on Dick Cheney's influence in the Bush administration, which culminated in a book entitled *The Co-Presidency of Bush and Cheney* (2009). Research for the book, conducted over three years, involved numerous interviews of key Bush-Cheney administration and campaign staff and an analysis of key policy decisions.

THE TRANSITION:
CHENEY GAINS CONTROL OF THE APPOINTMENT PROCESS

Although he had been involved earlier in the campaign in the foreign policy advisory group known as the Vulcans, his primary role in the campaign had been to manage the vice-presidential search. From April through July 2000, Cheney interviewed candidates for the vice-presidential position.

However, each candidate that Cheney reviewed seemed to have personal, financial, or professional disqualifiers. When Cheney presented his dilemma to Bush over lunch at the Crawford ranch on July 25, 2000, Bush unexpectedly asked Cheney to take the job. After accepting, Cheney's role during the general election was relatively minor. He never left the shadow of Bush and dutifully followed the direction of the Austin campaign staff, led by Karl Rove. But on election night, even before the final results had been determined in the battle between Bush and Gore, Cheney's role dramatically changed as he took command of the transition. He was no longer in the shadow of Bush or of the campaign staff.

As Cheney and his entourage sat in the suite of the Four Seasons Hotel in Austin on election night, waiting for the election to be decided, Cheney began to manage the transition. For the next four days Cheney, David Addington, and Scooter Libby, among others, remained in the suite, crafting the framework of the transition in spite of the legal challenge being waged over Florida's vote count by the Gore campaign (Hayes 2007). Overseeing the transition was a role that Bush had assigned to Cheney in August, soon after the Republican convention in Philadelphia.

The transition, however, faced a financial problem: since federal law barred either campaign from gaining access to the $5.27 million available to the president-elect until the election results were finalized, Cheney chose to establish a privately funded transition office in McLean, Virginia, using funds from the newly created Bush-Cheney Presidential Transition Foundation, Inc.

While they waited in Austin, Libby and Addington became Cheney's first appointments to the transition team. At the same time, Cheney also began building his staff for the vice president's office and named Libby as the vice president's national security advisor and chief of staff and Addington as the legal counsel. In addition to Libby and Addington, Paul Wolfowitz and Stephen Hadley, Cheney's deputies in the Department of Defense under George H.W. Bush, had remained in Austin to work on the transition. Their jobs, too, were determined as they waited with Cheney. Wolfowitz would become deputy secretary of defense and Hadley would be deputy national security advisor in the Bush administration.

As transition director, Cheney moved quickly to hire the myriads of political appointees that would be needed for the administration. Over six thousand political jobs would be filled across fourteen cabinet-level offices. Reporting to Cheney as the senior member of the transition team was Clay Johnson (Burke 2004; Kumar 2002). Johnson, a close friend of Bush and member of his gubernatorial staff, had been tapped by Bush in the spring of 2000 to begin informal transition planning (Johnson 2002). Cheney still had a relatively small staff and relied heavily on his daughter, Liz Cheney, and on Libby and Addington. Two other senior staff, David Gribben and Juleanna Glover Weiss, moved from the campaign to the transition team.

Once the election results were resolved, Cheney could finally begin a formal transition process—having run an informal one for over a month. Cheney's job, over the next five weeks, was to fill more than 6,400 jobs in the new administration, including 1,125 that would require Senate confirmation (known as PAS for presidentially appointed, Senate-confirmed).

Cheney's pro-business agenda focused on the agencies that controlled energy and environmental regulations. He began with the White House, where he installed James Connaughton to head the Council on Environmental Quality. Connaughton, a lawyer who represented General Electric in its lawsuits against EPA and its Superfund requirements, in turn named Philip Cooney, a lobbyist with the American Petroleum Institute, as his chief of staff. Cheney's appointees in the Department of the Interior, key to opening federal land for oil and gas drilling, included Stephen Griles, a lobbyist for energy companies, as deputy secretary, and Jeffrey Jarrett, a coal company executive, to run the Office of Surface Mining. To many, Cheney's appointees resembled putting a fox in charge of the hen house.

The fox was everywhere, as it turned out. At the Office of Management and Budget (OMB), Cheney placed John D. Graham in charge of the Office of Information and Regulatory Affairs (OIRA). Before his appointment to OIRA, Graham had been director of Harvard University's Center for Risk Analysis (HCRA). The HCRA was widely criticized by public interest groups and others for its pro-business tilt when it minimized the health risks from industrial pollution. At Agriculture, Cheney installed Mark Rey, a logging executive, to manage the national forests. At Energy, Cheney installed not only Spencer Abraham, a long-time opponent of environmental regulation of the auto industry, but as his deputy, Francis Blake, a General

Electric lawyer who opposed EPA demands on industrial cleanup. These are a small sampling of the many pro-business appointments Cheney made in agencies dealing with environmental and energy regulations.

Cheney had notably little influence over the Department of Health and Human Services, whose policies built the moral and civil society that Bush addressed in his faith-based agenda. These appointments came from the circle of campaign advisors involved in the faith-based issues, such as abstinence education, abortion, and funding for faith-based organizations such as Prison Ministries.

In general, Cheney controlled the staffing within the agencies that dealt with economic, environmental, and energy policy, allowing him to build an administration focused on reducing regulatory controls on business and industry. His appointments to senior levels of the defense establishment (such as Stephen Hadley, Paul Wolfowitz, Douglas Feith, Stephen Cambone, and Richard Perle) allowed him to cement his influence in national security policy (Hayes 2007).

FULL TRANSPARENCY: CREATING THE SINGLE EXECUTIVE OFFICE

Using the transition to control the appointments process was only one of the tools that Cheney employed to influence administration policies for his pro-business agenda. Perhaps equally as important was integrating his staff into the White House policy apparatus: full transparency—a term coined by Libby—meant that every decision made in the White House had input from the vice president's staff, as well as from the vice president himself (Hughes 2004).

Every memo circulated within the White House included the vice president's staff on the routing list. Members of the vice president's staff were included in all meeting arrangements and could choose whether or not they wanted to attend (Frum 2007). Andy Card, among others, referred approvingly to the new arrangement as a single executive office.

Having successfully changed the organizational structure of the White House by creating a single executive office which fully integrated the vice president's staff, Cheney then had the Office of the Vice President deleted in the federal budget as a separate appropriation and consolidated into the larger appropriation for the Executive Office of the President (EOP). The Office of the Vice President became part of the same line item in the federal budget as the White House staff. The fiscal year 2003 budget was changed to include a line that read, "As part of the FY 2003 budget, the Administration is requesting a consolidation and financial realignment for the Executive Office of the President" (Executive Office of the President 2002, 383). The change allowed the twelve annual salary and expense accounts for the EOP agencies, including the vice president's office, to be consolidated into a single appropriation.

Cheney's staff became so interwoven with White House staff that when openings occurred on the White House staff, Cheney's staff filled them. For example, Cheney's legislative liaison, Candida Wolff, became White House legislative director when Nicholas Calio left, and Ron Christie, Cheney's deputy domestic policy advisor, became deputy director of the White House domestic policy office when a vacancy opened in that office (Bridgeland 2007; Calio 2007; Howard 2007).

Cheney was particularly successful at building bridges to the foreign policy machinery of the National Security Council (NSC) within the White House (Wilkerson 2006–2007). Libby, Cheney's top national security advisor and his chief of staff, was a regular participant in meetings of the National Security Council staff and was as engrained in discussions there as was any member of the White House staff. Libby was welcomed to the NSC meetings by his old friend Stephen Hadley, the deputy director of the National Security Council staff. Hadley and Libby had worked together at the Department of Defense for then secretary of defense Cheney. In essence, Cheney had a significant influence on decisions being made within the National Security Council and certainly more influence than his nemesis, Secretary of State Colin Powell (Wilkerson 2006–2007).

Crafting the White House staff and the vice president's staff into one fluid organization, with "full transparency" as Libby referred to it, was accentuated by Cheney's insistence on certain titles for his staff. As in any organization, titles matter, and Cheney ensured that his staff had the titles that mattered within the executive office. Cheney's staff had titles that paralleled the White House's, such as assistant to the vice president and deputy assistant to the vice president (Christie 2006).

He first ensured that two of his staff, Mary Matalin and Scooter Libby, had the coveted title of *assistant to the president* in addition to their title of assistant to the vice president. They remained part of the vice president's staff but, because of their additional title, were part of the 7:30 A.M. senior staff meeting held by Andy Card each morning and were included in all senior staff discussions. Cheney also had members of his staff, such as his speechwriter, John McConnell, and his counselor, Steve Schmidt, given the added designation *deputy assistant to the president*, further reinforcing the integration of the two staffs and their role in the broader organizational structure.

By the end of the first full month of the administration, Cheney had built a staff of eighty-five within the vice president's office. For every senior White House staff position Cheney created a similar staff position in the vice president's office. Cheney built a staff of eleven assistants to the vice president, including his chief of staff, counsel, staff secretary, press secretary, political affairs, legislative affairs, domestic policy, operations, and advance. Added to this list were not one but two assistants to the vice president for national security affairs—a signal that this would be the largest of the many staffs within the vice president's office. Each of these senior staff had a staff of deputy assistants and special assistants, in addition to other staff within each unit (list of staff from Evans 2002).

Policy expertise in the vice president's office mirrored (if not exceeded) that in the White House, particularly in the area of national security. The most dramatic example of this was found in the national security affairs staff, which included John Hannah (on loan to Cheney's office from John Bolton at the State Department); Eric Edelman, a foreign service officer who recently served as ambassador to Finland; and C. Dean McGrath Jr., who had been chief of staff for Representative Christopher Cox of California. McGrath and Cheney had been on a bipartisan panel on stolen Chinese military hardware years earlier. Matched with these policy experts were military staff, most of whom were detailed from defense agencies. In sharp contrast to the large, specialized staffing structure created in Cheney's office, Vice President Al Gore had only one national security advisor, Leon S. Fuerth.

Although Gore's staff had reached a similar size, numbering ninety at one point, its role was very different. Cheney's staff was built to parallel the White House staff, to ensure that the vice president's staff was fully integrated into the discussions at policy meetings. In contrast, Gore had no intention of having his staff participate in every White House policy discussion and join in every meeting, as Cheney did. Rather, Gore built his staff to handle specific assignments that President Clinton had assigned him, the largest of which was the National Performance Review, which worked with all fourteen cabinet-level agencies and the Office of Management and Budget to streamline government operations.

The staff that Cheney built was drawn largely from Congress, including Ethan Hastert, the son of Speaker of the House Dennis Hastert. Cheney's congressional hires were a nod to the close working relationship that he intended to build with Hastert and the Republican-controlled Congress, and it reflected his distrust of the executive branch. By the time Cheney returned to Washington, D.C., with the transition, he had been out of Beltway politics for eight years. While he still had connections in the military complex from which to pull staff for his national security section, he had few connections in the domestic arena of the executive branch (Schmitt 2001).

The executive branch, moreover, was likely to have Democrats tied to the Clinton administration, with a liberal approach to domestic policy issues. Cheney had served in Congress for ten years, and he still knew many Republican members who were eager to have their staffers working in the vice president's office.

It is worth noting that while the president's and vice president's staffs had full transparencies, they were focusing on different issues (DiIulio 2005–2007). There appear to be few cases in which clashes developed between the two staffs in domestic policy, since each had its own realm of influence. Not until the Valerie Plame incident, which involved controlling information on Iraq and pitted Scooter Libby against Karl Rove, did the two staffs clash.

CHENEY CREATES PARALLEL TRANSITION TEAMS
FROM HIS BUSINESS NETWORK

Although Cheney controlled the appointments process, others from the campaign had roles in the transition. Joshua Bolten, the campaign's policy director, took responsibility for creating the policy transition teams that would guide the incoming cabinet officers as they prepared to lead their agencies. Bolten brought in John Cogan, an economist from Stanford University and the architect of Bush's proposal for individual Social Security accounts, to work on specific economic issues, and John Bridgeland and Gary Edson from the campaign to manage broader economic and domestic policy (Cogan 2007; Bridgeland 2007).

Bridgeland and Edson assembled small task forces of three to four policy experts to oversee each department's transition. The task forces interfaced with the Clinton cabinet officers and staff, reviewed existing budgets and legislative mandates, met the political staff, and determined how Bush campaign goals would be interwoven into departmental priorities. The task forces were formally known as "policy coordinating groups," a purposefully different working title from Cheney's transition "advisory teams." Bolten knew exactly what he was doing by differentiating the working titles, separating the fluff of Cheney's advisory teams from the substance of the Bridgeland and Edson policy groups.

Cheney, however, was not willing to relinquish his influence over the departments to the Bolten-led task forces. At about the same time that Bolten announced the creation of the policy coordinating groups, Cheney established what he called advisory teams for each of the twelve domestic departments. Most of the 474 individuals Cheney named to the advisory teams were lobbyists or corporate executives who had a vested interest in the actions of the departments for which they were recommending personnel and policies. The *Washington Post* carried a quote that described Cheney's advisory teams as "a way for the Bush team to do a favor for people, to show who their friends are. You want your clients to read about all the access you have" (Mintz 2001). The intensity of the energy advisory team sent another signal. Cheney was making clear to his business constituency that this was going to be a business-oriented administration with an energy focus.

CHENEY BUILDS THE CABINET

While Cheney's advisory teams and Bolten's transition teams (policy coordinating groups) were doing their work, Cheney was developing a list of names for cabinet positions as part of his role as transition director. Some positions had obvious choices. Colin Powell had indicated his interest in serving as secretary of state during the campaign. Donald Evans, the campaign chair, was a logical choice for Commerce. Cheney's old friend and mentor Donald Rumsfeld wanted to return to the Defense Department to finish his plans for modernizing the military. For the Treasury Department was another colleague of Cheney's from the Ford administration, Alcoa chairman Paul O'Neill, who had been a senior staffer at OMB.

The rest of the cabinet had solid business credentials, which became the core requirement for Cheney. This would be a cabinet that protected business and industry from what Cheney saw as the intrusive nature of government regulation. Spencer Abraham, the defeated senator from Michigan, had a long voting history of support for the automobile industry, and he understood energy issues; Cheney recommended Abraham for Energy. To head the Interior Department, Cheney recommended Gale Norton, who had worked for a lobbying organization to reduce controls over federal parkland. For the Labor Department, he recommended Linda Chavez, who was immediately opposed by labor unions for her antiunion positions. Chavez eventually pulled out of the confirmation hearings and was replaced by Elaine Chao, who had few credentials in labor issues but was married to politically important Kentucky senator Mitch McConnell, and who brought ethnic and gender diversity to the cabinet.

One of the few cabinet positions that Cheney had little influence over was that of attorney general. John Ashcroft had the support of the elder Bush, who in 1991 had considered naming him attorney general to pull Christian conservatives into the reelection campaign. The younger Bush had at times been part of his father's campaign team, doing outreach to Christian conservatives. Tapping Ashcroft as attorney general would also be political payback. In late 1998, Ashcroft had launched his own brief campaign for the White House, winning the support of Pat Robertson's Christian Coalition and other conservative religious groups. But he withdrew in January 1999 before entering a single primary, and later endorsed the George W. Bush campaign.

Ashcroft was not a Cheney loyalist. As one of the few members of the cabinet who knew that his job was not due to Cheney, Ashcroft remained independent of the vice president. Several years later—in the aftermath of the September 11, 2001, terrorist attacks, when the vice president was overseeing policy decisions on the war on terror—Ashcroft would resist Cheney's proposals. For example, after the Abu Ghraib prison scandal erupted, regular battles erupted between the vice president, his counsel David Addington, and Ashcroft over interrogation law (Savage 2007).

When Ashcroft left after the first term, Cheney ensured that he would have an ally at the helm of the Department of Justice. He supported the nomination of Bush's White House legal counsel, Alberto Gonzales, who had proven very supportive of Cheney-driven policies on the war on terror. Gonzales was so supportive that he pushed Ashcroft to overturn a Justice Department decision that found the domestic wireless surveillance program illegal; in March 2004, after meetings with David Addington, Gonzales went to Ashcroft's intensive care hospital room to have him overturn the ruling. Ashcroft refused (Goldsmith 2007). Ashcroft and Powell had been the two cabinet appointments that Cheney had not controlled during the transition, and both later proved thorns in his side as he pushed a contro-versial set of policies, including wireless surveillance, refuting the Geneva Conventions' ban on torture, and the invasion of Iraq.

THE WHITE HOUSE STAFF DIVIDED

The pro-business orientation of the appointments in most of the depart-ments, which Cheney controlled, did not hold true for appointments to the White House staff, which he did not control. The White House staff was a different breed, split between the political pragmatists and the so-cial moderates. Rove and Hughes led the political pragmatists and Bolten, Bridgeland, and Edson led the social moderates—Bolten as deputy chief of staff, Bridgeland as director of the Domestic Policy Council, and Edson as deputy director of the National Economic Council. Their work during the transition managing the policy coordinating groups was widely viewed as professional, even-handed, and thoughtful—views that others would continue to have of them as they moved into the West Wing.

Bolten, Bridgeland, and Edson, and later John DiIulio, were the mod-erates within the White House who sought to build policy responses to campaign rhetoric. They were not endeavoring to build a new governing coalition, as was Karl Rove, or to tilt policy making toward business, as was Dick Cheney, or to create a moral and civil society, as was George W. Bush. Instead, they saw government as a bridge for citizens to use in building stronger communities.

This small band of policy wonks wanted to use the resources of the federal government to increase volunteerism and to create new partnerships between communities and citizens. Each member of the group had been drawn to the campaign's theme of compassionate conservatism, which implied a new role for government as the twenty-first century emerged, instead of the Reagan philosophy of limited government.

They were young moderates with few ties to old governing coalitions. Bolten, a former Goldman Sachs executive and a Princeton graduate with a law degree from Stanford, became a neutral broker in the chief of staff's office. Bridgeland, a Harvard graduate with a law degree from the University of Virginia, had served as chief of staff for moderate Cincinnati congressman Rob Portman. While in Portman's office, he had authored the Citizen's Service Act, which later framed the USA Freedom Corps, a program that he would direct. Gary Edson, another Stanford graduate, would lead the effort to create the Millennium Challenge Account for developing nations. John DiIulio, a Democrat and Harvard Ph.D. in political science, who was also drawn to the call of compassionate conservatism, would oversee the creation of the White House Office of Faith-Based Initiatives. They formed the core of centrist policy making in the senior levels of the White House (Bridgeland 2007; DiIulio 2005–2007).

What was emerging in the transition was a three-way split in the policy offices of the White House. The Cheney organization in the vice president's office focused on national security and energy policy, while the Bush organization in the president's office focused on education policy and a broad definition of compassionate conservatism; in most cases, these two spheres did not overlap. In the middle were the Bridgeland-Edson-DiIulio policy units in the White House. They endeavored to build a domestic policy agenda that did not intrude on either the Cheney or Bush organizations.

By the first weeks and months of the administration, three clear policy agendas were taking shape: Bush and the Christian conservatives, Cheney and the business interests, and the White House moderates. The dominant

Cheney = dominant agenda

agenda, however, was Dick Cheney's; he had used the transition to create an administration populated with business-oriented political appointees whose primary mission was to carry out policies benefiting their own business interests.

In the brief two and a half months between the election and the inauguration, Cheney successfully used the transition to build an administration stacked with those who shared his pro-business agenda in the domestic policy agencies, and with those who shared his worldview in the foreign policy agencies. He would later ensure that key legal offices were filled by lawyers who supported his expansive view of presidential power.

Cheney's control of staffing did not extend to the president's own staff in the White House. As it turned out, the White House staff differed in its ideological consistency from the business-oriented, limited-government Cheney appointees. The White House had social moderates running the domestic policy arm, who were committed to a certain degree of government activism. These social moderates tried to move forward the centerpiece of Bush's campaign pledge for compassionate conservatism: funding for faith-based groups and for increased volunteerism. Added to the mix of policy moderates was Bush himself, who was personally more interested in building programs that supported his moral values, such as abstinence education, adoption rather than abortion, banning federally funded stem cell research, and similar programs.

What Cheney understood, more than Bush or the social moderates on the White House staff, was the enormous reach of the federal government. Although Bush and the White House staff controlled a small but important mix of social policy areas, Cheney controlled through his appointments the much larger mix of economic, national security, environmental, and energy policy.

CONCLUSION:

JUDGING BUSH

The legacy of the Bush administration will unquestionably be the war in Iraq, a policy orchestrated by Cheney and a small group of Cheney-appointed senior officials in the Department of Defense, such as Donald Rumsfeld, Paul Wolfowitz, Douglas Feith, and Stephen Cambone. During the transition, Cheney easily had moved into office a group who had long sought to overturn the existing regime in Iraq.

The war itself is only part of the Cheney legacy, which includes the decisions on warrantless surveillance, harsh interrogation practices, abrogation of protections under the third Geneva Convention, and a refusal to use the judge advocate general staff in detainees' trials—decisions managed by Cheney's appointees.

Those decisions received the approval of both the White House legal office under Alberto Gonzales and the Department of Justice's Office of Legal Counsel. Without the legal staff put in place by David Addington in Cheney's office, the decisions would not have been approved. One lawyer whom Addington did not choose was William Taft IV in the Department of State, who adamantly opposed many of the decisions that the Cheney-appointed lawyers rendered. But his voice was silenced by the Office of Legal Counsel, which Cheney controlled. The degree to which Cheney managed both the prosecution of the war and the control of the prisoners of war was possible only through his control of the transition and the appointments process.

Similarly, his ability to move forward his pro-business policies, focused on antiregulatory action, was possible because of the key appointments he made across the administration. These antiregulatory policies were a significant factor in the economic chaos of the fall of 2008, when the stock market plunged 500 points in one day and 400 points immediately after. The failure of some of the largest corporate entities in the nation, such as AIG, Merrill Lynch, and Lehman Brothers, was caused by a culture of antiregulation that Dick Cheney enabled.

While Cheney was integrally involved in both domestic and foreign policy, his role in demanding new interpretations of presidential power cannot be overlooked. David Addington, Cheney's legal counsel, was responsible for writing signing statements that asserted a line-item veto into legislation which removed the president from controlling executive branch decisions. Whether the signing statement dealt with the president's right to open mail or with the Endangered Species Act and sonar policy for submarines, Addington and Cheney ensured presidential control. Charges of an imperial presidency should be directed at Cheney, not Bush.

For the purpose of this volume, I will frame the influence that Cheney wielded in terms of his strategic, political, and tactical competence. From a tactical perspective, he successfully captured the appointments process during the transition to build a pro-business administration and successfully integrated his staff into the single executive office within the White House. In addition, he implemented a massive outsourcing effort to reduce the size of the career bureaucracy. However, the policies that Cheney oversaw became the administration's greatest failures largely due to his strategic failures. He failed to build the political coalitions to support his policies largely because of the narrow political interests they served. The strategic failure to integrate career professionals in the federal bureaucracy into the policy process led to failures in every policy area in which Cheney was involved.

The final criterion employed in this book in judging the Bush administration is integrity, which Cheney frequently lacked. His determination to move forward his policy proposals often ignored the policy recommendations of career professionals and refuted the arguments of international experts. Whether arguing that factory pollutants did not contribute to global warming, that Saddam Hussein had weapons of mass destruction, or that his office was not part of the executive branch, Cheney skewed the evidence to satisfy his position.

Cheney's portfolio of energy, environmental, economic, and national security policy has provided the administration's greatest failures. Policy areas that Cheney was not involved in, such as education reform, expansion of volunteer programs, and federal funding for faith-based initiatives, have been more successful. But the legacy of the Bush administration is largely one of failure, with most of the blame falling squarely on the shoulders of the vice president, Dick Cheney.

REFERENCES

Bridgeland, John. 2007. Interview with the author, November.
Burke, John P. 2004. *Becoming President: The Bush Transition, 2000–2003*. Boulder, CO: Lynne Rienner.
Calio, Nicholas. 2007. Interview with the author, October–November.
Christie, Ron. 2006. *Black in the White House: Life Inside George W. Bush's West Wing*. New York: Nelson.
Cogan, John. 2007. Interview with the author, November.

DiIulio, John. 2005–2007. Interviews with the author, various dates.

Evans, Eleanor, ed. 2002. *Capital Source, Fall 2002: The Who's Who, What, Where in Washington*. Washington, DC: National Journal Group.

Executive Office of the President. 2002. Office of Management and Budget. *Budget of the U.S. Government, FY 2003*. Washington, DC: U.S. Government Printing Office.

Frum, David. 2007. Interview with the author, November.

Gellman, Barton. 2008. *Angler: The Cheney Vice Presidency*. New York: Penguin.

Gerson, Michael J. 2007. *Heroic Conservatism: Why Republicans Need to Embrace America's Ideals (And Why They Deserve to Fail If They Don't)*. New York: HarperCollins.

Goldsmith, Jack. 2007. *The Terror Presidency: Law and Judgment Inside the Bush Administration*. New York: Norton.

Hayes, Stephen F. 2007. *Cheney: The Untold Story of America's Most Powerful and Controversial Vice President*. New York: HarperCollins.

Howard, Jack. 2007. Interview with the author, October–November.

Hughes, Karen. 2004. *Ten Minutes from Normal*. New York: Penguin.

Johnson, Clay. 2002. "The 2000–01 Presidential Transition: Planning, Goals and Reality." *PS: Political Science and Politics* 35(1): 51–53.

Kumar, Martha. 2002. "The Presidential Transition of 2001: Scholars Offer Expertise and Analysis." *PS: Political Science and Politics* 35(1): 6–8.

Mintz, John. 2001. "Transition Advisers Have Much to Gain." *Washington Post*, January 17, p. A15.

Savage, Charlie. 2007. *Takeover: The Return of the Imperial Presidency and the Subversion of American Democracy*. New York: Little, Brown.

Schmitt, Eric. 2001. "Cheney Assembles Formidable Team." *New York Times*, February 3. http://query.nytimes.com/gst/fullpage.html?res=9907E7DC133EF930A35751C0A967 9C8B63 (Accessed August 15, 2008).

Warshaw, Shirley Anne. 2009. *The Co-Presidency of Bush and Cheney*. Stanford, CA: Stanford University Press.

Wehner, Peter. 2007. Interview with the author, November.

Wilkerson, Lawrence. 2006–2007. Interviews with the author, various dates.

CHAPTER 4

President Bush as Chief Executive

JAMES P. PFIFFNER

AS CHIEF EXECUTIVE, the president is formally responsible for the execution of the laws and the management of the executive branch. This
does not mean that the president personally directs most executive branch
activities, but the president or presidential surrogates, often political appointees, oversee and supervise the most important activities of the executive branch. Presidents are personally most directly involved with the
management of the White House staff, policy making at the top levels of
the executive branch, and the place of the presidency in the constitutional system. This chapter will examine several of President Bush's actions
as chief executive at these three levels of presidential responsibility. Although only a few executive actions will be analyzed, these policies had
far-reaching, historic consequences and are among the most important of
the Bush administration: the war in Iraq, detainee policy, and claims to
constitutional executive power.

The first section will examine decision making in the White House on
two key actions of historic importance: the decision to go to war in Iraq
and the decision to suspend the Geneva Conventions. In making each of
these decisions, important White House staff or cabinet members were
excluded or marginalized. The second section will deal with two key decisions on carrying out the above policies: how to occupy Iraq and how
to interrogate detainees in the war on terror. In each of these cases, the
administration ignored the advice of career professionals in the military
services. The third section will examine President Bush's extraordinary
claims to executive power under the Constitution in several important
policy areas. In each of these cases, Bush tried to exclude the other two
branches of government, Congress and the federal court system, from
controlling or overseeing his decisions.

MANAGING WHITE HOUSE POLICY MAKING

Public policy at the presidential level is so complex, and the organization of the White House is so differentiated, that a regular policy process is virtually essential to good policy making. The process should not be rigidly bureaucratic, but for important decisions there should be a procedure in place to ensure that all of the relevant White House and cabinet officials have an opportunity to "sign off" on proposed policies. As a matter of prudence the president should want to ensure that his or her decision is based on the full range of relevant information (George 1972; Pfiffner 2005).

On some of the most important decisions of the Bush administration, it appears that no systematic policy process was followed and that key people who should have had an opportunity to make their views known to the president were excluded or marginalized. Of course, a fully informed president will not necessarily make wise decisions, but an ill-informed president is more likely to make mistakes.

This section will examine two key decisions made by President Bush and argue that there were important shortcomings in the way that he made these decisions—primarily the exclusion or marginalizing of key personnel or the absence of a full airing of the issues and deliberation with all of the principals.

Deciding to Go to War in Iraq

The most important decision with respect to Iraq was that the invasion of the country was necessary in order to depose Saddam Hussein. In the decision to go to war in Afghanistan, President Bush deliberated openly with his war cabinet and followed a rational process in making the major decisions in a relatively short time. In contrast, the decision to invade Iraq seems to have been made over the course of a year or so and was characterized by incremental and disjointed rather than comprehensive decision making along the way. Bush had probably made up his own mind about war sometime early in 2002, but other members of his administration became aware of his decision at different times over the next year.

President Bush did not make public his decision to pursue Iraq until the State of the Union address on January 29, 2002, though even then he was somewhat vague about the way in which he stated his intention.

entertain dissenting opinions

(In November 2001, he had ordered Donald Rumsfeld to prepare operational plans for a war against Iraq.) Bush announced his decision with a high level of generality, including Iraq, Iran, and North Korea in what he called an "axis of evil." In the speech Bush declared, "I will not wait on events while dangers gather. I will not stand by as peril draws closer and closer" (Bush 2002). In April 2002, the administration started talking about "regime change" in Iraq, and Bush told a British reporter, "I made up my mind that Saddam needs to go" (Woodward 2004, 119).

stubborness & inability to

According to State Department director of policy and planning Richard Haass (who had worked on the NSC staff on Middle East issues for George H.W. Bush), Condoleezza Rice told him that the president had made up his mind by July 2002. Haass said that he broached the issue of war with Iraq with Rice: "I raised this issue about were we really sure that we wanted to put Iraq front and center at this point, given the war on terrorism and other issues. And she said, essentially, that that decision's been made, don't waste your breath" (Lemann 2003, 36).

On August 5, 2002, at Colin Powell's initiative, Rice arranged for Powell to spend two hours with the president in order to explain his own reservations about war with Iraq. He argued that war with Iraq would destabilize the whole Middle East; an American occupation would be seen as hostile by the Muslim world; and an invasion of Iraq should not be undertaken by the United States unilaterally. Powell didn't think the president understood the full implications of an American invasion. He told the president that if the United States invaded Iraq, it would tie down most of the army and the United States would be responsible for twenty-five million people: "You will become the government until you get a new government" (Woodward 2004, 150–51).

The relative informality of the decision-making process is illustrated by the way the president informed his secretary of state that he had made up his mind. The president asked Rice and White House counselor Karen Hughes their opinion about going to war with Iraq, but he didn't ask Powell. Once he finalized the decision to go to war, Bush immediately informed Rumsfeld but not Powell. In fact, the president informed Prince Bandar, the Saudi Arabian ambassador to the United States, of his decision before he informed Powell (Woodward 2004, 151–52, 165). The president had to be prompted by Rice to inform Powell that he had made up his mind to go to war. On January 13, 2003, the president brought Powell in for a twelve-minute meeting to inform him of the decision to go to war and ask him to support his decision. The president stressed that it was a "cordial" conversation and that "I didn't need his permission" (Woodward 2004, 269–74). The deliberations about war were not definitive enough or inclusive enough for the secretary of state (the only NSC principal with combat experience) to know that President Bush had made the decision to go to war.

The seeming lack of deliberation is striking. Though there were many meetings on tactical and operational decisions, there seemed to be no meetings where the entire National Security Council (NSC) engaged in face-to-face discussions of all the options, including the pros and cons of whether or not to go to war. In part, this may have been due to the shift in Rice's role away from the honest broker role she played in the decisions about Afghanistan. According to John Burke, in the decisions about Iraq, Rice did not act as a broker (Burke 2005). Instead, the president decided to use her talents as a confidant and articulator of his views.

Suspending the Geneva Conventions

The Geneva Conventions were revised after World War II, partly in response to Nazi atrocities committed against wartime captives. In the fall of 2001, however, the Bush administration felt tremendous pressure not only to pursue those who had committed the 9/11 atrocities but also to prevent future attacks, which it assumed were in planning stages. In order to obtain crucial intelligence, the United States would have to depend much more on the interrogation of prisoners to reveal plans for future attacks. Thus, the traditional interrogation techniques developed by the U.S. military and limited to the strictures of the Geneva Conventions would not be sufficient, in the Bush administration's judgment. In late 2001 and early 2002 the administration went about exempting U.S. interrogators from the Geneva rules.

The purpose of the suspension of the Geneva Conventions by the administration was to ensure that captives in the war on terror did not have to be treated according to the Geneva rules; thus, interrogators could apply harsh techniques to gain intelligence on terrorist activities.

In addition, the administration wanted to ensure that its interrogators did not get charged with war crimes; the U.S. War Crimes statute referred to the Geneva rules, and if Geneva did not apply, the war crimes statute was unlikely to be invoked regarding the harsh treatment of detainees. As White House Counsel Alberto Gonzales stated in a memo to Bush, "A determination that GPW [Geneva Conventions Prisoner of War requirements] is not applicable to the Taliban would mean that Section 2441 [War Crimes Act] would not apply to actions taken with respect to the Taliban" (Gonzales 2002).[1]

The decision was made when Colin Powell was out of the country, and when he objected upon his return, his warnings were ignored. Suspending the Geneva agreements drastically changed what had been U.S. policy for the treatment of prisoners since George Washington told his troops not to abuse British captives. It also reversed what had been firm Defense Department guidelines for the treatment of prisoners during wartime. The president was successful in exempting interrogators from having to conform to Geneva rules, but the Supreme Court in its *Hamdan* decision ruled that the president is required to abide by the Geneva Conventions.

The judge advocate generals of the services, however, were not consulted about the decision to abandon the Geneva Conventions (Sands 2008, 32). That is, those who because of their training and years of experience were among the most informed and qualified lawyers on the laws of war were excluded from being consulted on this important decision.

MANAGING THE EXECUTIVE BRANCH

The White House staff exists to facilitate decision making by the president, but most policies have to be implemented by the departments and agencies of the executive branch. The president is the chief executive officer of the United States and has authority (within the law) over the implementation of public policy. Thus, the relationship between the direct representatives of the president in the White House and cabinet officers who administer the major departments is crucial to successful implementation of public policy. Likewise, good relationships between the president's political appointees and the career services, which actually carry out policy, are essential. The consequences of Bush's policy victories, treated in the first section, led to administrative failures that were often due either to career professionals being excluded from having input into policies about which they were expert or to their advice being ignored by political appointees. Examples of these problems of implementation include military decisions about how to conduct the war in Iraq and the decision to use certain "alternative interrogation techniques" to extract intelligence from detainees suspected of terrorism.

Deciding How to Occupy Iraq

Once military victory in Iraq had been achieved, several key decisions were made that gravely jeopardized U.S. chances for success in Iraq: (1) the decision to make Paul Bremer, alone, the supreme U.S. authority in Iraq; (2) the decision to bar from government work those who ranked in the top four levels of Saddam's Baath Party and the top three levels of each ministry; and (3) the decision to disband the Iraqi army and replace it with a new army built from scratch. These fateful decisions were made against the advice of military and CIA professionals and without consulting important members of the president's staff and cabinet.

The decision to give Paul Bremer sole authority in Iraq without the corepresentative of the president, Zalmay Khalilzad, as had been planned, was made by President Bush during an informal lunch with Bremer, without consulting his secretary of state or national security advisor (Gordon and Trainor 2006, 475). According to Colin Powell, "The plan was for Zal to go back. He was the one guy who knew this place better than anyone. I thought this was part of the deal with Bremer. But with no discussion, no debate, things changed. I was stunned." Powell observed that President Bush's decision was "typical." There were "no full deliberations. And you suddenly discover, gee, maybe that wasn't so great, we should have thought about it a little longer" (Cohen 2007).

The decision by Bush to put Bremer fully in charge led to the first of the other two blunders. In order to rid the country of any important vestiges of Saddam's brutal regime, Bremer issued his de-Baathification order (Coalition Provisional Authority [CPA] 2003). This included up to eighty-five thousand people who constituted the civilian managerial-level techno-crats that managed the economic and energy infrastructure of the country.

Despite Undersecretary of Defense for Policy Douglas Feith's assertion that the decision had been cleared in an interagency process, the military had a distinctly different understanding of what the policy had been and thought that the CPA order cut too deeply into the administrative infrastructure of the country. The CIA was not consulted, and George Tenet said, "In fact, we knew nothing about it until de-Baathification was a fait accompli . . . Clearly, this was a critical policy decision, yet there was no NSC Principals meeting to debate the move" (Tenet 2007, 426). The lack of an NSC meeting to fully deliberate before President Bush's decision was characteristic of the Bush presidency.

The second key decision was to disband the Iraqi army. This move threw hundreds of thousands out of work and immediately created a large pool of unemployed and armed men, who felt humiliated and hostile to the U.S. occupiers. According to one U.S. officer in Baghdad, "When they disbanded the military, and announced we were occupiers—that was it. Every moderate, every person that had leaned toward us, was furious" (Ricks 2006, 164). The prewar plans of the State Department, the Army War College, and the Center for International and Strategic Studies had all recommended against disbanding the army (Fallows 2004, 74).

In an NSC meeting on March 12, 2003, there had been a consensus that the U.S. forces would use the Iraqi army to help provide internal and external security in postwar Iraq. But one week after the de-Baathification order, Bremer issued CPA Order Number 2 on May 23, 2003, which dissolved the Iraqi security forces. There had been an NSC meeting in which Bremer, via teleconference, had casually mentioned his intentions, but other participants did not conclude that President Bush had made a decision about disbanding the army.

Importantly, Colin Powell was out of town when the decision was made, and he was not informed about it, much less consulted. Even President Bush did not remember deciding. When asked in 2006 by his biographer, Roger Draper, about the decision, Bush replied, "Well, the policy was to keep the army intact. Didn't happen" (Draper 2007, 211, 433). "Yeah, I can't remember, I'm sure I said, 'This is the policy, what happened?'" (Andrews 2007). What is known is that the decision was made against the judgment of military planners and without consultation with Secretary of

State Colin Powell, chair of the Joint Chiefs of Staff General Myers, or CIA director George Tenet.

The security forces included 385,000 in the armed forces, 285,000 in the Interior Ministry (police), and 50,000 in presidential security units (Ricks 2006, 162, 192). Of course, those in police and military units (for example, the Special Republican Guard) that were Saddam's top enforcers had to be barred from working in the government. But many officers in the army were professional soldiers, and the rank-and-file enlisted soldiers constituted a source of stability and order.

Both the de-Baathification and the disbanding decisions fueled the insurgency by (1) alienating hundreds of thousands of Iraqis who could not support themselves or their families; (2) undermining the normal infrastructure necessary for social and economic activity; (3) ensuring that there was not sufficient security to carry on normal life; and (4) creating insurgents who were angry at the United States, many of whom had weapons and were trained to use them. It is probable that a more thorough consultation process, including military leaders, before these decisions were made would have given President Bush a much more realistic understanding of what the likely consequences would be.

Deciding How to Interrogate Detainees

There were three key decisions that determined that the treatment of terrorist suspects would not be handled according to traditional U.S. policy. The first was President Bush's military order of November 13, 2001, which said that the president could designate terrorist suspects as "enemy combatants" who could be detained indefinitely, who would have no access to civil courts, and who would be tried for war crimes by military commissions. The second was the suspension of the Geneva Conventions, discussed above. And the third was the decision by Donald Rumsfeld to allow a range of interrogation techniques that went beyond those allowed by the Geneva Conventions.

The military order by President Bush on November 13, 2001, was handled very closely and controlled carefully by Vice President Cheney. Because Cheney did not want any changes or challenges to his draft of the order, he explicitly excluded National Security Advisor Rice and Secretary

of State Colin Powell and drastically limited any input from military lawyers in the Department of Defense. Cheney was successful in getting the
order signed by the president without any changes, but the decision led to
a flawed legal framework for dealing with detainees in the war on terror
that depended on military commissions not authorized by law.

The combination of these two key decisions, along with Rumsfeld's
decisions about interrogation techniques, led to the torture and abuse of
detainees at Guantánamo, Bagram Air Force Base in Afghanistan, and
Abu Ghraib in Iraq. The methods authorized by Rumsfeld exceeded those
specified in the Army Field Manual on interrogations (pages 34–52). Army
training involves familiarity with the Geneva Conventions, and interrogation techniques allowed in the field manual range from kindness to trick-
ery, but none of them approach physical abuse or torture.

In the summer of 2002, with hundreds of detainees at Guantánamo,
the administration was frustrated by the dearth of actionable intelligence
being obtained by the interrogation methods that were in force at Guantánamo and which conformed to the Geneva Conventions. Administration
lawyers and the military intelligence leadership at Guantánamo began to
explore additional techniques based on U.S. training for soldiers who would
be in danger of capture by the enemy. The approach of the training was
to subject U.S. soldiers in training to the types of torture techniques that
were used by the Chinese on captured U.S. pilots in order to get them to
falsely confess to committing atrocities. U.S. trainers trained Guantánamo
interrogators in how to "reverse engineer" the resistance training received
by U.S. soldiers into counterresistance methods for getting terrorist suspects in Guantánamo to reveal more intelligence. Strenuous objections by
military lawyers for the armed services were ignored by Rumsfeld when
he approved the techniques.

The techniques were then codified in a memorandum signed by Donald Rumsfeld, which authorized the use of a range of techniques that
would have been forbidden by traditional policies. His December 2, 2002,
memorandum authorized the use of stress positions, hooding, isolation for
up to thirty days, deprivation of light and auditory stimuli, twenty-hour
interrogations, removal of clothing, and the use of dogs to intimidate detainees. According to Lawrence Wilkerson, chief of staff to Colin Powell

at the time, Rumsfeld's handwritten appendage to the December 2 memo sent the message that anything goes in the interrogation of suspected terrorists; it said, "Carte blanche, guys" (Mayer 2007, 7).

After serious objections from a range of lawyers in the Pentagon that the techniques probably violated both U.S. and international law, Rumsfeld withdrew the memo on January 15, 2003, and appointed a working group of lawyers to examine the legality of interrogation techniques. The working group was closely controlled by political appointees, and it ignored the objections of career military lawyers. The working group (without notifying the military lawyers who dissented) recommended a list of techniques on April 4, 2003, and Rumsfeld approved some of them on April 16. Hooding, stress positions, and the use of dogs were dropped, and dietary manipulation, environmental manipulation, and sleep adjustment were added; isolation was retained.

Although the dry, legal terms used in the memoranda do not seem excessive, the actual implementation of these techniques by young, untrained soldiers and contractors resulted in extremely harsh treatment of detainees that amounted to torture at Guantánamo, Bagram Air Force Base, and Abu Ghraib. That a number of detainees died after being beaten and suffocated demonstrated that the treatment was indeed harsh (Schmitt 2004; Allen 2006). It might be argued that the legally authorized techniques, if carefully applied, would not necessarily amount to torture, but the consequences of authorizing harsh treatment predictably led to excesses in implementation.

MANAGING PRESIDENTIAL POWER

After the atrocities of 9/11, the president had the duty to protect Americans. The problem, however, was that President Bush pushed the reasonable duties of the executive beyond the bounds that the Constitution established. He imprisoned hundreds of suspected terrorists indefinitely without charging them and denied them the opportunity to argue their innocence before an independent judge. He allowed, and arguably encouraged, interrogating them with harsh techniques that many consider to be torture. He claimed the unilateral authority to conduct surveillance secretly on Americans without obtaining warrants required by law. And

Patriot
Act

he asserted that he was not bound by provisions of laws that he himself deemed to impinge on his executive authority.

Suspending the Geneva Conventions and Torture

George W. Bush has been the only U.S. president to defend publicly the right of United States personnel to torture detainees. Probably the president did not intend for U.S. personnel to commit the egregious acts of torture that resulted in the death of many detainees. But he did argue that U.S. personnel needed to use aggressive techniques when interrogating prisoners captured in the war on terror. Despite his declarations that "we do not torture," the aggressive interrogation procedures that were used by U.S. personnel (military, CIA, and contractors) in Guantánamo, Afghanistan, and Abu Ghraib are considered by most of the world to be torture. The Bush administration, in determining the legal basis of interrogation policy, used a narrow and technical definition of *torture* set forth in an Office of Legal Counsel memorandum of August 2002. President Bush vigorously argued that it was essential to the war on terror to continue to pursue "the program" of aggressive interrogation when he argued against the Detainee Treatment Act of 2005 and in favor of the Military Commissions Act of 2006.

Despite Article I, Section 8 of the Constitution, which provides that Congress shall have the power "To make Rules for the Government and Regulation of the land and naval Forces," the Bush administration denied that the president could be bound by public law with respect to torture. According to this argument, Congress cannot regulate presidential actions when he is acting as commander in chief, nor can any law prohibit the president from using torture. Any law intending to do so "must be construed as not applying to interrogations undertaken pursuant to his Commander-in-Chief authority" (Bybee 2002, 34).

The Privilege of Habeas Corpus

In 2003 and 2004 the Bush administration incarcerated hundreds of persons who were suspected of cooperating with the Taliban regime in Afghanistan and fighting U.S. troops. The administration argued that those incarcerated had no right to appeal to U.S. courts for writs of habeas corpus and that the courts had no jurisdiction to make judgments on these executive branch actions. President Bush was asserting authority that had been denied English kings since before Magna Carta (1215). Article I of the Constitution provides that "The Privilege of the Writ of Habeas Corpus shall not be suspended, unless when in Cases of Rebellion or Invasion the public Safety may require it." Note that this provision was placed in Article I, which deals with the powers of Congress, not in Article II, which specifies presidential authority.[2]

The president's military order of November 13, 2001, provided that enemy combatants would be tried by military commission and that the only appeal they could make would be within the executive branch. That is, the detainees would be charged by the executive, imprisoned by the executive, tried by the executive, and any appeal would be decided within the executive branch. The administration argued strenuously in court that U.S. courts had no jurisdiction to hear habeas appeals. When prisoners in Guantánamo attempted to make habeas corpus appeals, the administration argued that as enemy combatants they had no such right and that the president alone could determine their fate.

The Supreme Court delivered several setbacks to President Bush's claims to executive power. In *Hamdi v. Rumsfeld* (542 U.S. 507, 2004) the Court ruled that U.S. citizens had the right to challenge their imprisonment at Guantánamo in court. In *Rasul v. Bush* (542 U.S. 466, 2004) the Court held that noncitizens could challenge their detentions through habeas corpus petitions. In *Hamdan v. Rumsfeld* (126 S.Ct. 2749, 2006) the Court ruled that the president was bound by the Geneva Conventions. And in *Boumedienne v. Bush* (No. 06–1195) the Court ruled that detainees in Guantánamo had a constitutional right to habeas corpus.

Warrantless Electronic Surveillance by the National Security Agency

In December 2005 the *New York Times* revealed that the Bush administration had been secretly monitoring telephone calls and e-mail between suspected foreign terrorists and people within the domestic United States without the warrants required by law. President Bush ordered the National Security Agency to set up the Terrorist Surveillance Program in the fall of 2001. The legal right of the executive branch to conduct electronic surveillance on foreign intelligence targets is not in dispute, but the right of the government to eavesdrop on or wiretap suspects within the United States without a warrant is limited by the Fourth Amendment and the law. The applicable law was the Foreign Intelligence Surveillance Act (FISA), which was passed in 1978 in reaction to wiretapping abuses in the 1970s. FISA required that any surveillance of persons in the United States could be undertaken only after a warrant was received from a special court set up to examine national security warrant applications.

The administration argued that getting a FISA warrant was too cumbersome and slow, and thus it had to set up a secret program for the National Security Agency to conduct the warrantless surveillance in secret. The record of the FISA court, however, does not seem to indicate that the administration had trouble obtaining warrants. From the time that the court was created in 1978 to the end of 2005, it issued 18,748 warrants and refused only 5 (Baker and Babington 2005). If speed was an issue, FISA provided that surveillance could be commenced immediately and the executive could come to the court within seventy-two hours for a retroactive warrant.

The question here is not whether there was a serious threat from terrorism or whether the government ought to be able to wiretap U.S. citizens without a warrant. It may or may not be good policy to allow the government to conduct such surveillance, but the constitutional process for making such decisions entails the legislative process and judicial interpretation of the law. President Bush claimed that despite the laws enacted by Congress and duly signed by the president, he had inherent authority to ignore the law and set up a secret surveillance program that could act without warrants. The question is one of constitutional presidential authority versus the constitutional rights and duties of the other two branches. The Constitution does not give the president the authority to ignore the law. The wisdom of surveillance policy is a separate issue.

Jack Goldsmith, President Bush's conservative director of the Office of Legal Counsel, who was involved with policy making regarding the Terrorist Surveillance Program, said, "After 9/11 they [Cheney and his counsel David Addington] and other top officials in the administration dealt with FISA the way they dealt with other laws they didn't like: they blew through them in secret based on flimsy legal opinions that they guarded closely so no one could question the legal basis for the operations" (Goldsmith 2007, 181).

Signing Statements

Although many other presidents have issued signing statements, President George W. Bush used signing statements to an unprecedented extent. He issued more than one thousand constitutional challenges to provisions in 150 laws in his first six years in office (Savage 2007). He used signing statements to assert the unilateral and unreviewable right of the executive to choose which provisions of laws to enforce and which to ignore. For instance, he used them to indicate that he did not feel bound by all of the provisions of laws regarding reporting to Congress pursuant to the PATRIOT Act; the torture of prisoners; whistle-blower protections for the Department of Energy; the number of U.S. troops in Colombia; the use of illegally gathered intelligence; and the publication of educational data gathered by the Department of Education (Savage 2007, 228–49).

The implications of these sweeping claims to presidential authority are profound and undermine the very meaning of the rule of law. Despite the Constitution's granting lawmaking power to the Congress, the Bush administration maintained that executive authority and the commander-in-chief clause can overcome virtually any law that constrains the executive. President Bush was thus claiming unilateral control of the laws. If the executive claims that it is not subject to the law as it is written but can pick and choose which provisions to enforce, it is essentially claiming the unitary power to say what the law is. The "take care" clause of Article II can be effectively nullified. Even if President Bush did not act on his claimed authority to ignore the law, his claims were dangerous in that he was publicly reserving the right for himself or any of his successors to nullify any law that the executive unilaterally judged to impinge on presidential prerogatives.

Even though some limited circumstances might justify the president not obeying a law, expanding those limited circumstances to more than one thousand threats to not execute the law constitutes an arrogation of power by the president. The Constitution does not give the president the option to decide *not* to faithfully execute the law. If there is a dispute about the interpretation of a law, the interaction of the three branches in the constitutional process is the appropriate way to settle the issue. The politics of passage, the choice to veto or not, and the right to challenge laws in court all are legitimate ways to deal with differences in interpretation. But the assertion by the executive that it alone has the authority to interpret the law and that it will enforce the law at its own discretion threatens the balance set up by the Constitution.

CONCLUSION:
PRESIDENT BUSH AS CHIEF EXECUTIVE

As chief executive, President Bush did not subject some of his most important decisions to systematic deliberation. At the implementation stage, he and his political appointees often did not consult with or heed the advice of uniformed and civilian professionals. At the constitutional level, President Bush aggressively asserted extraordinary claims to exclusive executive authority and argued that his actions could not be limited by the other two branches of government.

 In the terms of the criteria set out in this book, President Bush was a very effective politician, whose skill led to tactical victories; but his policies resulted in strategic blunders that will haunt the United States for generations. Although at the personal level President Bush adhered to the moral standards of sexual probity and decorous behavior, his misleading the country in gaining support for the war in Iraq (Pfiffner 2004) and his encouraging and condoning torture (Pfiffner 2008, 2009) were profound moral failures.

Perhaps the most important principle established by the Supreme Court during the Bush presidency was Justice Sandra Day O'Conner's statement in the majority opinion in *Hamdi*: "We have long since made clear that a state of war is not a blank check for the President when it comes to the rights of the Nation's citizens."

NOTES

1. Alberto Gonzales argued that the war on terror was "a new kind of war" that made the Geneva Conventions "obsolete." Despite the fact that suspects of terrorism might not fit the prisoner-of-war status specified in the Geneva Conventions, they did fit the fourth Convention specifications: "those who, at a given moment and in any manner whatsoever, find themselves, in

the case of a conflict or occupation, in the hands of a party to the conflict." Common Article 3 of the Conventions provides that all detained persons must be treated "humanely" and prohibits "outrages upon personal dignity, in particular, humiliating and degrading treatment."

2. Defenders of President Bush's policies have pointed out that President Lincoln suspended habeas corpus at the beginning of the Civil War. Lincoln took his action in April 1861, when Congress was not in session. When it returned to Washington in July, Lincoln asked Congress to ratify his action, and it did. Lincoln did not assert that as president he had the constitutional authority to deny habeas corpus (Pfiffner 2008, 94–97).

REFERENCES

Allen, Scott A., et al. 2006. "Deaths of Detainees in the Custody of US Forces in Iraq and Afghanistan from 2002 to 2005." *Medscape.com*, December 5. http://www.medscape .com/viewarticle/547787 (Accessed June 23, 2008).

Andrews, Edmund. 2007. "Envoy's Letter Counters Bush on Dismantling of Iraq Army." *New York Times*, September 4. http://www.nytimes.com/2007/09/04/washington/04bremer .html (Accessed July 13, 2008).

Baker, Peter, and Charles Babington. 2005. "Bush Addresses Uproar over Spying." *Washington Post*, December 20, p. A8.

Burke, John. 2005. "Condoleezza Rice as NSC Adviser: A Case Study of the Honest Broker Role." *Presidential Studies Quarterly* 35(3): 554–75.

Bush, George W. 2002. *Weekly Compilation of Presidential Documents, Administration of George W. Bush* (January 29), pp. 133-39.

Bybee, Jay S. 2002. "Memorandum for Alberto R. Gonzales, counsel to the President, Standards of Conduct for Interrogation under 18 U.S.C. Sc. 2340–2340A (August 1, 2002)." Reprinted in *The Torture Papers*, ed. Karen Greenberg and Joshua Dratel. 2005. New York: Cambridge University Press, 172.

Coalition Provisional Authority. 2003. *Coalition Provisional Authority Order Number 1: De-Ba'athification of Iraqi Society CPA/ORD/16 May 2003/01*. Baghdad, Iraq: Coalition Provisional Authority.

Cohen, Roger. 2007. "The MacArthur Lunch." *New York Times*, August 27. http://select.nytimes .com/2007/08/27/opinion/27cohen.html?_r=1 (Accessed November 28, 2008).

Draper, Robert. 2007. *Dead Certain: The Presidency of George W. Bush*. New York: Free Press.

Fallows, James. 2004. "Blind into Baghdad." *Atlantic Monthly* (January/February): 52–74. http://www.theatlantic.com/doc/200401/fallows (Accessed November 28, 2008).

George, Alexander L. 1972. "The Case for Multiple Advocacy in Making Foreign Policy." *American Political Science Review* 66(3): 751–85.

Goldsmith, Jack. 2007. *The Terror Presidency*. New York: Norton.

Gonzales, Alberto. 2002. "Memorandum for the President. Decision RE Application of the Geneva Convention on Prisoners of War to the Conflict with al Qaeda and the Taliban (January 25, 2002)." Reprinted in *The Torture Papers*, ed. Karen Greenberg and Joshua Dratel. 2005. New York: Cambridge University Press, 118–21.

Gordon, Michael, and Bernard Trainor. 2006. *Cobra II*. New York: Pantheon.

Lemann, Nicholas. 2003. "How It Came to War." *New Yorker* 79(6): 36.

Mayer, Jane. 2007. "Whatever It Takes." *New Yorker*, February 19 and 26, pp. 66–82. http://www.newyorker.com/reporting/2007/02/19/070219fa_fact_mayer (Accessed November 28, 2008).

Pfiffner, James P. 2004. "Did President Bush Mislead the Country in His Arguments for War with Iraq?" *Presidential Studies Quarterly* 34(1): 25–46.

———. 2005. "Presidential Decision Making: Rationality, Advisory Systems, and Personality." *Presidential Studies Quarterly* 35(2): 217–28.

———. 2008. *Power Play: The Bush Presidency and the Constitution.* Washington, DC: Brookings Institution.

———. 2009. *Torture as Public Policy.* Boulder, CO: Paradigm Press.

Ricks, Thomas. 2006. *Fiasco.* New York: Penguin.

Sands, Philippe. 2008. *Torture Team.* New York: Palgrave Macmillan.

Savage, Charlie. 2007. *Takeover: The Return of the Imperial Presidency and the Subversion of American Democracy.* Boston: Little, Brown.

Schmitt, Eric. 2004. "Army Report Says Flaws in Detention Didn't Cause Abuse." *New York Times*, July 23. http://query.nytimes.com/gst/fullpage.html?res=9903E4DB163DF930A 15754C0A9629C (Accessed November 28, 2008).

Tenet, George. 2007. *At the Center of the Storm: My Years at the CIA.* New York: HarperCollins.

Woodward, Bob. 2004. *Plan of Attack.* New York: Simon & Schuster.

PART TWO

Institutions and the Policy Regime

CHAPTER 5

Reactionary Ideologues and Uneasy Partisans

Bush and Realignment

LARA M. BROWN

EXAMINING GEORGE W. BUSH'S PRESIDENCY by electoral cycle reveals that his political competence or his "ability to reshape the political regime" backfired (see Chapter 1).[1] Bush's strident partisanship helped him pass conservative policies in his first term and alter the political landscape in the 2002 and 2004 elections, but his unbending ways brought about a legislative stalemate in his second term and electoral backlashes in 2006 and 2008 (Ceaser and Busch 2005; Cook 2008; Sabato 2008).[2] His "compassionate conservatism" attracted religiously devout individuals (evangelical Christians and Hispanic Catholics) to the Republican Party, but it stoked rather than bridged the ideological polarization already present in the electorate (Abramowitz 2006; Campbell 2006; Miller and Schofield 2008).[3] Bush's many early successes bred contempt among his opponents, and his unwillingness to compromise made him vulnerable to his critics when failures occurred (for example, the Iraq War, Social Security reform, and Hurricane Katrina). Hence, he did not effect a realignment akin to that in 1896, as he and his advisor Karl Rove anticipated (Lemann 2003; Traub 2006).[4] The Republican Party is roughly situated in the electorate where it was in 2000, after Democratic president Bill Clinton's two terms (see Table 5.1). Bush was therefore both politically competent *and* a political failure.

Similar to Richard Nixon, Bush's moral competence or "trustworthiness" appears largely responsible for the paradox (see Chapter 1). Several of his highly publicized decisions (for example, awarding Halliburton no-bid government contracts, retaining Defense secretary Donald Rumsfeld after revelations of prisoner abuse at Abu Ghraib, and firing U.S. attorneys for partisan reasons) struck political observers as not only bold but brazen.

TABLE 5.1

Support by Group for the Republican Presidential Nominee, 1996–2008

Group	1996 Dole	2000 Bush	2004 Bush	2008 McCain
	Measured in percent (percentage of total electorate in parentheses)			
All	41	48	51	46
Men	44 (48)	53 (48)	55 (46)	48 (47)
Women	38 (52)	43 (52)	48 (54)	43 (53)
Whites	46 (83)	54 (81)	58 (77)	55 (74)
Blacks	12 (10)	9 (10)	11 (11)	4 (13)
Hispanics	21 (5)	35 (7)	44 (8)	31 (9)
Asians	48 (1)	41 (2)	44 (2)	35 (2)
East	—	39 (23)	43 (22)	40 (21)
Midwest	—	49 (26)	51 (26)	44 (24)
South	—	55 (31)	58 (32)	54 (32)
West	—	46 (21)	49 (20)	40 (23)
Democrats	10 (39)	11 (39)	11 (37)	10 (39)
Republicans	80 (35)	91 (35)	93 (37)	90 (32)
Independents	35 (26)	47 (26)	48 (26)	44 (29)
Liberals	11 (20)	13 (21)	13 (21)	10 (22)
Conservatives	71 (33)	81 (29)	84 (34)	78 (34)
Moderates	33 (47)	44 (50)	45 (45)	39 (44)
Level of Polarization* (Number of states)	24	30	33	33

SOURCES: CNN's exit polls, available online at: (1996) http://www.cnn.com/ALLPOLITICS/1996/
elections/natl.exit.poll/index1.html and http://www.cnn.com/ALLPOLITICS/1996/elections/natl.exit
.poll/index2.html; (2000) http://www.cnn.com/ELECTION/2000/results/index.epolls.html; (2004)
http://www.cnn.com/ELECTION/2004/pages/results/states/US/P/00/epolls.0.html; (2008) http://www
.cnn.com/ELECTION/2008/results/polls/#USP00p1; 1996 regional totals unavailable.

*Level of polarization is a measure used by Galston and Nivola (2006, 13–14), which counts the
number of states (including the District of Columbia) where the winning candidate's vote share was
more than either 5 percentage points above his national average or 5 percentage points below his
national average.

Bush further courted controversy with his seemingly blind loyalty to some in his administration, for example, his nomination of Harriet Miers to the Supreme Court and his intervention in a Justice Department investigation of "the domestic eavesdropping program" to protect Alberto Gonzales (Waas 2007, 34). In these ways, he was his own worst enemy. By the end of his presidency, rather than uniting behind him, many independents and moderates had united against him (Jacobson 2007; Brody 2008).[5] This left 2008 Republican presidential nominee Senator John McCain of Arizona, a frequent Bush critic and perceived reformer, with little room to maneuver and long electoral odds that proved intractable. Thus, Bush's presidency—even in failure—was not without lasting impact.

1999–2000:

COMPASSIONATE CONSERVATISM STEALS THE SHOW[6]

Even before Bush announced his presidential campaign in March 1999, the majority of Republicans backed his candidacy (Kristof 2000). Speaker Newt Gingrich's confrontational political strategy (for example, the budget shutdown and the multiple investigations of Clinton, which culminated in impeachment proceedings) had not only failed to produce large majorities in both chambers but had cost the Republicans seats in the House in the 1998 midterm election.[7] Bush's gubernatorial reelection in Texas that year offered them hope. Earning 69 percent of the vote, Bush had done well among constituencies not typically supportive of Republicans, including African Americans, women, and Hispanics, the latter who were of particular interest because their numbers are rapidly growing in the population and because many are religiously devout and, presumably, socially conservative (Berke 1998).[8] Bush had also described himself as someone who lives on the "sunrise side of the mountain" and holds a "philosophy, which is conservative and compassionate and full of hope" (Verhovek 1997). Bush seemed the antithesis of Gingrich's contemptuous and combative persona (Gould 2003, 463–65).[9]

While some compared Bush to Ronald Reagan, his "compassionate conservatism" was not the small government and states' rights philosophy of Reagan.[10] Brooks explains that "Bush understood that the simple government-is-the-problem philosophy of the older Republicans was obsolete" and views him as a Republican who grasps "the paradox that if you don't have a positive vision of government, you won't be able to limit the growth of government" (2004). Bush had a positive vision. He argued that the federal government should be used to institutionalize conservative principles, such as fostering more competition in education with vouchers, protecting life by promoting abstinence and limiting access to stem cells, ensuring an ample supply of labor by encouraging immigration, and giving people more choice in directing their investments in Social Security. Hence, Bush was socially and economically conservative, but he was also a governmental activist. Rove saw the parallels between Bush and William McKinley, whose conservative activism (for example, intervening in coal mine strikes in Ohio; promoting high tariffs and the gold standard) had generated widespread support a century earlier from social activists (such as those in the temperance movement) and economic conservatives on Wall Street (Morgan 2003; Harpine 2005). Rove also wanted to create "a long-lasting, dominant Republican majority" much as McKinley had in the late 1890s (Lemann 2003, 68).[11]

By December 1999, Bush had "a volunteer army approaching 4,000 people to organize events, work the phones, hand out fliers, and get people to the polls in each of the early primary states" (Neal 1999). His advisors thought that even if Bush's main competitor, McCain, won a state, he would "have little time to take advantage of that momentum" because Bush held such "an overwhelming money and organizational advantage" (Neal 1999). They proved prescient. McCain beat Bush in New Hampshire by over 18 percentage points (48 to 30), but two weeks later Bush won South Carolina's primary with the support of evangelical Christians (Jacobson 2007, 51). McCain went on to win six more states, but Bush won the rest of the early contests, including the delegate-rich states of California, New York, and Ohio, which secured him the nomination.

At the Republican National Convention, Bush's speech stressed character, hoping "to make Clinton's moral legacy weigh more heavily than his economic legacy in voters' minds," even though his opponent was Vice President Al Gore (Crotty 2001, 2–3; Jacobson 2007, 53). In September, the campaigns were tied, and while most believed that Gore would best Bush in the debates, he did not (Milkis and Nelson 2003, 407).[12] Over the next month, Gore lost his way, running "a populist-style, 'people, not the powerful' campaign better suited for a candidate challenging an incumbent in economic hard times than for a vice-president seeking to extend his party's control of the presidency in good times" (Milkis and Nelson 2003, 406). While Democrats questioned his experience and gravitas, Bush stayed on message (Jacobson 2007, 54).

On Election Day, an unusual event occurred: the candidates nearly tied. The outcome depended on the winner in Florida, whose popular vote on election night had Bush ahead by a margin of 1,784 votes out of nearly six million cast. Without Florida's 25 electoral votes, each candidate was short of the 270 needed to win (Gore 267, Bush 246). Thus began a series of recounts and legal challenges. A Supreme Court ruling on December 12 effectively allowed the certified popular vote count to stand as final, making Bush the president by virtue of his winning Florida by 537 votes (Crotty 2001, 36–78; Milkis and Nelson 2003, 409–11).

While the election was as close as could be imagined, Bush drew many more people into the GOP than his Republican predecessor Robert Dole (Table 5.1). While Dole earned just 21 percent of the Hispanic vote, Bush won 35 percent. Hispanic votes surely helped Bush prevail in Arizona and Nevada, which had gone for Clinton in 1996. A larger percentage of women also supported Bush than had backed Dole (43 to 38). Whites had split between Clinton and Dole (44 to 46), but they solidly chose Bush over Gore (54 to 42). Those votes likely contributed to Bush's success in states throughout the Midwest and the South, like Missouri, Ohio, Clinton's home state of Arkansas, and Gore's home state of Tennessee. In sum, while Bush went to Washington without a mandate, he did possess a governing philosophy and a "small"[13] but broad coalition of voters supporting him.

2001–2002:
THE WORLD TURNS UPSIDE DOWN

Given how evenly divided Congress was (see Table 5.2), many commentators thought that Bush would build bridges across the partisan divide and govern as a moderate (for example, see Klein 2000). Bush, however, began his presidency by pushing a large tax cut favored by conservative

TABLE 5.2

Number of Republicans in the Congress, 1988–2008

	1988	1990	1992	1994	1996	1998	2000	2002	2004	2006	2008
House	175	167	176	230	228	223	221	229	232	202	178
Senate	45	44	43	52	55	55	50	51	55	49	41

SOURCES: Congress and party division data available at: (House) http://clerk.house.gov/art_history/house_history/partyDiv.html; (Senate) http://www.senate.gov/pagelayout/history/one_item_and_teasers/partydiv.htm.

Republicans (Ceaser and Busch 2005, 37). Though he downsized his $1.6 trillion proposal to $1.35 trillion, his compromise did not win him any new friends but instead carried a price: Senator Jim Jeffords, a liberal Republican from Vermont, announced on May 24 that he was leaving the Republican Party and becoming an Independent who would caucus with the Democrats (Jacobson 2007, 72).[14] Republicans lost majority control of the Senate. After the tax cut passed in May, an ABC News–*Washington Post* poll showed that the public was less than impressed: they thought "by a 30-point margin that Bush ha[d] tried harder in the last four months to push 'his own agenda' in Congress than to compromise with the Democrats" ("Sharp Challenges . . ." 2001). While Bush's aggregate approval rating stood at 55 percent, his approval rating by region reveals that his support was higher in the Midwest and the South (56 and 63 percent) than in either the West or the East (44 and 49 percent). Bush was serving his electoral base.

Along with the world, Bush's presidency turned upside down on September 11, 2001. The terrorist attacks on the World Trade Center and the Pentagon "dramatically altered" Bush's standing among the public, as a rally-round-the-president effect took hold (Brody 2008). Under the mantle of commander in chief, he responded forcefully and unequivocally, advocating a "neo-conservative" philosophy, which sought to protect America by spreading democracy throughout the world. He explained, "Either you are with us, or you are with the terrorists . . . any nation that continues to harbor or support terrorism will be regarded as a hostile regime" (Ceaser and Busch 2005, 41). Over the next fifteen months, those words effectively silenced criticism—foreign and domestic—aimed at Bush and

his administration.[15] As Jacobson describes, "In the days that followed
. . . the president was now to be evaluated as the defender of the nation
against shadowy foreign enemies rather than as a partisan figure of dubious legitimacy" (2007, 80–82).

While the Democrats tried associating the struggling economy and the
spectacular collapse of Enron (the Texas-based energy company whose
chief executive officer had multiple ties to the administration) with Bush
and the Republicans in the 2002 election, their efforts were futile. The
public focused on foreign policy and national security, even though Bush
signed into law that year major domestic legislation, including education
reform (No Child Left Behind Act), campaign finance reform (Bipartisan Campaign Reform Act), and another large tax cut (Job Creation and
Worker Assistance Act). On election night, Republicans picked up six
seats in the House, extending their majority to double digits, and two in
the Senate, restoring their majority control. Republican electoral success
was related to four factors: (1) Bush cornered the Democrats on the vote
authorizing the use of force against Iraq in the October before the election; (2) Republicans worked postcensus to gerrymander congressional
districts; (3) the National Republican Party initiated what became known
as their "72-Hour Task Force," a sophisticated turnout project dependent
on community volunteers; and (4) Bush campaigned heartily for Republican
candidates across the country.[16] Bush also outmaneuvered the Democrats
on the organization of the Department of Homeland Security, managing
to make it appear as though the Democrats were exploiting the tragedy
of 9/11 for political gain (Ceaser and Busch 2005, 52–53). Hence, Bush's
decisions in the lead-up to the election and throughout 2002 demonstrate
how politically astute—strategically and tactically competent—he and the
Republicans were in the months after the attacks.

2003–2004:
NATIONAL SECURITY BECOMES THE NATIONAL FOCUS

The 2004 electoral cycle was a continuation of the 2002 cycle, which had
national security and foreign policy as its focus; however, the 2004 cycle
was more partisan and more polarized (Jacobson 2005). It was also a
referendum on Bush (Campbell 2005, 234). Deciding against persuading

swing voters, Bush courted evangelical Protestants and other moral "traditionalists" (orthodox Jews and conservative Catholics).[17] Believing these voters would agree with his conservative values, he sought to turn out larger numbers of them. Bush's policy positions (such as standing against new lines of stem cells for research) and political rhetoric (a "crusade"[18]) aided his cause (Jacobson 2007, 91–94).

While the administration had begun making its case against Saddam Hussein (his suspected ties with terrorists and the possibility of his possessing weapons of mass destruction) prior to the 2002 election, the drumbeat for a preemptive ("preventive") war grew louder with Bush's State of the Union address on January 28, 2003. Making his political opponents sound naïve, Bush said, "Trusting in the sanity and restraint of Saddam Hussein is not a strategy, and it is not an option" (Ceaser and Busch 2005, 58). The argument gained legitimacy with Secretary of State Colin Powell's presentation to the United Nations on February 5. On March 19, a coalition led by the United States invaded Iraq. Less than one month later, on April 9, Baghdad fell and Saddam fled. On May 1, Bush, in celebratory fashion, landed a jet on an aircraft carrier. Speaking under a banner that read "Mission Accomplished," he explained that major combat operations in Iraq were complete and were a success. Unfortunately, the Iraq War was far from over.

Sensing an opening, Bush's critics began airing their concerns. That summer, former ambassador Joseph Wilson wrote an opinion-editorial in the *New York Times* that questioned prewar intelligence on Iraq.[19] The administration's response was to discredit Wilson by leaking the identity of his wife, Valerie Plame, who was a CIA operative, to the press (and the public). Inciting controversy in intelligence circles in Washington, the leak led to a special investigation conducted by the Justice Department that reached into the White House (McClellan 2008). Outside the Beltway, "Bush came under increasing fire from the crowded Democratic field and from liberal groups organized around the goal of preventing his reelection" (Ceaser and Busch 2005, 61).

While the Republicans continued to support Bush, Bush supported them.[20] In May, he signed another major tax cut (Jobs and Growth Tax Relief Reconciliation Act), reducing the rates on capital gains and raising the alternative minimum tax exemption (Gale and Harris 2008).[21] Bush also signed the Medicare Prescription Drug, Improvement, and Modernization Act. The Republican leadership in the House went to extraordinary measures to deliver this bill to the White House. They scheduled the vote for 3:00 A.M. and kept open the roll call for nearly three hours, strongarming members who were against not only the expansion of the program but also the enormous projected cost of about $400 billion over ten years. While the American Association of Retired Persons (AARP) supported the legislation, Democrats decried it as a corporate "giveaway," owing to the subsidies for large employers and the prohibition on the government negotiating drug discounts.[22]

By March 2004, Senator John Kerry from Massachusetts had won the Democratic presidential nomination, in part because many thought his decorated service in the Vietnam War and his foreign policy experience in the Senate would provide him ample cover to criticize Bush. Not having had a nomination contest, Bush was prepared. He questioned Kerry's record and lodged character attacks; by summer he had damaged Kerry's reputation (Nagourney and Seelye 2004).[23] While the race remained close throughout the campaign, Bush won "a narrow but unambiguous victory—50.7 percent of the popular vote to Kerry's 48.3 percent" (Jacobson 2007, 186). Deepening his electoral base, Bush won 78 percent of the votes of white evangelical Protestants, whose turnout was 63 percent (Dionne 2006, 203). Bush increased his support among women, earning 48 percent, and Hispanics, earning 44 percent. Regionally, he carried the Midwest (51%) and the South (58%).[24] Republicans also enjoyed a net gain of seats in the House and the Senate (three and four, respectively). Thus, Jacobson aptly concludes, "In any close election, every contribution to victory is arguably decisive, but there is no question that the superior turnout and loyalty of Republicans was the *sine qua non* of Bush's reelection" (2007, 197).

Even though the Democrats remained on the defensive on issues in 2003 and 2004, the cracks were beginning to appear in Bush's patriotic (also known as partisan) persona.[25] Not unlike Nixon's reelection campaign in 1972, Bush's team engaged in questionable practices in its desire to secure a win. While some of the more serious issues are still being investigated by congressional committees (for example, the leaking of the identity of

CIA operative Plame in 2003, the deletion of White House e-mail between 2003 and 2005, and the firing of U.S. attorneys because of their reluctance to prosecute allegations of voter fraud in 2004), current evidence suggests that Bush overreached, crossing ethical and perhaps legal lines.[26] Thus, Bush's moral competency began to compromise his political competency and tarnish his presidential legacy.

2005–2006: WHO DOES THIS GUY THINK HE IS?

On November 4, 2004, Bush held a press conference and described his interpretation of the election results:

I earned capital in the campaign, political capital, and now I intend to spend it . . . and I'm going to spend it for what I told the people I'd spend it on, which is—you've heard the agenda: Social Security and tax reform, moving this economy forward, education, fighting and winning the war on terror [White House Press Office, 2004].

Shortly thereafter, Bush launched a massive effort to overhaul Social Security but did not put forth a detailed proposal. Instead, he offered up some broad goals and essentially told Congress to do the rest, leaving his fellow partisans without much to defend and a lot to accomplish. While Bush stumped across the country, he was unsuccessful in rousing the electorate. Not feeling grassroots pressure, Democrats stonewalled his reform. By the summer, the push ended as a "bipartisan consensus" to do nothing emerged (Jacobson 2007, 217). Bush's attempt failed partly because by framing the reform as a mandate (derived from a highly polarized and relatively close election), he infused the debate with partisanship when bipartisanship was needed. Playing into the already prevailing "fog of war" meme on Iraq, Bush seemed ineffectual as a political leader for the first time in a long time.

On other domestic issues, however, Bush enjoyed more success. He signed the Class Action Fairness Act in February, requiring class-action lawsuits to be filed in federal courts. While he was praised by Republicans and the business community, it is notable that the bill takes power away from the states and protects corporations because of the large number of conservative federal judges who are likely to rule against these suits. This was not a "small government" or states' rights measure, but then neither were some of Bush's other signature pieces of legislation, like No Child Left Behind and the Medicare Prescription Drug Act (Ceaser and Busch 2005, 64). Still, he was committed to one major conservative tenet: low taxes. In 2006, he extended many of the previously approved tax cuts for longer periods (Tax Increase Prevention and Reconciliation Act).

Amidst these policy debates, more controversies swirled:

In January 2005, it was discovered that the Bush administration had been paying conservative journalists (Armstrong Williams and Maggie Gallagher) to promote administration policies.

While the Abu Ghraib torture scandal had been in the news since 2004, Charles Graner, a former soldier thought responsible for the outrageous abuses, was found guilty and sentenced to prison that same month.

In March, conservatives in Congress worked to save the life of Terri Schiavo, a woman who had been on life support for years but whose family was divided on whether or not she should be removed from her feeding tube. In a show of solidarity with evangelical Christians, Bush flew to Washington from his Texas ranch to sign legislation removing her case from the Florida courts to the U.S. courts.

In October, Special Prosecutor Patrick Fitzgerald indicted Lewis "Scooter" Libby, Vice President Dick Cheney's chief of staff, on perjury, obstruction of justice, and false statements relating to the CIA leak scandal.

In January 2006, the Republican lobbyist Jack Abramoff, who had publicly been under investigation for over a year, pled guilty in a federal corruption case, implicating some Republicans in Congress as well as some key administration officials.

Hence, Bush was politically vulnerable when Hurricane Katrina came ashore in September 2005, destroying much of New Orleans and a large swath of the Gulf Coast. Bush's apparent indifference and incompetence in responding to the crisis crystallized what many already believed: he was out of touch with the country's needs and the American people (Cook 2008, 51). Worse, he did not seem to be making any progress abroad either.[27]

As the 2006 midterm election cycle got under way, most observers believed that the Republicans would suffer losses but would likely retain their majorities in Congress because of institutional advantages (gerrymandered districts, incumbency) and geographical good fortune (the Senate races were in "red" states like Virginia, Missouri, and Montana). While the number of scandals among Republicans increased during the year (Representatives Bob Ney and Tom Delay resigned for reasons related to the Abramoff investigation), in late September, when Representative Mark Foley (R-FL) was discovered to have been inappropriately text-messaging a congressional page, support plummeted. An ABC News–*Washington Post* poll released on October 23 noted that "47 percent of registered voters say it would be a good thing if control of Congress switched to the Democrats" (Langer 2006). When the results came in, the Republicans had lost thirty seats in the House and six in the Senate; the Democrats had become the majority party on Capitol Hill. The country had turned away from Bush's Republican Party.

2007–2008:
YOU'RE NOT SURPRISED, ARE YOU?

Though Secretary of Defense Donald Rumsfeld resigned (read "was dismissed") almost immediately after the election, Bush hardly seemed chastened. For while the country wanted out of the Iraq War, Bush sided with John McCain, who had proposed a troop surge. As Cooper and Sanger (2007) describe, "Bush insisted [on *60 Minutes*] that he has the authority as commander-in-chief to execute his strategy, no matter what kind of objections Congress raises. 'In this situation, I do, yeah,' he said. 'Now, I fully understand they could try to stop me from doing it. But I made my decision, and we're going forward.'" Bush seemed stubborn—tone-deaf rather than loyal.

Making matters worse, Congress seemed powerless (some suggested "gutless") to stop Bush. Democratic Speaker of the House Nancy Pelosi took impeachment "off the table," and the Democrats worried they would be demonized as unpatriotic partisans who did not support the troops if they failed to authorize funding requests for Iraq and Afghanistan. Hoping the electorate's indignation over Bush and the Republicans would catapult their next presidential nominee into the White House, the Democrats in Congress played it safe, avoiding issues that might provoke partisan confrontations.[28] In 2007, Washington was at a standstill, and the approval ratings of Congress took a nosedive.[29] The announcements of numerous presidential aspirants—five of them senators—kicking off their campaigns altered the political calculus. All of the aspirants, of both parties, directly attacked or purposely distanced themselves from Bush, which meant that he became one of the earliest lame ducks in modern history.

As Bush's presidency came to a close, he enjoyed something of a slight rebound. Over the summer of 2008, there were rumblings that victory in Iraq, a widely believed lost cause, might once again be possible. Then, when gasoline prices topped $4.00 a gallon at the pump and public dismay soared about the rising cost of energy, Bush repealed an executive order that prohibited offshore oil drilling along the coasts. A Gallup poll released in mid-August notes, "While George W. Bush's 33% job approval rating is still low from a historical perspective, it is an improvement from the 28% readings he received in April, May, and June, and is his best rating since February" (Jones 2008). Bush's recovery was short-lived. On September 15, Lehman Brothers filed for bankruptcy and marked the start of Wall Street's financial meltdown. The economic crisis that ensued spun increasingly out of control and continued on through the November election that resulted in the Democratic Party's presidential nominee, Senator Barack Obama from Illinois, winning 365 electoral votes and 53 percent of the popular vote.

SPECULATING ABOUT THE BUSH LEGACY: THE ERA OF SMALL GOVERNMENT IS OVER[30]

While McCain was not an administration loyalist, he and Bush agreed on a number of policy issues (like comprehensive immigration reform) and philosophical stances (a strong defense and the "preemptive" doctrine). They also were both Republicans. For some, the rejection of McCain's candidacy equated to the repudiation of Bush's presidency, particularly his compassionate conservatism at home and his neoconservatism abroad. While this narrative is convenient, it does not appear to comport with the postelection political environment.

A December 2008 poll showed Alaska governor Sarah Palin and former Arkansas governor Mike Huckabee, two compassionate conservatives, as the "leading contenders" for the Republican nomination in 2012 (Davis 2008). Along with this, Democratic president Barack Obama announced that he intended not only to continue with some of Bush's policies (such as a military surge in Afghanistan) and retain some of Bush's appointees (Secretary of Defense Robert Gates) but to launch a "21st Century New Deal" (Allen and Martin 2008). He also invited the Reverend Rick Warren, an evangelical pastor, to give the inaugural invocation. Bush's ideological legacy, which included a positive vision for the federal government and expansive executive powers, appears likely to continue into the foreseeable future.

It is unlikely, however, that Bush would view either McCain's loss or Obama's agenda as a validation of his political competency. While some have suggested that Bush may have realigned the electorate away from the Republicans, this seems to ignore the reality that even though more voters considered themselves Democrats in 2008, the ideological composition of the electorate was largely unchanged from 2004 (Table 5.1).

Table 5.2 reviews the electoral fortunes of the Republicans in Congress and shows that in 2008 they were about where they were in 1988, after President Ronald Reagan's two terms. Still, they endured a wild political ride under Bush: he helped push Republicans in the House to their highest levels since 1994 but also to their lowest levels since 1992. More generally, Bush's actions unsettled partisans and emboldened ideologues on both sides of the aisle. His moral incompetence eventually outweighed his political competency. Even though his presidency tarnished the Republican Party, it did not damage conservatism, the philosophy. Thus, while the 2008 election favored the Democratic Party, the legacy that Bush left the country was polarization and partisanship. The more things change, the more they remain the same.

NOTES

The author would like to extend her sincere appreciation to Bob Maranto, Tom Lansford, Jeremy Johnson, Jim Pfiffner, and the anonymous reviewers for their insightful comments and helpful suggestions on this chapter.

1. Throughout the chapter, when referencing Bush's competence (political, strategic,

tactical, and moral), I am referring to his political team's competence, which includes those decisions made by his strategist Karl Rove.

2. While this chapter proceeds chronologically rather than thematically, it is important to note that party politics are driven not by a parsimonious theory but by the conditions and events that create opportunities in the political environment on which politicians may capitalize to their benefit or neglect to their detriment (Riker 1986).

3. Whether these changes have occurred among political elites or among the broader electorate is debatable. Still, the consensus is that change has occurred and its consequences are not insignificant (Nivola and Brady 2006, 2008).

4. While this chapter is framed around realignment theory and Bush's efforts at restructuring the partisan coalitions in the electorate, it does not endorse realignment theory. It discusses it because Karl Rove suggested that realignment was one of Bush's political goals. Agreeing with Mayhew (2002), I believe that realignment theory has problems. Most notably, it argues that partisan cleavages arise from exogenous events or organic shifts at the grassroots level (Burnham 1970; Sundquist 1983). It seems more likely that aspirants and presidents try to alter partisan coalitions in order to win (elections, midterm elections, etc.). Thus, my perspective is that most presidents try and fail; a few succeed, but many enjoy partial success, meaning that parties evolve more slowly than the theory suggests.

5. In 2008, only conservatives continued to support Bush. See http://www.gallup.com/poll/113083/Conservative-Republicans-Still-Widely-Support-Bush.aspx (Accessed December 15, 2008).

6. Some portions of this section have been drawn from a case study presented in another work (Brown 2009).

7. The year 1998 was the first time since 1934 that the president's party had not lost seats in the House in a midterm election.

8. In a poll done by the Democratic Leadership Council entitled "Hispanic America 2002," 82 percent agreed that "prayer is an important part of my life." See http://www.dlc.org/documents/Bendixen.ppt (Accessed December 17, 2008).

9. For example, Gingrich once said, "It is impossible to maintain civilization with twelve-year-olds having babies, fifteen-year-olds killing each other, seventeen-year-olds receiving diplomas they cannot read" (Gould 2003, 465).

10. Many of the comparisons centered on his being a Western governor who was optimistic about the government and believed in the ingenuity and strength of the American people. For a more complete analysis, see Keller (2003).

11. While Mayhew (2002) finds that there is little evidence to view 1896 as a critical election, for this chapter, his work is not pertinent. See note 2.

12. An ABC News–*Washington Post* poll from September 2000 showed both candidates earning the support of 47 percent of likely voters. See http://abcnews.go.com/images/pdf/827a1PostLaborDayPoll.pdf (Accessed August 7, 2008).

13. Bush's coalition included a wide swath of voters across a majority of states, but numerically it was smaller than Gore's coalition.

14. Though Jeffords left the Republican Party for a number of reasons, including the belief that his views were not respected, he was initially opposed to Bush's $1.6 trillion tax cut proposal, which he said was "too expensive" (Mitchell 2001). During the first four months of 2001, Jeffords was a key player in the tax cuts negotiations and his actions forced what became a key compromise (Rosenbaum 2001). See also Gellman (2008, 61–80).

15. For example, the ABC television network canceled Bill Maher's show, *Politically*

Incorrect, because he said, "We have been the cowards, lobbing cruise missiles from 2,000 miles away. That's cowardly. Staying in the airplane when it hits the building, say what you want about it, it's not cowardly" (Tapper 2002).

16. For a more detailed discussion, see Jacobson (2003); Lemann (2003); Sabato (2003).

17. While Republicans heavily favored Bush in 2004, his support among Independents fell. See presidential approval by party at http://www.gallup.com/poll/1723/Presidential-Job -Approval-Depth.aspx (Accessed December 6, 2008).

18. Gary Jacobson thoughtfully describes the ways in which "Bush deliberately adopted Christian dualism's language of good and evil to refer to his new mission" and that "although he stopped referring to the war on terrorism as a 'crusade' after the term triggered a counterproductive backlash among Muslims, he left the sense that it was just that" (2007, 92).

19. An ABC News–*Washington Post* poll released in June 2003 revealed that "The number of Americans who say the United States is sustaining an 'unacceptable' level of military casualties in Iraq has grown sharply, a trend that could signal limited patience for a long and violent occupation . . . the number calling casualties 'unacceptable' has jumped by 16 points, to 44 percent." See http://abcnews.go.com/images/pdf/928a1IraqUpdate.pdf (Accessed August 12, 2008).

20. The partisan divide in support for the Iraq War grew during the electoral cycle, reaching "an average of about 63 percentage points in the last quarter of 2004" (Jacobson 2007, 131).

21. Further details are available through the Tax Policy Center, a nonprofit organization, at http://www.taxpolicycenter.org/briefing-book/background/bush-tax-cuts/change.cfm (Accessed August 12, 2008).

22. Echoing many Democrats during the debate, California State Democratic Party chair Art Torres called the Medicare prescription drug benefit a "corporate giveaway" on August 30, 2005. See http://www.sfgate.com/cgi-bin/article.cgi?f=/c/a/2005/08/30/MNGSBEFAFN1 .DTL&hw=sterngold&sn=001&sc=1000 (Accessed December 17, 2008).

23. Ceaser and Busch note, "Bush raised a record $84 million by October 1, 2003 . . . [his] strategists had been . . . laying the groundwork for a massive organizational effort modeled on 2002" (2005, 65). See also Bai (2004); Shaw (2006).

24. Exit poll data are available at http://www.cnn.com/ELECTION/2004/pages/results/ states/US/P/oo/epolls.o.html (Accessed August 12, 2008).

25. While I have no doubt that Bush is a patriot, it is also clear that in hindsight his administration used patriotic themes as covers for partisan maneuvering. For further discussion, see Crotty (2004).

26. For reports on the state of these investigations, see the U.S. House Committee on Governmental Oversight and Reform's online archive at http://oversight.house.gov/ investigations.asp?id=101 (Accessed August 12, 2008).

27. An ABC News–*Washington Post* poll showed that "George W. Bush's job approval rating slipped to a career low 45 percent." See http://abcnews.go.com/Politics/PollVault/ story?id= 1080163&page=1 (Accessed August 15, 2008).

28. "Barring a burst of legislative activity after Labor Day, this group of 535 men and women will have accomplished a rare feat. In two decades of record keeping, no sitting Congress has passed fewer public laws at this point in the session—294 so far—than this one." *Wall Street Journal*, August 19, 2008, at http://online.wsj.com/article/SB121910897089651793 .html?mod=googlenews_wsj (Accessed August 19, 2008).

29. An ABC News–*Washington Post* poll released in June 2007 noted, "Six weeks ago the Democrats held a 24-point lead over Bush as the stronger leadership force in Washington; today that's collapsed to a dead heat. The Democrats' overall job approval rating likewise has dropped, from a 54 percent majority to 44 percent now—with the decline occurring almost exclusively among strong opponents of the Iraq War." See http://abcnews.go.com/Politics/story?id=3242551&page=1 (Accessed August 20, 2008).

30. During Clinton's administration, the size of the federal workforce decreased, and in his last State of the Union address, his theme continued his 1995 pledge that "the era of big government was over" (Clinton 2004, 694).

REFERENCES

Abramowitz, Alan. 2006. "Disconnected or Joined at the Hip? Comment." In *Red and Blue Nation? Characteristics and Causes of America's Polarized Politics*, ed. Pietro S. Nivola and David W. Brady. Washington, DC: Brookings Institution, 72–85.

Allen, Mike, and Jonathan Martin. 2008. "Obama Unveils 21st Century New Deal." *Politico.com*, December 6. http://www.politico.com/news/stories/1208/16258.html (Accessed December 6, 2008).

Bai, Matt. 2004. "Who Lost Ohio?" *New York Times*, November 21, section 6, p. 67.

Berke, Richard L. 1998. "Grand Old Problem: The Republican Middle Looks for an Edge." *New York Times*, November 8, p. D1.

Brody, Richard A. 2008. "The American People and President George W. Bush: The Fall, the Rise, and Fall Again." *The Forum* 6(2): article 1. http://www.bepress.com/forum/vol6/iss2/art1 (Accessed December 5, 2008).

Brooks, David. 2004. "How to Reinvent the G.O.P." *New York Times*, August 29, section 6, p. 32.

Brown, Lara M. 2009. "A High Speed Chase: Presidential Aspirants and the Nomination Process." In *Understanding the Presidency*, 5th ed., ed. James P. Pfiffner and Roger H. Davidson. New York: Longman, 88–111.

Burnham, Walter. 1970. *Critical Elections and the Mainsprings of American Politics*. New York: Norton.

Campbell, James E. 2005. "Why Bush Won the Presidential Election of 2004: Incumbency, Ideology, Terrorism, and Turnout." *Political Science Quarterly* 120(2): 219–41.

———. 2006. "Polarization Runs Deep, Even by Yesterday's Standards: Comment." In *Red and Blue Nation?: Characteristics and Causes of America's Polarized Politics*, ed. Pietro S. Nivola and David W. Brady. Washington, DC: Brookings Institution, 152–62.

Ceaser, James W., and Andrew E. Busch. 2005. *Red over Blue: The 2004 Elections and American Politics*. Lanham, MD: Rowman & Littlefield.

Clinton, Bill. 2004. *My Life*. New York: Knopf.

Cook, Charlie. 2008. "2006: An 'Abby Normal' Election." In *The Sixth Year Itch: The Rise and Fall of George W. Bush's Presidency*, ed. Larry J. Sabato. New York: Pearson Longman, 47–64.

Cooper, Helene, and David E. Sanger. 2007. "Bush Administration, Under Criticism, Warns Iraq to Fulfill Its End of the Bargain." *New York Times*, January 27. http://www.nytimes.com/2007/01/21/world/middleeast/21options.html?_r=3&scp=6&sqsurge+bush&st=nyt&oref=slogin (Accessed August 18, 2008).

Crotty, William. 2001. "The Election of 2000: Close, Chaotic, and Unforgettable." In *America's Choice 2000*, ed. William Crotty. Boulder, CO: Westview Press, 1–35.

————, ed. 2004. *A Defining Moment: The Presidential Election of 2004*. New York: M. E. Sharpe.

Davis, Susan. 2008. "Palin, Huckabee Lead GOP Contenders for 2012." *Washington Wire-WSJ.com*, December 5. http://blogs.wsj.com/washwire/2008/12/05/palin-huckabee-lead -gop-contenders-for-2012/ (Accessed December 6, 2008).

Dionne, E. J., Jr. 2006. "Polarized by God? American Politics and the Religious Divide." In *Red and Blue Nation?: Characteristics and Causes of America's Polarized Politics*, ed. Pietro S. Nivola and David W. Brady. Washington, DC: Brookings Institution, 175–205.

Gale, William, and Benjamin Harris. 2008. "The Bush Tax Cuts: How Did They Change the Tax Code?" *Tax Policy Center*, January 23. http://www.taxpolicycenter.org/briefing -book/background/bush-tax-cuts/change.cfm (Accessed August 12, 2008).

Galston, William A., and Pietro S. Nivola. 2006. "Delineating the Problem." In *Red and Blue Nation?: Characteristics and Causes of America's Polarized Politics*, ed. Pietro S. Nivola and David W. Brady. Washington, DC: Brookings Institution, 1–47.

Gellman, Barton. 2008. *Angler: The Cheney Vice Presidency*. New York: Penguin.

Gould, Louis. 2003. *Grand Old Party: A History of Republicans*. New York: Random House.

Harpine, William D. 2005. *McKinley and Bryan in the 1896 Presidential Campaign*. College Station: Texas A&M University Press.

Jacobson, Gary C. 2003. "Terror, Terrain, and Turnout: Explaining the 2002 Midterm Elections." *Political Science Quarterly* 118(1): 1–22.

————. 2005. "Polarized Politics and the 2004 Congressional and Presidential Elections." *Political Science Quarterly* 120(2): 199–218.

————. 2007. *A Divider, Not a Uniter: George W. Bush and the American People*. New York: Pearson Longman.

Jones, Jeffrey M. 2008. "Bush's Job Approval Inches Up to 33%." *Gallup.com*, August 15. http://www.gallup.com/poll/109570/Bushs-Job-Approval-Inches-33.aspx (Accessed August 20, 2008).

Keller, William. 2003. "Reagan's Son." *New York Times*, January 26, section 6, p. 26.

Klein, Joe. 2000. "Winners and Losers." *New Yorker*, November 20, p. 35.

Kristof, Nicholas. 2000. "For Bush, His Toughest Call Was the Choice to Run at All." *New York Times*, October 29, p. A1.

Langer, Gary. 2006. "Midterm Election: Referendum on War." *ABCNews.go.com*, October 23. http://abcnews.go.com/Politics/Story?id=2600146&page=1 (Accessed August 15, 2008).

Lemann, Nicholas. 2003. "The Controller." *New Yorker*, May 12, p. 68.

Mayhew, David R. 2002. *Electoral Realignments: A Critique of an American Genre*. New Haven, CT: Yale University Press.

McClellan, Scott. 2008. *What Happened: Inside the Bush White House and Washington's Culture of Deception*. Washington, DC: Public Affairs.

Milkis, Sidney M., and Michael Nelson. 2003. *The American Presidency: Origins and Development, 1776–2002*, 4th ed. Washington, DC: CQ Press.

Miller, Gary, and Norman Schofield. 2008. "The Transformation of the Republican and Democratic Party Coalitions in the U.S." *Perspectives on Politics* 6(3): 433–50.

Mitchell, Alison. 2001. "Two Moderate Republicans Oppose Bush Tax Plan as Democrats Offer Their Own." *New York Times*, February 16, p. A16.

Morgan, H. Wayne. 2003. *William McKinley and His America*, rev. ed. Kent, OH: Kent State University Press.

Nagourney, Adam, and Katharine Q. Seelye. 2004. "The Massachusetts Senator: Kerry Struggling to Find a Theme, Democrats Fear." *New York Times*, May 2, section 1, p. 1.

Neal, Terry. 1999. "Bush Campaign Counts on Vast Network." *Washington Post*, December 22, p. A4.

Nivola, Pietro S., and David W. Brady, eds. 2006. *Red and Blue Nation?: Characteristics and Causes of America's Polarized Politics*. Washington, DC: Brookings Institution.

————, eds. 2008. *Red and Blue Nation?: Consequences and Correction of America's Polarized Politics*. Washington, DC: Brookings Institution.

Riker, William H. 1986. *The Art of Political Manipulation*. New Haven, CT: Yale University Press.

Rosenbaum, David. 2001. "Republicans Admit Lack of Votes for Full Bush Tax Plan in Senate." *New York Times*, April 6, p. A1.

Sabato, Larry J., ed. 2003. *Midterm Madness: The Elections of 2002*. Lanham, MD: Rowman & Littlefield.

————. 2008. "Historical Imperative?" In *The Sixth Year Itch: The Rise and Fall of George W. Bush's Presidency*, ed. Larry J. Sabato. New York: Pearson Longman, 1–46.

"Sharp Challenges for Bush On Policy and Politics Alike." 2001. *ABCNews.go.com*, June 4. http:// abcnews.go.com/images/PollingUnit/853a1Politics.pdf (Accessed August 11, 2008).

Shaw, Daron R. 2006. *The Race to 270: The Electoral College and the Campaign Strategies of 2000 and 2004*. Chicago: University of Chicago Press.

Sundquist, James. 1983. *Dynamics of the Party System: Alignment and Realignment of Political Parties in the United States*. Washington, DC: Brookings Institution.

Tapper, Jake. 2002. "The Salon Interview: Bill Maher." *Salon*, December 11. http://dir.salon .com/story/people/interview/2002/12/11/maher/ (Accessed August 12, 2008).

Traub, James. 2006. "The Submerging Republican Majority." *New York Times Magazine*, June 18, section 6, p. 30.

Verhovek, Sam. 1997. "Bush Runs in Texas, But Bigger Quest Is Suspected." *New York Times*, December 4, p. A18.

Waas, Murray. 2007. "Internal Affairs." *National Journal*, March 17, p. 34.

White House Press Office, 2004. "President Holds Press Conference." Washington, DC: White House, November 4. http://www.whitehouse.gov/news/releases/2004/11/20041104-5 .html (Accessed December 6, 2008).

CHAPTER 6

Diminishing Returns

George W. Bush and Congress, 2001–2008

ANDREW RUDALEVIGE

ON SEPTEMBER 24, 2008, President George W. Bush addressed the nation from the White House. In the wake of huge market swings and bank failures, he urged passage of a $700 billion bailout of the financial industry. "Without immediate action by Congress," he warned, "America could slip into a financial panic . . . Our entire economy is in danger" (Bush 2008b).

Congressional leaders soon announced that agreement had been reached on the outline of a bill—only to find opposition from disgruntled House Republicans and unease, too, among some Democrats. Negotiations continued, the president and his team exerting pressure on legislators even over the weekend and to the point of, in one case, literally begging for votes. On Monday morning, Bush renewed his televised case. The act was not a rescue of rich bankers or a harbinger of socialism, he stressed. Instead, "every member of Congress and every American should keep in mind: A vote for this bill is a vote to prevent economic damage to you and your community" (Bush 2008c).

Yet, that evening, the House voted by a 228–205 margin to reject the bill. Republican members voted more than 2–1 against it, the group that had supported Bush in near lockstep for over seven years now ignoring him. The next day, the stock exchange suffered its largest single-day drop in two decades. Fingers pointed in all directions, but most of them wound up aimed at the president. Later in the week, a version of the legislation did pass, bearing scant resemblance to the administration's original proposal (having grown from 3 pages to 450) and still opposed by a majority of GOP representatives. The president nonetheless gamely praised the law and his role in having "Republicans and Democrats . . . come together to pass a good bill" (Bush 2008d).

The episode illuminated key facets of the American presidency as it relates to Congress. The role of president as legislative leader is not intuitive, given the separated institutions devised in the Constitution, but that expectation was on clear display. The president was the national focal point, and confusion and crisis demanded a presidential response: Congress itself looked immediately to the executive branch for proposals to deal with the financial meltdown. The bully pulpit of the presidency was in full prime-time view; and the effort (however halting in effect) to use public pressure and private suasion to move legislative outcomes toward executive preferences was hardly subtle. All these elements are fundamental to the modern presidency.

But the highly salient failure of the first House vote highlighted too that presidents cannot command congressional action. By that point in the Bush presidency, legislators did not find him very persuasive. Only three of ten Americans approved of Bush's job performance; the ongoing campaign to succeed him had sucked most of the political air—and airtime—out of the White House beat. While in the past, on issues from Medicare expansion to executive wiretapping, Bush had been able to pressure members of both parties to suspend their ideological scruples, this time the administration's proposal came under attack from all sides. Republicans attacked public sector intrusion into private markets; Democrats lambasted the administration's previous laissez-faire attitude toward financial regulation and bruited analogies to Iraq's absent weapons of mass destruction. "Just as we should have asked more questions . . . before we found ourselves in this war," Senator Richard Durbin (D-IL) growled, "we need to ask questions today about where this is leading" (Herszenhorn 2008). Both sides cautioned they would not again grant enormous discretionary powers to the president without strict oversight procedures.

All this provides a frame to help us "judge Bush" in the arena of presidential-congressional relations. It recalls, if by contrast, his impressive earlier success in gaining congressional support for key administration priorities, whether through legislative action or inaction. It shows the important role of context, especially crisis and timing, in that achievement. And it also shows that the administration's attitudes and actions vis-à-vis Congress ultimately damaged its credibility, its leeway, and thus its legislative legacy. Its successful short-term tactics produced diminishing strategic returns—on its investment of political capital, on its electoral support, and on its policy legacy.

BALANCING THE BRANCHES

The U.S. Constitution begins with an unusually clear claim, vesting "all legislative powers herein granted" in Congress. But like other aspects of American government's "separated institutions sharing power," legislative endowments bridge rather than divide the branches (Neustadt 1990, 29). Presidents must call on legislators to confirm executive branch nominees and to ratify treaties. Further, the Constitution enjoins presidents to propose "necessary and expedient" measures and gives them the power to veto legislative enactments. The first provides the potential to set the congressional, and national, agenda; the second, an important tool in determining policy outcomes.

Early presidents were hesitant to use these tools. But over time, the president's legislative program and success in persuading Congress to accept its components has become key to assessing his overall success. As Carter and Clinton official Stu Eizenstat put it, "People judge strong presidents versus weak presidents on the basis of whether they perceive that the president is able to get the Congress to do what he wants" (Eizenstat 1982, 105).

Presidents are rarely happy with their ability to do that. Indeed, political scientist Michael Genovese's *Memo to a New President* advises that "there is no way to convey to you at this point the utter frustration and anger to which the Congress will drive you" (2008, 161). Despite deeply held images of presidential authority, from the "Johnson treatment" to George W. Bush's post–9/11 bullhorn, presidential sway over Congress is normally measured by degrees, not decree. As even Johnson colorfully conceded, the president can't "start yelling 'frog' at everybody, and expect 'em to jump" (Rudalevige 2005, 429).

Further, much of presidents' ability to persuade legislators to jump their way is gallingly out of their control, constrained by political context. The most important determinant is the number of congressional seats held by the president's copartisans, along with the proximity of his policy preferences to those of House and Senate majorities. Presidents working with large majorities of like-minded allies not surprisingly get more of what they ask for than do presidents in divided government or presidents with divided parties. And other aspects of the political environment matter too. How strong is the national economy? How effective is the party leadership in Congress? How unified is the president's electoral coalition and the interest-group universe? How successful was the president's predecessor? Stephen Skowronek (1994) shows that where presidents fall in these aspects of "political time" and their ability to discern the tenor of that time, has important implications for their chances of achieving lasting policy change.

Other factors stem from the more immediate context provided by what scholars have called "focusing events" (Kingdon 1995). In times of national crisis, legislators are far more likely to defer to presidential initiative. "History," as Bush aide Karl Rove mused, "has a way of intruding on you," and those intrusions shape presidential opportunities (Balz and Fletcher 2005, A1).

Presidents are not without strategic options, though. They have some discretion, for example, over the makeup and ambition of their agenda. They may highlight foreign affairs, where they are often given more leeway; they may attempt a focused "rifle" rather than a widespread "shotgun" approach (Pfiffner 1996). Timing—the ability to interpret and exploit the above contexts—matters greatly, but time on the whole is not on presidents' side: postwar history before George W. Bush shows a significant decline in the legislative success of second-term chief executives. After eight years, as one aide said of LBJ, they "can't get Mother's Day through" (Rudalevige 2006, 433).[1]

THE CONGRESSIONAL RECORD, 2001–2008

Early in his own eighth year, President Bush went on the attack against the "irresponsible" Congress. Americans, he said, were worried about issues ranging from gasoline prices to the mortgage crunch. "I've repeatedly submitted proposals to help address these problems. Yet, time after time, Congress chose to block them" (Bush 2008a).

This complaint could have been lifted from anywhere in presidential history. But if Bush's sentiments were timeless, the return of that normalcy to interbranch relations was still notable. After all, for much of his administration Bush oversaw one of the more successful legislative presidencies of modern times, working with Congresses that had largely let him direct national affairs without much oversight, passing bills he wanted—and, as importantly, stopping bills he didn't (Rudalevige 2006; Sinclair 2007). Indeed, for more than five years Bush did not veto a single bill, the longest such streak in two centuries. His focused initial agenda, disciplined copartisans, and (not least) the shock of the 9/11 attacks provided political resources, leveraged skillfully into consequential policy change.

The First Term

The context for such success was not immediately obvious: Bush was elected in 2000 with a minority of the popular vote and a slim, disputed Electoral College majority, while Republicans lost seats in both chambers. Bush, however, chose to behave as though he had a clear mandate for his campaign platform. The strategy worked. Education reform and tax cuts were the president's clear priorities; both passed, in forms well acceptable to the president. The No Child Left Behind Act (NCLB) was the grandest restructuring of the federal role in education since the 1960s; the 2001 tax reductions were the largest since Reagan's, even before they were further extended and augmented. Both measures attracted bipartisan support.

Other elements of the administration's agenda made less progress, especially once the Senate flipped to the Democrats following James Jeffords's decision to leave the GOP caucus. But while the terrorist attacks of September 11, 2001, may not have "changed everything," as commonly propounded at the time, they clearly changed the Bush presidency. Bush's public approval ratings quickly brushed 90 percent, from 50 percent the week before; and a powerful national address on September 20 coined additional political capital. Even before the president spoke, Congress had passed a joint resolution granting him discretionary authority to use "all necessary and appropriate force" against the facilitators of the attacks. The sweeping expansion of federal law enforcement powers known as the PATRIOT Act passed soon afterward. And in 2002, legislators voted by large margins to authorize war against Iraq, again at the president's discretion.

Democrats were able to use their Senate majority to block some measures (such as the administration's energy bill) and modify others; and Bush picked his fights. For example, he decided to avoid the criticism that would have come with vetoing a new campaign finance law. But the president was able to push through his main objectives, especially where these dealt with national security, even tangentially (such as economic recovery measures—largely further tax cuts—and the renewal of "fast track" trade authority). During the midterm elections, the president bucked history by campaigning vigorously, and successfully, for GOP candidates as Republicans expanded their House majority and retook the Senate. Chastened Democrats agreed to the president's version of a bill creating a huge new Department of Homeland Security, which included new personnel provisions despised by public sector unions, and confirmed a number of bottled-up judicial nominees.

With party control restored in 2003, the president again kept his legislative agenda short. It led off with a third successful round of tax cuts, followed by a base-pleasing ban on late-term abortions.

Other major acts funded military operations and occupation in Iraq subsequent to the March 2003 invasion. These generally received wide support. At the same time (as discussed below) Congress did not interfere in the president's wide-ranging claims to executive power concerning a war on terror. A rare case of legislative initiative in the national security arena was a measure reorganizing the intelligence community in the wake of its pre–9/11 failures. The president was unenthusiastic but ultimately pledged his support, though molding the final product to grant him more autonomy.

As his first term ended, President Bush had succeeded both in passing his program and in fomenting partisan polarization. The two went together, since the latter was both a result and cause of the president's success. As House Speaker Dennis Hastert (R-IL) noted, his aim was a "majority of the majority" rather than to pass a bill that required Democratic votes, even where they were available (Babington 2004). *Congressional Quarterly* data show that from 2001 to 2004 the average Republican House member voted with the president almost 85 percent of the time; in the

Senate, GOP loyalty topped 90 percent. Democratic House members, by contrast, supported the president on fewer than three in ten votes. These figures may even understate the partisan divide: on votes where the parties split during this period, Republicans voted with their party's majority between 89 and 92 percent of the time, with more than four-fifths of Democrats doing the same. From the late 1960s through the 1970s, by contrast, figures for both parties rarely hit 70 percent and were often in the fifties.[2] Further, the sheer number of these party votes also rose—from fewer than four in ten of all roll calls in the 1970s to well over half from the 1990s on. And in Bush's first term, Republicans won nearly 90 percent of such votes (Sinclair 2006, 6; Zeller 2008, 3335).

The "majority of the majority" strategy exacerbated these patterns but was also a tactically astute exploitation of broader underlying trends—for instance, the slow diminution of intraparty diversity, as between Southern Democrats and their more liberal counterparts, or between Northeastern Republicans and their more conservative copartisans. Over time, the parties grew more internally homogenous, but the divisions between them grew wider. At the same time, legislative leaders of both parties had learned to utilize the powers granted them (ironically enough) in the 1970s, giving them additional authority over participation and agenda-setting in committee and on the floor (Sinclair 2006). The result was that the minority caucus, especially in the House, could be ignored, given a united and disciplined majority.

A Tale of Two Congresses

As we have seen, the GOP—and Bush—had just that. And in November 2004, the president defeated Massachusetts senator John Kerry with just under 51 percent of the popular vote, while Republican legislative majorities grew. The close tally suggested that the divisions in Congress were reflected nationally but also that the president's leadership in Iraq and on the economy had received the benefit of public doubt.

Flush with victory, President Bush laid out his second-term agenda: restructuring Social Security, expanding NCLB, and simplifying the tax code. In foreign affairs he stressed "fighting and winning the war on terror," along with expansive inaugural claims about American intentions to support the growth of democracy "in every nation and culture." His reelection provided a new mandate for his program, said the president: "I earned capital in the campaign . . . and now I intend to spend it" (Bush 2004).

If Bush was spending, the expanded GOP caucus on Capitol Hill seemed to augur willing business partners. Two early victories for the president came on legislation limiting class-action litigation and bankruptcy protection.

Bush's big-ticket items, however, ran into more resistance. The president's extensive road show on behalf of his Social Security plan—"60 Stops in 60 Days"—failed to convince the public that the program needed the addition of private retirement accounts. Facing legislative ambivalence, at best, the administration never submitted a complete proposal on the subject. Tax code reform was relegated to a study commission and did not reemerge. Nor did various efforts to reauthorize NCLB gain traction: Democrats who had supported the bill in 2001 resented what they saw as inadequate funding for its provisions, and Republicans distrusted the expanded federal role in education generally. A major effort in 2006 to reform immigration laws also fell by the wayside, with an insufficient number of Republicans willing to support its amnesty provisions and the "majority" strategy having eroded the odds of garnering Democratic support.

In any case, by then the president's domestic agenda had been blown far off course by the storms that hit the Gulf Coast in the late summer of 2005. In 2001, events, and the administration's reaction to them, had recharged presidential clout; in 2005, they drained it. Most damaging was Hurricane Katrina, which wreaked havoc along the Southern shoreline and especially in New Orleans. Officials at all levels reacted poorly, but the federal government took the most blame, especially after Bush seemed to fail to grasp the scope of the crisis. His misguided compliment to soon-to-be-fired FEMA director Michael Brown—"Brownie, you're doing a heck of a job"—became a catchphrase that rebounded against the president (Hsu and Glasser 2005).

At the same time, the conflict in Iraq grew increasingly deadly for American troops and Iraqi civilians alike. Elections in January 2005 raised hopes, but subsequent delays in forming a government, continued investigations into prisoner abuse, and a nihilistic insurgency quickly dampened them. American public opinion turned on the administration: by March a solid majority of the public believed the war had not been worth fighting. Nevertheless, an $80 billion spending request for Iraq and Afghanistan was approved in May, to be followed by $50 billion in December and $69 billion in mid-2006.

On security issues, then, the administration continued to advance its legislative agenda. In late 2005, Congress made efforts both to ensure humane treatment of those captured in the war on terror and to prevent them from using American courts to press their cause. The administration resisted the first, issuing a controversial signing statement that signaled it would not comply; but it welcomed the second. However, in 2006 the Supreme Court held that the military tribunals unilaterally set up by the president to try detainees violated U.S. statutory and treaty obligations. In response the president proposed, and Congress passed, the Military Commissions Act of 2006, which gave the administration explicit power to name "enemy combatants" and to strip them of their habeas corpus rights.[3] The 2001 PATRIOT Act was reauthorized in 2006 as well, largely along the expansive lines Bush desired.

During this period, the president was also able to seat two new members on the Supreme Court, John Roberts and Samuel Alito, as discussed in Chapter 8 of this volume. The process was not entirely smooth, since for the Alito seat Bush first nominated White House Counsel Harriet Miers; she was pressured to withdraw after questions arose about her qualifications and core beliefs. But both Roberts and Alito soon proved to be reliable conservative voices on the Court and looked likely to remain so for years to come. They came on top of 315 other Bush appointees to the federal bench confirmed by the Senate during his presidency—in the aggregate, a consequential legacy.[4]

On the whole, then, President Bush could justifiably claim in late 2006 that "we had a pretty successful couple of years when it comes to legislation." Citing yet another tax cut bill ($70 billion in May 2006), trade initiatives, a transportation bill, and an energy exploration act, he argued, "it's been a pretty substantial legislative record if you carefully scrutinize it" (Bush 2006; Stevenson 2005). His record on winning specific roll call votes had remained strong at 81 percent, better than that of Dwight Eisenhower,

Ronald Reagan, or Bill Clinton in their sixth year in office (Barshay 2007). Roll call statistics can be misleading—after all, the administration's Social Security and education initiatives, and the Miers nomination, can hardly be considered successful simply because they never came to a vote. But in as many cases the president was able to forestall likely floor defeat. For instance, though legislators vehemently opposed the administration's support for a Dubai-based company's bid to operate several American ports, they did not ultimately force the issue. On the whole, though, when push came to shove, Republican party leaders pressured their rank and file to vote with the president or not to vote at all.

But if the 109th Congress reflected in retrospect the best of times, worse was to come. In the November 2006 midterm elections, Democrats won sweeping victories, gaining thirty seats in the House and six in the Senate to regain majorities in both chambers. The results catapulted previously marginalized administration antagonists into key posts. For instance, acerbic Bush critic Henry Waxman (D-CA) took the gavel at the House Oversight and Government Reform Committee, with a wide brief to conduct investigations into any topic. Not surprisingly, the number of oversight hearings soared in 2007, covering everything from the status of Iraqi reconstruction to the storage of White House e-mail.

The president continued to push an aggressive legislative agenda, though largely through the resurrection of older proposals newly framed to match new problems (Eggen 2008a; Sanger and Rutenberg 2007). This suggested either principled consistency or ideological rigidity; either way it was not a tactic finely tuned to the new partisan reality. Bush thought that education and immigration were prime areas for agreement, for example, but did not give enough ground to suit Democrats. U.S. Representative Rahm Emanuel (D-IL) complained that Bush and his aides "think being stubborn is tough. Stubborn is not tough; it's stubborn" (Baker 2008). Democrats were equally stubborn. Using one rough measure to suggest "success," the president's record of winning roll call votes on which he had taken a position fell from an impressive 80 percent or so from 2001 to 2006 to just 38 percent in 2007. The rate of party-line votes rose, too, to over six of ten roll calls in 2007, with unprecedented Democratic unity (over 90 percent) driving the total ("When the President . . ." 2008, 133; Zeller

2008, 3338). In short, both sides talked of bipartisanship but tended to mean concession *by* others rather than compromise *with* them.

The president's ability to just say No had its own substantive impact. As Bush legislative liaison Candi Wolff noted, "[even] in the eighth year of the presidency and in this environment, [his] veto was pretty strong" (Davis 2008). By August 2007, the president had already issued twice as many formal veto threats as in any other year of his presidency (Jackson 2007). And after just one veto in his first six years, Bush vetoed eleven bills in the 110th Congress alone.

To be sure, a handful of these were overridden; like Jimmy Carter thirty years earlier, Bush discovered that disrupting local water projects was a sure way to unite Congress. Still, the president was able to fend off a long series of Democratic attempts to impose conditions on funding Iraq or place time limits on U.S. involvement there. He vetoed efforts to expand children's health insurance and to limit CIA interrogation tactics. And since, even outside veto overrides, Senate action often requires sixty votes (for cloture), even a minority there could block movement. Majority Leader Harry Reid (D-NV) grew frustrated, accusing the president of "pulling the strings on the 49 puppets he has here in the Senate" to prevent progress (Herszenhorn 2007). Here, as throughout his administration, legislative stalemate tended to favor the president's preferences by enhancing his freedom of action.

Still, as the 110th Congress progressed, there were exceptions to the lack of cooperation, such as the $152 billion economic stimulus bill passed in early 2008. A fair amount of quiet give-and-take, channeled by veto bargaining but going beyond it, led to other legislation as well (Eggen and Kane 2008). Democrats were able to use the "must pass" status of military appropriations bills to impose their own policy preferences: while Bush won $162 billion in no-strings funding for the wars in Iraq and Afghanistan, Democrats added billions in new benefits for returning troops and increased aid to the jobless. Bush's large-scale AIDS relief package was approved, but so was a housing bill aimed to provide mortgage help and new aid to poor neighborhoods. The Higher Education Act was reauthorized (five years late) along with other measures designed to make college more affordable. A major nuclear cooperation deal with India was approved in October 2008.

These outcomes showed that the normal bargaining dynamic of presidential-congressional relations had returned, after a six-year hiatus. But even here there was continuing legislative deference in providing discretionary authority to the president in the national security arena. In 2007, for instance, Congress approved the Protect America Act, legitimating the surveillance program begun after 9/11 in violation of the Foreign Intelligence Surveillance Act (FISA). In early July 2008, after a pause, Congress revisited the issue and broadened FISA, while granting telecommunications companies who had participated in the program immunity from prosecution.

It is worth highlighting the administrative autonomy thus endorsed. The president's unilateral strategies are in fact part of Bush's relations with (and success in) Congress: part of that success was in cordoning off substantial zones of authority where he could avoid Congress altogether by acting alone. Even before 9/11, the Bush administration had asserted a wide range of claims aimed at rolling back legislative entitlements developed after Watergate; afterward, not surprisingly, the pace picked up, grounded in the quick, secret action needed to wage a war on terror. As the Justice Department's John Yoo testified, "extensive congressional discussion will often be a luxury we cannot afford" (Owens 2006, 270).

Indeed, in claiming sole authority over all aspects of the detention regime housed at Guantánamo Bay, and through the wiretapping program, the administration went further, affirmatively rejecting the conclusions of any such discussion. It argued that legislative action in those domains was actually unconstitutional interference with the president's power as commander in chief (see Rudalevige 2006). By 2008 the administration was concluding a status-of-forces agreement with Iraq concerning the American presence there, arguing that it could be implemented without legislative approval. This provoked some congressional bluster—Representative Gary Ackerman (D-NY) raged that "The trouble with the administration is that it thinks that the Constitution is optional" (U.S. Congress 2008)—but, as before, little congressional action.

BUSH, CONGRESS, AND COMPETENCE

The narrative above suggests a straightforward arc tracing a largely successful legislative presidency through 2004, tailing off somewhat (at least domestically) in 2005 and 2006, until meeting a brick wall after the 2006 elections. This is true enough so far as it goes. But it disguises a mass of discordant data comprising deference and dissent, capability and contempt. Judgment of Bush's dealings with Congress must grapple with an administration and a period of history that (like Walt Whitman) "contained multitudes."

It is useful to return then to the organizing framework proposed in the first chapter of this volume. It centers on the notion of competence, divided into the political, strategic, tactical, and moral. One could add to this a temporal dimension, considering within each category both the short term, and the long. If so, one might conclude that the Bush record is a model of short-term success at the cost of long-term sustainability.

The Bush presidency will long be studied for its command of partisan politics and its ability to shape a responsive executive branch staffed with what one aide called "loyal Bushies." Its expertise in the mechanics of campaigning carried over to issue management. September 11, 2001, obviously set the stage; but President Bush and his team utilized well the opportunities they had, from the desire for public unity after the 2000 election and the aftermath of the attacks to the mantle of "wartime president" worn so ostentatiously in 2004. Bush and a steadfast Republican leadership in Congress, especially in the House, showed that a firm grip on the legislative and public agendas could produce meaningful policy change.

Bush's core proposals were large, but the list was short; and (with the prominent exceptions of NCLB and, eventually, the 2008 financial rescue act) they were passed not from the middle out but from the right wing in. President Bush issued bold blueprints and refused to "negotiate against myself"; the House, able to rely on restrictive rules to limit debate and amendment, sought to find a bare 218 votes to pass a proposal; the Senate, with its more consensual rules, passed a more moderate version; and conference committees were then used ruthlessly to come down near the House version, sometimes by excluding Democratic conferees from participation. As Jack Howard of the Bush legislative affairs office categorized the sequence, "You push the House to get as much as you can, take what you can from the Senate and use the conference process to push it back toward the House some" (Barshay 2007).

The 2003 Medicare prescription drug benefit bill exemplifies this mastery of small-bore politics and process. While in the Senate, the president turned to Ted Kennedy (D-MA) to craft a measure; in the House, the president instead sought to build the bill he really wanted. Because of conservative members' objections to the bill's cost, when the fifteen-minute vote on passage was called at 3 A.M., the president's bill had lost, 215–219. Rather than close the vote, though, House leaders worked the floor, and the president worked the phones, twisting arms and making offers. By 5:00 A.M. the president had 216 votes; at 5:51 A.M., he had 218.

The conference committee, as appointed, contained ten Republicans and seven Democrats. But only two of the latter were ever admitted to its deliberations, and its report tilted heavily toward the House bill. Helped by Senate Democrats wary of voting against what was, after all, a massive expansion of a public health care program, the report was nonetheless adopted (Sinclair 2007).

The tactics in this exaggerated example were used in more refined ways to win a series of legislative victories. However, the reliance on those targeted mechanics did not—perhaps to the surprise of their architects—carry over to reshaping voter loyalties or the broader party system. Despite the impressive Republican victories of 2002 and 2004, in 2006 and 2008 Independent voters showed they had not realigned to the GOP.

Perhaps this was because administrative responsiveness had been favored over managerial competence; after a bill became a law, the victory it represented was not always institutionalized. Even the Medicare bill cost far more than its public projections.[5]

But nor did those victories aggregate to build something larger. The Bush administration strategy for legislative acquiescence was long grounded in aggressive use of executive prerogative and fierce partisan loyalty, in the demand for compliance rather than the offer of consultation. Even as that strategy thrived, it bred resentment among those who would shortly be able to implement their anger. Prior to the 2006 election, Representative David Obey (D-WI) had griped that "this administration thinks that Article I of the Constitution was a fundamental mistake" (Caruso 2003, 2258); in 2007, Obey became chair of the House Appropriations Committee. Yet, even Republicans had long complained of being shut out and taken for granted (Stolberg 2006). The result was that repeated tactics, whether rhetorical or procedural or attitudinal, yielded diminishing returns. If some of the rising rancor over time was the natural result of divided party control, and some was simply a matter of time itself—reflecting both election-year inertia and the lame duck status of a late-term president— a fair amount seems to be blowback, the negative consequences of past actions, however successful those actions might have seemed at the time (Johnson 2004). As we have seen, the hostility over the banking bailout was a reciprocal image of congressional docility in earlier days. "Like the Iraq War and the Patriot Act," one House member complained (Eggen 2008b), "this bill is fuelled on fear and hinges on haste."

Strategic competence, as the term is used in this volume, deals with a broad impact on the policy regime; here too the signs point in two directions. The legislative results of the 2001–2008 period led to truly important policy change, in foreign affairs, of course, but also in K–12 education, the tax code (with seven major tax relief packages enacted in eight years, most of whose "temporary" provisions have been extended or made permanent), farm subsidies, homeland security, deregulation, and Medicare. The president's wins in these areas reshaped the distribution of government resources in ways that reshaped society's approach to government action, rewarded his electoral coalition, and bid (he hoped) to expand it.[6]

But one wonders whether this success will also consume itself over time. Fiscal conservatism was largely abandoned to tax cuts, to the enormous military buildup of the war on terror, and then to pent-up Democratic priorities. Vice President Dick Cheney set the tone: "Reagan proved deficits don't matter," he told the cabinet in pressing for tax cuts in the 2003 round; "this is our due" (Suskind 2004, 291). Congress went along with that rationale and added insult to injury by consistently failing to pass budgets on time or in conjunction with a coherent budget resolution guiding spending and revenue choices. Instead, the massive spending increases incorporated by the programmatic changes led to a flood of red ink. In fiscal 2001, the federal budget showed a $128 billion surplus; by fiscal 2009, the deficit had shot past $1 trillion.

As a result, the national debt increased by $4 *trillion* in these eight years, meaning that 9 percent of federal spending simply pays interest on that debt.

This was before any of the financial sector's assets were purchased, before needed revisions to the Alternative Minimum Tax (AMT), before repair of the nation's crumbling transportation infrastructure, before restoring solvency to Social Security, before developing new energy sources, before extending health care coverage to recession-stressed families or providing disability benefits to veterans of the Iraq War. As of the end of 2007, the Government Accountability Office estimated that commitments totaled a staggering $53 trillion in future unfunded liabilities (Walker 2008, 7). The long-term view is one of open-ended commitment often entered into for short-term political gain and without much scrutiny. On fiscal matters, then, and on other intergenerational concerns from energy independence to immigration reform, there is a long list of major issues for which the legislative legacy of the Bush years is one of neglect.

This implies, at least, the final issue of moral competence, though that is not a frame of reference often used in presidential-congressional relations.[7] The mismatch of commitments to resources, bequeathed to one's successors, does perhaps suggest a likely shortfall in responsible governance. More immediately, trustworthiness, or its lack, did become a troubling issue over time. Consider the dire terms in which President Bush put the case for the urgency of the financial rescue bill. This made sense: warning of imminent danger had been a successful formula for the president in areas ranging from the invasion of Iraq to the debate over surveillance law, and rarely was sufficient information to justify the claims either volunteered or demanded. But by 2008 the president's credibility had been whittled away. "The only thing we have to fear," Representative Louis Gohmert responded, "is the fear-mongering." This, from a Texas Republican. Presidential persuasion—one component of presidential power—had drained, at least in part, from self-inflicted wounds.

If so, Bush's most lasting achievement as regards Congress may be the tools he has bequeathed his successors for *avoiding* Congress, from the expansion of executive privilege to the systematic use of signing statements. But that too was a two-way street. If the executive branch had a certain contempt for the notion of a coequal branch, Congress shared that contempt (Mann and Ornstein 2006). It is worth emphasizing that much of the president's legislative success must be attributed to a set of congressional leaders who did not challenge his ideas and would not let him fail. As former Republican representative Mickey Edwards told a Senate committee in September 2008, "the Congress has failed to live up to its assigned role as the principal representative of the people. . . . You are not a parliament," where the executive and legislative functions are fused, he reminded his former colleagues, "you are a Congress—separate, independent, and equal" (2008).

Acting on those constitutional principles makes presidential leadership more challenging. But they are nonetheless the ultimate grounds for judgment—of the Bush presidency, of Congress, and, not least, of our own roles as citizens of a democratic republic.

NOTES

1. That is, a resolution honoring Mother's Day. The empirical figure is a 20 percentage point decrease from first term to second, starting with Eisenhower, in success on contested votes as defined by Bond and Fleisher (1990).

2. The first figures refer to roll call votes on which the president took a position; the second, to votes where a majority of one party opposed a majority of the other. See Rudalevige (2006); Zeller (2008, 3335).

3. In *Boumediene v. Bush* (2008), the Supreme Court found this latter provision to be unconstitutional.

4. Figures are through December 15, 2008, and are from the Senate Judiciary Committee. See http://leahy.senate.gov/issues/nominations/index.html.

5. The public estimate was $400 billion over ten years. Arguably, the bill's passage was attained only by the administration's decision to withhold from Congress higher cost projections ($534 billion) developed by Medicare actuaries. But in 2005, Medicare projected the cost as at least $720 billion.

6. For example, to elderly voters, who supported Al Gore in 2000 but Bush in 2004 and McCain in 2008. Outreach to black and (more damaging) Latino voters was less successful.

7. It doesn't help, perhaps, that moral judgments of this administration tend to correlate so exactly with the judge's partisan predilections.

REFERENCES

Babington, Charles. 2004. "Hastert Launches a Partisan Policy." *Washington Post*, November 27, p. A1.

Baker, Peter. 2008. "The Final Days." *New York Times Magazine*, August 31, p. MM26.

Balz, Dan, and Michael Fletcher. 2005. "Looking to Apply Lessons Learned." *Washington Post*, January 20, p. A1.

Barshay, Jill. 2007. "Popularity Not Required." *CQ Weekly*, January 1, pp. 44–47.

Bond, Jon R., and Richard Fleisher. 1990. *The President in the Legislative Arena*. Chicago: University of Chicago Press.

Bush, George W. 2004. President's Press Conference. Office of the White House Press Secretary, November 4.

———. 2006. Press Conference by the President. Office of the White House Press Secretary, December 20.

———. 2008a. Press Conference by the President. Office of the White House Press Secretary, April 29.

———. 2008b. President's Address to the Nation. Office of the White House Press Secretary, September 24.

———. 2008c. President Bush Discusses Financial Rescue Legislation. Office of the White House Press Secretary, September 29.

———. 2008d. President Bush Discusses Emergency Economic Stabilization Act. Office of the White House Press Secretary, October 7.

Caruso, Lisa. 2003. "You've Got to Know When to Hold 'Em." *National Journal*, July 12, p. 2258.

Davis, Julie Hirschfeld. 2008. "Democrats Exact Price from Bush for War." *USA Today*, August 2. http://www.usatoday.com/news/topstories/ 2008-08-02- 4094996487_x.htm (Accessed December 30, 2008).

Edwards, Mickey. 2008. "On the Subject of Restoring the Rule of Law." US Congress. Senate. Committee on the Judiciary. Subcommittee on the Constitution. 110th Congress, 2nd Session, September 16.

Eggen, Dan. 2008a. "For Bush in Last Year, It's the Principle." *Washington Post*, May 3, p. A1.

———. 2008b. "Bush's Warnings of Danger Are No Longer as Powerful." *Washington Post*, October 1, p. A10.

———, and Paul Kane. 2008. "Recent Bush Victories Smell of Compromise." *Washington Post*, July 13, p. A4.

Eizenstat, Stuart. 1982. Miller Center Interviews, Carter Project, Vol. 13, January.

Genovese, Michael A. 2008. *Memo to a New President*. New York: Oxford University Press.

Herszenhorn, David. 2007. "Reid's Chilly Relationship with Bush Enters Deep Freeze." *New York Times*, December 19, p. A20.

———. 2008. "Bailout Plan Talks Advance in Congress." *New York Times*, September 23, p. A1.

Hsu, Spencer, and Susan Glasser. 2005. "FEMA Director Singled Out by Response Critics." *Washington Post*, September 6, p. A1.

Jackson, David. 2007. "Squaring Off with Dems, Bush Makes More Veto Threats." *USA Today*, August 6, p. 7A.

Johnson, Chalmers. 2004. *Blowback*, 2nd ed. New York: Holt.

Kingdon, John W. 1995. *Agendas, Alternatives, and Public Policies*, 2nd ed. New York: HarperCollins.

Mann, Thomas, and Norman Ornstein. 2006. *The Broken Branch*. New York: Oxford University Press.

Neustadt, Richard E. 1990. *Presidential Power and the Modern Presidents*. New York: Free Press.

Owens, John E. 2006. "Presidential Power and Congressional Acquiescence in the 'War' on Terrorism." *Politics and Policy* 34(2): 258–303.

Pfiffner, James P. 1996. *The Strategic Presidency*, 2nd rev. ed. Lawrence: University Press of Kansas.

Rudalevige, Andrew. 2005. "The Executive Branch and the Legislative Process." In *The Executive Branch*, ed. Joel D. Aberbach and Mark A. Peterson. New York: Oxford University Press, 419–51.

———. 2006. "George W. Bush and Congress in the Second Term: New Problems, Same Results?" In *The Second Term of George W. Bush: Prospects and Perils*, ed. Robert Maranto, Douglas M. Brattebo, and Tom Lansford. New York: Palgrave Macmillan, 79–100.

Sanger, David, and Jim Rutenberg. 2007. "Bush, Pressing Modest Agenda, Insists U.S. Must Not Fail in Iraq." *New York Times*, January 24, p. A1.

Sinclair, Barbara. 2006. *Party Wars*. Norman: University of Oklahoma Press.

———. 2007. "Living (and Dying?) by the Sword." In *The George W. Bush Legacy*, ed. Colin Campbell, Bert Rockman, and Andrew Rudalevige. Washington, DC: CQ Press, 164–87.

Skowronek, Stephen. 1994. *The Politics Presidents Make*. Cambridge, MA: Harvard University Press.

Stevenson, Richard W. 2005. "Despite Problems, Bush Continues to Make Advances on His Agenda." *New York Times*, July 29, p. A20.

Stolberg, Sheryl Gay. 2006. "As Agenda Falters, Bush Tries a More Personal Approach in Dealing with Congress." *New York Times*, June 11, p. A35.

Suskind, Ron. 2004. *The Price of Loyalty*. New York: Simon & Schuster.

U.S. Congress. House of Representatives. Committee on Foreign Affairs. Subcommittee on the Middle East and South Asia and Subcommittee on International Organizations, Human Rights, and Oversight. 2008. *Declaration and Principles: Future U.S. Commitments to Iraq*. 100th Congress, 2nd Session, March 4. http://foreignaffairs.house.gov/110/ackerman030408.htm (Accessed April 14, 2009).

Walker, David M. 2008. *Making Tough Budget Choices to Create a Better Future* (GAO-08-604CG). Washington, DC: U.S. Government Accountability Office.

"When the President Has Won." 2008. *CQ Weekly*, January 14, p. 133.

Zeller, Shawn. 2008. "2008 Votes Studies: Party Unity." *CQ Weekly*, December 15, pp. 3332–38.

CHAPTER 7

Not Always According to Plan

Theory and Practice in the Bush White House

KAREN M. HULT, CHARLES E. WALCOTT, AND DAVID B. COHEN

JUDGING A PRESIDENT'S White House staff organization first requires that we ask an obvious but difficult question: *What does a strong staff organization do for a president?* That in turn begs another question: *What do we mean by a "strong" staff organization?* In this chapter, we will begin by advancing workable, if tentative, answers to such questions, then look more closely at the Bush White House's performance. Our focus is on *tactical competence*, since the most obvious benefit of a strong staff organization is its contribution to making and carrying out plans and decisions.

The question of what staff organization can contribute to presidential success is always vexing because definitions of success are varied and elusive. Inevitably, they depend on contestable evidence and differing judgments of observers. Here, we will avoid the most obvious thicket, leaving aside questions of whether a policy or action succeeded or failed. Instead, we will invoke *process* criteria, examining how the Bush White House operated, not whether those operations produced good or bad outcomes. Where success is subjective, at least a focus on process directs us to observables.

We examine three core tasks of any White House: maintaining orderly processes of consultation and decision making, developing and overseeing policy, and presenting the president to the public. These by no means exhaust the tasks that a modern White House is expected to perform. But they are a reasonable place from which an evaluation can proceed.

WHITE HOUSE DECISION PROCESSES

Processes for making decisions in modern White Houses tend to be carefully structured and managed, seeking to achieve what Alexander George called multiple advocacy (1974): making sure that relevant decision makers, especially the president, are armed with a full array of facts, arguments, and judgments before they make a choice, to facilitate informed decisions. It is a technique for avoiding what Irving Janis famously dubbed "groupthink," where one point of view prematurely prevails and dissenting views are silenced (1982).

In the contemporary White House, multiple advocacy is encouraged by an elaborate process known as "staffing." This entails identifying issues for decision and circulating decision memoranda to all interested members of the administration. The memoranda outline the issues to be presented for presidential decision and may include arguments pro and con. Officials—White House staffers, cabinet and subcabinet members, and others—are asked to register their opinions in writing for transmission to the president. Presidents may supplement the written process with as much face-to-face discussion and advocacy as they choose. George W. Bush preferred meetings that supplemented the written opinions, and he made himself more available to top aides and others than many of his predecessors.

The staffing process has been a formalized staple of White House decision making since the Nixon administration. One cannot demonstrate definitively that it makes for better decisions. Even so, it is likely that in the long run decision makers use the staffing process to the limits of their own capabilities, making a sound system of multiple advocacy a useful evaluative criterion for White House staffs. An effective staffing process also can help the White House in other ways. Richard Cheney, reflecting before he was vice president on his time as President Ford's chief of staff, contended that a key virtue is the appearance of fairness to all potential advisors.

If you don't trust the process, you're going to start looking for ways around it . . . All of a sudden you have people freelancing, trying to get around the decision- making process because they feel the process lacks integrity. So it's very, very important . . . to make certain that you have a guaranteed flow—you know what's going in; you know what's coming out. You know when it goes in that it's complete, that everybody's got their shot at the decision memo. You know if there's going to be a meeting, the right people are going to be in the meeting [cited in Kumar and Sullivan 2003b, 10].

Essential to this perception of fairness is that the manager of the process—generally either the chief of staff or the national security assistant—be seen (and be seen to act) as an honest broker rather than as an advocate for any particular policy, ideology, or group (Walcott et al. 2001, 479ff).

This balancing of inputs to the president is especially important in performing what many consider the basic function of the White House staff: the integration of considerations of good public policy with the demands of presidential politics. In recent administrations, notably that of Bill Clinton, the case can be made that political considerations and political advisors like Dick Morris at times took over the process, relegating policy considerations to secondary status (see, for example, Hult 2000). In a highly partisan environment, this is always a possibility and a concern. The capacity to maintain an appropriate focus on policy substance thus becomes another criterion by which a presidency may be judged.

POLICY DEVELOPMENT, MONITORING, AND IMPLEMENTATION

Beginning with the creation of the National Security Council (NSC) staff under Truman through the establishment of the first domestic policy staff under Johnson and continuing today, policy responsibilities gradually but consistently have migrated to the White House (see Warshaw 1997). More recently, Clinton created and Bush continued the National Economic Council (NEC), modeled largely on the other institutionalized policy staffs in the White House. This centralization of policy processes in the White House places them closer to the president and thus encourages responsiveness to presidential goals and interests (compare Moe 1985). As important, White House–based bodies are able to work across bureaucratic divisions and purposes. Nonetheless, policy councils have waxed and waned in their centrality across administrations. Moreover, the locus of debate and decision is not always in these formal bodies.

In focusing on policy, we also must return to politics. To the extent that Hult (2000) is justified in her concern that political concerns—electoral, organizational, coalitional—can come to dominate considerations of "good policy," participants in policy processes must be able to advocate for the latter. Policy goals and strategies cannot evolve in a political vacuum, but they must be protected from cooptation by political aims and, at best, integrated into an overall strategy of governance. Thus, effective design and use of policy machinery, the ability to improvise as necessary, and the capacity to integrate policy with politics become criteria on which an administration may be evaluated.

PRESENTING THE PRESIDENCY TO THE PUBLIC

The most impressive growth in the White House staff since Richard Nixon's inauguration in 1969 has come in the area of outreach, especially to the public, the media, and interest groups (Hult and Walcott 2004). Prior to this time, media outreach was largely limited to the interaction of the press office and the Washington press corps; interest in polling was growing, but polling was relatively primitive, and interest groups, though courted, were formally held at arm's length for reasons of appearance. Since then, media operations have expanded to encompass outreach to non-Washington media, electronic media, and the Internet as part of the "permanent campaign" (see Ornstein and Mann 2000; Heith 2004). Similarly, presidents have paid careful attention to polls and focus groups; they have placed their own polling operations into (or very near) the White House. At the same time, outreach to organized advocacy groups has been incorporated into the White House, and raising funds from these sources is a central element of the permanent campaign.

Whether effective fund-raising and public relations are necessary for the promotion of the public interest certainly can be debated. Nevertheless, the presentation of a strong presidential message, effective relationships with constituency groups, and appropriate sensitivity to public opinion constitute criteria by which a presidency can be judged.

DECISION PROCESSES IN THE GEORGE W. BUSH ERA

Like all two-term presidencies, as time passed and as the faces and names changed in the George W. Bush administration, the White House decision process evolved. The administration was plagued in its first five-plus years by decisions being rushed to judgment (the invasion of Iraq), taking too long (Hurricane Katrina), being based on misjudgments of likely reactions (Harriet Miers's nomination to the Supreme Court), or circumventing the normal decision process (warrantless surveillance). Yet, its final three years witnessed a marked improvement in the functioning of the staff and the processes leading to presidential decisions.

STAFF ORGANIZATION

At the top of the White House hierarchy is the chief of staff. The Bush White House benefited from remarkable stability, with only two individuals occupying this powerful and important position: Andrew Card (2001–2006) and Joshua Bolten (2006–2009). As administrator of the White House, broker of policy and political advice to the president, and guardian of the president's interests, the chief of staff is as crucial to the success of a presidential administration as anyone in the U.S. government except perhaps the president (Cohen 2002).

George W. Bush's selection of Card as his chief of staff before Election Day in 2000 was unsurprising given Card's experience as deputy chief of staff for President George H.W. Bush and his solid reputation among people in both political parties. During the transition, many observers noted that the two powerful Texas stalwarts in the White House, Karen Hughes as communications director and Karl Rove as special advisor, might challenge Card's authority, in effect creating a troika akin to Ronald Reagan's first-term staff organization. All three were powerful, independent voices who had Bush's ear and trust. Beyond that, the comparison fell flat. Card explicitly disputed the notion: "I told the President that if he wanted to have a troika, he should have a troika, but I didn't want to be one of the three; I would be out. I felt very strongly that the chief of staff should be *the* chief of staff, not *one of the* chiefs of staff" (Card 2007).[1]

On paper, the decision-making framework constructed before the inauguration held steady throughout the Bush presidency, especially in domestic policy. It reflected an organizational approach instituted by Card and by Bolten, who began his service in the White House as deputy chief of staff for policy (Bolten 2007). At the outset, three existing White House policy councils created an institutional "home" for most policy proposals the administration considered: the National Security Council staff, headed by the national security assistant; the Domestic Policy Council staff, led by the assistant to the president for domestic policy; and the National Economic Council staff, chaired by the president's chief economic advisor. On October 8, 2001, following the 9/11 terrorist attacks, President Bush added a fourth: the Homeland Security Council (which later was strengthened by the Homeland Security Act of 2002). To these one might add the Office of Management and Budget (OMB), which led discussion on budget issues (Patterson 2008, 40).

The purpose of the policy council system was to ensure that all interested stakeholders received a fair hearing in the policy process and that all proposed policies which warranted presidential attention reached the president. If the chief of staff determined that a presidential decision was needed, Bush would receive the necessary background materials to bring him up to speed on the issue, and "policy time" would be scheduled in the Oval Office. This face time with the president afforded administration officials the opportunity to hash out their issue positions in front of and with the president.

On many important issues, such as the No Child Left Behind bill, the decision process worked well. The Bush White House was quite disciplined, as evidenced particularly in the general absence of leaks that have bedeviled so many modern administrations. The first five years of the administration, however, were replete with examples of decision processes gone awry, instances in which the system broke down or at least where a parallel process operated.

These difficulties surfaced after 9/11 in matters dealing with national security and the "War on Terror." For example, Richard Clarke, a counterterrorism expert who served on the NSC staff under both Clinton and George W. Bush, argued that the decision process in the early part of the Afghanistan War was flawed and the circle of advisers, dominated by Vice President Cheney, was too closely knit around the president. Clarke partly blamed the lack of wider access to Bush for the U.S. failure to capture or kill Osama bin Laden in the hills of Tora Bora:

They [those counseling the president] ignored the advice of the experts in CIA, both in CIA headquarters and on the ground. They didn't allow anyone into the decision-making chamber other than the president and vice president, secretary of defense, and General [Tommy] Franks . . . no one on the NSC staff was allowed to get involved in any way in this war plan or war execution [Clarke 2006].

The second term brought a return to the standard procedures Card and Bolten instituted at the start of the administration, for several reasons. First, the light of day increasingly shone on the internal workings of the Bush presidency and soured the public's view of the administration, especially of the vice president. Cheney's public approval ratings at the beginning of the second term dropped precipitously as the Iraq War grew increasingly unpopular and as his role in pushing for the invasion of Iraq became more public. Other incidents, such as the unfortunate quail-hunting accident in which the vice president shot a companion in the face and the conviction of his former chief of staff, Lewis "Scooter" Libby, for lying to federal prosecutors, further eroded his stature (see Rothkopf 2005). Personnel changes also affected the power equation. Condoleezza Rice's shift to secretary of state and Stephen Hadley's elevation to national security assistant at the beginning of the second term; Bolten's move to chief of staff in April 2006; and Donald Rumsfeld's replacement in late 2006 by the more even-tempered Robert Gates brought new discipline to the national security and other decision processes.

POLICY DYNAMICS

The formal arrangements for handling policy in the Bush White House generally resembled those of his predecessors. Yet, existing arrangements and designated processes were not always used, and ad hoc, sometimes secretive structuring appeared as the administration strove to cope with the unexpected or the not-fully-understood. These arrangements in turn sometimes narrowed the range of policy and political advice available to top decision makers and led to reduced accountability.

Policy Councils

Even before 9/11 the domestic policy and economic policy staffs (which remained lodged together in the Office of Policy Development) were not as central as they had been under Clinton, particularly after the early tax cut victory in Congress. Although the House and Senate passed versions of Bush's signature education initiative, No Child Left Behind, the bill remained stalled in a conference committee until Senator Edward Kennedy joined forces with the White House to secure final passage in late December 2001. Meanwhile, a key presidential agenda item—to encourage greater participation of "faith-based" nonprofit organizations in helping deliver government-funded services—stalled in Congress. The new White House unit created to develop and shepherd such efforts, the Office of Faith-Based and Community Initiatives (OFBCI), suffered from early inconsistent leadership and lack of internal White House support. Ultimately, as with a range of other domestic policy objectives, faith-based efforts were pursued through executive branch rather than legislative action.

September 11, 2001, of course, pushed most domestic policy initiatives far down on the administration's agenda. After the attacks, too, then–NEC director Lawrence Lindsey reported that he had less "policy time" with the president (Maggs and Simendinger 2002, 2252–54). Economic problems continued, leading to the December 2002 dismissals of Lindsey and Treasury secretary Paul O'Neill and the February 2003 departure of Council of Economic Advisors chair Glenn Hubbard (Hult 2003, 65–66). At least until the 2004 election, Bush's economic team apparently "was selected for [its] presumed ability to 'sell' the . . . next round of tax cuts" (Hult 2003, 66). After the economic meltdown of 2008, Treasury secretary Henry Paulson took the lead in economic policy.

Among the structural effects of the terrorist attacks was the creation in October 2001 of the Office of Homeland Security (OHS), headed by an assistant to the president and charged with directing the staff of the new Homeland Security Council.[2] Modeled after the National Security Council, OHS was meant to be a coordinating body (see Newmann 2002). Yet, with neither statutory nor budget authority, its director struggled to pull together the activities of the more than forty agencies whose work fell under the umbrella of homeland security. Eventually, most of those agencies were placed in the Department of Homeland Security (DHS) when it opened in 2003. Nonetheless, the assistant for homeland security (homeland security advisor) and the Homeland Security Council remained at the White House due to the DHS legislation that made them permanent, leading to potential overlap and confusion.[3]

Office of the Vice President

More than any prior vice president, Dick Cheney and his staff shaped and oversaw numerous administrative initiatives, as is discussed in Chapter 3 of this volume. To be sure, his recent predecessors had offices in the West Wing, near the president, and they and their aides undertook significant responsibilities.[4] Yet Cheney's reach extended broadly across policy areas and reached deeply into executive branch departments like Defense and Justice; *Washington Post* reporters Barton Gellman and Jo Becker contend that the vice president had "an unrivaled portfolio across the executive branch," encompassing national security, homeland security, and domestic issues (Gellman and Becker 2007, A1; compare Draper 2007 with Gellman 2007a, b). Meanwhile, Cheney's staff was well integrated into the White House staff, with several having the title Assistant to the President and attending senior staff meetings. The independent role of the vice president and his office in policy processes at times undermined the chief of staff's and national security assistant's ability to be honest brokers (see Burke 2005).

Reflecting his strong interests in national security issues, Cheney's office of national security affairs had fourteen staffers (Patterson 2008, 238). Some believed it operated on occasion as a shadow NSC staff. For instance, the authorization for presidential use of force that Congress passed on September 18, 2001, was drafted by a "core legal team" of staffers from the White House Counsel's Office, the vice president's national security unit, and the deputy director of the Justice Department's Office of Legal Counsel (OLC). Among those excluded was John Ballinger, the lawyer for the NSC staff (Gellman 2007a, 143ff). Later, national security assistant Rice reportedly was not included in Cheney-run sessions on reauthorizing the administration's warrantless domestic surveillance program, which Attorney General John Ashcroft refused to approve from his hospital bed (Eggen 2007, A3; Gellman 2007a, 303–5). An unnamed White House official reported that "documents prepared for the national security adviser . . . were 'routed outside the formal process' to Cheney" (Gellman and Becker 2007, A1).

Among the better known of the vice president's national security efforts are those that produced President Bush's order that foreign terrorism suspects be held indefinitely by the United States without charges; if charges were filed, they would be heard in closed military commissions

(Bush 2001; see Pfiffner 2008, 104ff; Goldsmith 2007, 109ff). As Gellman and Becker recounted:

Vice President Cheney joined President Bush at a round parquet table they shared
once a week. Cheney brought a four-page text, written in strict secrecy by his
lawyer. He carried it back out with him after lunch. In less than an hour, the document traversed a West Wing circuit that gave its words the power of command.
It changed hands four times, according to witnesses, *with emphatic instructions
to bypass staff review* . . . Even witnesses to the Oval Office signing said they did
not know the vice president had played any part [2007, A1].[5]

Cheney's staffers also were prominent in many national security policy
decisions. Counsel David Addington was a key member of the administration group that drafted White House positions on the treatment of enemy
combatants at facilities such as Guantánamo. Jack Goldsmith, director of
the Office of Legal Counsel in 2003–2004, remembers only one of "about
100" meetings with White House Counsel Gonzales to discuss national
security issues when Addington was *not* present (Goldsmith 2007, 76).[6]

At the same time, the vice president devoted considerable attention and
energy to policy outside the sphere of national security, often focusing on
issues involving the economy. Initially, as might have been expected given
his experience in the petroleum business, he headed the administration's
review of the nation's energy policy. Later, he worked hard to help craft
the 2003 tax cut package, and he was a "vocal participant" at weekly lun-
cheon meetings of Bush's economic advisors (Becker and Gellman 2007,
A1).[7] Throughout the administration, Cheney chaired the President's Budget Review Board, which ruled on appeals of OMB decisions on proposed
funding for executive branch departments and programs. He and his staff
also monitored and participated in some agency activities. Oversight investigations by the U.S. House Select Committee on Energy Independence
and Global Warming, for example, uncovered evidence that the Cheney
office's opposition to a finding that greenhouse gases are dangerous and
should be regulated under clean-air laws led to regulatory initiatives being
rejected (see Hughes 2008).

Cheney also was distinctive among vice presidents in his and his staff's
involvement in a range of matters related to the Justice Department, some

going beyond the national security arena. His counsel was fully integrated into the operations of the White House Counsel's Office, and "received all of the important governmental documents that went to the Attorney General" (Goldsmith 2007, 76). More typical was the vice president's involvement in White House discussions about issues such as administration amicus briefs to the U.S. Supreme Court and Supreme Court nominees. Finally, like some of his predecessors, Cheney on occasion served as a troubleshooter and mediator on a diverse range of issues.

White House Counsel

The White House Counsel's Office was an arena for considerable activity in the Bush years. Over time, the office has evolved into a unit handling legal matters ranging from formulating and overseeing ethics requirements for White House aides, to handling security clearances for all presidential appointees, to examining draft statutes and executive orders and passed legislation, to overseeing presidential nominations to the federal courts (see Borrelli et al. 2001). But the Bush counsel's office also became more involved in policy making, hearkening back to the "special counsels" in the Kennedy and Johnson administrations. Primarily that meant its officials participated in more staff meetings of the cabinet councils.

The unit also provided direct input into a range of homeland and national security issues. Following 9/11, for example, a self-styled "War Council" met "every few weeks" in White House Counsel Gonzales's office or in Defense Department counsel William Haynes's Pentagon office; other members included Deputy Counsel Timothy Flanigan and vice presidential counsel David Addington. The council

plot[ted] legal strategy on the war on terror, sometimes as a prelude to dealing with lawyers from the State Department, the National Security Council, and the Joint Chiefs of Staff who would ordinarily be involved in war-related interagency legal decisions, and sometimes to the exclusion of the interagency process altogether [Goldsmith 2007, 22].

The lines between policy, politics, and advice at times blurred. The counsel's office evidently was involved in the firing of several U.S. attorneys following the 2004 election. Although it is not fully clear if the office was passing information and concerns from others in the White House (such as Karl Rove) to the Justice Department, Counsel Harriet Miers and her aide Colin Newman were on the sending and receiving ends of multiple e-mails (see Iglesias 2008). The unprecedented dismissal of federal prosecutors, apparently for political and ideological reasons, enmeshed the White House in another approval-sapping controversy; it also led to Attorney General Gonzales's resignation (see Lipton and Johnson 2007; Johnson 2008).

Fred Fielding (who served as counsel for Ronald Reagan from 1981 to 1986 and as deputy White House counsel to Richard Nixon) returned to steady the counsel's office. Although he presided over a staff bogged down with responding to requests for documents from the invigorated Democratic Congress, Fielding continued to participate in policy meetings.

Administrative Presidency?

Many of the policy-related activities in the Bush administration focused on the larger executive branch and relied on a variety of strategies. Some involved centralization, moving political and policy decisions closer to the president by placing them in the White House Office or the larger Executive Office of the President. For instance, the Bush administration continued the administrative clearance process of reviewing the rules and regulations proposed by departments and agencies, performed by the Office of Information and Regulatory Affairs (OIRA), a unit in OMB; this regulatory review process is designed to help ensure that agency decisions are consistent with presidential priorities (see, for example, Bush 2007). One illustration of the Bush OIRA's operation is its handling of a rule proposed by the National Oceanic and Atmospheric Administration that was designed to limit the fishing of krill, an important food source for whales and other animals; OIRA rejected the rule on the grounds that the supporting scientific findings were too "uncertain" (O'Connell 2008, 63–65).

An emphasis on political appointees directs attention to another strategy, politicization—the "core" of strategies exercised by administrative presidencies in which appointees are selected "strategically, based on their ideological policy congruence with the president" (Golden 2000, 5; compare Durant and Warber 2001; Nathan 1975, 1983; Moe 1985). From the start, the White House personnel office worked to screen applicants and attract loyalists to serve in the administration (see Aberbach 2004). It "wasn't enough for White House job seekers to be Republicans, or even friends of the Bushes—they had to agree with George W. Bush's ideology" (Draper 2007, 105). Although the definition of loyalty had a stronger ideological component than had been the case with Clinton or George H.W. Bush, little was unusual about its use, especially given the party polarization that existed in Washington and among policy activists. The White House exercised control over subcabinet personnel as well as cabinet and agency heads, offering cabinet members "a choice of subordinates already vetted by the White House personnel and political teams" (Rudalevige 2007, 140). Such efforts typically targeted parts of the federal executive: appointees requiring Senate confirmation increased more in apparently "liberal" agencies (such as the Consumer Product Safety Commission and the EPA) than in more "conservative" ones (Small Business Administration, Department of Defense) (Lewis 2008, 116, 127; see also DiIulio 2007). Like its predecessors, the Bush administration left some positions vacant or filled with "actings" (interim personnel) as ways of slowing or halting undesired action or avoiding Senate confirmation fights. Besides seeking bureaucratic responsiveness through appointments, the Bush team continued the Clinton practice of reducing the size of the permanent bureaucracy by outsourcing government functions to contractors.

This policy politicization had clear effects, frequently helping guide agency activities in directions consistent with President Bush's priorities. In 2001, for example, officials "rebuked Clinton-era environmental policies by easing wetlands rules affecting developers; reducing energy-saving standards for air conditioners; allowing more road-building and power lines in national parks; and easing restrictions on mining on public lands" ("White House: How Bush . . ." 2002). More generally, in enforcing clean-air laws, the EPA worked to revise, streamline, and in some cases abolish rules to give businesses more time to comply and to reduce compliance costs (for example, Drew and Oppel 2004).

At times, some Bush appointees overreached, as evidently happened with the U.S. attorneys. Legislative hearings also highlighted a range of other alleged abuses in the Justice Department, including its handling of national security letters and interference in tobacco and redistricting litigation (for example, Hulse and Shane 2007). Similarly, in 2004, the Congressional Research Service reported that the administrator of Medicare, political appointee Thomas A. Scully, violated federal law by directing Medicare's chief actuary, Richard Foster, to withhold information from Congress that indicated that the new Medicare prescription drug benefit would cost far more than the administration had stated (Pear 2004; see also Goldstein 2004).

POLITICS AND THE PUBLIC PRESIDENCY

With the emergence of cable television's all-news networks and then the Internet as a medium of communicating news and opinion, the old idea of a news cycle, dictated by the rhythms of newspaper publishing and network evening news, has died. In its place is the "24-hour news cycle," with its implication that the White House must be ready to respond to events occurring anywhere in the world at any time of the day or night. This requirement has shaped the challenges faced by White House staff members in the press and the communications offices. At the same time, presidents have learned to use media outlets to advance their messages continuously and to respond to crises and attacks immediately, in the style and with the techniques of presidential campaigns; thus the "permanent campaign." The phrase originated as a characterization of the Clinton presidency, but it applies at least as strongly to George W. Bush's own.[8]

Bush's initial trio of top advisors, Hughes, Rove, and Card, were, respectively, a communications expert, a political strategist, and a manager. This clearly signaled that the Bush White House was prepared from the outset to place communications strategy at the center of its approach to leadership. The result, in the felicitous title of George Edwards's book, was "governing by campaigning" (2008). This leadership strategy deemphasized traditional "inside the Beltway" negotiating in favor of taking the administration's case directly to the public, counting on public opinion to drive Congress toward the president's positions.

The Bush White House brought to a high level a set of techniques first introduced to the presidency by Richard Nixon (Hult and Walcott 2004, ch. 3) and honed under Ronald Reagan (see Edwards 2008, ch. 3). The key was a deliberate process of "prioritizing issues, creating events to emphasize a limited number of priorities, and rounding up people to talk about them" (Kumar 2007, 72). Martha Joynt Kumar has called the basic Bush approach "communicating on the President's terms" (2007, 80). This refers not only to the administration's proactive stance but also to its focus on the president himself as the one who announces policy—a strategy that both commands attention and minimizes the opportunity for leaks. Central to the Bush White House's communications approach was to stick strictly to plans, even to the extent of passing on unanticipated opportunities to communicate.

The strategy of controlling the message and its presentation worked well. Kumar notes that especially during the first term, Bush's communications team was more effective at taking and keeping the communications initiative than Clinton's advisors had been. Yet, this emphasis on following plans seemingly had a downside. Kumar argues persuasively that the Bush approach, while "strong where the Clinton one was weak," also was "weak where Clinton excelled," namely, in improvising and responding to unanticipated events (2007, 71). This became especially apparent in the second Bush term, as the war in Iraq soured, the president's initiatives, such as his Social Security reform, floundered, and his approval ratings dropped to record depths.

Karl Rove, the man many observers saw as Bush's most important advisor outside the national security team, was responsible for overall political strategy, which he oversaw through the Office of Strategic Initiatives (Hult 2003, 72). He presided over regular meetings to plan the president's travel schedule, the content of his public messages, and themes of the day. These meetings "provide[d] them with a direction for the months ahead even if events outside of their control [blew] them off course" (Edwards 2008, 31). Rove also oversaw other White House units dedicated to outreach, such as the Office of Public Liaison, and he was the key White House link to the administration's opinion pollsters. When Hughes left the White House, Rove in effect became the "face" of the administration's public relations as well as its political strategy.

Rove's centrality to important White House processes placed him in a strategic position at the intersection of policy and politics. This, and the general tilt toward placing message planning at the center of the White

House agenda, clearly continued the campaign's effort to build coalitions and "sell" the presidency. It also arguably continued or even amplified the Clinton White House's tendency to put policy in the service of politics. Where Clinton chose policy initiatives for their public acceptability during a time when his presidency was under fire, Bush made long-term political planning, aimed at building an enduring Republican majority, a dominant feature of policy decision making. Faith-based initiatives aimed at the Bush base constituency of religious conservatives. An even more ambitious effort sought to create an "ownership society" through such means as partial privatization of Social Security in the hope of replacing public dependence on government programs with a stake in the free market. The relatively narrow and compatible nature of the Republican base encouraged this approach, and the Bush White House, in a polarized environment, was more than content to govern with the primary intent of pleasing the base.

Nothing in this analysis need suggest that policy which is driven in part by political goals is bad policy. The question is how the factors of "good policy" and "good politics" are balanced and integrated. Much of the time, the Bush staff seems to have leaned more toward the political side than policy staffers would have liked. That underlay the complaint by John DiIulio, first White House leader of the faith-based program, about "Mayberry Machiavellis," who injected political considerations where they did not belong (Suskind 2003)—a claim that David Kuo, also a White House aide who worked on faith-based issues, supported (Kuo 2006).

The long-range planning effort was elevated in the White House when Rove was made deputy chief of staff for policy after the 2004 election. At the same time, however, the fortunes of the Bush administration were on the wane as his centerpiece Social Security reform proposal failed to elicit interest among either the public or Congress. When Rove finally left the White House after the 2006 Democratic rout, the political plan, much like the message-control communications strategy, was mostly a fond memory.

CONCLUSION

The structures and processes of George W. Bush's White House were designed by veterans of prior administrations. Not surprisingly, they generally conformed to the "standard model" of White House organization that has emerged in recent decades (Walcott and Hult 2005). That model is marked by careful and inclusive decision processes, along with specialized structures for policy, outreach, and management of the White House organization itself. The Bush White House was led at the outset by an experienced chief of staff, Andrew Card, then by his likewise experienced deputy, Joshua Bolten. Initially, it appeared that the first president to hold an M.B.A. had designed an orthodox staff organization that would be judged with approval by the Washington community.

In many ways, the system worked as anticipated. From the outset, the Bush White House proved itself disciplined, focused, and clearly effective, if somewhat opaque as seen from outside. Then came crises, beginning with the 9/11 attacks, then the Iraq War, continuing through Hurricane Katrina, and culminating in the meltdown of the mortgage market and Wall Street investment banks in 2008. Under these pressures, the carefully managed decision processes tended to break down, sometimes creating something of a free-for-all in which powerful insiders—Cheney, Rumsfeld, Paulson— could play policy entrepreneur and capture the initiative. At other times, as with Katrina, the administration's response was confused and responsibility hard to locate. All in all, when dramatic events breached the stern discipline of business as usual, the Bush White House's performance was disappointing. Perhaps discipline and planning on the one hand and improvisational flexibility on the other constitute a trade-off. Comparison of the Bush White House to Clinton's suggests that this may be the case.

When it came to President Bush's longer- and shorter-term policy and political messages, the story was much the same. Bush's approach to public relations depended on an ability to seize the agenda and control it. The longer-term political strategy was grounded in the tailoring of policy initiatives to the constituent elements of what was hoped to be a permanent electoral majority. That aspiration went unrealized.

The Bush staff organization started strongly, suffered its greatest problems in the middle years of the administration, then largely stabilized and worked as expected over the final years. Oddly, perhaps paradoxically, this correlates strongly but inversely with the overall success of the administration as measured by public approval ratings. It seems that whatever enhancement of tactical competence a presidency gets from strong staff organization need not translate to success on every dimension. Here, this observation tends to reinforce the conclusion that George W. Bush and his aides designed a system predicated on planning and control, a system that worked poorly when events conspired to frustrate the planning and challenge the control.

NOTES

1. Card's emphases.
2. OHS and the HSC were created by Executive Order 13228 on October 8, 2001.
3. The OHS, however, no longer exists.
4. For example, the Council on Competitiveness under Dan Quayle and the National Partnership for Reinventing Government under Al Gore.
5. Emphasis added. More broadly, Rothkopf (2005) has argued, "Although history has . . . shown that, given human nature, leaders come to depend on small clusters of close, trusted advisors, what happened during the first term of the presidency of George W. Bush was hardly anticipated by anyone—that the dominant role in that inner circle would be played by a vice president who would himself occasionally assume the role envisioned for the national security advisor and have unprecedented influence over the president" (392).
6. Among his other activities, Addington was "the chief legal architect of the Terrorist Surveillance Program" (181).
7. The description is reported as being chief of staff Bolten's.
8. Indeed, former Bush press secretary Scott McClellan (2008) charges that much of the White House operated as a permanent campaign.

REFERENCES

Aberbach, Joel D. 2004. "The State of the Contemporary American Presidency: Or, Is Bush II Actually Ronald Reagan's Heir?" In *The George W. Bush Presidency: Appraisals and Prospects*, ed. Colin Campbell and Bert A. Rockman. Washington, DC: CQ Press, 46–72.
Becker, Jo, and Barton Gellman. 2007. "A Strong Push from Backstage." *Washington Post*, June 26, p. A1.
Bolten, Joshua B. 2007. Interview conducted by David B. Cohen, October 25.
Borrelli, MaryAnne, Karen Hult, and Nancy Kassop. 2001. "The White House Counsel's Office." *Presidential Studies Quarterly* 31(4): 561–84.
Burke, John P. 2005. "Condoleezza Rice as NSC Advisor: A Case Study of the Honest Broker Role." *Presidential Studies Quarterly* 35(3): 554–75.
Bush, George W. 2001. Detention, Treatment, and Trial of Certain Non-Citizens in the War Against Terrorism. Military Order of November 13, 2001. *Federal Register* 66(222): 57833–36.
———. 2007. Executive Order 13422. *Federal Register* 72(14): 2763–65.
Card, Andrew H., Jr. 2007. Interview conducted by David B. Cohen, October 19.
Clarke, Richard. 2006. Interview on *Frontline*. January 23. http://www.pbs.org/wgbh/pages/frontline/darkside/interviews/clarke.html (Accessed September 28, 2008).

Cohen, David B. 2002. "From the Fabulous Baker Boys to the Master of Disaster: The White House Chief of Staff in the Reagan and G.H.W. Bush Administrations." *Presidential Studies Quarterly* 32(3): 463–83.

DiIulio, John J., Jr. 2007. "The Hyper-Rhetorical Presidency." *Critical Review* 19(2–3): 315–24.

Draper, Robert. 2007. *Dead Certain: The Presidency of George W. Bush*. New York: Free Press.

Drew, Christopher, and Richard A. Oppel Jr. 2004. "How Power Lobby Won Battle of Pollution Control at EPA." *New York Times*, March 6, p. A1.

Durant, Robert F., and Adam L. Warber. 2001. "Networking in the Shadow of Hierarchy: Public Policy, the Administrative Presidency, and the Neoadministrative State." *Presidential Studies Quarterly* 31(2): 221–44.

Edwards, George C., III. 2008. *Governing by Campaigning: The Politics of the Bush Presidency*. New York: Pearson Education.

Eggen, Dan. 2007. "Official: Cheney Urged Wiretaps; Stand-in for Ashcroft Alleges Interference." *Washington Post*, June 2, p. A3.

Gellman, Barton. 2007a. *Angler: The Cheney Vice Presidency*. New York: Penguin.

———. 2007b. "Cheney Shielded Bush from Crisis." *Washington Post*, September 15, p. A1.

———, and Jo Becker. 2007. "'A Different Understanding with the President.'" *Washington Post*, June 24, p. A1.

George, Alexander L. 1974. *Presidential Decisionmaking in Foreign Policy: Theory and Practice*. New York: Columbia University Press.

Golden, Marisso Martino. 2000. *What Motivates Bureaucrats? Politics and Administration During the Reagan Years*. New York: Columbia University Press.

Goldsmith, Jack. 2007. *The Terror Presidency: Law and Judgment Inside the Bush Administration*. New York: Norton.

Goldstein, Amy. 2004. "Probe Starts in Medicare Drug Cost Estimates." *Washington Post*, March 17, p. A1.

Heith, Diane. 2004. *Polling to Govern: Public Opinion and Presidential Leadership*. Stanford, CA: Stanford University Press.

Hughes, Siobhan. 2008. "Climate Report Cites Cheney's Office." *Wall Street Journal*, July 21, p. A2.

Hulse, Carl, and Scott Shane. 2007. "Congress Expands Scope of Inquiries into Justice Department Practices and Politics." *New York Times*, March 25, p. A25.

Hult, Karen M. 2000. "Strengthening Presidential Decision-Making Capacity." *Presidential Studies Quarterly* 30(1): 27–46.

———. 2003. "The Bush White House in Comparative Perspective." In *The George W. Bush Presidency: An Early Assessment*, ed. Fred I. Greenstein. Baltimore: Johns Hopkins University Press, 51–77.

———, and Charles E. Walcott. 2004. *Empowering the White House: Governance Under Nixon, Ford, and Carter*. Lawrence: University Press of Kansas.

Iglesias, David, with Davin Seay. 2008. *Justice: Inside the Scandal That Rocked the Bush Administration*. New York: John Wiley.

Janis, Irving. 1982. *Groupthink*, 2nd ed. Boston: Houghton Mifflin.

Johnson, Carrie. 2008. "Mukasey Appoints Prosecutor to Probe Gonzales's Role." *Washington Post*, September 29. http://www.washingtonpost.com/wpdyn/content/article/2008/09/29/AR2008092900980pf.html (Accessed September 29, 2008).

Kumar, Martha Joynt. 2007. *Managing the President's Message: The White House Communications Operation*. Baltimore: Johns Hopkins University Press.

———, George C. Edwards III, James P. Pfiffner, and Terry Sullivan. 2003a. "Meeting the Freight Train Head On: Planning the Transition to Power." In *The White House World: Transitions, Organization, and Office Operations*, ed. Martha Joynt Kumar and Terry Sullivan. College Station: Texas A&M University Press, 5–24.

———, and Terry Sullivan, eds. 2003b. *The White House World: Transitions, Organization, and Office Operations*. College Station: Texas A&M University Press.

Kuo, David J. 2006. *Tempting Faith: An Inside Story of Political Seduction*. New York: Free Press.

Lewis, David E. 2008. *The Politics of Presidential Appointments: Political Control and Bureaucratic Performance*. Princeton, NJ: Princeton University Press.

Lipton, Eric, and David Johnson. 2007. "For Gonzales, More Records, and Questions." *New York Times*, March 25. http://www.nytimes.com/2007/03/25/washington/25attorneys.html (Accessed November 17, 2008).

Maggs, John, and Alexis Simendinger. 2002. "White House: 'The President Has Confidence in Me.'" *National Journal*, July 27, pp. 2252–54.

McClellan, Scott. 2008. *What Happened: Inside the Bush White House and Washington's Culture of Deception*. New York: PublicAffairs.

Moe, Terry M. 1985. "The Politicized Presidency." In *The New Direction in American Politics*, ed. John E. Chubb and Paul E. Peterson. Washington, DC: Brookings Institution, 235–71.

Nathan, Richard P. 1975. *The Plot That Failed: Nixon and the Administrative Presidency*. New York: John Wiley.

———. 1983. *The Administrative Presidency*. New York: John Wiley.

Newmann, William W. 2002. "Reorganizing for National Security and Homeland Security." *Public Administration Review* 62(1): 126–37.

O'Connell, Anne Joseph. 2008. "Well-Regulated." *Democracy: A Journal of Ideas* 8(Spring): 63–65.

Ornstein, Norman J., and Thomas E. Mann, eds. 2000. *The Permanent Campaign and Its Future*. Washington, DC: American Enterprise Institute, Brookings Institution.

Patterson, Bradley H., Jr. 2008. *To Serve the President: Continuity and Innovation in the White House Staff*. Washington, DC: Brookings Institution.

Pear, Robert. 2004. "Agency Sees Withholding of Medicare Data from Congress as Illegal." *New York Times*, May 4, p. A23.

Pfiffner, James P. 2008. *Power Play: The Bush Presidency and the Constitution*. Washington, DC: Brookings Institution.

Rothkopf, David. 2005. *Running the World: The Inside Story of the National Security Council and the Architects of American Power*. New York: PublicAffairs.

Rudalevige, Andrew. 2007. "'The Decider': Issue Management and the Bush White House." In *The George W. Bush Legacy*, ed. Colin Campbell, Bert A. Rockman, and Andrew Rudalevige. Washington, DC: CQ Press, 135–63.

Suskind, Ron. 2003. "Why Are These Men Laughing?" *Esquire*, January, pp. 96–105.

Walcott, Charles E., and Karen M. Hult. 2005. "White House Structure and Decision Making: Elaborating the Standard Model." *Presidential Studies Quarterly* 35(2): 303–18.

———, Shirley Anne Warshaw, and Stephen J. Wayne. 2001. "The Chief of Staff." *Presidential Studies Quarterly* 31(3): 464–89.

Warshaw, Shirley Anne. 1997. *The Domestic Presidency: Policy Making in the White House.* Boston: Allyn & Bacon.

"White House: How Bush Flexes His Executive Muscles." 2002. *National Journal*, January 26. http://global.factiva.com/ha/default.aspx; Document ntljo000200201 25dy1q00006 (Accessed January 3, 2009).

CHAPTER 8

A Legal Revolution?

The Bush Administration's Effect on the Judiciary and Civil Justice Reform

LORI A. JOHNSON AND MICHAEL P. MORELAND

IT IS HARD TO RECALL now that before 9/11, George W. Bush ran for president primarily as a domestic policy reform candidate. When he campaigned for governor of Texas in 1994, his threefold platform was juvenile justice reform, education reform, and tort reform. The latter two issues went on to form a centerpiece of his 2000 campaign for the White House. In an interview given during the 2000 campaign, then-governor Bush also stated that he admired Justices Antonin Scalia and Clarence Thomas and would seek to nominate judges like them were he elected president. With tort reform and judicial nominations, President Bush campaigned on and sought to implement an agenda that had been at the heart of the conservative movement for twenty years. As summarized by Steven Teles in *The Rise of the Conservative Legal Movement* (2008), "[t]he Federalist Society represents, without a doubt, the most vigorous, durable, and well-ordered organization to emerge from th[e] rethinking of modern conservatism's political strategy" (179).

The task of this chapter is to assess how successful President Bush was in changing the face of the federal judiciary and reforming the civil justice system administered by it. In a presidency marred by low approval ratings and despondency even among conservatives, President Bush's judicial nominations and administrative and legislative tort reform achievements are a tale of relative success. We conclude that President Bush has brought about, if not a legal revolution, then at least a shift to the right of the federal judiciary and debates over the civil justice system.

THE FEDERAL JUDICIARY

Often, the most enduring impact a president has is through lifetime appointments to the federal judiciary. President George W. Bush followed the example of the Reagan administration in its judicial nominating efforts. The record of the Bush administration's efforts will be measured by the four categories of competence outlined in the Introduction.

Tactical competence is defined as effectiveness in the administration and daily operations of government. In this category, we will evaluate the processes used within the George W. Bush administration to select, vet, choose, and nominate highly qualified candidates for judgeships. According to Viet Dinh, the assistant attorney general who handled judicial nominations in the first two years of the Bush administration:

The legal legacy that the president leaves [is as] important as anything else we do in terms of legislative policy. . . . We want to ensure that the President's mandate to us that the men and women who are nominated by him to be on the bench have his vision of the proper role of the judiciary. That is, a judiciary that will follow the law, not make the law, a judiciary that will interpret the Constitution, not legislate from the bench [Goldman et al. 2003, 284].[1]

By all accounts, in the first term of the Bush administration this goal was accomplished by coordination of effort, dedication of resources, and careful prioritizing. Judicial nominations were a joint effort by Assistant Attorney General Dinh in the Department of Justice, Office of Legal Policy (OLP), White House Counsel Alberto Gonzales, and Associate White House Counsel Brett Kavanaugh. These officials were part of the Judicial Selection Committee (JSC), which was a collaborative effort of OLP and the White House Counsel. The JSC met at least weekly, or as needed, to discuss potential judicial nominees and where current nominees were in the confirmation process.

Beyond the involvement of the OLP and White House Counsel, not much else is known about the exact composition of the JSC. Although previous administrations had been willing to tell researchers the names of the specific people involved in the nomination process, the Bush administration was not. As described by Brett Kavanaugh, such secrecy, which became a hallmark of the Bush administration, was "part of a larger principle that we don't usually discuss who is involved in the deliberative process and who is making recommendations to the President" (Goldman et al. 2003, 285). A subsequent *New York Times* article about the controversial U.S. attorney firings mentioned a group, closely resembling the JSC, which met every Wednesday afternoon to strategize about judicial nominations. According to the article, the group was composed of staff from the White House Counsel's office, the chief of staff, the attorney general, and Karl Rove, and "each of them signs off on every nomination" (Kirkpatrick and Rutenberg 2007, A14; cited in Goldman et al. 2007, 254).

By Dinh's account, direct presidential approval of each nominee was required at two points in the process: (1) before any detailed vetting took place, and (2) after extensive vetting but before the formal nomination was made. This extensive involvement of the Oval Office in the selection process evidences the administration's commitment and prioritization of judicial selection.

One of the first steps taken by the administration that significantly changed the nomination process was to eliminate the role formerly played by the American Bar Association (ABA). Traditionally, the ABA had been involved at the beginning of the selection process, conducting an informal survey of lawyers and judges and providing assessment of the qualifications of the nominee. Shortly after taking office, George W. Bush announced that the ABA would no longer have "preferred status" in the selection process. Rather, the ABA would learn of the nomination at the same time as the public at large and could offer its assessment at that point. Conservatives had taken exception to the ABA's role ever since its active involvement in defeating Robert Bork's nomination to the Supreme Court (Teles 2008). The change of the ABA's role also enabled the administration to conduct the selection process without external scrutiny. According to Nan Aron with the Alliance for Justice, a liberal interest group:

I am absolutely convince[d] that the reason the administration removed the ABA . . . is not because they are afraid of the rating, because we all know that ratings were uniformly high. . . . It was their desire for total and complete secrecy, and that's another thing that's a huge departure [Goldman et al. 2003, 292].

While the majority of Bush's nominees received a "well qualified" rating by the ABA, the change in timing of its assessment may be significant. Aron and others questioned the ability of lawyers and judges to be candid in their assessment of a nominee once the nomination was made public and the success of a nomination was all but assured.

At the same time that the administration diminished the role played by the ABA in the process, it increased the role played by conservative groups such as the Federalist Society. In fact, the Federalist Society became a sort of "farm team" from which federal judicial nominees were selected. Membership in the Federalist Society was not a guarantee of a nomination, but for someone with judicial ambitions it was a place to get noticed. White House staff consulted frequently with Leonard Leo of the Federalist Society; Jay Sekulow of the American Center for Law and Justice; C. Boyden Gray, former White House counsel to George H.W. Bush and head of the Committee for Justice; and Edwin Meese III, attorney general during the Reagan administration and affiliated with the Heritage Foundation.

More evidence of the high priority placed on the judicial nomination process by the George W. Bush administration is the expedited timetable for the nomination process proposed just prior to the 2002 midterm elections. The timetable proposal recommended that (1) federal judges should give a year's notice of their intention to take retirement or senior status; (2) the president should nominate a replacement judge within 180 days of receiving such notice; (3) the Senate Judiciary Committee should hold hearings within 90 days of receiving a nomination; and (4) the full Senate should hold a floor vote within 180 days of the initial receipt of the nomination (Goldman et al. 2003, 292). While this expedited timetable reflected the administration's priorities, it proved overly optimistic. From the perspective of the Senate Judiciary Committee, the idea that all nominees could be processed within the same time frame, regardless of how controversial the nominee was or how extensive the record, was completely unrealistic.

The timetable also conveyed the administration's perspective on the Senate's role: every nomination should result in an "up or down" floor vote in the Senate. Previously, either the nomination would be withdrawn once it became clear that the nominee would not be confirmed, or the nomination would languish without a hearing in the Senate Judiciary Committee. It was rare for a controversial nominee to actually be voted down in the judiciary committee, much less on the floor of the Senate. The Bush administration, however, wanted to have a recorded vote from everyone in the Senate on every nominee.

The tactical success of the George W. Bush administration was greater in the first term than in the second. In part, the rate of nominations for judgeships slowed simply as the result of fewer vacancies. After Alberto Gonzales moved to the Attorney General's Office, he was replaced as White House counsel by Harriet Miers, who was perceived by many to be less interested in the judicial nomination process. Also, Brett Kavanaugh, recognized as a significant force in the nomination process in the first term, became staff secretary before his own nomination to the D.C. Circuit Court. The administration's practice of renominating previously unsuccessful candidates, even if they were highly unlikely to receive confirmation, also minimized their chances of filling vacancies quickly. As of May 2008, the Bush administration had put forward nominees for fewer than twenty of the fifty or so federal judicial vacancies.

Political competence refers to a president's ability to shape the political regime, especially in terms of the power dynamics between the two major political parties. In order to assess the George W. Bush administration's work in this category, we will consider the Senate confirmation stage of the nomination and how successful he was at getting his nominees through the judiciary committee, to a floor vote, and ultimately confirmed. Here, the administration realized early on it could nominate the conservative candidates it wanted, and even if they were not confirmed, it could use the issue of judges not being confirmed against the Democrats in the next election.

The George W. Bush administration managed to "stay the course" with its judicial nominees despite a challenging political landscape. The most important political challenge the administration faced was the confirmation of two justices to the Supreme Court in an extremely partisan atmosphere.

From the beginning, George W. Bush assumed the authority of a popular mandate for his presidency, despite the acrimonious and highly charged political environment. Several factors contributed to this environment: (1) an extremely close presidential election; (2) the failure of the Republican-controlled Senate to confirm some of President Clinton's judicial nominees; (3) the nomination of John Ashcroft as attorney general, given his involvement in obstructing the process for one of the Clinton judicial nominees; and (4) a Senate that was evenly divided between Republicans and Democrats. Then, in June 2001, Senator Jim Jeffords of Vermont changed political affiliation, thereby giving the Democrats control of the Senate and the judiciary committee.

Despite these challenges, in its first term the administration succeeded in obtaining confirmation of 85 percent of its nominees for district court positions and 53 percent of its appellate court nominees. This compares favorably with President Clinton's confirmation rates: 77 percent of nominees for district court positions and 55 percent of appellate court nominees.

In 2004, President Bush was reelected to a second term, and Republicans retained control of the Senate, emboldening President Bush to take further controversial actions. After the 2004 election, Bush made two recess appointments: Charles Pickering to the Fifth Circuit Court of Appeals and William Pryor to the Eleventh Circuit Court of Appeals. These recess appointments were perceived by Democrats to be an end run around the confirmation process and a "shot across the bow," indicating what they could expect in Bush's second term. Bush proceeded to renominate all the judges who had not been confirmed in the prior congressional session, including Priscilla Owen and Charles Pickering, who had received negative votes in the judiciary committee.

If Democrats wanted to block judicial nominees, their only tools were the "blue slip process"[2] and the filibuster. The Democrats had previously successfully filibustered several nominees, including Miguel Estrada, Priscilla Owen, and Charles Pickering. Such close attention to courts of appeal nominees is a fairly recent political phenomenon (Hartley and Holmes 2002). Republicans objected to the use of filibusters on judicial nominees (although they had used them in the past), arguing that they effectively changed the constitutional requirement of a simple majority to a supermajority, because ending a filibuster requires sixty votes on a motion to invoke cloture. In May 2005, the controversy escalated, and Republican majority leader Bill Frist threatened to use the so-called nuclear option—changing Senate rules to prohibit the filibuster of judicial nominations. If the "nuclear option" had succeeded, *all* Bush nominees would almost certainly have been confirmed, because the Republicans had the majority. At that point, a group of Democratic and Republican senators, known as the "Gang of 14," reached a compromise preserving the right of filibuster but only under "extraordinary circumstances." What exactly constituted extraordinary circumstances was not clear, but it seemed to rule out filibusters based only on partisan opposition rather than the qualifications of the nominee. Democrats agreed to allow floor votes on three of the more controversial nominees (Janice Rogers Brown, Priscilla Owen, William Pryor), all of whom were later confirmed.

Although the administration was not involved in the Gang of 14 compromise, it benefited from it later when its nominees to fill Supreme Court vacancies were protected from filibuster. In the summer of 2005, Justice Sandra Day O'Connor announced her retirement, pending confirmation of her replacement. President Bush nominated John Roberts of the D.C. Circuit Court of Appeals to fill the vacancy. In September 2005, Chief Justice William Rehnquist died; Bush withdrew Roberts's nomination for the O'Connor vacancy and renominated him to fill the chief justice position. Judge Roberts was well-prepared and impressive in the Senate Judiciary Committee hearings. Moreover, he was also well-known and liked by many Democrats, and a Roberts-for-Rehnquist switch would not do much to change the balance of the Supreme Court. Roberts was ultimately confirmed by a vote of 78 to 22.

Although President Bush nominated his White House counsel, Harriet Miers, to fill the O'Connor vacancy, she withdrew her nomination three weeks later, and Bush nominated Third Circuit judge Samuel Alito. Alito's hearings were rockier, including the tearful departure of his wife during the questioning. Alito was clearly more conservative than O'Connor, who had been a key swing vote, especially in abortion and affirmative action cases, and therefore more of a threat in changing the balance of the Court. Nevertheless, Democrats were not successful in competing with the White House and the Department of Justice to "define" Alito, and he was confirmed by a closer vote of 58 to 42. While there were certainly Democrats who wanted to filibuster the Alito nomination, most of the Democratic members of the Gang of 14 voted for cloture, which was invoked by a vote of 72 to 25.

After the Democrats regained control of the Senate in 2006, the administration initially maintained its strategy, renominating all unconfirmed candidates from the previous congressional session. For a Virginia vacancy on the Fourth Circuit, the administration ignored the recommendations of both home state senators and nominated its own candidate, who had no judicial experience ("Empty Seats . . ." 2007). The administration later tempered its approach, withdrew the names of the renominated candidates, and followed the recommendation of the Virginia senators, nominating Virginia Supreme Court justice G. Steven Agee, who was then confirmed by a 96 to 0 vote. The Bush administration's willingness to adjust to the new circumstances, especially given the president's low approval ratings in polls, meant that it was still somewhat successful in obtaining confirmation of its lower-court nominees in the last two years of the second term.

Strategic competence assesses a president's long-term influence on policy. For this measure, we will look at the number of judges George W. Bush was able to get confirmed and how they impact the balance of Republican and Democratic appointees on the circuit courts of appeal and the Supreme Court. The George W. Bush administration is certain to have a long-term impact on policy based on its success in placing so many conservatives on the federal bench. As of July 2008, 316 of the George W. Bush administration judicial nominees had been confirmed. While this is fewer than the 367 confirmed judges in President Clinton's two terms, there were also only 39 remaining judicial vacancies in Bush's last year in office, compared to over 100 in 1999, Clinton's last year in office. The breakdown of the appointments is as follows:

107th Congress (2000–2002): Eighty-three district court nominations confirmed (fifteen not acted upon); sixteen courts of appeal nominations confirmed (fifteen not acted upon)

108th Congress (2002–2004): Eighty-five district court nominations confirmed; eighteen courts of appeal nominations confirmed

By the end of the first term, 95 percent of district court nominees were confirmed and two-thirds of courts of appeal nominees were confirmed:

> *109th Congress (2004–2006)*: Two Supreme Court justices confirmed; fifteen courts of appeal nominations confirmed (twelve not acted upon, including two withdrawn); thirty-five district court nominations confirmed (twenty-eight not acted upon, including two withdrawn)

> *110th Congress (2006–2008)*: As of July 2008, the Senate had confirmed fifty-nine judicial nominees, with thirty-nine remaining judicial vacancies

The timing of George W. Bush's presidency was critical: it coincided with the retirement of many Republican-appointed judges. Of the 118 judicial retirements during the first term of the George W. Bush administration, 80 percent were appointed by Republican presidents and 49 percent were appointed by President Reagan. By the end of 2006, approximately 52 percent of all federal judges had been appointed by Republican presidents.

The impact of these appointments can be seen especially on the federal courts of appeal: Republican appointees are in the majority in ten out of thirteen appellate circuits, leaving only the Ninth Circuit with a Democratic-appointed majority and two circuits split evenly. In seven of the circuit courts of appeal, Republican-appointed judges hold 2–1 advantage, significantly affecting en banc decisions. Moreover, research has shown an "exaggeration effect" of such appellate majorities, because the three-judge panels that render most decisions are even more likely to be composed of a majority of Republican-appointed judges (Velona 2005).

Although there is always the risk that, once appointed, a judge's decisions will not conform to the expectations of the administration that appointed him or her, the George W. Bush administration seems to be doing better than most in this regard. Preliminary analysis shows that the judges appointed in his first term are the most conservative on record for modern administrations, comparable to those appointed during the Reagan administration (Carp et al. 2004). There is little doubt that Supreme Court decisions on partial-birth abortion, affirmative action, and gender discrimination have been affected by the replacement of O'Connor by Alito.

Moral competence refers to an administration's trustworthiness, particularly in terms of building a reservoir of goodwill among political elites of both parties and the general public. The aggressive political approach taken by the administration with the Senate evidenced a lack of interest in building trust across party lines. However, the administration was very focused on building trust within the conservative Republican Party base. This trust was jeopardized by two missteps that required corrective maneuvers.

The first misstep involved the Supreme Court nomination of White House Counsel Harriet Miers. Evidently, George W. Bush and his advisors believed that as long as the nominee was loyal to him and trusted by him, his personal relationship would translate into broad support across the Republican Party. This did not prove to be the case. Republicans objected to the Miers nomination on several grounds, including that (1) she was not considered qualified for a Supreme Court position, based on her experience; (2) her background in constitutional law was minimal; (3) her conservative credentials were in doubt; and (4) she was seen as a token female replacement for O'Connor's seat. Other conservatives were wary of appointing an "unknown," for fear she might turn into another Justice Souter (who was nominated by President George H.W. Bush but consistently voted with the liberals on the Court). Despite what some called an "embarrassing failure," the administration reestablished the trust of the party base by supporting Miers's withdrawal of her nomination and putting forward Samuel Alito. Alito's conservative credentials were impeccable and his record on the Third Circuit Court of Appeals allayed the fears of conservatives. The Miers nomination illustrated the president's desire to reward the loyalty of his staff but came at the cost of inspiring a conservative backlash.

The second misstep involved Attorney General Alberto Gonzales and the firing of seven U.S. attorneys appointed by Bush at the beginning of his presidency. Again, Bush believed that so long as he trusted the Department of Justice to assess federal prosecutors, who after all served at the will of the president, the decision to remove them would not be challenged by Republicans. Once the details emerged, Republicans joined Democrats in exerting pressure on the attorney general to resign. Similar to Miers, Gonzales had been a close personal advisor and confidant of

President Bush. However, even Republicans objected to his controversial politicization of the entire Justice Department. Once Gonzales resigned, Bush nominated federal judge Michael Mukasey, who like Justice Alito had unquestioned qualifications and a solid reputation. Mukasey was confirmed by a wide margin.

The George W. Bush administration successfully recovered from the self-imposed damage to its moral competence resulting from the Miers and Gonzales incidents.

LEGAL POLICY: TORT REFORM AND SOCIAL ISSUES

This portion of the chapter will discuss legal policy efforts during the Bush administration in two areas, tort reform and abortion.

Tort Reform

Tort reform has been an important, if prosaic, aspect of Republican campaigns for the past twenty years, dating at least to Peter Huber's popular 1990 book *Liability: The Legal Revolution and Its Consequences* and Walter Olson's 1991 book *The Litigation Explosion*. Pitting business interests against trial lawyers and consumer groups, tort reform initiatives have ranged from procedural reforms in such areas as class-action litigation to medical malpractice reform to federal preemption. In 2001, for the first time since tort reform became part of the national agenda, those who favored such reforms had an attentive Republican president and a Republican-controlled Congress. Abortion has, of course, been a hotly contested social issue since the Supreme Court struck down state restrictions on abortion in 1973. As with tort reform, a pro-life president came to office in 2001 backed by majorities in both houses of Congress. We will take up three legislative initiatives in this area: successful passage of the 2005 Class Action Fairness Act; the occasionally successful effort to enact various industry-specific tort reforms; and the 2003 ban on partial-birth abortion.

Enactment of the Class Action Fairness Act (CAFA) in 2005 was the culmination of an effort by business groups to limit the scope of class-action litigation and to make it easier to move claims from state court to federal court. For many years, defendants had argued that plaintiffs' attorneys filed claims in state courts in which plaintiffs could play a "home game" and extract a settlement from defendants who feared going to trial before a state court jury. The legislative priority of the Bush administration was to enact limitations on such suits.

The major provision of CAFA was expansion of federal diversity jurisdiction, that is, federal court jurisdiction over claims brought by plaintiffs under state law but between citizens (including corporations) of different states. Before enactment of CAFA, class-action cases—particularly expensive litigation with enormous potential liability for defendants—could be heard in federal court only if there was "complete diversity" between each plaintiff and each defendant. When filing such claims, then, plaintiffs' counsel would include a plaintiff who resided in the same state as the defendant and thereby force the case to be heard in state court. Plaintiffs were wary of federal courts on account of a series of U.S. Supreme Court cases that had sharply limited the availability of class certification under the federal rules and the general view that federal judges were more willing to dismiss claims.

Under CAFA, any class-action claim with more than one hundred class members can be heard in federal court so long as at least one class member is diverse from any one of the defendants. This expansion of federal jurisdiction shifts the resolution of class-action litigation into a forum in which defendants have friendlier U.S. Supreme Court precedent and a bench that has become more and more willing to enforce limits on federal judicial power.[3]

Beyond CAFA, the administration pursued a range of industry-specific reforms aimed at limiting litigation in particular contexts. The story with these narrower reforms is more mixed. With two exceptions—the Protection of Lawful Commerce in Arms Act and federal preemption—the proposals in this area were unsuccessful.

The firearms industry and groups such as the National Rifle Association had argued against lawsuits brought by municipalities and private parties alleging that gun manufacturers should be liable for injuries caused by their products (Lytton 2005). With enactment of the Protection of Lawful Commerce in Arms Act in 2005, such claims were barred and pending claims were dismissed. Passage of the bill was delayed by debate about inclusion of other gun-related measures and strong opposition from the gun-control lobby. After the 2004 election, however, Republicans in Congress were able to block unwanted amendments and overcome the objections of gun-control advocates. Notably, the Democratic leadership of the Senate shifted from an opponent of the bill, Senator Tom Daschle (D-SD), who was defeated for reelection in 2004, to a proponent of the bill, Senator Harry Reid (D-NV).

A notable failure of the Bush administration was its effort to enact legislation to resolve the crisis of asbestos litigation. The inability to pass such a bill is an interesting tale of how a president whose party is in control of both houses of Congress can still be frustrated in the legislative process.

Early on, the Bush administration expressed support for a legislative solution to the asbestos litigation problem. The closest the administration came to a legislative resolution was a bill cosponsored by Senators Arlen Specter (R-PA) and Patrick Leahy (D-VT), the so-called Fairness in Asbestos Injury Resolution Act. The act would have created a $140 billion trust fund financed by asbestos defendant companies and insurers. Plaintiffs would not have been permitted to bring lawsuits for asbestos-related injuries in court. Instead, they would have submitted an administrative claim for compensation with the trust fund and been compensated based on a statutory schedule.

The effort to resolve the asbestos litigation problem fell prey to objections from both the left and the right. The bill assumed potential liability of approximately $140 billion, but actuarial projections of payouts ranged from $120 billion to more than $300 billion. Liberals were concerned about unconstitutionally restricting victims' access to courts, that the fund payouts would be too low and unfair to victims, and that defendant companies and insurers were not paying enough into the fund. Conservatives worried that the fund would become insolvent, that smaller businesses should not have to pay into the fund, that there would be "leakage" of claims back into the tort system, and that overly broad medical criteria would provide payments to some who were not truly sick from asbestos-related diseases.

When the bill was brought to the Senate floor in February 2006, the administration expressed "serious concerns" about certain provisions in the bill. The bill was defeated when it fell one vote short on a budget point of order. Supporters of asbestos litigation reform were especially upset that ten Republican senators voted against the motion to waive the point of order. Even if the bill had survived the point of order, though, it still faced long odds in Congress.

The unsuccessful effort to enact asbestos litigation reform shows the limits of the administration's success in the area of civil justice reform. In particular, asbestos reform illustrates the difficulty of enacting legislation when the usual proponents of tort reform—the Chamber of Commerce, corporate interests, and conservatives—are divided among themselves, even with a sympathetic administration.

Another unsuccessful tort reform effort was in the area of medical malpractice reform. The Bush administration was initially dubious of federal efforts to reform the medical malpractice system, and President Bush acknowledged publicly that he believed the issue should be left to the states. In light of the expansive federal role in health care finance and the appetite for malpractice reform among physician groups, though, the administration moved late in President Bush's first term to support enactment of federal legislation.

The major flashpoint in the medical malpractice debate is and has been for some time the imposition of caps on damages. Most proposals allow plaintiffs to recover their "economic" damages (medical expenses incurred, lost wages) but would limit recovery for "non-economic" damages (pain and suffering) or for punitive damages against physicians or hospitals. At bottom, the argument centers on whether escalating damages have made it more difficult to obtain malpractice insurance. In his book *The Medical Malpractice Myth*, law professor Tom Baker argues that the link between high premiums and damages simply has not been demonstrated and that the real crisis is the high rate of medical error and the number of patients who go uncompensated at all (Baker 2005). By contrast, a 2003 report from the U.S. Department of Health and Human Services found that liability concerns drive the use of defensive practices such as ordering unnecessary tests and thereby driving up the overall cost of health care (U.S. Department of Health and Human Services 2003). High malpractice insurance premiums have led to a shortage of physicians in certain specialties such as obstetrics. In southeastern Pennsylvania, for example, a 2003 GAO report found that malpractice premiums for obstetricians increased 165 percent between 1999 and 2002 (U.S. General Accounting Office 2003).

Notwithstanding several speeches on the topic and regular inclusion of medical malpractice reform among his domestic policy priorities in the annual State of the Union address, President Bush was never successful in enacting a bill to limit malpractice damages. Bills to limit medical liability passed the House of Representatives every session, largely because the rules of the House permitted the Republican majority to bring measures to a final vote. In the Senate, however, medical malpractice reform legislation always fell well short of the sixty votes needed to break a filibuster, and Democratic interest groups such as the American Trial Lawyers Association were adamantly opposed to the bill. Even Democratic senators who supported class-action reform or limits on gun lawsuits were united in opposition to medical malpractice reform, leaving one to wonder whether the legacy of the administration on tort reform issues is one of success in light of CAFA and the Protection of Lawful Commerce in Arms Act or more one of legislative gridlock—even through no fault of the administration itself—that is so often a stumbling block to presidential success.

Not all civil justice reform need be enacted by legislation, however, and the Bush administration's success in expanding the reach of federal preemption of state tort claims is an example of how the regulatory process can achieve domestic policy goals amid legislative gridlock. Preemption is the straightforward constitutional doctrine that where federal and state law conflict, federal law trumps. The debate in recent years is over whether approval of products by federal agencies charged with ensuring the safety of products should prevent plaintiffs from later bringing certain claims alleging that they were harmed by the product. During the Bush administration, several federal agencies began to assert federal preemption of contravening state regulations or state tort law. The Food and Drug Administration (FDA), the Consumer Product Safety Commission, and the National Highway Traffic Safety Administration frequently acted to preempt state tort claims and illustrate how control of the administrative process can accomplish goals that elude the legislative process.

In February 2008, the Supreme Court ruled that FDA approval of medical devices preempts tort claims. The Supreme Court decided another preemption case on the scope of preemption in prescription drug cases in 2009 and held that FDA approval of prescription drug labels did not preempt state tort claims. While the issue of preemption often turns on mind-numbing fine points of statutory interpretation and agency expertise, the implications in a range of tort cases is profound. Plaintiffs argue that federal safety regulations establish only a safety floor and the prospect of tort liability encourages manufacturers to implement safety measures which are not required by the agency. Defendant manufacturers and the federal agencies argue that federal regulations set an optimal safety standard and that state court juries should not be able (indeed, are not equipped) to second-guess the agency's determination.

Social Issues and the Partial-Birth Abortion Ban Act

Opponents of abortion, constrained by the Supreme Court's rulings in *Roe v. Wade* (1973) and *Planned Parenthood v. Casey* (1992) in the scope of limitations that can be placed on abortion, tried during the 1990s to enact a prohibition on a particular abortion procedure, intact dilation and extraction, or "partial-birth abortion." President Clinton vetoed bills to prohibit partial-birth abortion in 1995 and 1997, but several states enacted bills similar to the federal proposal. The constitutionality of such state statutes was tested in 2000. By a 5–4 vote, the Supreme Court held in *Stenberg v. Carhart* that a Nebraska statute that prohibited partial-birth abortion but did not contain an exception for the health of the woman imposed an unconstitutional burden on the right to abortion. When President Bush came to office in 2001, the pro-life movement hoped that federal legislation could be enacted which would pass constitutional muster and that the replacement of one or more of the justices voting to strike down the Nebraska statute in *Stenberg* would affect the outcome of a constitutional challenge to any federal statute. They were successful on both counts.

In 2003, the Partial-Birth Abortion Ban Act passed the House 281–142, the Senate 64–34, and was signed by President Bush. Supporters of the bill hoped that the development of detailed congressional findings and a carefully crafted definition of precisely what type of procedure was being prohibited would help the statute survive constitutional scrutiny. While the statute included an exception for the life of the mother, like the Nebraska statute it did not include an exception for the health of the woman out of a concern that courts had so broadly interpreted "health" that the statute would accomplish little.

Meanwhile, as discussed above, Justice Samuel Alito replaced Justice Sandra Day O'Connor, who had voted to strike down the Nebraska statute in *Stenberg*. Opponents of the federal ban filed a constitutional challenge to the statute. Federal district courts in Nebraska, New York, and California held that the federal statute was unconstitutional, and the courts of appeal affirmed. In April 2007, the Supreme Court reversed the lower courts and held that the federal partial-birth abortion ban was constitutional by a vote of 5–4. Writing for the majority joined by Justice Alito, Justice Anthony Kennedy (who had dissented in *Stenberg*) argued that the government had a substantial interest in protecting fetal life and that the federal statute was narrowly tailored to advance this interest.

CONCLUSION

Because federal courts will review and interpret most of a president's domestic legislative agenda, the Bush administration's success in appointing federal judges will be critically important in maintaining its policy successes. Indeed, with the war on terror and its legal permutations, federal courts also have an increasing impact on the effectiveness of a president's foreign policy efforts as well. By passing tort reform legislation and using regulations to increase federal preemption, the Bush administration has further extended its impact on the outcome of litigation in tort cases and on social issues. While there were noted failures—judicial nominees unconfirmed, medical malpractice reform blocked—the overall record is one that shows many examples of tactical, political, strategic, and moral competence.

NOTES

1. Our analysis in this part of the chapter is aided immensely by the consistent and comprehensive research conducted by Sheldon Goldman and his colleagues. Their research on presidential impact on the judiciary has been published in *Judicature* for every presidency since the Carter administration.

2. With each nomination the judiciary committee sends a "blue slip" to the senators of the state in which the vacancy has arisen. If the blue slip is not returned by either senator, the committee does not schedule a hearing on the nomination. This process is intended to foster consultation between the White House and home state senators across party lines.

3. Another legislative proposal, the Lawsuit Abuse Reduction Act, would have built on CAFA and expanded the use of sanctions under the federal rules against attorneys for filing frivolous claims. The bill passed the House in October 2005 but was never brought to a vote in the Senate.

REFERENCES

Baker, Tom. 2005. *The Medical Malpractice Myth*. Chicago: University of Chicago Press.

Carp, Robert A., Kenneth L. Manning, and Ronald Stidham. 2004. "The Decision-Making Behavior of George W. Bush's Judicial Appointees." *Judicature* 88(1): 20–28.

"Empty Seats on the Bench: Realistic Nominations Might Get Them Filled." 2007. *Washington Post*, October 21, p. B6.

Goldman, Sheldon, Elliot Slotnick, Gerard Gryski, and Sara Schiavoni. 2007. "Picking Judges in a Time of Turmoil: George W. Bush's Judiciary During the 109th Congress." *Judicature* 90(6): 252–83.

Goldman, Sheldon, Elliot Slotnick, Gerard Gryski, Gary Zuk, and Sara Schiavoni. 2003. "W. Bush's Remaking the Judiciary: Like Father Like Son?" *Judicature* 86(6): 282–309.

Hartley, Roger E., and Lisa M. Holmes. 2002. "The Increasing Senate Scrutiny of Lower Federal Court Nominees." *Political Science Quarterly* 117(2): 259–78.

Huber, Peter W. 1990. *Liability: The Legal Revolution and Its Consequences*. New York: Basic Books.

Kirkpatrick, David, and Kirk Rutenberg. 2007. "E-Mail Shows Rove's Role in Fate of Federal Prosecutors." *New York Times*, March 29, p. 14A.

Lytton, Timothy D., ed. 2005. *Suing the Gun Industry: A Battle at the Crossroads of Gun Control and Mass Torts*. Ann Arbor: University of Michigan Press.

Olson, Walter K. 1991. *The Litigation Explosion: What Happened When America Unleashed the Lawsuit*. New York: Thomas Talley Books/Dutton.

Teles, Steven M. 2008. *The Rise of the Conservative Legal Movement*. Princeton, NJ: Princeton University Press.

U.S. Department of Health and Human Services (HHS). Office of the Assistant Secretary for Planning and Evaluation. 2003. *Addressing the New Health Care Crisis: Reforming the Medical Litigation System to Improve the Quality of Healthcare*. March 3. http://aspe.hhs.gov/daltcp/reports/medliab.htm (Accessed January 1, 2009).

U.S. General Accounting Office (GAO). 2003. *Medical Malpractice: Impact of Rising Premiums on Access to Health Care*. http://www.gao.gov/new.items/d03836.pdf (Accessed January 1, 2009).

Velona, Jess A. 2005. "Partisan Imbalance on the U.S. Courts of Appeals." *Judicature* 89(1): 25–34.

PART THREE

Domestic Policies

CHAPTER 9

George W. Bush's Education Legacy

The Two Faces of No Child Left Behind

FREDERICK M. HESS AND PATRICK J. MCGUINN

ASSESSMENTS OF THE BUSH PRESIDENCY will likely turn on his foreign policy legacy, particularly the war in Iraq and the nation's economic health. This is due both to their outsized significance and because the administration achieved only a few major legislative victories in programmatic domestic policy. The administration's signature domestic policy triumph was in education policy, where Bush's leadership was central to the passage of arguably the most important and controversial piece of education legislation in American history—the No Child Left Behind Act (NCLB). There, unlike in the 2003 Medicare bill, in which the administration grudgingly sought to shore up a Republican weakness, or the 2008 housing bill, where the administration responded to external forces and congressional pressure, the administration came into office calling for bold and expansive federal policy. In so doing, Bush broke with longstanding GOP opposition to an active federal role in school reform, as both the 1994 Contract with America and the 1996 Republican Party platform called for the abolition of the U.S. Department of Education. Bush was in many ways a revolutionary in education policy and the revolution he helped to initiate will long outlive his administration.

Education reform was a linchpin of Bush's "compassionate conservatism" and key to administration efforts to reassure suburban voters, woo traditionally Democratic constituencies in the black and Latino communities, and potentially weaken the two dominant teachers unions (the American Federation of Teachers and the National Education Association), which had long stood as pillars of the Democratic coalition. In Karl Rove's playbook for building a stable Republican majority, education was intended to demonstrate the ability of Republicans to deliver in an area where Democrats had long enjoyed a giant advantage but were hobbled by interest-group politics. This chapter will assess the political, strategic, and tactical competence of the Bush administration in the area of education policy and offer some reflections on the president's educational legacy. While the administration tackled a range of educational issues, history will mainly judge the president on the No Child Left Behind Act.

AN INSPIRATIONAL ACT OR AN INCOHERENT ONE?

Bush's approach to the 2001 reauthorization of the Elementary and Secondary Education Act (ESEA)—the primary federal statute addressing K–12 education—sought to inject assessment, accountability, and expanded school choice into federal education programs that had previously distributed billions of dollars in aid annually without any meaningful focus on student achievement or consequences for mediocre school performance. In January 2001, the Bush administration launched its first comprehensive domestic policy proposal when it released a blueprint for ESEA reauthorization (entitled "No Child Left Behind") that articulated a coherent strategy for reshaping the federal program. The proposal built on reforms championed by the Clinton administration during the 1994 ESEA reauthorization and were thought to have the potential to deliver considerable political benefits for the Republican Party. However, the choices the administration made in crafting and administering the new law proved controversial, and they leave room for two very different interpretations of its tactical competence and the legacy it will leave behind in education.

A generous assessment posits that the Bush administration consciously set out to change the culture of schooling in America—to focus reform efforts on proficiency in key academic subjects and to insist that educators find ways to boost performance for all students. In setting out the ambitious goal of "leaving no child behind," the administration won allies in the civil rights community, changed the calculus of school reform in urban districts, wrought a revolution in the transparency of educational outcomes, and dramatically raised expectations for educators. In this telling, NCLB proved catalytic in changing the conversation about education across the country among policymakers, educators, and the public at large. The law helped to institutionalize standards, testing, accountability, and choice into state education systems. It shifted the paradigm in education, and now even opponents of NCLB preface their criticisms by noting their support for the law's goals and the principles of assessment and accountability. To accomplish this cultural shift, the nuances of the law or of its implementation were never the central question; the most important question was not whether the provisions were well-designed but whether they created a sense of urgency and spurred innovation.

The skeptical view regards the Bush administration's educational ambitions as grandiose and questions the statute's design and the administration's heavy-handed approach to implementation. In lieu of contemporary conservatism's respect for self-interest and its attention to incentives, NCLB was a series of sloppy compromises, punctuated by aspirational goals stipulating that 100 percent of the nation's students would be proficient in reading and math by 2014. In this narrative, the law had more in common with the troubled initiatives of the Great Society than with anything one would expect to emerge under a conservative administration. The law offered scant incentive for schools or districts to move proactively while effectively encouraging states to game its accountability provisions, ultimately leading the U.S. Department of Education to rely on shaming as a primary tool of enforcement. The legacy of NCLB in this telling is problematic for Republicans, yielding an expansion of federal authority; electorally crucial suburbanites tending to blame NCLB for frustrations with their local schools; and, more generally, public opinion so sour on NCLB that Democratic congressman George Miller, a key author of the law, has termed it "the most tainted brand in America." Senator Edward Kennedy, another key administration ally in penning the law, has said, "No Child Left Behind, rather than being a flagship for improved strength and enhanced opportunity of education for the children, has become a symbol of controversial, flawed and failed policy" (Baker 2007, A1).

THE CONTEXT OF NO CHILD LEFT BEHIND

To understand the legacy of the Bush administration in education, it is necessary to sketch the contours of the national education policy landscape in 2001, at the dawn of the administration, and then in late 2008, at the administration's dusk. NCLB's passage in 2001 was preceded by nearly a decade's worth of efforts to reshape the Elementary and Secondary Education Act. Originated in 1965 as a key part of Lyndon Johnson's Great Society, ESEA was designed to promote greater educational opportunity for poor and minority children. ESEA's central provision, Title I, dispersed increasing amounts of federal funds to school districts across the country but demanded little in the way of accountability for student achievement.

Over the ensuing decades, there was little evidence that these investments improved the achievement of low-income or minority students, and there was growing concern about the rules and regulatory red tape that had gradually expanded (Hess and Petrilli 2006). The 1983 report *A Nation at Risk* emphasized the continuing failure of American schools, and, by the early 1990s, many policymakers and reformers in both parties had come to believe that ESEA needed a major overhaul. At the same time, the broader political environment remained unreceptive to new federal mandates governing educational accountability. Democrats frowned on such measures out of concern that they might shift the focus away from increasing financial resources for schools and due to opposition by the teachers unions. The GOP, meanwhile, still resisted federal intrusion in the historically locally controlled area of education.

During the 1994 ESEA reauthorization, Clinton—a "New Democrat"—sought changes that would push states to increase performance reporting and embrace educational accountability. Under this new ESEA and a companion piece of legislation, "Goals 2000," states were required to establish academic standards in each grade and create tests to assess whether students had mastered the standards. The tests were to be administered to all poor children at least once in Grades 3 through 5, 6 through 9, and 10 through 12. Enforcement by the U.S. Department of Education was lax, however, as Democrats opposed withholding funds from state education systems and Republicans resisted federal micromanagement of states. In the end, most states failed to comply: as late as 2002, two years *after* the target date for full compliance, just sixteen states had fully complied with the 1994 law (McGuinn 2005, 45).

Meanwhile, on the heels of the passage of the 1994 ESEA reauthorization, Republicans won control of both the House and Senate for the first time in decades, partly on the strength of their "Contract with America" and calls to abolish the U.S. Department of Education and roll back the expanse and power of the federal government more generally. Republican control of Congress dictated the context for the next ESEA reauthorization, slated for 1999. The Clinton administration forwarded a proposal that year which built on the 1994 reforms, with requirements that states regularly test *all* students, and which provided for a bigger federal role in ensuring state compliance. Conservative Republicans in Congress countered with a proposal called the Academic Achievement for All Act ("Straight A's"), which sought to reduce federal influence by combining most federal education programs into block grants. With the 2000 election nearing, the proposals died a quiet death.

BUSH, EDUCATION, AND THE 2000 ELECTION

During the 2000 election, Bush and his advisors developed a campaign strategy that accorded education a key role and—in a break with decades of GOP orthodoxy—envisioned expansive federal involvement in school reform. Seeking to narrow an enormous partisan deficit on education, the Bush team used the candidate's embrace of Texas's accountability system during his time as governor to demonstrate Republican bona fides on schooling and to demonstrate the party's commitment to the poor and disadvantaged. Bush's education proposals also served as the central component of the campaign's theme of "compassionate conservatism" appealing to moderate swing voters.

The tactic worked remarkably well. While polls showed that President Bill Clinton had thrashed Republican nominee Bob Dole in 1996 on the education question by roughly 50 percent, Bush ran almost dead even with Democratic nominee Al Gore in 2000. This proved especially significant in a year of peace and prosperity, when exit polls suggested that education topped the list of public concerns.[1] Republican pollster David Winston has noted that this "was a huge shift and is why Bush is president. . . . Education was THE deciding issue in 2000. The groups that were most interested in education were the key swing voters—independents, Catholics, married women with children" (Winston 2003). Bush's success in closing the education gap was not lost on congressional Republicans—even conservatives who had as recently as 1999 aggressively sought to reduce the federal role in schooling—and helped him move the GOP during the 2001 debate over NCLB.

The evolution of John Boehner (R-OH), the conservative chairman of the House Education and Workforce Committee, illustrates the extent to which Bush helped Republicans to shift positions. Boehner had been a leading opponent of federal influence in education in the 1990s, voting to eliminate the Department of Education and remarking in 1995 that "it is clear that the current experiment of having the federal government heavily involved in education has failed" (cited in Gorman 2001, 955). After Bush' election, however, Boehner acknowledged that "I think we realized in 1996 that our message was sending the wrong signal to the American people about the direction we wanted to go in education" (cited in Gorman 2001, 955). As a result, Boehner became a vocal supporter of NCLB and a key Bush ally in mobilizing Republican support for the bill. Boehner observed at the time that "the 2000 campaign paved the way for reform, and conservatives must capitalize by implementing the president's plan . . . conservatives have yearned for an opportunity to break the status quo in federal education policy. This could be our moment. On behalf of parents and students, let's seize it" (Boehner 2001, 2). Bush thus played a pivotal role in pushing the Republican Party to embrace a more ambitious and more politically salable—but substantially more interventionist and, arguably, substantially less "conservative"—position on K–12 schooling.

THE ENACTMENT OF NCLB

The opportunity for presidents to fundamentally reshape policy is partially due to their position in the partisan "regime cycle"—the confluence of existing statutes, the strength of the president's party, and of the popular and legislative appetite and enthusiasm for change (McGuinn 2006). Bush took office with one of the narrowest victories in presidential history and without a majority of the popular vote; while Republicans preserved their control of Congress, they did so by an exceedingly thin margin. In that environment, Bush rejected calls to embrace "conservative" principles in the ESEA reauthorization and instead sought bipartisan passage of NCLB. This approach—which was strikingly different from the more partisan tack the administration took on other issues, such as tax policy, Medicare, and Social Security—was due both to the fear that a more conservative bill might repel pro-accountability moderates from both parties and sink the legislation, and to the fact that Bush's substantive proposals were in many ways closer to the median Democratic position on education than to the Republican one (Maranto and Coppeto 2004).

This crucial tactical choice would have a significant impact on the measure's prospects for passage and on the specific provisions that emerged in the final bill. It forced Bush to accept a number of compromises with Democrats, including greatly increased federal funding for education, new federal regulations governing teacher quality, and a dramatic downsizing of proposals to reduce regulation and expand school choice. At the same time, the passage of NCLB on a 381–41 vote in the House of Representatives and on an 87–10 vote in the Senate enabled the president to secure his first major programmatic policy victory (excluding tax reduction) and to do so in a fashion that bolstered his claim to be a compassionate conservative able to work across party lines. This offered a particularly appealing image when the newly popular Bush signed the legislation just months after the terrorist attacks of September 11, 2001.

The Bush administration's tactical decision to sacrifice its initial design principles in order to win bipartisan support was perhaps most evident when it came to school choice and vouchers. Bush's initial blueprint for NCLB called for increased school choice, including funds to "assist charter schools with start-up costs, facilities, and other needs associated with creating high-quality schools" (Bush 2001). It also included a provision for school vouchers, stating, "If the school fails to make adequate yearly progress after three years, disadvantaged students within the school may use Title I funds to transfer to a higher performing public or private school, or receive supplemental education services (SES) from a provider of choice." However, concluding in the spring of 2001 that it lacked the votes to win on vouchers in the closely divided Congress, the administration allowed the proposal to die. Then-Undersecretary of Education Eugene Hickock would later explain that the president had no intention of "sacrifice[ing] accountability on the altar of school choice" (quoted in Rudalevige 2003, 5).

Under the final legislation, all the students in Title I schools deemed "in need of improvement" were to be given the option to transfer to another *public* school within the district or to a nearby charter school. No provision for vouchers was included, though public funds were allowed to be diverted to private providers of supplemental educational services (generally tutoring). While conservatives lamented a missed opportunity to establish a national voucher program, the transfer provision had the potential to shake up school systems, and the creation of SES provided an important precedent for sending federal funds to private educational providers. Three years later, Bush and the Republican Congress pushed further, enacting a modest but precedent-setting federally funded voucher program for nearly two thousand students in Washington, D.C.

The final version of NCLB required states to create accountability systems, annually test children in reading and math in Grades 3 through 8 (and once in high school), determine which students were proficient, identify schools where an insufficient number of students were proficient, ensure specified measures against schools that failed to make "adequate yearly progress," and set targets that would ensure 100 percent of children were proficient in reading and math by 2014. One of the most important mandates in the law is that school report cards must disaggregate student test score data for subgroups based on race or ethnicity, economically disadvantaged status, limited proficiency in English, and special education status. Crucially and controversially, a school that does not meet the proficiency target for *any one of these groups* is placed in "in need of improvement status." The disaggregated data has produced more information than ever before on the performance of disadvantaged students and has bolstered the claims of equity groups, particularly in urban areas. It has also angered suburban educators and parents, as many schools previously perceived to be high performing have been placed on NCLB's watch list due to failing subgroups.

The scope, specificity, and ambition of the law's mandates signaled something akin to a revolution in federal education policy. As written, however, the NCLB legislation was a complicated mix of federal mandates and state discretion: states are required to put standards and tests in place and create a system for dealing with failing schools, but they set the rigor of these themselves. As a prominent think-tanker explained in 2004, "To grasp why NCLB inspires both accolades and catcalls, not infrequently from the same observers, one should begin by noting that this legislation is both evolutionary and revolutionary. Many of its leading ideas have received bipartisan support over the years, while other aspects of the legislation are wholly new and more controversial" (quoted in Finn and Hess 2004, 36–37).

IMPLEMENTING NCLB

Given these cross-cutting currents, much would depend on the way in which the law was implemented by the Bush Department of Education and how the department handled states' requests for flexibility, extensions, and waivers. On this count, states hoped that the administration would be as amenable as the Clinton administration had been in implementing the 1994 legislation. Deeming it the most promising path to deliver the cultural shift it sought, the Bush administration initially took a hard line and pushed states to comply with the letter of the law. While this forced states to take the law's mandates more seriously than they otherwise would have, it unsurprisingly sparked vocal protests among educators, who complained that the law's goals and timetables were unrealistic and that the resources and guidance provided were insufficient.

Many congressional Democrats—including some of the legislation's initial supporters—quickly criticized the implementation approach of the administration and sought to distance themselves from how the law was put into practice. As Democratic House Education and Workforce Committee staffer Alex Nock noted, "The Department has really struggled in implementing the law—it's a difficult job, but they didn't do it right. They took too long to get out key regulations and guidance, issued contradictory guidance, and did a poor job with providing technical assistance" (Nock 2005). Later, Representative George Miller (D-CA), chair of the House Education and Workforce Committee and a key architect of NCLB would remark, "I would give [NCLB] an A in terms of the goals that it has set . . . in trying to develop a system to make sure that each and every child is proficient. I would give it an F for funding. . . . And on implementation, I would give it a C" (Miller 2006).

One awkward question was how the Bush administration would respond to states that pushed back against the law's requirements in the name of federalism. The administration faced a thorny choice: acquiescing and accepting the efforts to undercut NCLB, or aggressively challenging states that threatened to forfeit federal dollars in order to opt out of the NCLB regime. In a decision that caused consternation among conservatives concerned about federal overreach and the integrity of federalism, the administration opted to use every tool at its disposal to keep states in line. Given the noble promise of NCLB's pledge that every child would be proficient in reading and math by 2014, along with its belief that allowing states to backslide would launch the nation on a slippery slope and undercut its effort to transform the culture of schooling, the administration successfully brought substantial pressure to bear when Utah and Connecticut publicly challenged NCLB.

By 2004, however, more than a dozen states expressed interest in throwing off the mandates embodied in the ambitious law. In Virginia, the Republican-controlled House of Delegates voted 98–1 to condemn NCLB for "represent[ing] the most sweeping intrusions into state and local control of education in the history of the United States" (quoted in McDonnell 2005, 26). By 2007, the administration faced a full-fledged backlash among Republicans on the Hill. GOP congressmen and senators accused the administration of having abandoned conservative principles and tough-minded realism in the service of oversized ambition. By June 2007, fifty-two Republican House members and five GOP senators called for a repeal of the law in favor of a more flexible system of achievement standards. Republican House minority whip Roy Blunt would explain, "I always had misgivings. But I did vote for it on the basis that maybe he was right and this was his big domestic initiative and let's give him a chance. But all my concerns . . . have proven to be justified" (Baker 2007, A1).

The administration, resisting pushback from the teachers unions, congressional complaints, and critiques of various NCLB provisions, elected to stand fast. In 2006, Secretary of Education Margaret Spellings famously told reporters, "I talk about No Child Left Behind like Ivory Soap: It's 99.9 percent pure or something. There's not much needed in the way of change" (Associated Press 2006). Doubling down on that party line, Deputy Secretary Ray Simon echoed the once-popular Bush administration mantra on Iraq, telling *Washington Post* reporter Amit Paley, "We need to stay the course. The mission is do-able, and we don't need to back off that right now" (Paley 2007, A1).

A CIVIL RIGHTS MANIFESTO?

The great irony of NCLB is that this bill, which would be reviled by educators, education professors, and many progressives as a "Bush law," was at the time heralded by some prominent left-leaning school reformers as a stunning progressive coup and a fulfillment of LBJ's Great Society ambitions. Indeed, Robert Gordon, an education advisor to Democratic nominee Senator John Kerry during the 2004 general election, attacked the Democratic criticism of NCLB as shortsighted and a betrayal of liberal values. Writing in the *New Republic*, Gordon explained, "Progressives are misled by the logic of their own Bush-hatred: Bush is for NCLB, so NCLB must be bad. Never mind that President Clinton embraced accountability before President Bush. . . . At its heart, [NCLB] is the sort of law liberals once dreamed about. . . . The law requires a form of affirmative action: States must show that minority and poor students are achieving proficiency like everyone else, or else provide remedies targeted to the schools those students attend" (Gordon 2005, 25).

Political scientist E. E. Schattschneider noted long ago that "new policies create new politics," and it is now clear that NCLB has had a transformative effect not only on education policy but also on education *politics* (Schattschneider 1935). Bush's expansive efforts to pursue equal opportunity and court new constituencies yielded legislation that reflected the high hopes and ambitious design that characterized Democrat Lyndon Johnson's rhetorical aspirations for the initial ESEA. In January 2004, the centrist Democratic Leadership Council declared that NCLB "is a good law that should be strengthened, not abandoned. . . . Democrats . . . have a special responsibility to force change, in Washington, and at the state and local levels, to lift the measurable performance of schools. NCLB remains the best opportunity of this generation to do just that" (Democratic Leadership Council 2004).

Indeed, as Frederick Hess and Chester Finn have argued, "NCLB is, in fact, a civil rights manifesto masquerading as an education accountability system" (2007b, 40). At a 2007 NAACP conference, Education secretary Margaret Spellings would declare, "The No Child Left Behind Act . . . is not just an education law. It's a civil rights law" (quoted in U.S. Department of Education 2007). Many in the civil rights community have come to agree with this view of NCLB. In a remarkable development in 2006, the NAACP sided with the Bush administration's opposition to the state of Connecticut's lawsuit against NCLB. In 2008, the Leadership Conference on Civil Rights (the largest civil rights coalition in the country) announced its strong opposition to the "NCLB Recess until Reauthorization Act," which had been introduced in Congress. Their announcement stated that "LCCR believes that NCLB is a civil rights law, and that some of the requirements of NCLB constitute, in essence, the rights of children to obtain a quality education. . . . Even a temporary suspension of a civil rights law, and therefore the civil rights of our children, is unconscionable" (Leadership Conference on Civil Rights 2008).

Whether reflecting genuine sentiment or savvy tactical politics, the use of civil rights rhetoric by the Bush administration to defend NCLB has exacerbated deep divisions in the Democratic Party on education reform. In particular, it has exposed a major schism between teachers unions and civil rights groups—two of the most important Democratic constituencies. Many civil rights leaders believe that the law's disaggregated data and accountability provisions offer an unprecedented and powerful tool in the fight for educational equity. Many in the education establishment, however, believe that the law unfairly holds schools responsible for resolving educational problems that have their roots elsewhere, in broader social ills like poverty. The divergent views and mutual antagonism of these two groups led commentator Richard Kahlenberg to write an article entitled "How the Left Can Avoid a New Education War" (2008), and the split was on public display during a clash at the Democratic National Convention in Denver (Hoff 2008). Whether NCLB represented the Bush administration manipulating progressive allies for its own policy goals, the administration abandoning three decades of hard-won conservative insights out of fealty to grand aspirations, or a skillfully crafted compromise is a question whose answer is still unfolding.

BUSH AND THE NEW POLITICS OF EDUCATION

No Child Left Behind reshuffled, even if it did not abolish, the familiar politics of education. On the one hand, NCLB benefited from and helped to cement a powerful and unprecedented pro-accountability coalition that encompassed influential business and civil rights organizations, many of which have historically been political opponents. The pro-accountability Achievement Alliance, for example, has brought together progressive civil rights groups, such as the Citizen's Commission on Civil Rights, the Education Trust, and the Council of La Raza, with conservative business groups, such as the Business Roundtable—all in support of No Child Left Behind and the administration's efforts on school accountability.

As discussed above, Rove's hope that NCLB might fracture the Democratic coalition has shown some evidence of success. The desire of pro-reform Democrats to embrace accountability and separate themselves from union recalcitrance and the orthodoxies of the left-leaning education community has spurred the creation of new groups such as Democrats for Education Reform (DFER). DFER's website declares that "both political parties have failed to address the tragic decline of our system of public education, but it is the Democratic Party—our party—which must question how we allowed ourselves to drift so far from our mission. . . . We support leaders in our party who have the courage to challenge a failing status quo . . . through bold and revolutionary leadership" (2007). Another manifestation of the changing politics, and the split between the anti-accountability teachers unions and some of their allies in the civil rights community, is the emergence of the left-leaning Education Equality Group, which brought together the Reverend Al Sharpton with bêtes noires of the teachers unions like New York City schools chancellor Joel Klein, Newark mayor Corey Booker, and District of Columbia schools chancellor Michelle Rhee. These new coalitions have provided a bold challenge to the unions, have separated visible elements of the civil rights community from their traditional left-wing and teachers union allies, and have permanently altered the politics of the education debate.

At the same time, it would be naïve to imagine that the world was made completely anew by NCLB. During implementation, many of the traditional divisions in education quickly reasserted themselves, with conservatives increasingly bemoaning the expansion of federal power, some liberals complaining about the lack of sufficient resources, and teacher and administrator groups arguing that they should not be held accountable for the academic failings of disadvantaged students. The nation's largest teachers union, the National Education Association, which had been largely cut out of the legislative negotiations over NCLB, mobilized their members in opposition to the law and led a public campaign against it. As the Iraq War dragged on and the economy declined, NCLB also became associated with Bush's historically low public-approval ratings. By 2008, public opinion on education had shifted, with Americans split on NCLB and the Republicans again lagging far behind the Democrats (by 20 or 30 points in most polls) on which party could be trusted more on the question of education (Howell et al. 2008).

THE NEW WORLD OF EDUCATIONAL ASSESSMENT AND ACCOUNTABILITY

Despite all of the political controversy surrounding NCLB, one of the enduring legacies of the Bush administration will likely be the institutionalization of assessment and accountability in education. In this sense, NCLB's influence may ultimately be compared to the original ESEA in 1965, which for all its flaws and shortcomings cemented in place a new and substantial federal role in education. While it is impossible to predict the outcome of the pending congressional reauthorization of NCLB, signs indicate that the law's central principles are likely to continue—even if the name "No Child Left Behind" may be replaced and several of the law's original provisions substantially reworked.

Important to rendering any ultimate judgment on the impact of NCLB will be whether the ambitious ploy to set extravagant targets and thereby change the playing field ultimately works as intended, or whether it serves to undermine the credibility of educational accountability and to provoke a backlash. The polling data documents steady growth in public discomfort with NCLB and with many components of the law's accountability framework (Hess 2007). Coupled with the buyer's remorse so evident among conservatives on Capitol Hill and anger among suburban parents and politicians, these results suggest that the administration's vehement support for this awkwardly crafted law may ultimately do substantial damage to the reputation of accountability and to the Republican brand. Whether that indeed proves to be the case, and how such costs should be weighed against the law's successes, will only be known in the fullness of time.

Presidential scholars such as Stephen Skowronek have argued that the presidency can be effective as a "battering ram" in demolishing old systems but that it is not as good at building new ones (1997, 27–28). Similarly, scholar George Edwards (1990) has argued that presidential power works only at the "margins" and that presidents typically are "facilitators" and not "directors" of change—particularly because the president is forced to share power with members of Congress that have their own dynamics, priorities, and demands. As a result, Richard Neustadt (1990) has argued that presidents must persuade other political elites in order to advance their agenda. The case of NCLB illustrates how many of these limits play out in practice, as the Bush administration pursued transformative change within the constraints that shaped and restricted that change.

While the debate continues to rage about whether or not NCLB has boosted achievement and whether it has been good for America's students, the law clearly appears to have succeeded in changing the culture of schooling. As Phyllis McClure, a longtime member of the Title I Independent Review Panel, has observed, "NCLB has grabbed the education community's attention like no previous ESEA reauthorization. It has really upset the status quo in state and local offices. . . . For the first time, district and school officials are actually being required to take serious and urgent action in return for federal dollars" (McClure 2004). Moreover, one of the primary goals of Republicans has been to introduce market forces into education and to initiate what economist Joseph Schumpeter (1975) termed a process of "creative destruction," in which underperforming organizations give way to more-promising new entrants. Since the advent of NCLB, the educational status quo has been disrupted on the ground, and the number of charter schools, nontraditional superintendents, nontraditional teacher training programs, tutoring firms, and other new providers has increased steadily.

NCLB's requirement that states conduct annual testing and report student scores has forced states to build new data-gathering and -dissemination systems and has produced a greater degree of transparency in public education than ever before. Scholars Tiffany Berry and Rebecca Eddy have written that the law has "transformed the landscape of educational evaluation" and is "redefining what evaluation is within the education evaluation community" (2008, 2). By holding states clearly accountable for the performance of their public schools, NCLB has also prodded state departments of education to expand their capacity to monitor local districts, provide technical assistance, and intervene where necessary (see Hess and Finn 2007a). As Paul Manna (2006) has noted, reform-minded governors and superintendents have also used NCLB as political cover to advance school improvement agendas in the face of community, educator, or legislative resistance. In implementing NCLB, the Bush administration fundamentally altered the role of the federal Department of Education—shifting it from its historical role as a grant-maker and compliance monitor to a more active (if still relatively toothless) role as a compliance enforcer and an agitator. In addition, through the new District of Columbia voucher program, expanded funding for charter schools, and the creation of a new Office of Innovation and Improvement, the Bush administration has pushed the Education Department to be more supportive of alternative approaches to schooling. The creation of the Institute of Education Sciences shifted federal funding toward empirically validated education research that could generate improvement in student achievement. The administration has emphasized bottom-line results in student achievement rather than the traditional focus on regulation and process.

It is not yet clear to what extent the change in departmental profile and mission will outlast the Bush administration, or what direction the massive expansion of federal authority with regard to teacher quality, reading instruction, or addressing low-performing schools will ultimately take. In anticipating future developments, it is worth recognizing that the nature of bureaucracy dictates that trying to downsize or curtail an agency's mission is much like trying to stuff a genie back into a bottle. Particularly in the hands of a Democratic administration, this new capacity and mind-set might well be deployed in a manner that Bush partisans did not anticipate and did not intend—in which case, the administration's tactical victories could prove Pyrrhic for champions of limited government and conservative school reform.

CONCLUSION

For better or worse, the Bush administration has changed the world of K–12 schooling. The "rhetorical presidency" can be a powerful tool in influencing public opinion, and Bush effectively used the bully pulpit—particularly in the 2000 election campaign—to raise the profile of the education issue and the need to close racial and socioeconomic achievement gaps, with his powerful rhetoric about the "soft bigotry of low expectations." While opposition to NCLB proved a reliable applause line for Democratic presidential nominees in 2004 and 2008—a surprising turn for a bipartisan law that had been embraced by some progressives—no major Democratic candidate suggested a full-scale retreat from testing and accountability. During the 2008 campaign, Barack Obama called for more funding and major revisions to NCLB but voiced support for its core policies of standards, testing, and accountability. His endorsement of merit pay and charter schools, despite fervent union opposition, may suggest a changing political equilibrium on the left. John McCain, the Republican presidential nominee, indicated his firm support for NCLB, despite lingering opposition from the libertarian and states' rights wings of the GOP.

Today, the educational conversation in the United States is markedly different from what it was before Bush took office. Fundamental assumptions about the purposes and potential of schooling, the political alliances that dominate reform efforts, and public and elite expectations about the role of the federal government have all changed in important ways. Whether this will be good for school reform or good for the Republican Party over the long term is not yet clear. Indeed, the answer to such questions will be determined by which ultimately proves more lasting: the cultural transformation pushed by the administration, or the backlash, implementation headaches, and unanticipated consequences wrought by NCLB. Much will depend on the degree to which Barack Obama and the Democratic majorities in the 111th Congress opt to build on the consensus that has emerged on education policy, or to ostentatiously walk away from an unpopular law.

NOTE

1. Exit polls conducted by the Voter News Service revealed that in the 1996 election 78 percent of education voters supported Clinton and only 16 percent supported Dole. But among the 15 percent of voters who identified education as their top concern in 2000, 52 percent voted for Gore, while 44 percent voted for Bush (Barnes 2000, 3609).

REFERENCES

Associated Press. 2006. "Education Secretary: No Child Act Needs No Changes." August 30. http://www.msnbc.msn.com/id/14589472/ (Accessed September 27, 2006).

Baker, Peter. 2007. "An Unlikely Partnership Left Behind." *Washington Post*, November 5, p. A1.

Barnes, James. 2000. "The GOP's Shifting Terrain." *National Journal*, November 11, p. 3609.

Berry, Tiffany, and Rebecca M. Eddy. 2008. "Editor's Notes." In *New Directions for Evaluation, Special Issue: Consequences of No Child Left Behind on Educational Evaluation*, No. 117, ed. Tiffany Berry and Rebecca M. Eddy, 1–7. San Francisco: Jossey-Bass.

Boehner, John R. 2001. "Making the Grade: In the Hands of Parents, Information Is Like Rocket Fuel for Education Reform." *National Review Online*, April 6. http://republicans.edlabor .house.gov/archive/press/press107/jaboped4601.htm (Accessed December 7, 2002).

Bush, George W. 2001. "Blueprint for No Child Left Behind." Transmitted to Congress on January 23. http://www.whitehouse.gov/news/reports/no-child-left-behind.html (Accessed May 2, 2001).

Democratic Leadership Council. 2004. "An Educational Mission That Must Not Fail." *New Democrat Daily*, January 7. http://www.dlcppi.org/ndol_ci.cfm?kaid=110&subid =136&contentid =252307 (Accessed June 25, 2005).

Democrats for Education Reform. 2007. *Statement of Principles*, November 20. http://www .dfer.org/2007/11/statement_of_pr.php#more (Accessed May 12, 2008).

Edwards, George C., III. 1990. *At the Margins: Presidential Leadership of Congress*. New Haven, CT: Yale University Press.

Finn, Chester E., Jr., and Frederick M. Hess. 2004. "On Leaving No Child Behind." *Public Interest* 157: 35–56.

Gordon, Robert. 2005. "Class Struggle." *New Republic* 232(21/22): 24–27.

Gorman, Siobhan. 2001. "The Education of House Republicans." *National Journal*, March 31, p. 955.

Hess, Frederick M. 2007. "Accountability Without Angst? Public Opinion and No Child Left Behind." *Harvard Educational Review* 76(4): 587–610.

———, and Chester E. Finn Jr., eds. 2007a. *No Remedy Left Behind: Lessons from a Half-Decade of NCLB*. Washington, DC: American Enterprise Institute.

———, and Chester E. Finn Jr. 2007b. "Crash Course: NCLB Is Driven by Education Politics." *Education Next* 7(4): 40–45.

———, and Michael J. Petrilli. 2006. *No Child Left Behind: A Primer*. New York: Peter Lang.

Hoff, David J. 2008. "Democrats Air Dueling Ideas in Education: Broad Plans Divide Some, But Obama Seeks Middle." *Education Week* 28(1): 1, 22.

Howell, William G., Martin R. West, and Paul E. Peterson. 2008. "The 2008 *Education Next*-PEPG Survey of Public Opinion." *Education Week* 8(4): 12–26.

Kahlenberg, Richard D. 2008. "How the Left Can Avoid a New Education War." *American Prospect*, July 9. http://www.prospect.org/cs/articles?article=how_the_left_can_avoid_a _new_education_war (Accessed July 19, 2008).

Leadership Conference on Civil Rights. 2008. "Oppose the NCLB Recess Until Reauthorization Act." Letter of June 18. http://www.civilrights.org/library/advocacy-letters/pdfs/lccr _nclb_letter_061808.pdf (Accessed August 2, 2008).

Manna, Paul. 2006. *School's In: Federalism and the National Education Agenda*. Washington, DC: Georgetown University Press.

Maranto, Robert A., and Laura Coppeto. 2004. "The Politics Behind Bush's No Child Left Behind: Ideas, Elections, and Top-Down Education Reform." In *George W. Bush: Evaluating the President at Midterm*, ed. Bryan Hilliard, Tom Lansford, and Robert Watson. Albany: State University of New York Press, 105–20.

McClure, Phyllis. 2004. "Grassroots Resistance to NCLB." *Education Gadfly* 4(11). http:// www.edexcellence.net/gadfly/index.cfm?issue=140#a1723 (Accessed July 10, 2005).

McDonnell, Lorraine M. 2005. "No Child Left Behind and the Federal Role in Education: Evolution or Revolution?" *Peabody Journal of Education* 80(2): 19–38.

McGuinn, Patrick. 2005. "The National Schoolmarm: No Child Left Behind and the New Educational Federalism." *Publius: The Journal of Federalism* 35(1): 41–68.

———. 2006. *No Child Left Behind and the Transformation of Federal Education Policy, 1965–2005*. Lawrence: University Press of Kansas.

Miller, George. 2006. Speech, Fourth Annual No Child Left Behind Forum, "Assessing Progress, Addressing Problems, Advancing Performance." Conference, Business Roundtable, September 20.

Neustadt, Richard E. 1990. *Presidential Power and the Modern Presidents: The Politics of Leadership from Roosevelt to Reagan*. New York: Free Press.

Nock, Alex. 2005. Telephone interview, May 6.

Paley, Amit. 2007. "'No Child' Target Is Called out of Reach; Goal of 100% Proficiency Debated as Congress Weighs Renewal." *Washington Post*, March 14, p. A1.

Rudalevige, Andrew. 2003. "The Politics of No Child Left Behind." *Education Next* 3(4): 63–69.

Schattschneider, Elmer Eric. 1935. *Politics, Pressures, and the Tariff: A Study of Free Private Enterprise in Pressure Politics, as Shown in the 1929–1930 Revision of the Tariff*. New York: Prentice Hall.

Schumpeter, Joseph A. 1975. *Capitalism, Socialism and Democracy*. New York: HarperCollins.

Skowronek, Stephen. 1997. *The Politics Presidents Make: Leadership from John Adams to Bill Clinton*. Cambridge, MA: Belknap.

U.S. Department of Education. 2007. Secretary Spellings Delivers Keynote Address at NAACP 7th Biennial Daisy Bates Education Summit. May 19. http://www.ed.gov/news/ pressreleases/2007/05/05192007.html (Accessed March 2, 2008).

Winston, David. 2003. Telephone interview with Patrick J. McGuinn, May 9.

CHAPTER 10

The Politics of Economic Policy in a Polarized Era

The Case of George W. Bush

JEFFREY E. COHEN AND COSTAS PANAGOPOULOS

IN THE WANING DAYS of his presidency, George W. Bush's economic legacy appeared to be in tatters. The credit market freeze of 2008 shocked an already weak economy, leading to a deep and perhaps long recession. As Bush's job approval ratings sunk to 25 percent in the October 2008 Gallup Poll, among the lowest on record, many likened the president to Herbert Hoover as fears of depression mounted. A search of the Lexis-Nexis database for October 2008 found 1,955 U.S. newspaper articles that used the term "depression" in reporting on the economy. Another 240 mentioned Hoover and Bush in the same article. In a late October 2008 Pew Poll, 20 percent of Americans said the nation was in depression and 63 percent, in recession. The economy at the end of his term will surely cast a large shadow on Bush's economy legacy, at least until we understand better the sources and severity of the recession, the contribution of Bush's policies to it, and whether the administration's actions in fall 2008 helped the economy toward recovery.

In this chapter, we examine the larger picture of the economy under Bush, not merely this last act, which reveals several important themes and lessons about presidential policy leadership in an age of polarization. To set the stage, it helps to identify three economic periods during Bush's term. The first period lasted from the time Bush assumed office through 9/11 and into early 2002. The technology bubble had burst, and the nation dipped into a short and mild recession. For the next six years, the second period, the economy slowly recovered, until the summer of 2007 to the end of Bush's second term, the third period, when it appeared headed into a deep recession. Bush's economic policy accomplishments group into these periods, with some major enactments in the first period then not much until fall 2008, when crisis forced action that may ultimately prove to be innovative and far-reaching. Overall, the public barely credited Bush for good times but blamed him for bad times throughout his tenure. This is the ultimate puzzle that we address in this chapter: it tells us much about presidents and economic policy in the current era. We briefly review Bush's policy accomplishments and the economy's performance, turning in the last section to our puzzle.

BUSH'S ECONOMIC POLICIES AND ACCOMPLISHMENTS

Early indications suggested Bush would pursue an aggressive economic policy agenda, and that congressional Republicans would help deliver this to the White House. During his first term, Bush pushed a series of tax cut legislation through Congress, including the Economic Growth and Tax Relief Reconciliation Act of 2001, the Job Creation and Worker Assistance Act of 2002, and the Jobs and Growth Tax Relief Reconciliation Act of 2003. These policies were designed to decrease tax rates across the board, reduce the capital gains tax, increase the child tax credit, and eliminate the so-called marriage penalty, but Congress refused to make these cuts permanent, and they were set to expire in 2011.

Following these initial triumphs, congressional attention to Bush's economic policy priorities waned. Relying on presidential State of the Union addresses to identify priorities and major requests to Congress for past administrations (Light 1999; Cohen 1997) and using our own like calculations for the Bush administration, we observe that Bush's economic policy requests were few in number but tended toward high ambition.[1] In eight addresses, Bush submitted thirty-two economic policy proposals, but many were repeats because Congress had failed to enact them. For instance, the president asked to make the 2001 tax cuts permanent five times, for personal savings accounts six times each, and for earmark reform thrice. Eliminating repeats reduces the number of proposals to nineteen. Yet, Bush's economic policy goals were ambitious, especially his tax cuts if made permanent, and the personal savings account part of his Social Security reforms, both of which would restructure relations between government and society.

Congress ultimately extended and accelerated the 2001 tax cuts as part of a stimulus package for the economy in 2003 and delivered fast-track trade authority renewal to Bush (although the president had to sign on to provide support for trade-related dislocated workers). Bush also signed trade pacts with several nations but failed in his efforts to get a Central American Free Trade Agreement (CAFTA) similar to NAFTA.

Another cornerstone of the Bush administration's policies starting early in his first term was home-ownership expansion, a priority which some analysts believe had contributed to the economic disasters that ensued (Becker et al. 2008). Still, there was impressive growth in home ownership, especially for minorities and lower-income Americans who previously could not afford to own homes. The home-ownership rate soared to a high of 69.3 percent in the second quarter of 2004 but had dropped to pre-Bush levels by the end of 2008. As concerns about the implications of this growth were voiced in the administration, Bush proposed to create an agency to oversee Fannie Mae and Freddie Mac, but the bill faced strong opposition by Democrats in Congress and it was eventually abandoned. Critics believe that the White House also ignored other crucial economic warning signs related to Bush's home-ownership initiatives (Becker et al. 2008), since the administration continued to pursue home-ownership expansion in the face of these warning signs. Overall, little else was accomplished in terms of economic policy during the Bush years until 2008, when the economy edged toward collapse. The next section describes the trends in economic performance, followed by a discussion of the policy response to the crisis of fall 2008.

ECONOMIC PERFORMANCE DURING THE BUSH YEARS

Economic performance generally tells a bright story. After the economic downturn in 2001, the economy improved for the next five years until the mortgage and credit crisis and economic downturn of 2007–2009.

Macroeconomic Trends

We categorize the economy during the Bush years into three periods: (1) recession (March–November 2001); (2) recovery; and (3) economic downturn (summer 2007 into 2008). Unemployment rates provide a useful metric for tracing the health of the economy. Unemployment's high mark for Bush was lower than the peak for Clinton: 7.3 percent in January 1993, Clinton's first month in office, versus 6.3 percent in June 2003. Generally, unemployment, a lagging indicator, tends to rise for a time after a recession has begun to abate. Unemployment under Bush never fell as low as it did during the Clinton years. For Clinton, unemployment dipped to 3.9 percent in December 2000, fully 3.4 points lower than its highest mark under Clinton. For Bush, unemployment hit its low mark in January 2006 at 4.7 percent, only 1.6 points lower than its peak, at about half the rate of decline of the Clinton years. This relatively anemic unemployment performance in comparison to Clinton's led many to term the economy under Bush the "jobless recovery" ("Another Bush, Another Jobless Recovery" 2003, 43).

Inflation is another major macroeconomic marker with political implications. Across the Clinton years, excluding January 1993, the average annual rate of inflation was 2.5 percent. Inflation under Bush, from February 2001 through January 2008, was comparable at 2.7 percent but was more volatile for Bush than Clinton and started rising in September 2007. By June 2008, the annual inflation rate ran in the 4–5 percent range. Steep increases in oil prices played a role in stimulating inflation, while the combination of rising inflation and unemployment fueled fears of stagflation.

Economic growth, a third indicator with political implications, also reveals modest gains compared to the Clinton years. From 2001 through 2006, the economy grew at an average rate of 2.4 percent, with 2004 registering the highest annual growth rate of 3.6 percent. From 1960 to 2000, growth averaged 3.5 percent, about one point faster than during the Bush years. While long-term and cyclical factors may affect overall growth rates, on this count, like unemployment, the Bush record fares poorly compared to Clinton's. Still, Bush can claim that the economy improved under his watch, at least until the downturn in 2008.

Budget Deficits

Although not an economic indicator, the budget can have profound implications for the economy. From the surpluses amassed during the latter years of the Clinton presidency, and despite Bush's small government philosophy and a Republican control of Congress, deficits ballooned under Bush. Several factors account for the rise in deficits under Bush, including his tax cuts, modest economic growth, the wars in Afghanistan and Iraq, and the war on terror in general. After a high point in fiscal year 2004, the deficit began to contract through 2007, which was mostly a function of economic growth. Yet with the downturn of 2007–2008, projections in late 2008 predicted deficit growth into 2009 to hit over $400 billion or about 15 percent of total revenues. As the recession deepened, the Congressional Budget Office announced in January 2009 that the federal budget deficit was projected to surpass an unprecedented $1.2 trillion in 2009 (Montgomery 2009). In the aggregate, these predictions would match the levels of 2004, but at 15 percent they would be less severe than the nearly 22 percent registered in 2004 or the even deeper levels of the early 1990s. Far from being a budget balancer, Bush, like his model Ronald Reagan, presided over large deficits.

Economic Crisis

In late summer 2007, economic crisis hit the United States. It began with home mortgages, spread into credit markets, and then undermined the U.S. and global economies. Only when the crisis spread from mortgage-defaulting home owners to the financial system did the administration become energized, but the lead administration actor was Treasury secretary Henry Paulson, not the president.

The economy began its tumble as the rate of defaults on mortgages, especially subprime mortgages, began to rise. Subprime mortgages, invented in the mid-2000s, allowed financial companies to sell mortgages to people with fewer assets and lower credit ratings than had been the historic practice. Customers for these new types of mortgages presented a higher risk of default than more creditworthy, traditional borrowers. Financial markets thought they could reduce the risk of lending by bundling subprime mortgages with more secure mortgages into large packages. With such instruments they could entice investors with relatively high rates of return but presumably modest risk; the money from such investors was then used to underwrite new mortgages, leading to a large expansion of home ownership in the 2000s, especially to those whose financial standing would have precluded them from doing so in the past.

Consumers found it easy to obtain mortgages, and investors liked the high rates of return.

But default rates among subprime holders rose higher than expected by mid-2007, and the value of the financing instruments sold to investors plummeted. Many investors in these new instruments purchased their positions on margin, with borrowed money. The specter of huge losses led their lenders to call in the loans, and new investors willing to invest could not be found. Capital investment in the economy essentially froze up. Thus, subprime mortgage defaults spread across the entire financial system, leading to a loss of confidence. Money that could have been used for loans had to be kept on hand by banks to shore up financial shakiness and restore Wall Street's confidence in them. Lending nearly came to a halt, threatening the health of the wider economy, and fears of recession deepened.

Initially, both the administration and the Federal Reserve Board stumbled, acting neither swiftly nor decisively. Finally, in early-mid-2008, the Fed took charge with some bold and inventive policy initiatives, such as opening the discount window to investment banks and orchestrating and underwriting the J. P. Morgan Chase acquisition of Bear Stearns. In contrast, there was little early activity from the Bush administration other than to support Fed actions and to secure from Congress a modest stimulus package that gave tax rebates of $300–600 to most households as well as tax breaks to small businesses.

Furthermore, it was far from clear that fiscal action would solve the credit problem, which was essentially one of lack of confidence in credit markets. The panic resulting from the Bear Stearns implosion impelled Washington policymakers to further and broader action. By late July 2008, after much wrangling, Congress enacted a large-scale reform, the Money Service Business Act of 2008. The act provided funds to help some mortgagees nearing default, as well as financial support for two important government companies in the mortgage sector, Freddie Mac and Fannie Mae, which the markets feared were headed for bankruptcy. Freddie Mac and Fannie Mae provided most of the money for prime mortgages, that is, traditional, creditworthy mortgages. Their collapse could have had potentially catastrophic implications for the economy in general. Yet, the president hardly played a role in the passage of these provisions other than by withdrawing a veto threat aimed at the large sums budgeted toward mortgagees.

Crisis deepened in September and October 2008. Events moved swiftly, and government policymakers, primarily Treasury secretary Paulson and Fed chair Ben Bernanke, seemed to lurch from crisis to crisis, as no action they took seemed to prove systemically effective. Despite the Money Service Business Act, the government took over Fannie Mae and Freddie Mac on September 7, since both appeared heading into bankruptcy. By the next weekend, another venerable investment bank, Lehman Brothers, also headed toward failure. Despite government efforts, no buyer could be found, and Lehman failed on September 12.

Lehman's failure precipitated panic as investors felt unable to predict which companies the government would support, or "bail out". This uncertainty undermined three major financial companies in swift succession. The nation's largest investment and brokerage house, Merrill Lynch, sold itself to Bank of America. The federal government took over insurance giant AIG on September 16 and orchestrated J. P. Morgan Chase's acquisition of Washington Mutual on September 25. Wells Fargo purchased Wachovia in early October, and, fearing their possible demise, the last two large investment banks, Goldman Sachs and Morgan Stanley, decided to become bank holding companies. The American financial system underwent one of its most massive restructurings in history, creating a handful of massive banks and killing off the major stand-alone investment banks.

Wall Street panicked with steep market declines and a frozen credit market. Paulson and Bernanke proposed a $700 billion bailout program, announced on September 18, in which the government would buy what became known as toxic assets, that is, mortgage back securities, whose value no one could estimate. The public reacted negatively to the program, which many viewed as a bailout for Wall Street that provided no help for average Americans. Congress, Paulson, and Bernanke wrangled and negotiated over the details, but on September 29 the House defeated the plan by a vote of 228–205, with conservatives in the Republican Party and liberals in the Democratic Party opposing the plan. Stocks dived 9 percent in one day on news of the defeat in one of the worst days for the markets in history.

Congress and Paulson-Bernanke renegotiated, and supporters of the package used the stock plunge to demonstrate to voters the consequences of not taking action. President Bush began to speak publicly in hopes of calming the markets and steering the public to support a government rescue effort, but it is not clear that Bush's comments mattered much as markets continued to plunge. After initial setbacks, Congress finally passed a plan, with the Senate acting on October 1, by a 64–25 margin. On October 3, the House passed the Troubled Asset Relief Program (TARP) by a vote of 263–171. TARP still included the $700 billion provision but with greater congressional oversight of the powers given to the Treasury and more transparency. Passage of TARP did not soothe the markets: from October 3, the day of passage, until October 10 the markets dropped 18 percent, the most precipitous one-week decline in U.S. history.

The market declines and fears spread globally, precipitating European governments to action. The U.K. government partially nationalized British banks, and other European powers pledged to follow the British lead. Combined, the European Union nations would pump over $2 trillion into their economies and financial systems. As the end of the Bush administration approached, markets remained volatile and at depressed prices, unemployment spiked upward, and deep recession was a near certainty, leading to calls for a massive stimulus package. We note that Bush's successor, Democratic President Barack Obama, signed into law a $787 billion economic stimulus package on February 17, 2009.

As the administration rolled out the TARP money in November 2008, it decided to recapitalize banks rather than purchase toxic assets, in hopes of restoring confidence in the banks and help them resume lending. Then, in November 2008, the Big Three American auto companies, General Motors, Chrysler, and Ford came to Congress, requesting financial support lest they go bankrupt. After spirited congressional hearings with the auto executives, Republicans in Congress refused to sign on to an agreement brokered by the administration with the auto companies, the United Auto Workers, and congressional Democrats, and the bailout bill died. On December 19, President Bush, fearing massive job losses to an already faltering jobs market if the automakers went bankrupt, agreed to use some of the TARP money as a temporary financial bridge for the auto companies until the Obama administration took office.

The actions in fall and early winter 2008 represent a level of government intervention into the economy unseen for a generation. They also represent a stark departure from the Bush administration's deregulatory thrust. History may give Bush high marks for handling the credit crisis, but the administration seemingly reacted to the crisis in ad hoc fashion, not pursuing a grand economic vision rooted in strategic policy beliefs. Moreover, Secretary Paulson and Fed chair Bernanke provided most of the policy leadership; George Bush played essentially a supporting and secondary role and may not ultimately receive much personal credit for these policy moves. The public repudiation of the Bush administration, and Republicans generally, was palpable during the 2008 presidential election. The 2008 national exit polls indicate that the economy was far and away the chief concern for voters. Fully 85 percent of voters indicated they were worried about economic conditions and 54 percent of these voters chose Democrat Barack Obama over the Republican candidate John McCain.

PUBLIC OPINION AND ECONOMIC PERFORMANCE

We turn our attention to public perceptions about the economy and actual economic performance during the Bush years. We note a period of economic recovery between 2002 and 2006, but we argue that the public largely failed to credit Bush for the improved economic conditions. Rather, as the economy improved, Bush's poll ratings fell. How can we account for a president with few economic policy accomplishments, a relatively strong macroeconomy for most of his tenure, and low poll ratings? At least three factors conditioned the public reaction to the economy during Bush's tenure. First, the general economic improvement did not fall evenly across the population, and economic inequality, which had been rising for decades, increased during the Bush years, fostering a sense of economic insecurity for many. Second, international affairs trumped economics as the most important consideration in the public's evaluation of the president, and discontent with the war in Iraq spilled over to affect public assessments of Bush's presidency in general and across most policy areas, including economic issues. Third, partisan polarization meant that Democrats would give Bush little credit for anything good. And even some Republicans would grow weary of the Iraq War and frustrated with the weak economy of 2007–2008, withdrawing their support for Bush and further depressing his ratings.

For most of the Bush years, the economy improved, if not at the rates of the Clinton years. The public, however, did not seem to have credited Bush with the economic improvement of 2002–2007. Instead, public assessments of Bush's economic leadership, as well as its assessment of the state of the economy, ran in the opposite direction. Figure 10.1 plots economic approval and unemployment across the Bush years.[2] Contrary to existing research, we find a positive correlation of .2 (p = .08) between unemployment and economic approval from February 2001 through October 2008. However, the expected negative relationship emerges in 2007 as the economy began to slide. From January 2007 through October 2008, unemployment and economic approval correlate at –.95 (p = .000), which is strong given that only sixteen time points are under consideration. Why for so much of Bush's tenure did his economic approval ratings decline as

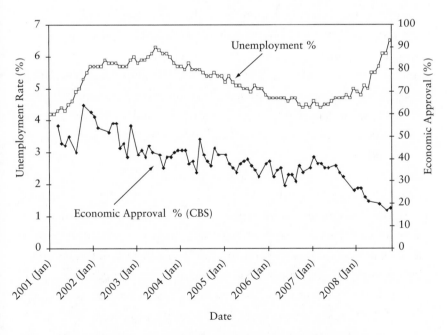

FIGURE 10.1. *Trends in Unemployment and Economic Approval, January 2001–October 2008, monthly.*

SOURCES: Unemployment (Bureau of Labor Statistics); economic approval (CBS–New York Times).

unemployment fell, the opposite of what we would expect and contrary to decades of research?

First, the public may have credited Alan Greenspan, the chair of the Federal Reserve Board, for the economy, not Bush. This assumes that the public understands the role that the president and the Fed play in economic policy making, a dubious assumption. Rather, we argue that three factors account for the relatively poor economic marks the public gave Bush: increasing economic inequality, partisan polarization, and the unpopular war in Iraq. Cumulatively, these factors would erect high barriers to the public crediting Bush with the economic improvements of 2002–2007; in fact, many citizens would fail to see 2002–2007 as a period of economic betterment. Even if the objective indicators suggested an improving economy, public perceptions of "tactical competence" on economic matters tell a different story.

While no major scandal plagued George W. Bush, unlike his predecessor, controversies abounded during Bush's presidency, many of which revolved around economic matters. Bush's ties to "big business" and to certain sectors of the economy—the oil industry, in particular—called into question the president's trustworthiness and integrity with regard to economic policy. Adding to public misgivings about the Bush's economic policy was that his rhetoric did not always match reality, especially with regard to growing economic inequality; the war in Iraq and partisan polarization also raised questions about his competence.

Increasing Economic Inequality

Economic inequality has been on the rise for the last twenty-five to thirty years (Piketty and Saez 2003; Bartels 2008). Using income-tax return data, economists Piketty and Saez estimate that the top 10 percent in terms of total income in 2005 owned approximately 44.4 percent of total income.[3] In contrast, that same top 10 percent held only 32.6 percent thirty years ago, in 1975; the concentration of wealth in the 1990s and 2000s rivals that of the 1920s, another period known for its inequality.

A host of factors may have contributed to this trend, including government policies, economic globalization, the restructuring of the U.S. economy, and the decline of labor unions (Piketty and Saez 2003). We cannot sort out this debate here. Although we do not have data yet for Bush's full two terms, the trend of increasing economic inequality continued from 2001 through 2005. In 2001, the top 10 percent owned 42.2 percent of total income, growing to 44.4 percent by 2005, although the rate of increasing inequality in the Bush years seemed slightly slower than during his father's or Clinton's terms.

This widening income-wealth gap has led to distinct perceptions of economic growth across income classes. We use the September 2007 NBC News–*Wall Street Journal* Poll to compare the economic perceptions of those in different income categories. The poll asked respondents, "I'd like you to rate economic conditions in America using a ten-point scale, on which a one means economic conditions are very bad, and a ten means economic conditions are very good. You may use any number from one to ten, depending on how you feel. Using this ten-point scale, how would you rate economic conditions in America today?" The results are clear. Except for those in the lowest income category (due to small sample sizes), positive perceptions of the economy rose with income levels. Only 17.7 percent in the $10,000–20,000 income range gave the economy positive marks, but 42.1 percent in the highest category, over $100,000, rated the economy as good. Rather than judging the economy as a whole, this finding suggests that people are considering only their own economic situation (a personal versus a sociotropic perspective), although the posed question clearly asks people to think about the national economy. Income differences also affect evaluations of Bush's handling of the economy. Whereas 71.5 percent in the lowest income group disapproved of Bush's handling of the economy in the same poll, in the highest income group only 58.7 percent rated him poorly—a 13 percentage point difference.

Party Polarization

Like income, partisanship colors public perceptions of the economy and Bush's handing of the economy. Simply put, Democrats were loath to credit Bush with any improvement in the economy, just as Republicans would defend him, no matter the true state of the economy. Democrats also perceived the economy to be in poor shape, and Republicans, in good shape, no matter the economy's actual condition. Again, the above poll illustrates this point. While approximately nine of ten Democrats disapproved of Bush's handling of the economy, nearly by the same margin Republicans approved—a striking difference. Just as partisanship colors public evaluations of the president, it colors evaluations of the economy. Where Republicans see a strong economy, Democrats see a poor one. Turning to the 10–point economic perception question, strong Democrats gave the economy a 4.5 rating, compared to 6.7 for strong Republicans, with Independents at 5.2, closer to the Democrats than the Republicans.

If Democrats and Republicans live in the same national economy, why should there be such large divergence in their economic perceptions? (Kramer 1983; Erikson 2004). Apparently, the actual state of the economy may have little to do with perceptions of the economy across individuals at any one point in time. Rather, people project their partisanship onto their evaluation of the economy. When people see such a different economy merely as a function of their partisanship, it is little wonder that objective economic performance barely affects attitudes about Bush and his economic leadership. For Republicans, this leads to rose-colored glasses; for Democrats, the tint has a darker hue. Thus, we cannot claim that economic assessments are realistic. They are, however, politically consequential.

The Iraq War

Finally, attitudes toward the Iraq War also strongly affect people's assessment of Bush's economic policies and the state of the economy.[4] Those who objected to the war or thought the policy a failure gave Bush poor marks, while viewing the economy as much weaker than those who supported the war. This depressed Bush's ratings since the heavy plurality disapproved of the war and Bush's war policies. But while the public linked the war to assessments of economic performance and Bush's economic leadership, it is not clear that the war substantially affected the economy.

Again the above poll is instructive. Fully 82 percent of respondents had consistent (approve-approve or disapprove-disapprove) answers to the war and Bush's economic-handling questions.[5] Respondent assessments of Bush's handling of the Iraq situation also affected perceptions of the state of the economy. On average, those who disapproved of Bush's handling of Iraq gave the economy a score of 4.7 on the 10–point economic percep-

tions scale, while those who approved rated the economy at 6.6.[6] Those
who disapproved of Iraq leaned toward seeing the economy in bad shape,
while those who approved leaned toward seeing it in good shape.

The Combined Impact of Class, Party, and War

Attitudes toward the Iraq War are intertwined with partisanship and approval of Bush in general. Gary Jacobson (2007a, 2007b) demonstrates
that as the war progressed, attitudes on it polarized, adding to the polarization in American politics and public opinion. Consequently, Bush became one of the most polarizing figures in recent American history. Thus,
the linkage between attitudes on Iraq and Bush's handling of the economy,
as well as assessments of the economy noted above, may be spurious. We
argue that this is not the case.

Using the above poll, we estimate two empirical models to explain
Bush's economic approval and respondents' assessments of the economy.
We expect economic approval to be a function of *economic perceptions,
approval of the war in Iraq, income, party identification,* and *ideology,*
while we expect economic assessments (measured using the 10-point scale)
to be a function of *approval of the war in Iraq, income, party identification,* and *ideology.*[7] Table 10.1 presents the results. Since the economic
approval question is dichotomous, probit is used. Regression is used for
the economic assessment equation.

With controls, attitudes about Iraq show a strong impact on Bush's
economic approval and on assessments of the economy. As probit estimates are not intuitive, we convert them to probabilities to get a sense
of the impact of Iraq War opinion on economic approval. War-approvers
have .43 higher probability of approving Bush's handling of the economy
than war-disapprovers, a whopping amount, considering the application
of controls and that all the control variables are also statistically significant.[8] Opinion about the economy tells a similar story. With controls for
partisanship, ideological identification, and income, war-approvers rate the
economy 1.19 steps better on the 10-point scale than war-disapprovers.[9]
Iraq War opinion strongly influences attitudes about Bush's handling of
the economy and perceptions of the economy. It is far from clear that the
war had any major implications for the economy. Still, the public linked

TABLE 10.1.

Impact of Iraq War Approval on Economic Approval and Economic Perceptions

Variable	Model 1: Economic Approval (Probit)					Model 2: Economic Perceptions (OLS)			
	b	SE	T	p^*	Impact**	b	SE	T	p^*
Iraq Approval	1.15	.14	8.00	.00	.43	1.19	.18	6.45	.000
Economic Perceptions	.30	.04	8.05	.000	.11	N/A			
Income	.05	.04	1.42	.07	.02	.07	.04	1.79	.03
Republican	.84	.15	5.72	.000	.31	.67	.18	3.70	.000
Ideology	.21	.06	3.50	.000	.08	.11	.08	1.40	.08
Constant	−3.49	.46	−7.55	.000		3.96	.47	8.50	.000
N /(Pseudo)R^2	726	.48				756	.21		

SOURCE: September 2007 NBC–*Wall Street Journal* Poll

NOTES: Robust standard errors in parentheses. Models include controls for additional demographic (age, gender, race) and socioeconomic (education) characteristics (not shown).

*One-tailed tests. ** Probability impact given a one-unit change in the independent variable.

Question Wording

Iraq Approval: In general, do you approve or disapprove of the job that George W. Bush is doing in handling the situation in Iraq?

Economic Approval: Do you generally approve or disapprove of the job that George W. Bush is doing in handling the economy?

Overall Approval: In general, do you approve or disapprove of the job that George W. Bush is doing as president?

Economic Perceptions: I'd like you to rate economic conditions in America using a ten-point scale, on which a one means economic conditions are very bad, and a ten means economic conditions are very good. You may use any number from one to ten, depending on how you feel. Using this ten-point scale, how would you rate economic conditions in America today?

Party Identification: Generally speaking, do you think of yourself as a Democrat, a Republican, an independent, or something else? [If Democrat or Republican, ask: "Would you call yourself a strong (Democrat/Republican) or not a very strong (Democrat/Republican)?" If Independent, ask: "Do you think of yourself as closer to the Republican Party, closer to the Democratic Party, or do you think of yourself as strictly independent?"]

Ideology: Thinking about your general approach to issues, do you consider yourself to be liberal, moderate, or conservative? [If Liberal or Conservative, ask: "Do you consider yourself to be very (liberal/conservative) or somewhat (liberal/conservative)?"]

Income: If you added together the yearly income of all the members of your family who were living at home last year, would the total be less than ten thousand dollars (1), between ten thousand dollars and twenty thousand dollars (2), between twenty thousand dollars and thirty thousand dollars (3), between thirty thousand dollars and forty thousand dollars (4), between forty thousand dollars and fifty thousand dollars (5), between fifty thousand dollars and seventy-five thousand dollars (6), between seventy-five thousand dollars and one hundred thousand dollars (7), or would the total be more than that (8)? [Numbers in parentheses are the codes for each income level.]

the war to assessments of Bush's economic leadership and the state of the economy. As the war prolonged and the public's disenchantment with it rose, Bush's economic poll ratings and assessments of the economy fell, despite the economy's upward trend.

CONCLUSIONS:

LESSONS FROM GEORGE W. BUSH'S EXPERIENCE

George W. Bush's experience offers some lessons about the impact of the economy on the presidency. Politically, public confidence in the economy and evaluations of presidential economic stewardship trump actual economic performance. People see the economy through the lens of personal experience and perceptions. Partisanship and economic class color perceptions of the state of the economy. Although Bush tried to convince the public that his economic policies led to economic improvement on his watch, he seemed unable to breach these perceptual barriers. Many people failed or refused to see any improvement in the economy, although Bush could easily point to certain types of objective economic improvements.

Bush, like Kennedy and Reagan, subscribed to trickle-down economic theory, in which a "rising tide would lift all boats." During Bush's tenure, the rising tide lifted only some boats, those that were already economically privileged, resulting in a widening gap in wealth. When economic growth does not lead to wealth being spread around society but instead remaining concentrated among the rich, the economy converts from a valence issue to a positional issue.

From a valence perspective, everyone likes economic growth because they will to some degree share in the increase in wealth. When viewed from a positional perspective, economic growth is good for some but not for others, and people perceive the president as pursuing the economic interests of some citizens but not others. Thus, many came to view Bush as the president of rich or corporate America, not as president of all the people. Consequently, economic improvement could not be translated into higher approval of the president—too many people did not share in the prosperity. But the danger for the president is that when the economy sours, not only will those who already dislike the president for economic distributional reasons fail to come to his support, but also those who

191

supported him because they prospered under his tenure might withdraw their support as their economic position erodes.

We can extend the general dynamics of economic responses to the president and the economy to other issues and to partisan polarization effects more generally. In fact, the widespread transformation of valence issues into positional ones along the same party lines may define the issue environment of political polarization. Under such conditions, no matter the policy option that a president pursues, it may be viewed as helping one class of citizens but not others, and may actually be viewed in zero-sum terms: helping some may even *harm* others.

Given this polarized environment, presidents naturally are on the lookout for policies that can be treated as valence issues. September 11, 2001, and the war on terror, at least for a period of time, united the nation and gave George Bush a valence issue with little downside. Thus, it is little wonder that Bush shifted his agenda to reflect this issue and that in 2002 and 2004 he and the Republicans more generally used the war on terror as the core of their reelection strategy. Around the margins this strategy proved successful in attracting some Independents and Democrats into the Republican reelection camp. For reelection, Bush and the Republicans did not need many such individuals, just enough for the margin of victory. But this strategy too proved short-lived as the situation in Iraq deteriorated and dragged out.

All in all, using the criteria set forth above—*strategic, political,* and *tactical competence,* and *integrity*—we conclude that the performance of the George W. Bush presidency along these dimensions is rather weak. At the very least, Americans—even Republicans by the end of his tenure— generally perceived weaknesses in Bush's handling of economic matters. By April 2008, according to a poll conducted by ABC News, 70 percent of Americans disapproved of Bush's handling of the economy, including 94 percent of Democrats, 75 percent of Independents, and even 37 percent of Republicans. Ratings in mid-2008 reveal that Bush garnered lower approval on the economy than on Iraq even. Perceptions of shortcomings along each of the dimensions discussed and described above certainly contributed to widespread public sentiment that Bush's performance on the economy was lackluster. And while history may permit *actual* economic performance to trump *perceptions* of economic performance (and thus view George W. Bush more favorably), we judge Bush's economic policies as mediocre at best.

NOTES

1. Bush also rarely used executive orders to make economic policy, issuing 37 from 2001 to 2007, 14 percent of all his executive orders. He also took few positions on economic roll calls, 115 from 2001 to 2007, about 31 percent of all position-taking, but of these, 42 were in 2007 (Ragsdale 2008, 458–59, 498). It is difficult to draw a line distinguishing economic policies because Bush justified many policies—including education, health, and immigration—in part on economic grounds and because all budget discussions involve the economy. We do not include the domestic or budget policies in our tally.

2. The economic approval data come from the CBS–*New York Times* polls and were accessed from the iPoll database of the Roper Center Online on November 15, 2008, http://www.ropercenter.uconn.edu/.

3. Data updated through 2005 can be accessed at http://elsa.berkeley.edu/saez/.

4. For a review of research on the impact of war on public opinion in general and the Iraq War in particular, see Berinsky and Druckman (2007).

5. The relationship is statistically significant and strong, with Kendall's Tau-b = 0.61 and Gamma = .91; both with p values < .001.

6. The difference in means is statistically significant at p < .001.

7. Both models include standard controls for respondents' socioeconomic and demographic characteristics.

8. Without these controls the probability effects of the Iraq War on economic approval is a massive .66.

9. Without the controls the effect is 1.9, p = .001.

REFERENCES

"Another Bush, Another Jobless Recovery." 2003. *Economist*, May 8, p. 43.

Bartels, Larry M. 2008. *Unequal Democracy: The Political Economy of the New Gilded Age*. Princeton, NJ: Princeton University Press.

Becker, Jo, Sheryl Gay Stolberg, and Stephen Labaton. 2008. "White House Philosophy Stoked Mortgage Bonfire." *New York Times*, December 21, p. A1.

Berinsky, Adam J., and James N. Druckman. 2007. "The Polls—Review: Public Opinion Research and Support for the Iraq War." *Public Opinion Quarterly* 71(1): 126–41.

Cohen, Jeffrey E. 1997. *Presidential Responsiveness and Public Policy-Making*. Ann Arbor: University of Michigan Press.

Erikson, Robert S. 2004. "Macro vs. Micro-Level Perspectives on Economic Voting: Is the Micro-Level Evidence Endogenously Induced?" Presented at the 2004 Political Methodology Meetings, Stanford University, Palo Alto, CA.

Jacobson, Gary C. 2007a. *A Divider, Not a Uniter. George W. Bush and the American People*. New York: Longman.

———. 2007b. "The Public, the President, and the War in Iraq." In *The Polarized Presidency of George W. Bush*, ed. George C. Edwards III and Desmond King. New York: Oxford University Press, 245–82.

Kramer, Gerald H. 1983. "The Ecological Fallacy Revisited: Aggregate- Versus Individual-Level Findings on Economics and Elections, and Sociotropic Voting." *American Political Science Review* 77(1): 92–111.

Light, Paul C. 1999. *The President's Agenda*, 3rd ed. Baltimore: Johns Hopkins University Press.

Montgomery, Lori. 2009. "Congress Urges Spending Restraint." *Washington Post*, January 8, p. A2.

Piketty, Thomas, and Emmanuel Saez. 2003. "Income Inequality in the United States, 1913–1998." *Quarterly Journal of Economics* 118(1): 1–39.

Ragsdale, Lyn. 2008. *Vital Statistics on the Presidency*, 2nd ed. Washington, DC: CQ Press.

CHAPTER 11

Hurricane Katrina and the Failure of Homeland Security

ANNE M. KHADEMIAN

MANY ACCOUNTS of the response to Hurricane Katrina in August 2005 place significant blame for the chaos and despair on the shoulders of the Bush administration (Cooper and Block 2006; Schneider 2005; U.S. Congress 2006). As much as the administration's response to the 9/11 terrorist attacks defined the first term of President George W. Bush, the dismal and consequently catastrophic federal response to Hurricane Katrina defined the second term—indeed, it served as a test of the capability of the homeland security policy domain forged in response to the attacks of 9/11, which has been judged by many to be a failure. This chapter examines the Bush administration's tactical competence and strategic competence in homeland security.

Much of the failed response to Katrina had its roots in administration policy and organizational decisions leading up to the formation of the Department of Homeland Security (DHS) and immediately afterward. This affected the capacity of agencies such as the Federal Emergency Management Agency (FEMA), which is responsible for leading emergency response efforts. Nevertheless, judging the Bush administration's success or failure in homeland security primarily by its response to Katrina should be undertaken with several points as context: the scale and power of Katrina, the challenges presented by emergency response across multiple levels of government, increasingly complex public problems, and the success stories that did take place must be considered in assessing the capacity of emergency response as a component of homeland security. The emergent policy area of homeland security has been etched by the Bush administration's response to 9/11, influencing the ways in which government responds to all emergencies or threats to America for years to come.

"THE HURRICANE IN QUESTION
IS STILL CALLED KATRINA"

On August 31, 2008, the eve of the Republican National Convention, Hurricane Gustav roared toward the Gulf Coast. The 2008 Republican nominee for president, John McCain, announced that convention activities would be scaled back so that preparations for the coming storm could take center stage. "We take off our Republican hats," he pronounced from a campaign event shortly after touring the emergency management center in Jackson, Mississippi, "and put on our American hats" (Gomez and Welch 2008). The mandated tone for the convention's opening days was to be somber with the focus on the safety of residents in harm's way. In Washington, President Bush declared a state of emergency for Louisiana and Mississippi, visited the headquarters of FEMA for an update on the preparations, transmitted a brief speech to the Republican National Convention via video conference, and then flew to Texas to meet with evacuees from Gustav and emergency workers and to check on preparations for the storm (Gomez and Welch 2008; Balz 2008). In an internal memorandum to DHS employees on September 1, Secretary Michael Chertoff emphasized his efforts to coordinate with the governors of Louisiana and Mississippi, the mayor of New Orleans, and state and local government officials; the prepositioning of DHS employees and resources from the Coast Guard, Customs and Border Protection, and the Transportation Security Agency; and the dangers posed by the still incomplete reinforcement of levees in New Orleans (Chertoff 2008).

The image of preparedness and focused attention on Hurricane Gustav's landfall was impressive. Yet, as the *Washington Post* reported on September 1, 2008, "the hurricane in question is still called Katrina"— not Gustav (Balz 2008). The canceled convention activities, high-profile visits to emergency management centers, reporting of preparations, and extensive efforts to coordinate were less about the impending storm and more about distancing the administration and the Republican nominee from the disastrous response to Hurricane Katrina three years earlier.

Beyond the political presentation of preparedness lingers the deeper question of *actual* preparedness. Is the federal government more prepared today for a natural disaster, or any disaster on American soil, than it was for Katrina?

The chaos and suffering in the wake of Katrina and the stunted response by the federal government—as well as the Gulf Coast state and local governments—are well known. Evacuation began late and many refused to evacuate or had no means to leave the city. When state and local officials realized the potential of the storm, the response was one of hurry and panic. Components of a response plan promised by FEMA during planning exercises in years preceding the storm were inadequate or nonexistent. As the levees gave way, there was a massive failure of regional communications and little ability to give guidance to those affected, to coordinate the relief efforts, or to get a clear picture of the extent of the catastrophe. Response agencies fell into disarray, including the New Orleans police force, which suffered abandonment of duty by officers in the middle of spontaneous street violence. Confusion reigned over supervision of the Superdome (a state-owned building) and the role of New Orleans police officers versus state troopers in maintaining order. Questions about the authority and roles of the Principal Federal Official (PFO) and the Federal Coordinating Officer (FCO) added to the confusion over chain of command. Emergency agencies at every level did not have the information or authority to respond effectively or quickly, in part since wireless and land communications had been destroyed by the hurricane. Thousands camped on rooftops, lingered in the claustrophobic Superdome, or waited anxiously in one of Louisiana's 113 state shelters, which were bursting at the seams (Senate Committee on Homeland Security and Governmental Affairs 2006; Cooper and Block 2006; Wise 2006; Menzel 2006).

In the wake of the storm, critics focused on a variety of failures in communication between the federal, state, and local governments, failures in preparation, and perhaps most critically, failure by the administration and its appointed leaders to take preemptive action. Indeed, the passive response of Mike Brown as director of FEMA[1] and Michael Chertoff as secretary of DHS reflected their lack of emergency management experience.

As reported by the Select Bipartisan Committee of the House of Representatives (U.S. Congress 2006) in the report *Failure of Initiative,*

passivity did the most damage. The failure of initiative cost lives, prolonged suffering, and left all Americans justifiably concerned our government is no better prepared to protect its people than it was before 9/11 [359].

In an effort to evaluate homeland security during the second Bush term, we turn first to a discussion of tactical competence as it relates to emergency response leading up to Hurricane Katrina.

TACTICAL COMPETENCE AND EMERGENCY RESPONSE

Tactical competence, as the volume's editors indicate, refers to a president's rational decision-making capability, the coherence of decisions within a policy domain, and an administration's ability to handle the basic duties of the government. Several components of the Bush administration's efforts to manage the policy domain of homeland security relate directly to the capacities for emergency response: (1) the clarity of the homeland security mission, (2) the emphasis on scaling back and privatizing federal emergency management efforts, and (3) the hierarchical approach to organizing for homeland security. Taken together, these components illustrate a diminished capacity for conducting emergency response.

Defining a Mission for DHS

At the core of tactical competence is the basic question, "competence for what?" In order to examine how well a president and an administration manage the fundamental duties of any given policy domain, we need a basic understanding of the president's definition of that domain and its policy goals. *Homeland security* was not a common term before 2001[2] but has since become the defining term of the Bush administration's domestic response to the attacks on September 11, 2001. The term represents the government's efforts, on the one hand, to prevent, deter, and respond to internal and external threats to the territory of the United States and, on the other hand, to prepare for and respond to accidents and hazards. However, finding the appropriate strategic balance between the two is at the heart of the question, "competence for what?"

The executive branch agencies and offices that today compose the domain of homeland security were in large part in place but spread across the government prior to the creation of the DHS as the fifteenth cabinet department in 2003.[3] The Coast Guard, the Secret Service, the Federal Protective Service, Customs, FEMA, and many other long-established organizations had coordinated with state and local government officials for emergencies, the safety of government officials and government buildings, enforcing immigration laws, providing for victims of disasters, protecting the nation's borders and coastlines, and facilitating commerce in and out of the United States. Bringing these entities together under one roof required a common focus or point of organization that could unite the new department. The "all hazards" doctrine articulated and advocated in large part by FEMA since the 1990s provided an obvious focus. Rather than focus on planning and preparation for different types of emergencies—from hurricanes and tornadoes to toxic chemical spills, fires, or terrorist attacks—emergency professionals focused on the *functions* of emergency management: *mitigation* (reducing the impact of future disasters), *preparedness* (training, technical assistance, and exercises), and *response and recovery* (immediate action upon a disaster, followed by restoration of the community). States and communities gradually moved toward this all-hazards approach with the support, cajoling, and grant guidance from FEMA under the Clinton administration, which was particularly evident in the emphasis on mitigation programs in all states. FEMA's efforts to establish uniform standards of all-hazards emergency management capabilities provided state governments with a means to benchmark their progress and to identify the gaps in emergency preparedness (Canada 2003).

The umbrella of homeland security prioritized terrorist attacks as the primary disaster requiring federal, state, and local attention. It gave new emphasis to the prevention of terrorist attacks. In a 2005 assessment of the grant distribution process in DHS, the Government Accountability Office (GAO) noted similarities between the capabilities needed by first responders for disasters and acts of terror. The *difference* in capabilities between dealing with natural or accidental disasters and acts of terror are found primarily in prevention. Intelligence gathering, investigation, apprehension, and counterterrorism are capabilities required for preventing terrorist attacks.

While mitigation efforts can minimize the damage or lessen the likelihood of an accident, prevention capabilities do not apply to natural or accidental disasters. As the key federal department responsible for ensuring that police, fire, emergency medical, and public health personnel are capable and readily coordinated to respond to large-scale crises, DHS embraced the all-hazards language and the concept of shared or overlapping capacities articulated by the GAO. However, DHS emphasized prevention capabilities and specialized preparation, response, and recovery for a terrorist attack in its grant-giving to state and local governments over the past five years (U.S. Government Accountability Office 2005; McCarter 2008). States and localities complain that the emphasis on international threats of terror skews the formula used for allocating money toward preventing terrorist attacks, in particular, and away from more dual-use equipment and training opportunities that are applicable to natural hazards as well as terrorism (U.S. Government Accountability Office 2005; McCarter 2008).

The "all hazards" doctrine is a comfortable conceptual fit with the multiple missions of DHS agencies and the role of DHS in facilitating the preparedness and coordination of state and local governments in the event of large-scale disasters. Yet, in practice, the primary emphasis in the missions of individual agencies now located within DHS and in the distribution of funds to states, metropolitan regions, and local governments has favored preventing and responding to terrorism. Out of $1.6 billion in grants allocated in fiscal year 2007, more than $1.1 billion went to the Urban Area Security Initiative, the State Homeland Security Program, and the Law Enforcement Terrorism Prevention Program. In contrast, $46 million was spent on Citizen Corps and the Metropolitan Medical Response System, both aimed at emergency management more generally (U.S. Department of Homeland Security 2007). There was consistency on the part of the Bush administration in funding the prevention and preparation for terrorism, as well as funding specialized equipment designed for responding to particular terrorist attacks. The difficulty was the thrust away from funding and encouraging training, equipment purchases, and planning activities that support an all-hazards balance which gives attention to emergency management capabilities. From fiscal 2001 to 2005, in the crucial years prior to Katrina, DHS grant-funding focused on terrorism exceeded funding for all hazards three to one (U.S. Government Accountability Office 2005, 38), while key FEMA mitigation programs created under the Clinton administration, such as Project Impact,[4] were cancelled (Elliston 2004).

In their comprehensive study of Hurricane Katrina and the federal government's response, Cooper and Block (2006) relate the story of five state emergency managers going to Washington, D.C., to meet with the deputy secretary for Homeland Security, Michael Jackson. "In plain language," they write, "the group told Jackson that the Department of Homeland Security's obsession with terrorist attacks had undermined the nation's readiness for natural disasters" (xiii). The group's warning was dismissed by Jackson only days before Hurricane Katrina hit ground.

Privatizing Emergency Response

Emergency response capabilities at the federal, state, and local levels were further strained by the initial effort of the Bush administration to minimize the role of the federal government in disaster relief. In testimony before Congress in 2001, the newly appointed FEMA director, Joseph Allbaugh, noted that the "original intent" of federal disaster assistance had shifted from a "supplement to State and local response efforts" to an "oversized entitlement program and a disincentive to effective State and local risk management" (Allbaugh 2001). Allbaugh viewed state and local governments as having the primary responsibility for emergency response, with expectations for "faith based organizations" and other nonprofit organizations to play a more prominent role in disaster relief (Allbaugh 2001; Schneider 2005).

When FEMA was moved to DHS in 2003, funding for the agency and its multiple grant programs aimed at training and enhancing first responder capability and emergency management skills was slashed, with resources transferred to other agencies focused on terrorism and weapons of mass destruction (Khademian 2004). Other organizations transferred into DHS met a similar fate. Consider the Federal Protective Service (FPS), a small agency that provides security for federal buildings, run by the Government Services Administration (GSA). FPS was relocated from GSA to DHS in 2003 and also suffered a 20 percent reduction in the number of full-time professional police officers, agents, and inspectors. In response to Hurricane Katrina, the agency placed thirty agents in New Orleans with instructions to "secure the federal buildings, patrol the city, and report up the chain of command" (Cooper and Block 2006, 175). The agency turned to contract employees to take on protection of disaster response centers, disaster medical assistance teams, and the New Orleans and Louisiana field offices of FEMA—responsibilities the agency did not have the resources or personnel to cover (Special Inspector General . . . , 2006). Reports of intimidation and excessive force exercised by employees of the contractor Blackwater (Scahill 2005, 2006) illustrate the downside of reducing the government's own emergency management capacity. Experienced in security work in insurgent-threatened Iraq, the skills of Blackwater employees were not the best fit (Scahill 2005, 2006).

After leaving FEMA in 2003, Joe Allbaugh and others with previous experience as the Bush administration's appointees served as consultants of companies ready to provide emergency management capacity in the wake of Hurricane Katrina (Reed et al. 2006). While relying on private companies for emergency management capacity, however, FEMA lacked capacity to oversee and manage the massive contracting effort (U.S. Congress 2006, 330–32). The Select Bipartisan Committee of the House of Representatives found that "FEMA suffered from a lack of sufficiently trained procurement professionals" (332). Only thirty-three out of fifty-five procurement slots in FEMA were filled at the time of Katrina, and officials interviewed for the select committee report noted that, at a minimum, the agency should have 172 procurement professionals. So, an effort to reduce federal emergency management capacity was not met with an increase in procurement capacity for overseeing the work by contracting companies. More generally, FEMA was not able to overcome state and local failings by taking a lead role in responding to Katrina. Asking states to exercise more emergency management responsibility, as the Bush administration did, is one thing; being able to compensate for state and local inadequacy, as in the case of New Orleans and the State of Louisiana, is a capacity FEMA was not able to provide in 2005.

Hierarchy and Competence: When a Network Is Needed
In his analysis of the organizational design of homeland security, Wise (2006) argues that the shared responsibility for homeland security tasks

across a wide range of government agencies, the shared authority across the federal system, and the complexity of the tasks suggest the need for a networked approach to implementation. Flexibility to draw on the multiorganizational capacities needed to effectively enact the functions of homeland security requires "matrix networks" that "dynamically interact" (Clayton and Haverty 2005) or a capacity for "contingent coordination" (Kettl 2003). Instead, the Bush administration opted for a hierarchical model of organization, centralizing authority within DHS and reorganizing, redefining, recreating, and, in some instances, reducing or expanding individual agency capacity when merged into the new department.

Initially, the Bush administration pursued a networked approach by establishing the Office of Homeland Security in the Executive Office of the President. The office was to "develop and coordinate the implementation of a comprehensive national strategy to secure the United States from terrorist threats or attacks" (Bush 2001) by working with executive branch agencies involved in preventing, preparing for, and responding to terrorism. Pressure from Congress for a new cabinet-level department and revelations about FBI failures to detect the activities of terrorists in America prior to the 9/11 attacks prompted the Bush administration instead to support an organizationally comprehensive approach (Kettl 2007).[5] While there were certainly political advantages to consolidating the work of DHS into a single agency and while the hierarchical nature of systems such as the National Incident Management System (NIMS) are reinforced by the hierarchical design, the ability to fully utilize local and state-based capacities as well as the capacities of organizations spread across the federal government could be more readily accessed with a network approach.

The impediments of a strict hierarchical approach to the tasks of preparation, response, and recovery can be seen in anecdotes of the Hurricane Katrina response effort. Consider the experience of Douglas Doan of DHS (Cooper and Block 2006). In the midst of the recovery effort, the National Guard needed relief supplies such as water, diapers, and baby formula for the victims of the storm. Doan was notified by Wal-Mart managers that the National Guard was taking these items; he labeled the circumstances "unusual procurement" (Cooper and Block 2006, 265) and partnered with Wal-Mart stores as supply stations for storm relief with the promise that

Wal-Mart would be paid for the goods. The media, residents, and analysts of the response effort widely recognized Wal-Mart as both efficient and generous, and Doan's actions represented the initiative and improvisation often needed for disaster relief response; but the accounting practices of DHS were fundamentally at odds (Horowitz 2008). When forced to resign and account for his actions, Doan wrote three lines on a piece of paper: "I did it. I would do it again. The President would agree with it" (Cooper and Block 2006, 265). It is curious that in an administration focused on partnerships with the private sector as a means to increase innovation and efficiency and scale back the size of government, the fundamentals of hierarchy and accountability systems prevented innovation when it was most needed.

Summary

The components discussed here together created a limited capacity for emergency management leading up to Hurricane Katrina and limited tactical competence for the policy domain of homeland security. The written mission of homeland security emphasizes an all-hazards approach, but in practice the resources of DHS are devoted to preventing, preparing for, and responding to terrorism. The infrastructure of emergency management was scaled back and the work turned over to contractors without sufficient resources left to FEMA to oversee the work. And the choice to centralize the work of homeland security has imposed a rigid structure that does not allow for the innovation and flexibility required for emergency response. In the next section, I note caveats on the negative performance of the administration.

SECOND THOUGHTS

In the hours before Katrina hit, an analysis by the DHS National Infrastructure Simulation and Analysis Center forecasted a breach of the levees, elimination of the communications network, and a city full of residents unable to evacuate and stranded on rooftops (Cooper and Block 2006, 132). When assessing the Bush administration's response to Katrina, many have noted the scale and power of a storm that might have overwhelmed the most sophisticated emergency response (Graumann et al. 2005; U.S. Congress

2006). Other contextual factors that could be considered in assessing the response effort include the organizational incentives in place for leaders of emergency response efforts, and the broader efforts to adjust government capacity to increasingly complex public problems. It is also important to note the accomplishments of DHS in responding to Katrina.

The Organizational Incentives of Emergency Response

Much of the criticism aimed at FEMA after Katrina struck focused on the hesitation and delay of the agency leading up to and in the immediate aftermath of the storm. FEMA and the administration held off taking any direct action until three days after the storm hit New Orleans, and then only in response to a desperate request from Mayor Nagin of New Orleans (Schneider 2005). Sobel and Leeson (2006) offer an explanation that generalizes the sluggish response: "[t]he incentive to be overly cautious and thus err on the side of type-two errors." Type 1 errors result from aggressively taking actions that may backfire and harm the public. Type 2 errors involve caution to the degree that earlier or more assertive action would have prevented harm to the public. "Any government agency for which errors of overcautiousness are less visible and less likely to evoke criticism than errors of undercautiousness," they write, "faces this incentive" (59).

This dynamic, Sobel and Leeson argue, typifies emergency response efforts in general: better to go in cautiously when the potential for visible mistakes by an agency is high. Donahue and Tuohy (2006) offer a similar argument about the predictable dynamics of emergency response in an analysis of the lessons never learned in emergency management. Despite repeated lessons about the failure of command and control in disasters, command-and-control processes still top the list of problems in the postdisaster assessment—a central problem with the Katrina response effort. The reason, Donahue and Tuohy (2006) argue, is complex, but rests in large part on the lack of an agency's motivation to make changes in longstanding practices, fear of very visible failure in the midst of the institutional change, resource constraints, and the inability to model the unknown in response exercises.

Findings by the select committee appointed in the House of Representatives to review the events of Hurricane Katrina resulted in similar questions about the capacity of government agencies, in particular those involved in emergency management, to learn. The committee posed a series of questions: "How can we set up a system to protect against passivity? Why do we repeatedly seem out of synch during disasters? Why do we continually seem to be one disaster behind?" (U.S. Congress 2006, 359). The bottom line, as suggested by Sobel and Leeson (2006), is that a broader government agency dynamic is in place that transcends and influences the performance of any set of organizations in any administration.[6]

Wicked Problems and Government Capacity

Efforts to assess the tactical competence of the Bush administration's emergency response efforts can also be placed in the context of broader government challenges to address problems that have become increasingly "wicked" in complexity and durability. As early as 1967, scholars and practitioners from different disciplines recognized that the dynamic complexity of many public problems defies the boundaries of established policy and management systems (Churchman 1967; Rittel and Webber 1973; Roberts 2000). In the past two decades, this clash between wicked problems and traditional management systems has become unworkable in many policy domains, requiring a rethinking of the systems and the role for managers (Kettl 2002; O'Toole 1997; Weber and Khademian 2008).

Emergency response and the challenges of homeland security meet the criteria for a wicked problem. The vast number of groups, organizations, and layers of government involved in the effort defy any organizational boundaries and require complex coordination. The meaning of an all-hazards approach and the capacities needed to accomplish an all-hazards approach, remain in dispute. The policy domain of homeland security is not unique in confronting the challenges of multiple jurisdictions, relentless problems, and lack of problem clarity. Hence, part of the response to Hurricane Katrina can be understood in this broader context of government struggling to develop the capacities for increasingly wicked problems. As stated by the Select Bipartisan Committee, "The preparation for and response to Hurricane Katrina show we are still an analog government in a digital age" (U.S. Congress 2006, 1).

Finally, while criticisms of the administration's response to Katrina dominate the recovery assessment, successful efforts are part of the story as well. The U.S. Coast Guard, in particular, prepositioned boats and helicopters in anticipation of the storm, and rescued more than thirty-three thousand people from flooded homes and rooftops; and Coast Guard personnel took initiatives to redirect resources to meet immediate emergent needs (Menzel 2006). Creative efforts of the FPS to secure federal buildings and provide direct emergency information to DHS and the White House are also notable (Cooper and Block 2006, 175).

STRATEGIC COMPETENCE

Strategic competence is evident in the long-term impact a president has on the policy regime. The defining feature of the Bush administration's response to the terrorist attacks of 9/11 has been to forge a policy domain by merging and blending organizations and activities long scattered across the government to find a common focus within the Department of Homeland Security and a policy convergence around terrorism. In some respects, the effort is simply a continuation of an ongoing battle over the location of key government activities and the emphasis each received. FEMA, for example, was created in 1978 to consolidate all federal emergency management functions related to natural disasters and to national security (or civil emergency) preparedness (Bea 2002). The fit of these two functions, however, was poor (Schneider 1995; National Academy of Public Administration 1993). National security issues dominated the agency to the detriment of its capacity to respond to natural disasters—a concern that became evident in the feeble response of FEMA to Hurricane Hugo in 1989 and Hurricane Andrew in 1992. Under the leadership of Director James Lee Witt throughout the 1990s, the agency was reorganized to emphasize all-hazards management and was widely recognized for its significant improvement in managing disasters and its guidance and support of state and local governments to prepare for disasters (Ellig 2000). Witt's support of state and local government preparedness, partnerships with the private sector, and facilitation of federal agency coordination forged key capacities essential to the task. Yet, after the September 11, 2001, terrorist attacks, the concern once again was that emergency management planning and preparation might be slighted in an all-hazards emergency management approach (Bea 2002); assessments of the federal response effort to Hurricane Katrina affirm that concern.

It is, however, the scale and depth of the Bush administration's efforts to reconfigure the domain of homeland security that is distinctive. Creation of DHS was the largest reorganization in the federal government since the 1940s and certainly the most complicated. The effort entailed twenty-two federal agencies, 180,000 government employees, maintenance of legacy missions, and in many cases, a new emphasis on elements of the homeland security mission (Kettl 2007, 53). Once DHS was created, budget priorities across these agencies shifted to a focus on preventing, preparing for, and responding to acts of terror, most evident in the diminishing resources for FEMA. The shift too in the focus of grant money to state and local governments quickly reflected the shift in priorities (Khademian 2004).

From the perspective of strategic competence, the Bush administration forged a homeland security domain with the primary concern of preventing, preparing for, and responding to terrorist attacks. The policy literature provides some insights regarding the likely durability of this shift, as well. Significant shocks can destabilize policy domains, facilitating changes that go well beyond incremental adjustments in budgets and priorities (Baumgartner and Jones 1993; Birkland 1997; Kettl 2007). The terrorist attacks of 9/11 jolted the patchwork domain of emergency management and civil defense, once defined by an incremental tug-of-war between the priorities of emergency management versus the priorities of civil defense (Bea 2002). In the creation of DHS, as well as the 2004 reorganization of the intelligence community, the passage of the U.S. PATRIOT Act, extensions of the surveillance powers of the federal government, and the creation of state-level offices of homeland security across the nation, the domain of what is now called homeland security has shifted to reflect the central priority of terrorism. Katrina was a shock to the capacity of this system and prompted numerous efforts to study, learn from, and improve upon the response to this and future storms. Yet emphasis given to emergency response seems to be incremental and superficial, rather than deep and significant. Any change to reemphasize the capacities of emergency management as a central priority will likely be up to leadership in the next administration.

NOTES

1. See the e-mail correspondence between Brown, FEMA employees, and other response officials for an up-close account of the detached leadership effort, http://i.a.cnn.net/cnn/2005/images/11/03/brown.emails.pdf.

2. The term "homeland" was used in a 1998 report *Catastrophic Terrorism: Elements of a National Policy*, by Carter, Deutch, and Zelikow, John F. Kennedy School of Government, http://www.hks.harvard.edu/visions/publication/terrorism.htm.

3. The legislation creating the Department of Homeland Security was passed in 2002, but the department was officially raised in March 2003.

4. Project Impact emphasized mitigation efforts in communities before disasters hit. The focus was on building public-private partnerships, "seeding" mitigation projects that private contributions would enhance, forging planning efforts, and supporting mitigation education and outreach programs. Between 1997 and 2001, when it was cancelled, Project Impact provided $77 million to states and territories (U.S. Government Accountability Office 2002, 12–16).

5. Intelligence-gathering organizations such as the FBI, the CIA, and NSA remained independent of DHS. In 2004, however, Congress passed the Intelligence Reform and Terrorism Prevention Act to create a director of national intelligence (DNI) of the National Intelligence Program (NIP) to coordinate and direct the resources—or "connect the dots"—of the many agencies involved in intelligence gathering, support for operations, and analysis. While not as dramatic as the consolidation of organizations within one executive branch department, the legislation provided central tendencies for intelligence organizations involved in national intelligence (Public Law No. 108–458 Intelligence Reform and Terrorism Prevention Act of 2004).

6. As a caveat, however, the leadership of James Lee Witt has been evaluated as highly successful in overcoming the incapacity to learn and the hesitation to act, both prominent characteristics of the agency before Witt's tenure from 1992 to 2000 (Khademian 2004). Witt's departure, and the move to DHS, are markers for the transformation in tactical competence.

REFERENCES

Allbaugh, Joe M. 2001. "Testimony of Federal Emergency Management Agency Director Joe M. Allbaugh, Before the Veterans Affairs, Housing and Urban Development and Independent Agencies Subcommittee of the Senate Appropriations Committee." May 16. http://www.fema.gov/about/director/allbaugh/testimony/051601.shtm (Accessed September 14, 2008).

Balz, Dan. 2008. "The Hurricane in Question Is Still Called Katrina." *Washington Post*, September 1, p. A1.

Baumgartner, Frank, and Bryan Jones. 1993. *Agendas and Instability in American Politics.* Chicago: University of Chicago Press.

Bea, Keith. 2002. *Proposed Transfer of FEMA to the Department of Homeland Security.* Congressional Research Service. July 29. http://www.law.umaryland.edu/marshall/crsreports/crsdocuments/RL31510_07292002.pdf (Accessed May 14, 2008).

Birkland, Thomas. 1997. *After Disaster: Agenda Setting, Public Policy and Focusing Events.* Washington, DC: Georgetown University Press.

Bush, George W. 2001. "Establishing the Office of Homeland Security and the Homeland

Security Council, Executive Order 13228 of October 8, 2001." *Federal Register* 66(196): 51812–17.

Canada, Ben. 2003. *Homeland Security: Standards for State and Local Performance.* CRS Report for Congress, January 2. Washington, DC: Congressional Research Service, Library of Congress.

Chertoff, Michael. 2008. "Gustav Preparations." *Leadership Journal* (U.S. Department of Homeland Security), September 1. http://www.dhs.gov/journal/leadership/2008/09/gustav-preparations.html.

Churchman, C. West. 1967. "Wicked Problems." *Management Science* 4(14): B141–42.

Clayton, Ross, and Dan Haverty. 2005. "Modernizing Homeland Defense and Security." *Journal of Homeland Security and Emergency Management* 2(1): Article 7.

Cooper, Christopher, and Robert Block. 2006. *Disaster: Hurricane Katrina and the Failure of Homeland Security.* New York: Times Books.

Donahue, Amy K., and Robert V. Tuohy. 2006. "Lessons We Don't Learn: A Study of the Lessons of Disasters, Why We Repeat Them, and How We Can Learn from Them." *Homeland Security Affairs* 2(2). http://www.hsaj.org/pages/volume2/issue2/pdfs/2.2.4.pdf (Accessed July 26, 2006).

Ellig, Jerry. 2000. *Learning from the Leaders: Results-Based Management at the Federal Emergency Management Agency.* Arlington, VA: Mercatus Center at George Mason University. http://www.mercatus.org/uploadedFiles/Mercatus/Publications/ MC_GAP _RBMatFEMA_000329.pdf.

Elliston, John. 2004. "A Disaster Waiting to Happen." Indyweek.com, September 22. http://www.indyweek.com/gyrobase/Content?oid=oid%3A22664.

Gomez, Alan, and William Welch. 2008. "GOP Suspends Convention Sessions Due to Gustav." *USA Today*, August 31. http://www.usatoday.com/news/washington/2008 –08-31–gopconvention_N.htm.

Graumann, Axel, Tamara Houston, Jay Lawrimore, David Levinson, Neal Lott, Sam McCown, Scott Stephens, and David Wuertz. 2005. *Hurricane Katrina: A Climatological Perspective.* Technical Report 2005-1. Asheville, NC: U.S. Department of Commerce, National Oceanic and Atmospheric Administration, National Climatic Data Center. http://www.ncdc.noaa.gov/oa/reports/tech-report-200501z.pdf.

Horowitz, Steven. 2008. *Making Hurricane Response More Effective: Lessons from the Private Sector and the Coast Guard During Katrina.* Mercatus Policy Series: Policy Comment No. 17. Arlington, VA: Mercatus Center at George Mason University.

Kettl, Donald F. 2002. *The Transformation of Governance: Public Administration for Twenty-First Century America.* Baltimore: Johns Hopkins University Press.

———. 2003. "Contingent Coordination: Practical and Theoretical Challenges for Homeland Security." *American Journal of Public Administration* 33(2): 253–77.

———. 2007. *System Under Stress: Homeland Security and American Politics.* Washington, DC: CQ Press.

Khademian, Anne M. 2004. "Strengthening State and Local Terrorism Prevention and Response." In *The Department of Homeland Security's First Year: A Report Card*, ed. Donald Kettl. New York: Century Foundation, 97–117.

McCarter, Mickey. 2008. "Grant Funding Formula Disregards All-Hazards Threats." *Homeland Security Today*, July 2. http://www.hstoday.us/content/view/4090/128/.

Menzel, Donald. 2006. "The Katrina Aftermath: A Failure of Federalism or Leadership?" *Public Administration Review* 66(6): 808–12.

National Academy of Public Administration. 1993. *Coping with Catastrophe: Building an Emergency Management System to Meet People's Needs in Natural and Manmade Disasters.* Washington, DC: NAPA.

O'Toole, Laurence J. 1997. "Treating Networks Seriously: Practical and Research-Based Agendas in Public Administration." *Public Administration Review* 57(1): 45–52.

Reed, Betsy, Adolph Reed Jr., and Adolph Reed. 2006. *Unnatural Disaster: The Nation on Hurricane Katrina.* New York: Nation Books.

Rittel, Horst W. J., and Melvin M. Webber. 1973. "Dilemmas in a General Theory of Planning." *Policy Sciences* 4: 155–69.

Roberts, Nancy C. 2000. "Wicked Problems and Network Approaches to Resolution." *International Public Management Review* 1(1): 1–19.

Scahill, Jeremy. 2005. "Blackwater Down." *The Nation,* September 21. http://www.thenation .com/doc/20051010/scahill.

———. 2006. "In the Black(water)." *The Nation,* May 22. http://www.thenation.com/doc/20060605/scahill.

Schneider, Saundra. 1995. *Flirting with Disaster: Public Management in Crisis Situations.* Armonk, NY: M. E. Sharpe.

———. 2005. "Administrative Breakdowns in the Governmental Response to Hurricane Katrina." *Public Administration Review* 65(5): 515–17.

Senate Committee on Homeland Security and Governmental Affairs. 2006. *Hurricane Katrina: A Nation Still Unprepared (A Report).* Washington, DC: U.S. Government Printing Office.

Sobel, Russell, and Peter Leeson. 2006. "Government's Response to Hurricane Katrina: A Public Choice Analysis." *Public Choice* 127(1–2): 55–73.

Special Inspector General for Gulf Coast Hurricane Recovery DHS. 2006. "Revised Report: Management Advisory Report on Armed Guard Services Provided by Blackwater Security Consulting, LLC Under contract HSCEFC-05-J-F00002." Report Number GC-HQ-06–17.

U.S. Congress. Select Bipartisan Committee to Investigate the Preparation for and Response to Hurricane Katrina. 2006. *A Failure of Initiative: Final Report of the Select Bipartisan Committee to Investigate the Preparation for and Response to Hurricane Katrina.* 109th Congress, 2nd Session, H. Rept. 109–377. Washington, DC: U.S. Government Printing Office.

U.S. Department of Homeland Security (DHS). 2007. *FY 2007 Homeland Security Grant Program.* Washington, DC: DHS. http://www.dhs.gov/xlibrary/assets/grants_st-local _fy07.pdf (Accessed September 14, 2008).

U.S. Government Accountability Office (GAO). 2002. *Hazard Mitigation: Proposed Changes to FEMA's Hazard Multihazard Mitigation Programs Present Challenges.* Washington, DC: GAO.

U.S. Government Accountability Office (GAO). 2005. *Homeland Security: DHS' Efforts to Enhance First Responders' All-Hazards Capabilities Continue to Evolve.* Washington, DC: GAO.

Weber, Edward, and Anne M. Khademian. 2008. "Wicked Problems, Knowledge Challenges, and Collaborative Capacity Builders in Network Settings." *Public Administration Review* 26(2): 334–49.

Wise, Charles. 2006. "Organizing for Homeland Security After Hurricane Katrina: Is Adaptive Management What's Missing?" *Public Administration Review* 66(3): 302–18.

PART FOUR

Crusade
The Bush Foreign Policies

CHAPTER 12

Is the Bush Doctrine Dead?

ROBERT G. KAUFMAN

WORLD WAR IV began on September 11, 2001, with attacks on the World Trade Center and the Pentagon, which murdered more than two thousand Americans (Podhoretz 2007, 12). The Bush Doctrine—the George W. Bush administration's strategy for defining and waging this war—will go down as the president's most pivotal and controversial legacy.

Two main premises inform the Bush Doctrine. First, the events of 9/11 rudely demonstrate the inadequacy of deterrence, containment, or ex post facto strategies when dealing with terrorists and rogue regimes; therefore, the United States cannot rule out using force preemptively rather than reactively. Second, the root cause of 9/11 and similarly inspired aggression is a culture of tyranny and oppression in the Middle East, which spawns fanatical, aggressive, secular, and religious despotisms; therefore, the United States must promote stable, liberal, and democratic regime change in the region (Kaufman 2007, 157–82).

The Bush Doctrine, particularly its application to Iraq, has evoked ferocious criticism. Prominent foreign policy realists rejected President Bush's emphasis on the importance of regime type and ideology in assessing America's true national interests. They doubt whether democratic regime change can succeed in the Middle East, or whether it matters very much in the grand scheme of things. What matters most for these realists is stability and equilibrium, which in their view the Bush administration squandered by waging an unnecessary, costly, futile war of preemption in Iraq that has left the United States less secure. To their way of thinking, the United States could have safely relied on strategies such as containment and deterrence to deal with regimes such as Iran and Iraq (Walt 2005).

The most politically potent assault on the Bush Doctrine has come from Western European elites and liberal multilateralists regnant in the

Democratic Party since 1968. Like President Bush and unlike his realist critics, liberal multilateralists of all varieties stress the importance of liberal democratic institutions for mitigating rivalry and fostering legitimacy. Yet this group also fears what former Democratic senator J. William Fulbright of Arkansas called the "arrogance of American power" as much as the external threat ranged against the United States (Fulbright 1966). Although liberal multilateralists concede that the United States must occasionally use force unilaterally or with a smaller coalition of the willing rather than the unanimous approval of the NATO alliance or the United Nations, they do not consider the American invasion of Iraq in 2003 such a case. Multilateralists assail the Bush Doctrine for relying too much on hard power while slighting soft power, the ability to get what one wants through negotiation, cooperation, and the attraction of American culture and values (Nye 2004, 3–10).

Like Bush's realist critics, liberal multilateralists such as Barack Obama have called for negotiation rather than confrontation with Iran. Obama has pledged to withdraw American troops from Iraq promptly, because he believes the United States cannot win the war in Iraq, a war we should not have launched in the first place (Obama 2007).

This chapter makes the opposite case: eventually, George W. Bush's presidential reputation will soar high above the smog of his low late-term approval ratings. What is novel about the Bush Doctrine—the need to employ force preemptively in some circumstances—is necessary in light of the insidious convergence between radicalism and the spread of weapons of mass destruction (WMD). What is familiar about the Bush Doctrine—a commitment to stable, liberal, democratic regime change as a war aim to represent the real root cause of the conflict—represents one of the most venerable traditions in American grand strategy since Woodrow Wilson. Despite the sobering difficulties American forces have encountered in their efforts to create a free and democratic Iraq, the United States stands a good chance of achieving a decent outcome if it does not snatch defeat from the jaws of victory by withdrawing too soon.

This chapter proposes the Truman administration as a hopeful analogy for contemplating the legacy of President Bush. The lacerating controversies over the Korean War of 1950–53 did not invalidate President Truman's policy of vigilant containment that contributed so mightily to winning the Cold War against a Soviet empire that was truly evil and mortally dangerous. Whatever happens in Iraq, the Bush Doctrine has established the political fault lines for the debate over American grand strategy for decades to come. The chapter has two major parts. The first explains why the Bush Doctrine ranks high, alongside the Truman Doctrine, in terms of strategic, tactical, and moral competence. The second part explains why the Iraq War ranks higher in terms of tactical competence than Bush's critics realize, especially since the surge of June 2007. It closes with some observations about how events beyond the Middle East may bear on the Bush Doctrine and the president's ultimate legacy.

CRITIC OF THE CRITICS

The virtues of the Bush Doctrine become manifest by scrutinizing the principal objections to it. Start with the claim that a strategy of preemption violates elementary principles of justice, particularly the requirements of modern (though not traditional) just war theory, that force be used only as a last resort (Powell 1992–93). St. Thomas Aquinas' traditional and superior formulation wisely did not stipulate this as a requirement (Aquinas 1948, 577–81); for we know from history that sometimes using force sooner can save much blood, toil, and tears later. Consider two prime examples, of many: had the democracies heeded Winston Churchill's advice and stopped Hitler at various watersheds during the 1930s, particularly when he invaded the Rhineland on March 7, 1936, in violation of two international treaties, we could have averted the most destructive war in history. Indeed, Hitler admitted as much (Hilgruber 1981). In May 1981, Israel launched a preventive strike against Iraq's nuclear reactor at Osirak; otherwise, Saddam Hussein may well have possessed a nuclear capability when he invaded Kuwait in the summer of 1990, which may have deterred the United States from responding decisively or raised exponentially the cost or risk of such a response.

The Bush Doctrine does not hold preemption as the norm but as a carefully delineated exception to diplomacy and other less stark options. In the United States, formidable constraints exist on the abuse of preemption in the form of separation of powers and public accountability. These constraints also operated robustly during the debate leading up to the American invasion of Iraq in March 2003. The United States did not rush to war but resorted to it only after a year of extensive debate at home and abroad, after more than a decade of Saddam's brazen defiance, and years of failure of the more conciliatory alternatives. The United States had ample moral as well as geopolitical reasons to remove Saddam, given the paramount importance of preventing a single hostile power from dominating the Middle East, and Saddam's aspirations to do just that. It was President Clinton who officially made Iraqi regime change U.S. policy by signing the Iraqi Liberation Act of 1998. President Bush transformed rhetoric into reality (Shawcross 2004).

No president can resort to preventive or preemptive use of force cavalierly. Whether preemption is appropriate depends on the circumstances: the gravity of the danger; the availability of plausible alternatives for meeting the threat; and a calculation of the probable costs of acting or deferring action against a gathering danger.

Take the related claim that preemption may be justified in rare circumstances but not in today's Middle East, where the strategies of containment and deterrence that worked so well during the Cold War are plausible alternatives. The strategy of containment and deterrence are not effective against certain types of threats. Our greatest Cold Warriors, such as Presidents Truman and Reagan, who rightly equated Nazi Germany and the Soviet Union on the scale of danger and evil, drew this critical distinction between the two empires: the Soviet Union calculated risk less recklessly than did Nazi Germany, using Marxist-Leninist ideology that assumed time was on its side, combined with the traditional impulses of Great Russian History (Kengor 2006). We could deter the Soviet Union by sustaining what Winston Churchill called an imbalance of power on behalf of the forces of freedom. Conversely, we could not deter Nazi Germany, because Hitler was bent on war (Churchill 1948, 345–47).

This distinction between Stalin's Soviet Union and Hitler's Germany applies in large measure to the post-9/11 world. On one hand, the United States can prudently rely on some hybrid strategy of containment, deterrence, and engagement to deal with the challenge of a rising, still authoritarian, and expansionist China, whose leadership calculates cost and risks in a way conducive to the success of this strategy (Friedberg 2000, 26–32). On the other hand, the United States could not have prudently relied on deterrence or containment against reckless actors such as Saddam Hussein, especially now that the convergence between mounting radicalism and the spread of WMD has magnified the cost of waiting too long. Saddam's propensity to take risk fell closer on the spectrum to Hitler's than Stalin's. The sanctions regime that was integral to any plausible policy of containing Saddam had begun irrevocably to break down and hurt innocent Iraqis rather than the evil regime. In these circumstances, using force to remove Saddam averted much blood, sweat, and tears later—for Americans and Iraqis.

What about the objections of liberal multilateralists that the Bush Doctrine undermines the principles of multilateralism and collective security? (Ikenberry and Kupchan 2004, 38–49). To make the United Nations the arbiter of international legitimacy is a triumph of hope over experience. Neither the United Nations nor its predecessor, the League of Nations, has ever served as an effective substitute for an American-led alliance system. The inability of the United Nations to operate effectively against powerful aggressors is intrinsic to the institution. The United Nations lacks the three prerequisites for strong, effective action: sufficient independent power, sufficient consensus, and sufficient willingness to make the requisite effort to deal with powerful aggressors. The only two successful examples of collective security in history—Korea in 1950 and the Gulf War of 1991—are the exceptions to the rule of UN inaction (Kaufman 2001).

The United States enlisted the support of the United Nations to resist North Korea's invasion of South Korea only because the Soviet Union, one of the five permanent members of the council with a veto, boycotted the Security Council for the UN's refusal to recognize the People's Republic of China. Neither the Soviet Union nor any other major power has repeated that mistake.

The United States secured the approval of the UN Security Council to liberate Kuwait only because of an equally rare convergence of circumstances. When Iraq invaded Kuwait in 1990, the impending disintegration of the Soviet Union and diplomatic fallout still resonating over China's brutal suppression of its students at Tiananmen Square gave Moscow and

Beijing powerful but evanescent incentives not to incur America's ill will. Also, French fears about the consequences of then impending German unification inclined France to be significantly less obstructionist than usual. So, these states did not veto effective military action to liberate Kuwait (Muravchik 2005, 117–72).

Since the Gulf War of 1991, the failures of the security council have dwarfed the marginal contributions that peacekeeping missions have made in such places as Haiti, Cambodia, and East Timor. In 1994, UN intervention in Bosnia was too weak to succeed but large enough to thwart effective action until stronger NATO forces could intervene. In 1999, the United States (under President Clinton) and its NATO allies, including France, bypassed a gridlocked UN Security Council to wage war against Serbia for its atrocities against Muslim Kosovars. For more than a decade, Saddam Hussein defied a total of seventeen UN resolutions with impunity. Add to these examples the genocide of Rwanda, the slaughter in Darfur, and the nuclear program of a fanatical Iran to the litany of the United Nation's dismal record in the realm of international security (Bolton 2007, 220–412).

The system of the UN Security Council that gives each of the five permanent members the veto means effectively that France, Russia, or China could thwart any American use of force deemed illegitimate—were we unwise enough to make the United Nations the arbiter of legitimacy for the use of force. Eliminating the security council veto would make matters worse, because it would leave the United States prey to an unsavory combination of hostile and illiberal regimes that have dominated the UN General Assembly since the 1960s (Rabkin 2004, 180–86).

Nor can the United States make the NATO alliance of twenty-seven members the arbiter of legitimacy for when and how to use force, especially in light of France's record in the alliance. Misguided French attempts to use NATO to constrain what they call American hyperpower date back to the founding of the French Republic in 1958 under the viscerally anti-American Charles de Gaulle (Aron 1990, 286–300, 347–48).

Then there is the objection that the Bush Doctrine's commitment to spreading stable, liberal democracy to the Middle East is arrogant, untenable, and imprudent (Scowcroft 2006, 13–15; Goldberg 2005, 60). Yet all regimes do not behave essentially alike. A vital distinction exists between stable, liberal democracies and totalitarian regimes animated by malevolent, messianic ideologies.

The United States has encouraged the spread of stable, liberal democracies for an excellent reason: such regimes are more likely to cooperate and unlikely to fight one another even when they do disagree (Weart 1997). Regime type and ideology account not only positively for the democratic peace so beneficial for American security but negatively for the most menacing aggression against the United States since 1900.

As a caveat, the United States should not court enormous risk to establish democracy everywhere on any pretext. The United States will remain the world's dominant power for decades to come, especially in the military realm. Yet even our abundant resources are finite. Sometimes the prospects for democratic forces succeeding are too remote or our stake in the outcome too limited to justify American involvement. The United States also must give priority to extending the zone of democratic peace to East Asia, Europe, and the Middle East: these are the major power centers of the world, where the absence of liberty could prove to be most perilous. However laudable a goal, promoting democracy never suffices as justification for going to war absent immediate or impending threats to America's vital interests or the vital interests of its allies.

Since Woodrow Wilson proclaimed World War I as a war to end all wars, American presidents have rightly identified the regime type of our adversaries as the root cause of conflict; thus, they have defined democratic regime change as a primary war aim. The tragedy of Wilson is that he, the United States, and its principal allies failed to establish on a durable foundation the peace that ended World War I. The United States withdrew from Europe too soon, naïvely relying on a hapless League of Nations rather than the robustness of American power to uphold the peace. During World War II, the great democratic war leaders Churchill and Roosevelt did not make the same mistake: they would settle for nothing less than the unconditional surrender of the Nazi and Imperial Japanese regimes in a manner so devastating that neither the German nor Japanese people could deny it. They insisted on imposing stable, liberal democracy, there and elsewhere, to address the real root cause of the most destructive war in history (Beschloss 2002, 13–19). We succeeded magnificently. During the Cold War, our most dauntless Cold Warriors identified the Soviet regime as the root cause of the struggle; thus, the policy of vigilant containment sought to bring down the Soviet regime by sustained, comprehensive, long-term pressure (Spalding 2006). That strategy also succeeded magnificently, especially during the final phase of the Cold War under Ronald Reagan (Schweizer 2002).

One major cause of the Iraq War of 2003 was the ambiguous outcome of the Gulf War of 1990–91, which left Saddam in power. President George W. Bush did not make the same mistake. He understood that a just and durable peace required democratic regime change.

Many thoughtful critics of the president counter that unlike Europe and Japan after World War II, the conditions are not propitious for stable, liberal democracy to succeed in the Middle East. Critics point not only to the sectarian violence and insurgency in Iraq but also to the success of ter-rorist organizations such as Hamas in Palestine as evidence of the folly of the Bush administration's policy of encouraging democracy in the Middle East. Their argument runs as follows: the United States cannot impose de-mocracy by force; it must wait for it to emerge organically, when a mature civil society is in place (Fukuyama 2006, 30–45).

Although these are serious arguments, Bush's case is more compelling. Few in 1945 were optimistic about establishing stable, liberal democra-cies in Germany or Japan, or throughout a defeated, demoralized Europe, which was confronting a malevolent, powerful, and insatiably expansion-ist Soviet Union. The only experience the Germans or Japanese had with democracy prior to 1945 had ended badly: the reviled Weimar Republic between 1918 and 1933 in Germany and the maligned Taisho democracy in Japan during the 1920s. The Marshall Plan and the NATO alliance so pivotal to Western Europe's democratic resurgence came about in response to conditions in Europe that had deteriorated for a full two to four years after the end of World War II.

Keep in mind that many of the same critics of President George W. Bush denounced President Reagan during the 1980s for his insistence on democratic regime change in Eastern Europe (O'Sullivan 2006, 68–87): Reagan was right. Democracy has often succeeded in places such as South

Korea, India, South Africa, the Philippines, and El Salvador, where many of the purported prerequisites for democracy were wholly or partially lacking. In the Middle East, with the dangerous intersection of radicalism, tyranny, and proliferation of WMD, the United States does not have the luxury of waiting for the organic growth of democracy any more than it did with Nazi Germany and imperial Japan.

Those who would rely on authoritarian regimes as the bulwark of American foreign policy in the Middle East confuse rigidity for stability: many autocratic regimes, such as Saudi Arabia, are neither durable in the long run nor all that reliably moderate. Even in places such as the Palestinian territories, where elections have yielded results we rightly deplore, a brutal and corrupt PLO under Yasir Arafat, bent on Israel's elimination, offered no better alternative for peace, provisional justice, or stability (Ross 2004, 768). With wisdom and tenacity, President Bush reiterated to the Knesset that a just and lasting resolution of the Israeli-Palestinian conflict depends on the emergence of a more decent, responsible Palestinian entity committed to free and fair elections, liberty, tolerance, compromise, transparency, and the rule of law (Abramowitz 2008).

Even if democracy will not succeed swiftly or in all places in the Middle East, promoting it is the more prudential strategy than the alternative of neglecting the real root cause of 9/11 and similarly inspired aggression. Fareed Zakaria, one of President Bush's most thoughtful critics, concedes that America will be honored and respected in the long run if Iraq, Afghanistan, and perhaps an independent Palestine and democratic Lebanon become thriving countries with open, tolerant, and modern political and economic systems (2005).

IRAQ VINDICATED

Theoretical arguments alone will not suffice to salvage President Bush's battered reputation: results matter decisively. Are not the critics right, even supposing the Bush Doctrine has some or perhaps even considerable merit in principle, that the Iraq War is the graveyard of Bush's foreign policy vision? Have not the spiraling cost of the war, the faulty intelligence to justify it, the failure to find weapons of mass destruction, and the raging sectarian violence of post-Saddam Iraq conspired to discredit the Bush Doctrine beyond repair? The likely if contingent answer to these questions is No.

The 2003 invasion of Iraq was long overdue. Saddam was a symbol of defiance to American power in a region seething with defiance, especially in the wake of 9/11. Saddam not only had once possessed WMD but had used them, against Kurds, Shiites, and Iranians. During the Gulf War of 1990–91, Iraq launched Scud missiles into Israel. Saddam acted to the end as if he possessed WMD; every reputable intelligence service in the world shared the American assumption that he still possessed them, an error for which Saddam, not President Bush, was to blame. According to the Kay Commission and Duelfer Report, Saddam never wavered in his determination to resume his acquisition of WMDs once the already porous UN sanctions inevitably broke down. Nor could the United States have relied prudently on the UN inspectors to verify Saddam's compliance with the disarmament resolutions, which the United Nations lacked the will to enforce. Saddam exploited the utterly corrupt UN oil-for-food program to buy off the French, Russian, and the Chinese and abet his plans for developing a WMD capability (Duelfer 2004).

For decades, Saddam demonstrated a predisposition to take enormous risks that rendered inadequate the options of containing or deterring him. He mounted an assassination attempt against an American president, maintained a regime hideous even by the low standards of the Islamic Middle East, and routinely assisted homicide bombers on the West Bank of Palestine and in Gaza, if not al-Qaeda directly. Saddam had ample opportunity to save himself and his regime by complying with the UN sanctions, which would have deprived Bush of the political support necessary to remove him. Also, the strategy of containing Iraq had reached the point of diminishing moral and strategic returns. Sanctions imposed terrible suffering on innocent Iraqis, without eradicating Saddam's regime, the source of their misery and of the gathering danger to Iraq's neighbors (Pollack 2002).

Nor does the situation in Iraq justify the extreme pessimism of Bush's critics. Granted, Americans should not minimize the significant difficulties that lie ahead. The United States has lost more than four thousand servicemen and women in Iraq, every one of whom is precious. The economic cost of the war seems high, though it is markedly less burdensome than

Vietnam measured as a percentage of gross domestic product (1.6 percent annually versus less than 1 percent for Iraq) (Zakaria 2008, 182). The first phase of the war, the conventional military campaign that culminated in the fall of Baghdad in May 2003, went splendidly: the United States defeated the regular armies of Saddam in less time and with less cost than even the optimists expected (Keegan 2004). However, the second phase of the war, from May 2003 until the surge of June 2007, confounded the administration's expectations. As even informed defenders of the war admit, serious errors occurred in this second phase: the failure to police the Iraqi-Syrian border; the lack of postinvasion planning; the lack of ground troops; the lack of coordination of oversight; the lack of electricity; failure to anticipate the intensity of sectarian violence; and the mishandling of the trial of Saddam Hussein (Feith 2008, 504–28).

Yet, compare the costs of the Iraq War of 2003 to conflicts of similar or even lesser magnitude. The United States lost more than four thousand dead pacifying the Philippines between 1898 and 1902, a figure comparable to the number of servicemen killed in Iraq. More than fifty-eight thousand American soldiers lost their lives in the Vietnam War, which ended in defeat. The tragic loss of American lives in Iraq also pales in comparison to the numbers of U.S. servicemen killed in the Civil War (660,000, Union and Confederate), World War II (290,000), World War I (116,000), and the Korean War (38,000) (Boot 2002, 125). For all the heartbreak of the war, the United States already has achieved a great deal: removing Saddam's tyranny; negotiating an interim constitution; restoring full sovereignty; holding free national elections; drafting and ratifying a permanent constitution; mitigating sectarian violence; introducing a sound currency; improving Iraq's neglected infrastructure; and training, equipping, and improving an Iraqi security force.

Since the surge of June 2007, the situation in Iraq has improved considerably. The United States military has learned how to win a counterinsurgency war, a lesson the American military took much longer to master fighting in Vietnam. Violence has plummeted 90 percent and deaths 70 percent from their presurge peaks. Reliable estimates predict the Iraqi economy grew at the prodigious rate of 8 percent in 2008 (Feaver 2008).

The surge has even achieved significant progress in some of the most recalcitrant enclaves. In Basra, joint American-Iraqi operations have inflicted a huge defeat on the Mahdi Army of radical Shiite cleric Muqtada al-Sadr. Army Lieutenant General Martin Dempsey, the interim commander of the U.S. Central Command, reported that "our forces and Iraqi forces have certainly disrupted al-Qaida, probably to a level we haven't seen" since the invasion in 2003 (Burns 2008). Spurred by this success, the government of Prime Minister Nouri Kamel al-Maliki initiated a major offensive against large Shiite enclaves of Sadr City, achieving what *New York Times* reporters Michael R. Gordon (a critic of the war) and Alissa Rubin call "a dramatic turnaround from the bitter fighting that has plagued the Baghdad neighborhood for two months" (2008, 1). Winning on the battlefield has generated corresponding political progress, bolstering the authority and legitimacy of the Maliki government and encouraging Sunnis to reenter rather than resist it (West 2008). By staying the course, the United States can establish a stable, prosperous, and democratic Iraq that protects the rights of its citizens, poses no threat to its neighbors, and contributes to winning the war on terror (Hanson 2008).

Such an outcome would raise Bush to the lofty heights of Truman. It could serve as a catalyst to transform the entire Middle East. Witness, for example, several other significant developments, which have contingently confirmed Bush's determination to push for regime change and democratization: the dismantling of Libya's WMD program; the breakup of Pakistani A. Q. Khan's nuclear smuggling ring; a possibility of ending Syrian tyranny in Lebanon; the quiescence of the so-called Arab Street, which was supposed to erupt in outrage at the American invasion of Iraq; and mounting demands for reform in the region. Saad Ibrahim, a democratic activist in Egypt, originally opposed the war but changed his mind: "It has unfrozen the Middle East, just as Napoleon's 1798 invasion did. Elections in Iraq force theocrats and autocrats to put democracy on the table, even if only to fight against us" (quoted in Wehner 2006).

Conversely, the United States will lose in Iraq and much elsewhere in the Middle East if American forces leave prematurely. None of the alternatives to staying the course—gradual or complete withdrawal of American troops, accelerating the transfer of responsibility to the Iraqi Army, engaging Syria or Iran, or any combination thereof—would provide even the semblance of a decent interval for staving off a defeat that would embolden our adversaries and result in the slaughter of hundreds of thousands of Iraqis who counted on us.

Meanwhile, critics continue to judge Bush's technical competence by a utopian standard of measure, which even the greatest leaders of democracy in wartime could never meet. Do the abuses of Abu Ghraib that should appall us constitute the aberration or the essence of American behavior in Iraq? Does not the Bush administration's assiduous and largely successful efforts to minimize civilian casualties compare favorably to the way in which any other great power has ever waged a war against such an implacable foe?

Should we rate Abraham Lincoln poorly for the torrent of miscalculations and disasters, which rendered the Civil War by far the most costly in our history? Have the Bush administration's mistakes or miscalculations reached the level of FDR's and the U.S. military's in World War II: the surprise attack on Pearl Harbor (despite abundant evidence that Japanese attacks were imminent); the defeats in the Philippines and at the Kasserine Pass; the bloodshed of Tarawa; Anzio; the Battle of the Bulge; Iwo Jima; and Okinawa? Does any sensible person deny Churchill's greatness despite his major mistakes: the Dardanelles; the Norway Campaign of 1940; the debacle in Greece and Crete in 1941; the 1942 sinking of the *Prince of Wales* and the *Repulse*; the 1942 fall of Singapore; and his illusions about Greece and Italy as the soft underbelly of Nazi Europe? Should we deny Truman's ranking as a great foreign policy president because of the catastrophic intelligence failures and miscalculations that beset his administration's conduct of the Korean War? (Beisner 2006, 393–416).

Is President Bush's vaunted failure to prepare adequately for the postwar occupation of Iraq unique among our great commanders in chief? Consider the monumental failures that arose in the conception and implementation of Reconstruction in the South after the American Civil War. Consider the more than five years of trial and error it took for the United States to devise and implement an effective plan for reconstructing Germany and Japan after World War II.

Is not the Bush administration's detention of suspected terrorists on Guantánamo that has so exercised his critics morally and practically defensible? What happens when we obliterate the distinction between uniformed soldiers and those who fight disguised as civilians? Does that not obliterate the traditional just war distinction between civilians and combatants? Will we not erode that critical distinction, to the detriment of the innocent, by applying a flawed criminal justice model for dealing with terrorists, or according them the rights of uniformed soldiers under the Geneva Convention?

Critics exaggerate likewise the damage the war in Iraq has inflicted on America's alliances, and underestimate the costs of inaction. Actually, the diplomatic controversy with Europe over the Iraq War may improve America's military and diplomatic situation in the long run: by eradicating Saddam's tyranny, the United States not only bolstered its credibility but exposed to the new Europe—Eastern Europe and our traditional British allies—the depth of French antipathy to the very existence of American power. Ultimately, most of Europe will recoil from France's agenda of weakening a United States that continues to underwrite Europe's freedom and prosperity. This has already begun to happen with the most important NATO allies that have led the opposition to Bush, even in France: witness the German and the French voters' replacement of their virulently anti-American leaders with robustly pro-American ones. President Sarkozy is indeed the most pro-American leader in the history of the French Fifth Republic. As the logic of the Bush Doctrine correctly anticipated, the United States has found an authoritarian Russia more challenging than a democratic one on a wide array of issues, though not as dangerous or categorical an adversary as the Soviet Union under communism. Nevertheless, the disturbing antidemocratic trends in Russia under Putin also will impel our NATO allies to cooperate more with the United States, disagree less, and moderate those disagreements that do arise.

President Bush bequeathed his successors an even stronger hand in East Asia, where constructively managing the rise of China lurks as the largest long-term challenge for American grand strategy. Geopolitically, the United States has a vital interest in preventing any single hostile power from dominating East Asia, the world's most powerful region based on traditional geopolitical criteria. A dynamic but still authoritarian China growing at an annual rate of more than 9 percent may develop the capacity and perhaps harbor the ambition to attain such dominance. The Bush administration buttressed the already strong alliance between the United States and democratic Japan, grounded in shared values; a well-justified alarm about North Korea's nuclear ambitions; and a complementary perception of the imperative of channeling China's dynamism in a constructive direction through a combination of economic engagement and military containment (Pyle 2007, 310–62).

The logic of the Bush Doctrine, the critical distinction it draws between tyrannies and stable, liberal democracies, also has accelerated the emerging strategic partnership between the United States and democratic India. This surely will stand as one of President Bush's most vital and enduring achievements, which will benefit the United States mightily for decades to come. India is a potentially powerful and philosophically congenial ally. Its economy, the world's fourth largest, will soon surpass Japan's as the world's third largest. The Bush administration prudently committed the United States to help India become a great power, a goal congenial with the global implications of the Bush Doctrine. America and India largely agree about the two paramount strategic challenges of the twenty-first century: preventing China from dominating East Asia and defeating radical Islam (which also menaces India) (Blackwill 2005, 10). India and Japan constitute the foundation of an American-led alliance system in East Asia essential for containing an authoritarian China's military while engaging the Chinese economically. This mixed strategy accords well with the premises of the Bush Doctrine: it identifies China's authoritarian regime as the wellspring of China's potential ambitions to displace the United States as the preeminent power in East Asia. It also defines our ultimate goal as political liberalization of the Chinese regime, leading to stable, liberal democracy; for peace with an authoritarian, Communist China will never be secure (Menges 2005, xxiii–xxiv).

Iran poses the most daunting immediate problem for the Obama administration. Again, the Bush Doctrine offers a better framework than the alternatives for choosing the least bad option. The militant mullahs have embarked on a perilous course: developing a nuclear and ballistic missile capability; supporting terrorism; fueling insurgencies in Iraq, Lebanon, and Palestine; striving to drive the United States out of the Middle East; and ultimately destroying Anglo-American civilization. Iran already has three thousand nuclear centrifuges in operation capable of producing uranium for nuclear weapons. The pledge of Iranian president Mahmoud Ahmadinejad to see Israel "wiped off the map" reveals in bold relief the politics of hate and confrontation that animate the current Iranian regime. Negotiations and engagement, the preferred strategy, have yielded nothing but Iranian defiance (Berman 2005). The United States cannot prudently tolerate a nuclear-armed Iran. Neither deterrence nor containment would suffice against a regime determined to return the world to the twelfth century, eradicate Israel, and impose a caliphate on the United States. If Iran obtains nuclear weapons, their militant rulers will become even more aggressive (Ledeen 2007).

President Bush rightly identified the nature of the Iranian regime as the source of the danger and prescribed democratic regime change as the remedy. He refrained, however, from using force preemptively against Iran, because until recently the Iranian mullahs have been more deterrable and less prone to taking precipitous risk than was Saddam. Moreover, the cost and risk of direct military action is greater. Iran is much larger than Iraq, its geography more forbidding, and its nuclear programs more difficult to preempt. An attack on Iran would cause enormous economic hardship: oil prices would skyrocket. Iranians also have a long history of ferocious hostility to foreign intervention, particularly American intervention. Unlike Saddam's Iraq, a plausible scenario exists for achieving democratic regime change in Iran that does not entail the use of force there: inspiring the large pro-American opposition in Iran to depose the militant mullahs by creating a successful democracy in neighboring Shiite Iraq and defeating Iran's chief surrogates, such as Syria, which are more vulnerable to direct military force (Pollack 2004, 266–424).

Yet time may run out on President Obama for pursuing nonmilitary solutions to the gathering danger of a radical, nuclear Iran. In the spring of 2007, Iran's president announced the regime's determination to install an additional six thousand nuclear centrifuges. The Iranians have become even more incendiary in causing trouble in Iraq, the West Bank, Lebanon, and Syria. All this may overwhelm the presumptions in favor of robust containment and against preemption if the internal dynamics in Iran cannot produce benign regime change soon enough to stave off a nuclear-armed

Iran under the ayatollahs (Gerecht 2008, 10).

Finally, this chapter predicts that the general principles of the Bush Doctrine will survive and thrive. Sooner or later, the gathering dangers of Iran, the global aspirations of dictators in Beijing, the neoauthoritarian revival of Putin's Russia, and other devils lurking around the corner in international relations, even in the best of times, will reveal the grave deficiencies of any of the plausible alternatives to the Bush Doctrine: an unrealistic realism that does not take regime type or ideology seriously; or a naïve liberal multilateralism that overestimates the harmony of interests among men and states. Sooner or later, Bush will receive his due as one of the nation's great foreign policy presidents, on par with President Truman.

REFERENCES

Abramowitz, Michael. 2008. "Bush's Comments in Israel Fuel Anger; Linking of Nazis, Iran Seen as Jab at Obama." *Washington Post*, May 16, p. A8.

Aquinas, Thomas. 1948. *Summa Theologica*. Chicago: Encyclopedia Britannica.

Aron, Raymond. 1990. *Memoirs: Fifty Years of Political Reflection*. New York: Holmes and Meier.

Beisner, Robert. 2006. *Dean Acheson: A Life in the Cold War*. New York: Oxford University Press.

Berman, Ilan. 2005. *Tehran's Rising: Iran's Challenge to the United States*. Lanham, MD: Rowman & Littlefield.

Beschloss, Michael. 2002. *The Conquerors: Roosevelt, Truman, and the Destruction of Hitler's Germany, 1941–1945*. New York: Simon & Schuster.

Blackwill, Robert D. 2005. "The India Imperative." *National Interest* 80: 8–16.

Bolton, John. 2007. *Surrender Is Not an Option: Defending America at the United Nations and Abroad*. New York: Threshold Editions.

Boot, Max. 2002. *A Savage War of Peace: Small Wars and the Rise of American Power*. New York: Basic Books.

Burns, Robert. 2008. "Commander: Al-Qaida in Iraq at Its Weakest." May 21. http://news .yahoo.com/s/ap/20080521/ap_on_go_ca_st_pe/us_iraq (Accessed July 13, 2008).

Churchill, Winston. 1948. *The Gathering Storm*. Boston: Houghton Mifflin.

Duelfer, Charles. 2004. *Comprehensive Report of the Special Advisor to the DCI on Iraq's WMD*. September 30. https://www.cia.gov/library/reports/general-reports-1/iraq_wmd _2004/index.html (Accessed July 13, 2008).

Feaver, Peter D. 2008. "Anatomy of the Surge." *Commentary* 125(4): 24–28.

Feith, Douglas. 2008. *War and Decision: Inside the Pentagon at the Dawn of the War on Terrorism*. New York: HarperCollins.

Friedberg, Aaron L. 2000. "The Struggle for Mastery in Asia." *Commentary* 109(5): 26–32.

Fukuyama, Francis. 2006. *America at the Crossroads: Democracy, Power, and the Neoconservative Legacy*. New Haven, CT: Yale University Press.

Fulbright, James William. 1966. *The Arrogance of American Power*. New York: Random House.

Gerecht, Reuel Mark. 2008. "Countering Iran: How to Deal with the Clerics in Iran." *Weekly Standard* 13(34): 10.

Goldberg, Jeffrey. 2005. "Breaking Ranks: What Turned Brent Scowcroft Against the Bush Administration." *New Yorker*, October 31, pp. 59–66.

Gordon, Michael R., and Alissa J. Rubin. 2008. "Operation in Sadr City Is an Iraqi Success, So Far." *New York Times*, May 21, p. 1.

Hanson, Victor Davis. 2008. "Nothing Succeeds Like Success." *Commentary* 125(4): 19–23.

Hilgruber, Andreas. 1981. *Germany and the Two World Wars*. Cambridge, MA: Harvard University Press.

Ikenberry, G. J., and C. A. Kupchan. 2004. "Liberal Realism: The Foundations of a Democratic Foreign Policy." *National Interest* 77(4): 38–49.

Kaufman, Robert. 2001. "The UN Record." *The World and I* 16(9): 34–39.

———. 2007. *In Defense of the Bush Doctrine*. Lexington: University Press of Kentucky.

Keegan, John. 2004. *The Iraq War*. New York: Knopf.

Kengor, Paul. 2006. *The Crusader: Ronald Reagan and the Fall of Communism*. New York: Regan Books.

Ledeen, Michael. 2007. *The Iranian Time Bomb: The Mullah Zealots' Quest for Destruction*. New York: Truman Talley Books.

Menges, Constantine. 2005. *China: The Gathering Threat*. Nashville, TN: Nelson Currant.

Muravchik, Joshua. 2005. *The Future of the United Nations: Understanding the Past to Chart a Way Forward*. Washington, DC: American Enterprise Institute.

Nye, Joseph. 2004. *Soft Power: The Means to Success in World Politics*. New York: PublicAffairs.

Obama, Barack. 2007. "Renewing American Leadership." *Foreign Affairs* 86(4): 2–16.

O'Sullivan, John. 2006. *The President, the Pope, and the Prime Minister: Three Who Changed the World*. Washington, DC: Regnery.

Podhoretz, Norman. 2007. *World War IV: The Long Struggle Against Islamo-Fascism*. New York: Doubleday.

Pollack, Kenneth. 2002. *The Threatening Storm: The Case for Invading Iraq*. New York: Random House.

———. 2004. *The Persian Puzzle: The Conflict Between Iran and America*. New York: Random House.

Powell, Colin. 1992–93. "US Forces: Challenges Ahead." *Foreign Affairs* 71(5): 32–45.

Pyle, Kenneth. 2007. *Japan Rising: The Resurgence of Japanese Power and Purpose*. New York: PublicAffairs.

Rabkin, Jeremy. 2004. *The Case for Sovereignty: Why the World Should Welcome American Independence*. Washington, DC: American Enterprise Institute.

Ross, Dennis. 2004. *The Missing Peace: The Inside Story of the Fight for the Middle East Peace*. New York: Farrar, Straus, and Giroux.

Schweizer, Peter. 2002. *Reagan's War: The Epic Story of His Forty-Year Struggle and Final Triumph over Communism*. New York: Doubleday.

Scowcroft, Brent. 2006. "A Modest Proposal." *National Interest* 83: 13–15.

Shawcross, William. 2004. *Allies: The U.S., Britain, Europe, and the War in Iraq*. New York: PublicAffairs.

Spalding, Elizabeth E. 2006. *The First Cold Warrior: Harry Truman, Containment, and the Remaking of Liberal Internationalism*. Lexington: University Press of Kentucky.

Walt, Stephen. 2005. *Taming American Power: The Global Response to U.S. Primacy*. New York: Norton.

Weart, Spencer. 1997. *Never at War: Why Democracies Will Not Fight One Another*. New Haven, CT: Yale University Press.

Wehner, Peter. 2006. "The Wrong Time to Lose Our Nerve." Opinionjournal.com, April 4. http://www.opinionjournal.com/editorial/feature.html?id=110008182 (Accessed July 13, 2008).

West, Bing. 2008. *The Strongest Tribe: War, Politics, and the Endgame in Iraq*. New York: Random House.

Zakaria, Fareed. 2005. "What Bush Got Right." *Newsweek*, March 14, pp. 22–26.

———. 2008. *The Post-American World*. New York: Norton.

CHAPTER 13

Forging an American Empire

LAWRENCE J. KORB AND LAURA CONLEY

ALTHOUGH PRESIDENTIAL LEGACIES often become clear only in the long term, the historical analysis of George W. Bush's two terms in office will focus intently on the conduct and outcome of his foreign policy. The man who came to the Oval Office with a domestic policy agenda and no international experience will be remembered less for his attention to such initiatives as raising test scores or expanding trade liberalization than for taking the United States into wars in Afghanistan and Iraq, particularly the latter.

Bush's intense involvement in international politics was unexpected but necessary after the attacks of September 11, 2001. Less than ten months after coming into office, he ordered U.S. troops into Afghanistan; in early 2003 he sent them to Iraq. He argued that it was necessary to remove the regime of Saddam Hussein in order to prevent the dictator from using weapons of mass destruction (WMD) against the United States or giving them to terrorist groups like al-Qaeda. The invasion and occupation provoked intense backlash and became Bush's most contentious policy.

Whether viewed through a realist or idealist lens, or a combination of both, foreign policy is a tool for furthering state interests. Thus, the evaluation of Bush's policy in this chapter will ask how effectively he defined and pursued the long-term foreign policy goals of the United States, and whether he adopted the appropriate tactical paths to advance the interests of the state. On balance, the chapter will argue that his presidency was marked by a lack of both strategic and tactical competence unprecedented in the nation's history.

As a comprehensive strategy document issued early in Bush's first term, the 2002 National Security Strategy (NSS) offers a good framework from which to judge Bush's competence in the execution of foreign policy. While an administration's outlook may change over time, the Global War on Terror (GWOT)—the major foreign policy thrust of the Bush presidency—has its foundations in this document. Therefore, it is logical to ask how effectively the administration accomplished the tactical goals set out in the NSS before questioning whether the administration's subsequent actions demonstrated long-term strategic competence.

As president, Bush used foreign policy primarily as a tool to sustain and increase a U.S. global preeminence that no longer exists. After 9/11 it should have been apparent that the United States would have to work multilaterally to guarantee its own security. The strategic environment that existed in the first decade after the Cold War had given way to a more dangerous and challenging situation, in which the United States would have to learn to work with other nations and deal effectively with rising powers and nonstate actors.

Bush dismissed this crucial change in the strategic environment and implemented a foreign policy predicated on the idea that protecting national security necessitated the unhindered projection of American power. Moreover, he defined power almost exclusively as hard power and consequently relied heavily on the military to carry out his policies, to the exclusion of other tools of statecraft. Ultimately, Bush overrode both allies and opponents in a vain effort to forge a new empire of American influence in the Middle East. In doing so, he made significant tactical errors, leading to devastating strategic failures.

FOREIGN POLICY BEFORE SEPTEMBER 11, 2001

Bush's foreign policy legacy is sharply bifurcated by the terrorist attacks of 9 / 11. While the first nine months of his presidency contained the philosophical underpinnings for his later actions, his engagement in the international arena was limited. He sought involvement in foreign affairs only when he believed it would strengthen national interest, and shied away from cooperation for the sake of multilateral gains. He consistently rejected international agreements with the potential to limit U.S. activities, and let lapse some of the key foreign policies of the previous administration.

As president-elect, Bush took a first definitive step toward rejecting international restrictions by stating that he had no intention of pursuing ratification of the International Criminal Court (ICC) treaty. Although

President Clinton had expressed some doubts about ratification, he had signed the treaty with faith that signatory status would allow the United States to shape the court in such a way as to avoid potential problems (Myers 2001). Bush did not see the same utility and withdrew before U.S. military forces could be subject to prosecution by an international court.

The ICC treaty was the beginning of a trend. Despite a campaign promise to regulate carbon dioxide emissions, Bush withdrew U.S. participation from the Kyoto Protocol (Ifill 2001). He also unsigned the Comprehensive Test Ban Treaty, which had been signed by Clinton but not ratified by the Senate; rejected a draft agreement intended to give teeth to the 1972 Biological Weapons Convention; and announced his intention to withdraw from the Anti-Ballistic Missile Treaty in order to deploy a national missile defense system. Finally, Bush stepped back from Clinton's engagement with North Korea and the Middle East peace process. Together, these actions were indicative of his strong tendency to define the utility of foreign policy in terms of narrow national self-interest. The international consequences of nonparticipation were of secondary concern.

FOREIGN POLICY AFTER SEPTEMBER 11, 2001

The events of 9/11 made it politically and strategically impossible for the Bush administration to remove itself from the international arena. However, the president's aversion to restrictive multilateral regimes did not diminish. In his first major post–9/11 action, Operation Enduring Freedom (OEF) in Afghanistan, this philosophy determined the composition of the mission. Bush conducted OEF as a loose coalition of troops rather than under the aegis of NATO or any other international organization. He did so even though NATO had invoked Article Five, the mutual defense clause of the Atlantic Treaty, for the first time in its history after 9/11 (Daley 2001). NATO later entered Afghanistan as the operator of the International Security Assistance Force, but the United States continued to maintain a separate command structure for some American troops until mid-2008, when NATO and American troops, with the exception of special operations forces, were placed under a single commander (Gilmore 2008).

The ad hoc coalition model was also Bush's instrument of choice in

Iraq. Although his administration initially involved the United Nations in assessing Iraq's alleged WMD capabilities, it quickly became apparent that international cooperation was of interest only if it did not hinder the push to remove Saddam Hussein. Indeed, Iraq had long been a priority for some top Bush advisors. During his confirmation, future deputy secretary of Defense Paul Wolfowitz stated frankly in regard to regime change in Iraq that "if there's a real option to do that, I would certainly think it's still worthwhile" (Ricks 2006, 27).

The war in Iraq was a policy failure from the beginning. The United States invaded with unrealistic expectations for the duration of the war and a "coalition of the willing" that was not large enough to confront the emergence of a multifaceted insurgency. More than five years after the invasion, American forces had dealt with multiple civil wars and suffered more than four thousand casualties, while coalition partners increasingly scaled back or removed their troop presence.

In making the decision to go to war in Iraq and Afghanistan, Bush eschewed not only international restrictions but also disagreement and uncertainty at home. Indeed, his decision-making process, based on his "instinctive reactions," restricted negotiation and compromise (Woodward 2008, 431). Bob Woodward writes that after 9/11 Secretary Rice suggested that Bush try to assuage concerns about his Afghanistan policy among members of his war cabinet by asking for their opinions and ideas. Bush agreed to do so. However, at the meeting he "went around the table asking everyone to affirm allegiance to the plan" rather than opening the policy up to criticism. Indeed, once set on a decision, Bush would not waver. Woodward notes that in regard to the war in Iraq, Bush "had never questioned its rightness, and its rightness made it the only course" (432).

THE BUSH DOCTRINE

Bush's determination to avoid international restrictions is laid out most forcefully in the 2002 NSS. This document, which was reiterated in 2006, notes up front that although the United States will work with partners, its policies will be "based on a distinctly American internationalism that reflects the union of our values and our national interests" ("National Security Strategy . . ." 2002, 1). As becomes apparent later in the document, this uniquely Bush approach, which overturned fifty years of American practice, can lead to unilateral, preventive military action.

The NSS's overarching goal is to enable the United States to triumph over global threats and capitalize on its power and influence to usher in "decades of peace, prosperity, and liberty" ("National Security Strategy . . ." 2002, 1). Although these goals are not markedly different from past U.S. policy, they are a particularly blunt presentation of these intentions. The more controversial aspects of the policy are found in the tactical prescriptions offered to attain this new "Pax Americana." In particular, the strategy contains a number of concepts unique to the Bush administration's approach.

First, the NSS identifies terrorism and unstable, rogue regimes as singular, even existential threats to U.S. security. Second, it assumes that the United States will maintain military dominance into the foreseeable future as a bulwark against rival great powers and other threats. Third, it foresees that a coalition of powers will confront global threats, and that these same countries will recognize the legitimate right of the United States to lead this effort. Finally, the NSS outlines a plan to combat terrorism by pursuing the spread of political and economic openness around the world; in other words, by making the world democratic (Korb 2003, 16–18).

The section of the NSS that drew the most virulent criticism, however, even from America's closest allies, was Bush's declaration that the United States would "not hesitate to act alone, if necessary, to exercise our right of self-defense by acting preemptively against . . . terrorists, to prevent them from doing harm against our people and our country" ("National Security Strategy . . ." 2002, 6). This statement, which was interpreted by some analysts as the basis of a new preventive-war "Bush doctrine," was reflected in the administration's willingness to invade Iraq over the objections of key allies and without a UN resolution.

Before launching the invasion, Bush made clear his impatience with international partners. He demanded that Hussein and his sons leave Iraq within forty-eight hours and remarked that "The United Nations Security Council has not lived up to its responsibilities, so we will rise to ours" (Bush 2003). In his view, the international community was no longer needed to make American military action legitimate or lawful.

TACTICAL COMPETENCE

After years of the United States waging war in Afghanistan and Iraq, criticisms of Bush's tactical competence have emerged from foes and allies alike. Both L. Paul Bremer, the former U.S. head administrator in Iraq, and General Eric Shinseki, army chief of staff from 1999 to 2003, have criticized the Bush administration for entering Iraq with too few troops to stabilize the situation after the removal of the regime (Wright and Ricks 2004). A detailed view of Bush's tactical competence, encompassing five policy areas from the NSS, reveals a pattern of incompetent policy management, in which the struggle to subdue global terrorism and rogue regimes without international support has led to military, political, and diplomatic failures.

"Champion Aspirations for Human Dignity"

In the NSS, the Bush administration committed itself to safeguarding "the nonnegotiable demands of human dignity," among them "the rule of law, limits on the absolute power of the state" and "equal justice." It also contained a strong commitment to opposing any violations of these concepts through international forums ("National Security Strategy . . ." 2002, 3). Yet, after 9/11 the Bush administration began to systematically violate basic principles of equal justice. The inhumane treatment of prisoners at Abu Ghraib by U.S. forces, the application of enhanced interrogation techniques on suspects in U.S. custody, the rendition of prisoners to countries that routinely practice torture, and efforts by the Bush administration to deny detainees at Guantánamo the ability to challenge their detentions in court all undermined Bush's efforts to serve as a leader in this area.

The use of enhanced interrogation techniques on detainees was a particularly egregious tactical failure. The president and his staff claimed that nonroutine techniques were needed in order to gain information vital to national security. Such techniques included subjecting detainees to cold temperatures, head slapping, and waterboarding. The legitimacy of these operations was based on a 2002 Department of Justice memo, which argued that all interrogation techniques were legal unless they caused pain comparable to that experienced during organ failure (Shane et al. 2007). This unprecedented redefinition of U.S. human rights policy led to allegations of possible torture from leading humanitarian organizations, including the International Committee of the Red Cross.

The United States' failure to lead by example was particularly devastating given the unconventional opponents that American forces were facing in Iraq and Afghanistan. The U.S. Army and Marine Counterinsurgency Manual lays out the consequences of ceding the moral high ground in such a conflict, whether through torture or the denial of basic legal rights. The manual analyzes the experiences of French troops during the Algerian revolution, when torture was employed as a tactic to defeat the Front de Libération Nationale (FLN). In that conflict, the "failure to comply with moral and legal restrictions against torture severely undermined French efforts and contributed to their loss despite several significant military victories" (Petraeus and Amos 2006, 7–9). A similar lesson was learned by the British government, which abandoned a policy of preemptively imprisoning suspected members of the Irish Republican Army in the 1970s after it became apparent "that this policy generated sympathy for the IRA and aided recruitment efforts" (Roth 2008, 9–16).

In the global war on terror, these tactics were similarly self-defeating. Former CIA officer Marc Sageman testified before the Senate Committee on Homeland Security and Governmental Affairs that although followers of radical Islam found much to dislike in the actions of the U.S. government prior to the invasion of Iraq, the Bush administration's policies in the years following that event contributed to the radicalization of future jihadists. He argued that Muslims were reacting with moral outrage—one of four factors leading to radicalization—to the U.S. involvement in Iraq and the experiences of Muslims in Abu Ghraib and Guantánamo (Sageman 2007). In allowing these abuses to proceed, Bush failed to uphold his own rhetorical commitment to equal justice. This glaring tactical failure strengthened the future ranks of the enemy he sought to defeat.

"Strengthen Alliances to Defeat Global Terrorism"

After the 9/11 attacks, the United States increasingly abandoned traditional alliances in favor of Bush's coalitions of the willing. Instead of partnering with others to develop a mutually acceptable and thus mutually actionable plan for combating terrorism, Bush sacrificed international goodwill for control. This tendency was consistent with the NSS, in which the president declared that while the United States would need the help of allies to defeat terrorism, it reserved the freedom to act alone if necessary. This is ostensibly an uncontroversial statement, but under the Bush administration it became a tactically counterproductive policy of limited and conditional engagement.

Bush received widespread support for his initial efforts to pursue the terrorists responsible for the 9 / 11 attacks. The most notable demonstration of this support came from NATO allies. However, the president opted to pursue the Taliban and al-Qaeda in Afghanistan with limited assistance. While this decision ensured that even well-meaning allies would not interfere with U.S. command of the operation, it also meant that the United States would not receive the military and economic contributions of many countries that had offered assistance. The United States even blocked the deployment of a UN-authorized multinational force to Afghanistan in late 2001, until the British could assure that U.S. Central Command would control the forces (Ford 2001).

Bush's aversion to allowing other countries to restrain his antiterrorism policies also shaped the coalition for Iraq. Although the president initially took his case against Hussein to the UN Security Council, the invasion was conducted without the sanction of NATO or any other international institution. Certainly, Bush was capable of acting without such approval. However, in doing so, he damaged relations with longtime allies—particularly the French and the Germans, who his secretary of Defense branded "old Europe" for their lack of cooperation—and gave credence to criticism that his administration endorsed not only preemptive but also preventive war (Purdum 2003).

Bush's choice not to create a broad international consensus around American actions severely damaged U.S. standing in the world. In Turkey, a staunch NATO ally and bulwark against the spread of radicalism in the volatile Middle East, only 9 percent of citizens surveyed in 2007 held a favorable view of the United States. In the 1999–2000 survey, the United States had a 52 percent favorability rating in Turkey, which dropped to 30 percent by 2002. U.S. favorability in Germany sunk from 78 percent in 1999–2000 to 60 percent in 2002 and 30 percent in 2007 (Pew Global

Attitudes Project 2007). The NSS envisioned the United States "forging new, productive international relationships and redefining existing ones in ways that meet the challenges of the twenty-first century" ("National Security Strategy . . ." 2002, 7). Instead, Bush's swift, nonnegotiable expansion of the American presence in the Middle East alienated key allies, further complicating his efforts to pursue terrorists and bring about peace and prosperity around the globe.

"Work with Others to Defuse Regional Conflicts"

In addition to outlining Bush's intentions to work with allies to fight terrorism the NSS highlighted his commitment to work with other nations to address intractable regional conflicts in areas whose chronic instability could be fertile ground for breeding future terrorists. Among the hot spots Bush proposed to engage, the Israel-Palestine and India-Pakistan conflicts stand out as areas where he failed to follow through on his commitment to confront instability. Moreover, when Bush did get involved, he sacrificed opportunities to work for broad solutions in favor of pursuing short-term, individual priorities in the war on terror. Ironically, these missed opportunities undermined his efforts in that struggle as well.

As early as February 2001, when violence erupted between Israel and Palestine, Bush decided not to continue the negotiations begun between the parties under the previous administration. A State Department spokesman declared that "The ideas and parameters that were discussed in the last few months are—were—President Clinton's parameters and, therefore, when he left office, they were no longer a US proposal or presidential proposal" (Goldenberg 2001). After 9/11, when Afghanistan and Iraq began to draw the administration's full attention, the Israel-Palestine conflict, despite its prominence in the NSS and its fundamental relevance to the history of foreign involvement in the Middle East, was completely ignored.

In early 2002, when a Hamas suicide bombing prompted Israel to surround the compound of Palestinian prime minister Yasir Arafat, Bush sent Colin Powell to the region. However, Bush and his national security advisor, Condoleezza Rice, rendered Powell ineffective by limiting his authority to pressure the involved parties (Bumiller 2007). Furthermore, Bush did not make any investment in peace between the parties until right before his invasion of Iraq, when he acceded to British requests to give rhetorical support for a Middle East "road map" to peace. To initiate wars in Afghanistan and Iraq without having first made a serious and sustained commitment to alleviating hostilities between Arabs and Israelis was foolhardy at best and contrary to the policies of virtually all administrations of the past fifty years.

After 9/11, it became increasingly obvious that resolving regional conflicts was less important to the United States than unilaterally pursuing its efforts in the war on terror. Nowhere was this more blatant than in the administration's policy toward Pakistan, where Bush's engagement did not demonstrate a coherent approach to alleviating regional tensions, and may actually have aggravated them.

General Pervez Musharraf, the unelected president of Pakistan when the 2001 terrorist attacks occurred, quickly won the Bush administration's support with his denunciations of terrorism and his initial assistance in capturing al-Qaeda operatives. However, Musharraf and his government failed to capture Osama bin Laden and his top assistant and did not assert sufficient authority over the volatile Federally Administered Tribal Areas to stop them from becoming a safe haven for jihadists. In fact, South Asia scholar Daniel Markey reports that early in the U.S.-Pakistan partnership, Musharraf's government did not seriously pursue Taliban fighters in Pakistan "because some members of the military still viewed them as potentially valuable assets for projecting Pakistani influence into Afghanistan and because their long history of a close working relationship make it hard to cut ties overnight" (Markey 2007, 85–102). While Markey argues that the military may be amenable to a change of heart, Bush was unable to bring about such a change by the end of his presidency, even after Musharraf's resignation.

Moreover, Bush's approach to engaging with Pakistan did not seem to acknowledge that country's longstanding conflict with India, which the NSS had sought to address. In July 2008, the administration foolishly proposed using almost $230 million of its counterterrorism aid to Pakistan to upgrade the country's fleet of F-16s, an aircraft more useful in Pakistan's potential war with India than in counterinsurgency operations. In fact, from 9/11 to mid-2008 the U.S. government gave Pakistan over $10 billion in military aid. About half was designated for counter-insurgency efforts, although "congressional auditors have said that Pakistan did not spend much of that money on counterinsurgency" (Schmitt 2008). Additionally, the Bush administration maintained its close relationship with Musharraf even though Pakistan was known to use its allies in Afghanistan to strengthen its regional position against India. The revelation in August 2008 that the Pakistani intelligence service, the ISI, aided militants responsible for a suicide attack on the Indian embassy in Kabul is another example of the results of putting antiterrorism policies before the United States' overall security interests.

Not only did the Bush administration provide aid to Pakistan without a reliable mechanism to ensure that the funds were used to support the war on terror, it also angered the Pakistanis by offering India a lucrative nuclear deal. This agreement, which was announced in 2005, proposed to allow India to acquire civilian nuclear technology from the United States, without requiring it to abandon its nuclear weapons programs or sign the Nuclear Non-Proliferation Treaty. The Pakistani government declared in July 2008 that the deal would set a precedent for further proliferation and would "increase the chances of a nuclear arms race in the sub-continent" ("International Agency . . ." 2008).

Although the Bush administration declared its intent to work with international partners to confront instability, the president's single-minded focus on antiterrorism policies undermined his ability to address entrenched regional conflicts. Even for those countries with which Bush found it expedient to engage, the incoherence of his administration's policies did little to resolve longstanding conflicts.

"Prevent Our Enemies from Threatening Us . . . with Weapons of Mass Destruction"

The NSS committed Bush to preventing the proliferation of WMDs using a variety of tools, among them "diplomacy, arms control, multilateral export controls, and threat reduction assistance" in concert with like-minded partners ("National Security Strategy . . ." 2002, 14). North Korea proved to be a particular challenge to this goal and joined the club of nuclear powers during Bush's time in office. While the failure to prevent this development cannot be laid entirely at the president's feet, Bush's hard line on negotiations with North Korea during his first term was an ineffective method for dealing with the problem.

When Bush took office, North Korea's plutonium enrichment program was ostensibly frozen under the 1994 Agreed Framework negotiated by the Clinton administration. In late 2002, however, after the Bush administration refused to live up to the terms of the 1994 agreement and broke off talks, North Korea openly admitted to the United States that it was developing a nuclear program by enriching uranium. By October 2006, after resuming its plutonium enrichment program and expelling United Nations inspectors, the North was able to conduct its first nuclear weapons tests. The Bush administration's policy to address these developments suffered from a lack of attention and a preference for confrontational rhetoric over diplomatic engagement.

In the summer of 2002, before the North Koreans admitted to the existence of their nuclear program, they appeared ready to increase openness. They proposed a meeting between Secretary of State Colin Powell and the North Korean foreign minister. They also implemented some economic reforms and expressed willingness for high-level talks with South Korea. Rather than capitalizing on this moment of opportunity to open a dialogue with the North Koreans, which would have been supported by the South Korean government, Bush permitted Powell only a brief, informal conversation with the minister at an international conference (Laney and Shaplen 2003, 16–30).

A few months after having been roundly rejected by the West, the North Koreans announced the existence of their nuclear program and offered the United States a nonaggression pact. Again, the Bush administration rejected the overture, this time with retaliation. Bush stopped shipments of heavy fuel oil to the North, a move which prompted the North to announce that it would begin reprocessing spent nuclear fuel rods. The situation reached a crisis point in 2006 with North Korea's first nuclear test.

By 2006, the Bush administration was engaged in two wars that were not going well and was losing domestic support for its foreign policies. Therefore, following the nuclear test, Bush was left with no choice but to engage North Korea. In 2008, as a part of multilateral talks, the North agreed to pursue disarmament in return for international aid. Whether this will reduce the nuclear threat will depend in large part on whether President Obama chooses to continue the policies of his predecessor or return to the approach of the Clinton administration.

Bush's largest nonproliferation success was Libya's decision to abandon its WMD programs in December 2003. While this was an encouraging development, it is not one for which the Bush administration can take full credit. The invasion of Iraq may have generated some pressure to disarm, but as Dafna Hochman points out in *Parameters*, the journal of the Army War College, the U.S. action in Iraq did not slow down any other known proliferation programs, and may actually have caused Iran and North Korea to accelerate their nuclear programs. Additionally, Libyan officials reportedly made an offer to disarm during secret talks with the Clinton administration in 1999 (Hochman 2006, 66). Thus, Bush's largest nonproliferation success might well have been built on the diplomacy of his predecessors.

"Develop Agendas for Cooperative Action with Other Main Centers of Global Power"

Despite Bush's propensity for prioritizing U.S. antiterrorism goals over international alliances, the 2002 NSS did indicate a desire to pursue U.S. goals "by organizing coalitions—as broad as practicable—of states able and willing to promote a balance of power that favors freedom" ("National Security Strategy . . ." 2002, 25). The strategy placed a heavy emphasis on improving NATO's ability to take action but also indicated an interest in working with other emerging powers. In practice, however, the Bush administration's selective approach to international arrangements also marked its relationships with regional hegemons. Bush cooperated with countries willing to follow U.S. strategy and dismissed those who disagreed.

Although Iran is not mentioned in the NSS as a key country—indeed, no country in the Middle East is labeled as such—it is undoubtedly a significant actor in its region. However, Bush not only spent the better part of his presidency refusing to negotiate with Iran over its nuclear ambitions but put at risk the one area where Iran was willing to work with the United States: Afghanistan.

During the U.S. invasion of Afghanistan, Iran supported the U.S. cause in overturning the Taliban government and getting the Northern Alliance to support President Hamid Karzai. Iran also provided substantial reconstruction assistance after the Taliban were successfully ousted and Karzai took office (Montero 2006). Despite its contributions, Bush labeled the nation one of the axis of evil countries in January 2002, thus attempting to isolate Iran diplomatically and strategically.

When President Nixon went to China in 1972, he scored a diplomatic coup against the Soviet Union and reinvigorated diplomacy with a country that, though not a friendly ally, was undoubtedly a significant global power. Although the circumstances were not entirely analogous, Bush faced a similar situation in the Middle East. In the global war on terror the Bush administration confronted a new kind of enemy—stateless actors—whose allegiance was to ideology rather than nationality. By forming a working partnership, though not an alliance, with Iran, Bush could have found an ally against two common enemies, the Taliban and the regime of Saddam Hussein. Instead, he chose to alienate Iran and pursue American policies without compromise. Moreover, by removing Saddam Hussein from power in Iraq, he increased permanently Iran's power and influence in the greater Middle East.

STRATEGIC COMPETENCE

In the NSS, Bush made a commitment to pursue global security under American leadership. However, he approached this long-term, strategic goal under the assumption that security could only be guaranteed through military dominance and the creation of an informal empire of American influence in the greater Middle East. This vision led him to rely almost exclusively on military power to carry out his primary policy objective, winning the global war on terror.

Bush's short-term, tactical errors were numerous. In his pursuit of victory in the war on terror he alienated allies, undermined the U.S. human rights record, ignored potentially explosive regional conflicts, refused to negotiate with potential nuclear states, and antagonized rising world powers. However, his heavy focus on the military as the primary tool of statecraft and his belief in its ability to bring about long-term peace may represent a greater foreign policy failure. As a strategic leader, he inflicted long-term damage on the U.S. military and set the United States on a path that could lead to failure in the war on terror.

In making the war in Afghanistan, and later the war in Iraq, the central efforts of the war on terror, Bush pushed the military almost to the breaking point. The all-volunteer force was not, as General John Abizaid, a former head of U.S. Central Command, noted, "built to sustain a long war" (Ryan 2006). By 2008, with the United States still fighting on both fronts, the truth of this statement became apparent. With both active duty forces and Army National Guard and Reserve units facing repeated deployments abroad, the U.S. Army saw desertion at its highest level since 1980 and suicide at its highest point in more than fifteen years. Soldiers consistently received less than the Department of Defense's recommended two-to-one ratio of time at home to combat deployment, and the Bush administration's efforts to increase the size of the ground forces were tardy at best. These increases, which were desperately needed to relieve the stress on U.S. armed forces, were relatively small additions that would not be completed until 2012.

The damaging effects of Bush's policies on the military were compounded by the president's failure to set the United States on the right path to fight the war on terror. Although Bush was widely supported in responding to the 9/11 attacks with military force, this is not the only, or the most effective, approach to fighting terrorism. In 2008, the RAND Corporation released a study of 648 terrorist groups in the second half of the twentieth century. The study's authors posed a simple question: How do terrorist groups end? Through analysis of such diverse actors as al-Qaeda, the IRA, and the Khmer Rouge, they determined that the most common path to ending terrorism came through transitioning terrorists to legitimate political actors. This result occurred 43 percent of the time. In only 7 percent of the cases was military force the decisive factor in bringing terrorism to an end (Jones and Libicki 2008, 19).

While the RAND study is not a total condemnation of the policies of the Bush administration, it casts serious doubt on the president's heavy reliance on military force as the primary instrument in the war on terror. In his pursuit of victory, Bush ignored the lessons of history. Instead of bringing to bear American diplomatic, political, and cultural expertise to defeat al-Qaeda and put the United States on a path to productive global leadership, he staked the security of the American people and the lives of American troops on the instrument least likely to achieve his goals.

CONCLUSION

From his first days in office, President Bush was so confident in American power that he adopted a policy of dealing with international challenges unilaterally if he could, and multilaterally only if he had to. This was the exact opposite of all the American presidents since World War II. The approach, from Truman to Clinton, was multilaterally if we can, unilaterally only if we must. Many analysts had hoped that the attacks of 9/11 would compel Bush to change his approach, but this proved not to be the case.

Bush compounded the situation in two ways. First, he established a new international norm for using military force. Rather than using military force to respond to an attack or to deal with an imminent threat, he decided it was appropriate to wage a preventive war, that is, to use military power to deal with a future potential threat. This was the basis for his invasion and occupation of Iraq, a policy that ignored the traditional doctrine of leveraging military superiority for deterrence and containment.

Second, for too long he refused to negotiate directly with our potential adversaries, like Iran and North Korea, without preconditions that would have required them to undermine their leverage in the negotiations. Had his predecessors followed such a policy, it is unlikely that the United States and the Soviet Union would have concluded any arms control agreements, or that China would have cooperated with the United States against the Soviet Union.

Zbigniew Brzezinski, national security advisor during the Carter administration, has remarked that Bush's war in Iraq is a "historic, strategic, and moral calamity" and that U.S. policy in the Middle East demands a "strategy of genuinely constructive political engagement" (Brzezinski 2007). Had Bush begun his presidency, or even his response to 9/11, with such a commitment to cooperative diplomacy, his policies might not have failed strategically and tactically.

REFERENCES

Brzezinski, Zbigniew. 2007. "SFRC Testimony." In *Securing America's Interests in Iraq: The Remaining Options. Iraq in the Strategic Context. Session 2.* U.S. Congress. Senate. Committee on Foreign Relations, 110th Congress, 1st Session, February 1. http://foreign.senate.gov/testimony/2007/BrzezinskiTestimony070201.pdf (Accessed August 21, 2008).

Bumiller, Elisabeth. 2007. "Rice's Turnabout on Mideast Talks." *New York Times*, November 26. http://www.nytimes.com/2007/11/26/washington/26rice.html (Accessed 2008).

Bush, George W. 2003. "President Says Saddam Hussein Must Leave Iraq Within 48 Hours," March 17. http://www.whitehouse.gov/news/releases/2003/03/20030317-7.html (Accessed August 25, 2008).

Daley, Suzanne. 2001. "After the Attacks: The Alliance; For First Time, NATO Invokes Joint Defense Pact with U.S." *New York Times*, September 13, p. A17.

Ford, Peter. 2001. "Coalition Allies Lament: It's Still 'America First.'" *Christian Science Monitor*, December 27. http://www.csmonitor.com/2001/1227/p1s3-wogn.html (Accessed August 25, 2008).

Gilmore, Gerry J. 2008. "Pentagon Proposes Change to U.S. Command Structure in Afghanistan." *American Forces Press Service*, August 8. http://www.defenselink.mil/News/newsarticle.aspx?id=50748 (Accessed August 25, 2008).

Goldenberg, Suzanne. 2001. "Bush Disowns Clinton Peace Proposals for Middle East." *Guardian*, February 10. http://www.guardian.co.uk/world/2001/feb/10/usa.israel (Accessed 2008).

Hochman, Dafna. 2006. "Rehabilitating a Rogue: Libya's WMD Reversal and Lessons for U.S. Policy." *Parameters* 36(1): 63–78.

Ifill, Gwen. 2001. "Bush and the Environment." *NewsHour with Jim Lehrer*, March 29. http://www.pbs.org/newshour/bb/environment/jan-june01/bushenv_3-29.html (Accessed August 25, 2008).

"International Agency Approves Nuclear Inspection Deal for India." 2008. *International Herald Tribune*, August 1. http://www.iht.com/articles/2008/08/01/asia/india.php (Accessed August 12, 2008).

Jones, Seth G., and Martin C. Libicki. 2008. *How Terrorist Groups End: Lessons for Countering al Qa'ida.* Santa Monica, CA: RAND Corporation. http://www.rand.org/pubs/monographs/MG741-1/ (Accessed August 25, 2008).

Korb, Lawrence J. 2003. *A New National Security Strategy in an Age of Terrorists, Tyrants, and Weapons of Mass Destruction.* New York: Council on Foreign Relations.

Laney, James T., and Jason T. Shaplen. 2003. "How to Deal with North Korea." *Foreign Affairs* 82(2): 16–30. http://www.foreignaffairs.org/20030301faessay10336/james-t-laney-jason-t-shaplen/how-to-deal-with-north-korea.html (Accessed August 25, 2008).

Markey, Daniel. 2007. "A False Choice in Pakistan." *Foreign Affairs* 86(4): 85–102. http://www.foreignaffairs.org/20070701faessay86407/daniel-markey/a-false-choice-in-pakistan.html (Accessed August 25, 2008).

Montero, David. 2006. "Iran, U.S. Share Afghan Goals." *Christian Science Monitor*, May 4. http://www.csmonitor.com/2006/0504/p06s02-wosc.html (Accessed August 25, 2008).

Myers, Steven Lee. 2001. "U.S. Signs Treaty for World Court to Try Atrocities." *New York Times*, January 1. http://query.nytimes.com/gst/fullpage.html?res=9D0CE0D7153BF932A35752C0A9679C8B63 (Accessed 2008).

"The National Security Strategy of the United States of America." 2002. http://www.whitehouse.gov/nsc/nss.pdf (Accessed August 20, 2008).

Petraeus, David H., and James F. Amos. 2006. *Counterinsurgency.* Washington, DC: U.S. Department of the Army. http://usacac.army.mil/cac/repository/materials/coin-fm3-24 .pdf (Accessed August 22, 2008).

Pew Global Attitudes Project. 2007. *Rising Environmental Concern in 47–Nation Survey: Global Unease with Major World Powers.* Washington, DC: Pew Research Center. http:// pewglobal.org/reports/pdf/256.pdf (Accessed August 25, 2008).

Purdum, Todd. 2003. "Threats and Responses: Washington; Rebuffing 2 Allies, U.S. Pushes Demand That Iraq Disarm." *New York Times,* January 24. http://query.nytimes.com/gst/ fullpage.html?res=9B0CE1DC1639F937A15752C0A9659C8B63 (Accessed 2008).

Ricks, Thomas. 2006. *Fiasco: The American Military Adventure in Iraq.* New York: Penguin.

Roth, Kenneth. 2008. "After Guantanamo: The Case Against Preventive Detention." *Foreign Affairs* 87(3): 9–16. http://www.foreignaffairs.org/20080501facomment87302/ kenneth -roth/after-guant-namo.html (Accessed August 25, 2008).

Ryan, Kevin. 2006. "Stretched Too Thin." *Washington Post,* December 18, p. A25.

Sageman, Marc. 2007. "Radicalization of Global Islamist Terrorists." In *Violent Islamic Extremism: The European Experience.* U.S. Congress. Senate. Committee on Homeland Security and Governmental Affairs. 110th Congress, 1st Session, June 27. http://hsgac .senate.gov/public/_files/062707Sageman.pdf (Accessed August 25, 2008).

Schmitt, Eric. 2008. "Plan Would Use Antiterror Aid on Pakistani Jets." *New York Times,* July 24. http://www.nytimes.com/2008/07/24/world/asia/24pstan.html?scp=1&sq=&st=nyt (Accessed August 2008).

Shane, Scott, David Johnston, and James Risen. 2007. "Secret U.S. Endorsement of Severe Interrogations." *New York Times,* October 4. http://www.nytimes.com/2007/10/04/ washington/04interrogate.html (Accessed 2008).

Woodward, Bob. 2008. *The War Within.* New York: Simon & Schuster.

Wright, Robin, and Thomas E. Ricks. 2004. "Bremer Criticizes Troop Levels." *Washington Post,* October 5, p. A1.

CHAPTER 14

Fighting Two Wars

TOM LANSFORD AND JACK COVARRUBIAS

PRESIDENT GEORGE W. BUSH left office in 2009 with the United States fighting two wars, Afghanistan and Iraq. Bush became the first president since Lyndon B. Johnson to exit the White House with the nation engaged in significant combat operations. In both Afghanistan and Iraq, the initial war strategy achieved its objectives. In Afghanistan the Taliban regime and al-Qaeda were overthrown, while in Iraq Saddam Hussein was deposed. However, insurgencies in the two nations bedeviled U.S. and allied military planners and eroded the credibility of the United States. Concurrently, public confidence in the Bush administration declined precipitously. Bush's personal approval ratings averaged only 28 percent by 2008, only a few points higher than Harry S Truman, whose approval ratings had dropped to 22 percent in 1952, also in the midst of a highly unpopular war (and who also left the resolution of a major conflict to his successor).

Exacerbating public perceptions and arguably military effectiveness was the ongoing transformation of the military to a leaner, more agile force instigated by Bush's appointee as secretary of Defense, Donald Rumsfeld. Tasked with modernizing and streamlining what was viewed as a bloated Cold War–era military, Rumsfeld proceeded to reassert civilian authority over a Joint Chiefs of Staff that was largely a holdover from the Clinton administration and not trusted by the Bush administration. Rumsfeld's often antagonistic attitude toward the generals in pushing transformation alienated military leaders who had become used to more autonomy and who openly countered any suggestion at cutting programs. By the invasion of Afghanistan, then Iraq, military brass was often cut out of the chain of command, with Rumsfeld's team micromanaging operations. Rumsfeld used this position to demonstrate the effectiveness of the "new," leaner military, though the public discourse often portrayed the Pentagon as divided and ill prepared.

During the invasion of Afghanistan (Operation Enduring Freedom), the United States implemented an innovative tactical strategy that relied on special operations units, supported by air power and indigenous forces, to overwhelm the Taliban and its allies. The "Afghan Model" of U.S. warfare was in many ways the culmination of longstanding trends and doctrine in the nation's military and the result of lessons learned from the 1991 Gulf War through the various interventions of the 1990s. The Afghan Model's core principle, that U.S. technology and firepower could devastate an opponent with only a relatively small number of troops, would form the basis for U.S. strategy during the invasion of Iraq. The military successes of the Afghan Model were replicated in Iraq, albeit on a far larger scale as conventional ground units were integrated into a campaign that emphasized what popularly became known as "shock and awe."

The political components of the Afghan Model were not as successful. After the fall of the Taliban, the United States implemented among its wartime coalition a division of labor whereby the nation's forces continued war-fighting missions, mainly anti-Taliban or anti–al-Qaeda operations, while other allies were delegated to oversee nation-building efforts and reconstruction. The United States sought to replicate this model in Iraq but was never able to deploy a robust coalition capable of stabilizing the country or ensuring security. The result was the escalation of the ongoing insurgency. Meanwhile, the failure of the Bush administration to grow its Afghan coalition has resulted in an expansion of Taliban–al-Qaeda operations there. Ultimately, both wars reinforce the necessity of coalition-building and reaffirm the utility of past U.S. security doctrines.

In judging the Bush administration on its handling of the two wars in Afghanistan and Iraq, it is difficult to determine if the long road will view these two conflicts as a strategic success or a setback. It is apparent, however, that the Bush years will certainly be influential in how the United States does business with the international community for the foreseeable future. Moral competence and tactical competence are a bit easier to look at in the present. In terms of moral competence, the Bush administration's failings have been discussed repeatedly over the last several years but not without a great deal of political spin and assumed facts. The inability of the administration to deal with this debate in the face of its being a moving target is at least some indication of the administration's political competence. Of course, the ability of the administration to continue these military operations into and through the end of the second term is also an important indicator of political competence—or perhaps political failure elsewhere. Congressional approval ratings were dismal since the Democratic takeover in January 2007, averaging around 18 percent in August–September 2008. Judging the Bush administration along the dimension of tactical competence, at least in regard to committing to wars in Afghanistan and Iraq, takes a bit of background understanding of how U.S. military doctrine has transformed military capabilities.

U.S. MILITARY DOCTRINE AND MULTIPLE WARS

Since the end of World War II, U.S. military strategy has been based on the capability to fight two wars simultaneously. The doctrine reached its peak under President John F. Kennedy, whose security strategy was based on the ability of the United States to fight two major wars and one minor conflict at the same time (the so-called two-and-a-half-war approach) (Eland 2001, 18). This required the U.S. military to be prepared, for instance, to fight a major war in Europe and one in the Pacific, while still maintaining the capability to fight a regional foe in Latin America or Africa. Successive presidents reduced this approach. For example, Richard Nixon implemented the one-and-a-half war, whereby the Defense Department had to be prepared to fight both a major and regional war at the same time. President George H.W. Bush cut the requirement further so that U.S. forces had to have the readiness to concurrently win two regional conflicts (Eland 2001, 18).

In 1993, Secretary of Defense Les Aspin announced the results of the Bill Clinton administration's "Bottom-Up Review" (BUR) of U.S. military doctrine and capabilities. The BUR called for the United States to continue to be able to fight two regional wars, such as the 1991 Gulf War, but it recommended $105 billion in defense-spending reductions through 1999 and drastic reductions in deployable forces. Significantly, the BUR recommended methods to continue to reduce troop strength while maintaining war-fighting capabilities. For instance, the "win-hold-win" strategy held that the United States should maintain force levels so that it could quickly win one regional conflict while using airpower or naval assets or even coalition assets to "hold" the second theater until forces from the first could be redeployed (Aspin 1992, 2–3). The administration's 1997 *Quadrennial Defense Review* (QDR) affirmed the main tenets of the BUR, including the "hold" element. Also, in spite of growing evidence that smaller conflicts, such as Bosnia, were more likely than large, Iraq War–style operations, the 1997 QDR left the main force structures, themselves a legacy of the Cold War, in place (Larson et al. 2005).

The initiatives to reduce troop strength and cut defense spending in the 1990s represented another pattern in U.S. national security policy. Concurrent with the strategic imperative to fight two simultaneous wars, successive presidents since World War II have endeavored to reduce the nation's standing military forces but maintain capabilities by increasing reliance on advanced armaments and weapons system. Dwight D. Eisenhower's "New Look" strategy emphasized the use of nuclear weapons as a substitute for maintaining a large standing army. Jimmy Carter initially sought to reduce the nation's reliance on nuclear weapons while also continuing the troop cuts begun in the aftermath of the Vietnam War (Auten 2008).

One method to maintain capability and still reduce expenditures was to increase the military's reliance on the Army Reserve and the National Guard. At the end of the Vietnam War, the army's chief of staff, Creighton B. Abrams, undertook a reorganization of the service. Abrams shifted a number of missions to the Reserves and National Guard, ranging from combat operations to logistics to transport. This trend continued through the end of the twentieth century. In addition to reductions in expenses, Abrams had another objective: in light of the erosion of public sentiment during the Vietnam War, the chief of staff wanted to ensure that future conflicts would have broad support. He and his staff concluded that since Reserve and National Guard units would have to be mobilized prior to the onset of fighting, Congress and the president would authorize military action only when there was broad public support (Snow 2008, 251–52). Furthermore, because of the reliance on the Reserves and National Guard, conflicts would have to be relatively short, since the units could only be mobilized for limited periods without causing a backlash.

When George W. Bush entered office in 2001, he ordered Secretary of

Defense Rumsfeld to conduct a review of U.S. forces. Rumsfeld was tasked to transform the military into a lighter, more lethal force, which used fewer conventional forces but integrated the technological and communications advantages of the United States. Like his immediate predecessors, Rumsfeld sought to transform the U.S. military from its Cold War posture to a leaner force that could maintain its ability to fight two simultaneous conflicts and was also capable of undertaking the disparate missions which emerged in the 1990s. However, Rumsfeld also encountered significant resistance from the military establishment and its civilian leadership (Snow 2008, 110). Both elements sought to retain Cold War strategy and tactics, which concentrated on the defense of Europe and which emphasized the use of large, conventional formations and weapons systems (Snow 2008, 112).

One of Rumsfeld's long-term plans was an effort to integrate a new approach to the nation's military operations, network-centric warfare. First developed in the late 1990s, network-centric warfare is a concept that "broadly describes the combination of strategies, emerging tactics, techniques, and procedures, and organizations that a fully or even a partially networked force can employ to create a decisive warfighting advantage" (U.S. Department of Defense 2005, 3). Simply put, network-centric warfare is a description of the ability to integrate information, communications, tactics, and weaponry from senior commanders down to the soldiers in the field so that everyone has complete tactical awareness. This allows for "on time" delivery of weaponry, including precision-guided munitions, and ensures that forces and weaponry are concentrated at the right place at the right time. The concept is "characterized by the ability of geographically dispersed forces to create a high level of shared battlespace awareness that can be exploited via self-synchronization and other network-centric operations to achieve commanders' intent" (Cebrowski and Garstka 1998, 28). Network-centric warfare is therefore a force-multiplier that takes advantage of information, communications, and tactical awareness.

Of specific concern for Rumsfeld, and his predecessors, was asymmetric warfare. Asymmetric warfare is a tactic in which an actor seeks to concentrate his advantages against the weaknesses of an opponent. Throughout history, asymmetric warfare has emerged in conflicts in which one military power is so dominant that an opponent avoids direct conventional engagements and instead uses unconventional or guerilla tactics which allow the opponent to concentrate its forces against a specific weakness of the larger force. Again, throughout history, weaker forces have sought to gain equality or superiority of power by attacking outposts or small deployments in such a way that the insurgents could gain temporary numeric parity or superiority and then retreat before larger forces could engage them. The North Vietnamese employed asymmetric warfare against the United States to great effect during the Vietnam War, as did the Mujahedeen against the Soviets during the Soviet occupation of Afghanistan. As a result, U.S. military planners sought to develop tactics that would negate asymmetric warfare through intelligence, communications, and the rapid deployment of aerial and over-the-horizon munitions.

THE AFGHAN MODEL

The 2001 terrorist attacks provided Rumsfeld with an opportunity to formulate and implement innovative tactics. The resultant Afghan Model alternatively fused and rejected a number of disparate trends in U.S. security strategy and military tactics. It also provided a means to overcome asymmetric warfare. Indeed, the Afghan Model was a form of asymmetric warfare in which the United States was able to concentrate its technological and tactical advantages against the weakest points of its opponent.

The Afghan Model brought together the main strategic tenets of the Weinberger-Powell Doctrine with network-centric warfare. The Weinberger Doctrine was developed by Secretary of Defense Caspar Weinberger in 1984 to provide overarching guidelines on the use of force by policymakers. The doctrine articulated six main points: (1) military force should be used only to protect the vital interests of the nation or an ally; (2) there had to be clear military and political objectives before operations began (in other words, there had to be a clearly defined end state that marked the point at which U.S. forces would be withdrawn); (3) the mission had to have adequate forces and resources; (4) there should be constant analysis to ensure that the forces were sufficient for the mission, and force structures should be adjusted based on those assessments; (5) operations had to have the support of the public and the nation's political leadership; and (6) military operations were a last resort, after all other options were exhausted (Twining 1988). Colin Powell refined the doctrine while he was chair of the Joint Chiefs of Staff to include a requirement that the United States be able to employ overwhelming force in military operations.

Unlike missions in the 1990s, the Afghan Model minimized coalition operations. Military conflicts in the 1990s, including the 1991 Gulf War and the Kosovo War, highlighted a variety of potential problems common to coalition warfare. For instance, U.S. officers reported that some of their European allies allowed political considerations to interfere with military operations during the Kosovo War. There were also problems with coordination of mission and differences in capabilities among the allies (Clark 2001). A Defense Science Board report noted that the "Kosovo conflict underlined the considerable gap in capability between the European and United States' forces" (Bender 1998, 8). The executive summary of a 1999 conference by the Institute for Strategic Studies at the National Defense University summarized both the positive and negative implications of coalition planning in declaring that "The consensus building process forces open debate in national capitals; decision-making is incremental and iterative, and tends to result in non-decisive engagement in the early going" (Institute for Strategic Studies 1999). In planning Operation Enduring Freedom in Afghanistan, U.S. defense officials deliberately sought to avoid large-scale coalition missions and instead utilize only those allied forces and weaponry that were highly compatible and had optimum interoperability with American forces (Lansford 2002).

Operation Enduring Freedom

In planning Operation Enduring Freedom, Rumsfeld was tasked to accomplish four major goals: (1) the destruction of terrorist networks and infrastructure in Afghanistan, including bases and training facilities; (2) the capture or death of senior al-Qaeda leadership; (3) the overthrow of the Taliban regime; and (4) the minimization of civilian casualties and the delivery of appropriate humanitarian aid to compensate for any disruptions among the civilian population. The initial planning incorporated the main tenets of the Weinberger-Powell Doctrine and integrated the principles of network-centric warfare.

Military scholar Stephen Biddle noted that through the resultant Afghan

Model "a novel combination of special operations forces (SOF), precision-guided munitions (PGMs), and an indigenous ally destroyed the Taliban's military, toppled their regime, and did so while neither exposing Americans to the risk of heavy casualties nor expanding the American presence in a way that might spur nationalist insurgency" (Biddle 2002, 1). The model emphasized the use of small, highly mobile forces that were tied into a broad support network and therefore able to direct the overwhelming firepower available to the coalition. Instead of deploying large conventional forces, the Afghan Model relied on allied indigenous forces, the anti-Taliban Northern Alliance. Michael E. O'Hanlon also pointed out that the operation demonstrated the success of the efforts at collaboration between the services and that it "showed that more joint-service experimentation and innovation are highly desirable, given that the synergies between special operations forces on the ground and Air Force and Navy aircraft in the skies were perhaps the most important keys to victory" (O'Hanlon 2004, 279).

Bush approved Operation Enduring Freedom on October 1, 2001. Combat operations began on October 7. The United States deployed two aircraft carrier battle groups to the region and inserted special operations forces into Afghanistan to coordinate with the Northern Alliance and other anti-Taliban elements. The United States selectively utilized allied assets, including, for instance, French, British, and Italian air units. The initial phase of the operation emphasized air and missile strikes to destroy the military infrastructure and capabilities of the Taliban and al-Qaeda. Rumsfeld sought to overwhelm the Taliban by attacking multiple targets with multiple weapons systems.

Coalition special operations forces identified targets and served as liaisons for coalition assets and on-the-ground anti-Taliban forces. This allowed the United States to use highly accurate and sophisticated precision-guided weaponry; approximately 70 percent of the munitions were precision-guided. Coalition personnel prespotted targets, which resulted in a high degree of accuracy. The United States also utilized other innovative weaponry such as unmanned aerial reconnaissance drones, which provided significant intelligence-gathering and attack capabilities at little or no risk to coalition personnel. U.S. military planners divided Afghanistan into thirty zones and assigned aircraft to each zone. Aircraft were deployed to each zone and remained on standby until they were assigned a mission or called on for ground support.

By October 20, the coalition had complete control of the air and had destroyed most of the Taliban's air defenses and communications infrastructure. By November 1, there had been more than two thousand combat sorties and the United States and its allies had delivered more than one million humanitarian rations to the Afghan people. At the end of November, the Taliban and al-Qaeda had lost about half of their territory to U.S. allies, led by the Northern Alliance. By December 2001, the Taliban and al-Qaeda had been dislodged and a pro-Western regime installed. By the end of the campaign, when Rumsfeld declared an end to major combat operations on May 1, 2003, the United States alone had carried out more than twenty-five thousand sorties and dropped more than ten thousand precision-guided bombs (more than were used in Kosovo and half as many as were deployed during the 1991 Gulf War) (O'Hanlon 2004, 271). Yet, the United States only used about sixty thousand service personnel, along with fifteen thousand allied personnel. Almost half of all coalition forces were stationed outside of the immediate theater in support roles (O'Hanlon 2004, 270–71). From 2001 through 2008, the coalition suffered only 980 killed, including noncombat deaths, although the majority of this number were killed after the end of major combat operations ("Afghanistan Foreign . . ." 2008).

Lessons from the Afghan Model

Operation Enduring Freedom accomplished most of its major goals. The Taliban was overthrown and the al-Qaeda network destroyed within the country. In addition, civilian casualties were, as O'Hanlon described them, "mercifully low" at about one thousand (O'Hanlon 2004, 275). However, the campaign failed to accomplish one of its major goals, the capture of senior al-Qaeda figures, including Osama bin Laden. This failure highlighted one of the main drawbacks of having minimal ground forces: the inability to seal borders or adequately surround enemy forces. Many of the core al-Qaeda leaders, and a significant number of fighters, were able to escape into Pakistan following the Battle of Tora Bora in December 2001. It is estimated that at least six hundred al-Qaeda personnel, including family members, fled during or after the battle (Smucker 2002). These and other al-Qaeda and Taliban members were able to establish a new, albeit smaller, network in the northwestern areas of Pakistan and launch attacks into Afghanistan. Tora Bora showed the limits of the Afghan Model, as many of the indigenous troops were unwilling to fight the kind of cave-by-cave attack that was necessary (and their hesitation created the opportunity for many al-Qaeda members to flee). Consequently, many senior military officers determined that U.S. forces would undertake major operations with local allies as the junior partner (Gellman and Ricks 2002). This strategy was also fraught with danger since it risked alienating the local populace and appearing imperialistic.

By contrast, the Afghan Model demonstrated three key advantages of network-centric warfare. First was the minimum number of troops deployed. Through the early phase of combat operations (into November), there were less than five hundred special operations forces on the ground in Afghanistan. This minimized U.S. casualties and also ameliorated concerns that a massive U.S. ground force might create a backlash and stir Afghan nationalism. Second, small special operations forces, when combined with strategic airpower and precision munitions, could achieve a degree of close air superiority that could dramatically change battle conditions and negate the numeric and conventional weaponry advantages of enemy forces. As Robert Luddy points out, "[s]trikes that took hours to coordinate in Desert Storm a decade earlier were carried out in Afghanistan and Iraq as quickly as 45 minutes from the time a target was identified" (Luddy 2005, 4). Luddy cites an illustrative example to demonstrate the impact of network-centric warfare in Afghanistan "even when using old technology: a Special Forces soldier on horseback sends targeting data from his laptop computer to a 40-year-old B-52H Stratofortress, which delivers a devastating blow to massed Taliban forces in less than 20 minutes" (Luddy 2005, 4).

Third, unmanned, high altitude reconnaissance aircraft (unmanned aerial vehicles, or UAVs) created an unprecedented level of strategic intelligence and surveillance for the United States. Flying from heights of 60,000 feet or just a few feet from the ground, UAVs provided the United States and its coalition allies a degree of strategic intelligence that was unparalleled in modern combat without placing personnel in harm's way. Luddy notes that a UAV offered two distinct advantages: "it was controlled through a communications network based from ground stations thousands of miles away, in Europe and California; and it flew not only pre-planned flight paths, but also in real time to locations as required by various missions" (Luddy 2005, 5). UAVs were so effective during Operation Enduring Freedom that the weapons systems created a new market in the defense trade ("Dutch, Canadians . . ." 2006). The drones proved so popular among theater commanders that a shortage emerged by 2008 as other nations sought to purchase the systems (Axe 2008). Meanwhile, low altitude UAVs proved an even more important weapon in support of ground forces. The UAV Predator provided a means to link the full spectrum of on-time intelligence resources. Predators often provided the "eyes and ears" for ground units. Luddy points out that ground forces used the Predators to "walk point" and provide real-time forward observation (2005, 5). The Predators were especially important at night or in bad weather since the drone's infrared and night-vision capabilities negated any disadvantage that the coalition forces may have had due to bad weather or low visibility. In addition, Predators armed with Hellfire missiles were capable of conducting immediate aerial attacks based on the very intelligence that they gathered.

Operation Enduring Freedom proved the utility of network-centric warfare and asymmetric tactics. In October 2001, shortly after Operation Enduring Freedom began, Rumsfeld established the Office of Force Transformation and tasked the new body to develop methods so that network-centric warfare would be integrated into planning and operations among the services. Rumsfeld sought to use the lessons and tactics that proved successful in Afghanistan in other operations (Moniz 2002). Specifically, Rumsfeld believed that the lessons from Afghanistan could be replicated in Iraq. Initially, the secretary of Defense hoped that the United States could encourage anti-Saddam elements in Iraq to overthrow the regime with the aid of U.S. special operations forces (Gordon 2002, A10). However, even as the United States drifted closer to war with Iraq, it became clear that the United States would have to undertake a conventional invasion to overthrow the Saddam regime since the anti-Saddam forces lacked the cohesion and military capabilities of the Northern Alliance (Ricks 2002).

Al-Qaeda and the Taliban regime represented a clear and present danger to the vital interests of the United States. Operation Enduring Freedom incorporated the main elements of the Weinberger-Powell Doctrine with one major exception: the operation lacked a clearly defined end state. U.S. military planners initially believed that Afghanistan would follow the model of Bosnia or Kosovo—after an initial deployment of U.S. forces during the war-fighting phase, international peacekeepers would be deployed and gradually relieve the American forces of security or humanitarian responsibilities. After the United Nations approved a multinational force, the International Security Assistance Force (ISAF), the United States initially retained operational autonomy in spite of efforts by other nations to have a unified command under the United Nations (Hoyos and Robinson 2001). Only after NATO took over command of ISAF did the United States agree to an integrated command (and then only as a way to coerce the NATO allies into greater troop contributions).

IRAQ

Iraq presented Pentagon planners with a much more challenging opponent than Afghanistan. Though degraded, the Iraqi Army was superior in size and weaponry to the Taliban and al-Qaeda fighters in Afghanistan. Most intelligence indicated that Iraq had been preparing for an invasion for at least a decade. The country was also larger, with more urban areas. (Cities are an especially difficult venue in which to conduct combat operations because of the confined nature of space, the presence of a large civilian population, and the concealment potential available to enemy forces.) In addition, in spite of the pro-Western Kurdish militias in the North, there was not an antiregime force such as Afghanistan's Northern Alliance capable of challenging the Saddam government. Weather conditions, including high heat and sandstorms, could seriously impede military operations. Lessons from the 1991 Gulf War highlighted the need to avoid major combat operations during the summer months.

The United States faced a new series of coalition obstacles in Iraq. In Afghanistan, the United States had been able to pick and choose between allied assets and use only those allied forces or weaponry that reinforced or complemented existing U.S. systems and forces. The diplomatic wrangling over Iraq constrained U.S. defense planners on several levels. The refusal of Turkey to participate in the invasion prevented the United States from undertaking a second-front, northern attack and freed the Iraqis to concentrate their defenses in the South. In addition, the absence of key allies such as France meant that the Iraqi coalition of the willing was far less robust than that of the smaller coalition of Operation Enduring Freedom.

Nonetheless, Rumsfeld and senior U.S. military officials believed that these obstacles could be overcome using lessons from the Afghan campaign, especially the use of special operations ground forces and precision-guided munitions. Furthermore, Iraq presented a target-rich environment that would allow the United States to showcase the full range of its military superiority (the overwhelming force required by the Weinberger-Powell Doctrine) in a campaign that would be described as "shock and awe." Rumsfeld planned to conduct the invasion of Iraq with less than half the troops that were involved in the 1991 Gulf War, using speed, network-centric warfare, and military superiority to compensate for less manpower.

Operation Iraqi Freedom

The invasion of Iraq—Operation Iraqi Freedom—began on March 20, 2003. U.S. forces numbered about 235,000 (168,000 were ground forces), with 46,000 British troops, 2,000 Australians, and a small number of Polish commandos. Iraqi forces numbered about 430,000, including both conventional and paramilitary units. The coalition quickly established air, naval, and communications superiority through aerial strikes and covert operations. Meanwhile, special operations forces worked with the Kurdish militias in a replication of the Afghan Model in the North, while armored columns advanced quickly from the South. The speed of the invasion was impressive from a military perspective. Within three weeks, U.S. forces were in Baghdad and most senior Iraqi political and military figures went into hiding. Saddam's two sons were killed in fighting on July 22, 2003, and Saddam himself was captured on December 13. Earlier, on May 1, Bush declared an end to major combat operations.

While the United States routed most organized Iraqi resistance, many Iraqi unconventional forces and ex-military joined an insurgency that developed into a sectarian conflict between the country's main religious and ethnic groups, the Sunnis, Shiites, and Kurds. U.S. forces became bogged down in the kind of internal strife that U.S. military planners had hoped to avoid since the Vietnam War (and which the Weinberger-Powell Doctrine had been developed to prevent). The insurgency proved costly in terms of economics and personnel. By 2008, the United States was spending about $6 billion per month in Iraq. In addition, while 173 U.S. service personnel were killed during the major combat operations in Iraq, by the summer of 2008 more than 4,000 U.S. service members had been killed while deployed in the occupation.

The growing unpopularity of the war had significant domestic implications for the Bush administration. Anti-war congressional Democrats and Republicans sought to force the administration to set a timetable for the withdrawal of U.S. forces from Iraq, something deeply opposed by the administration. During Operation Iraqi Freedom and the subsequent occupation, about 25 percent of the forces were Reserves and National Guard. Repeated deployments of some units were criticized by opponents of the conflict because of the physical, financial, and emotional toil on the reservists and their families. During the 2006 midterm elections, the Republicans lost control of Congress for the first time since 1994. Bush announced on November 8, 2006, the day after the elections, that Rumsfeld would resign as secretary of Defense. He was replaced by Robert Gates.

In February 2007, in an effort to stem the sectarian violence, the United States initiated a "surge" of thirty thousand additional troops. The additional troops were tasked to quell violence in order to allow Iraqi political reconciliation, which would in turn allow for the withdrawal of troops. The administration developed a series of benchmarks with which to judge Iraqi political and security progress (Beehner and Bruno 2008). By the fall of 2008, violence in Iraq had declined by 80 percent. Meanwhile, twelve of eighteen major benchmarks had been met, and there were minor withdrawals of forces. Nonetheless, the United States continued to station about 140,000 troops in Iraq.

Lessons from Iraq

The initial invasion of Iraq demonstrated that network-centric warfare and highly mobile forces could easily overcome numeric disadvantages. U.S.

forces easily overwhelmed the Iraqi defenders in a lightning campaign that highlighted U.S. advantages in tactics, weaponry, and communications. As was the case in Afghanistan, civilian casualties were low during the first phase of the Iraq War, as were coalition casualties. In spite of the success of the initial invasion, the United States quickly found itself drawn into combating a major insurgency and fighting two wars, Afghanistan and Iraq.

One of the tenets of the Weinberger-Powell Doctrine is the need for a clear end state. Unlike Afghanistan, there was not a central figure or political movement in Iraq around which most people could rally. The United States had not identified a leader of the stature of Hamid Karzai. Instead, Iraq was first governed by the U.S.-led Coalition Provisional Authority and then transitioned to civilian rule. While the overthrow of the Saddam regime was certainly a clear goal of the invasion, the planning for Operation Iraqi Freedom did not identify beforehand a clear end state. Meanwhile, the insurgency was initially fueled by the inability of the U.S.-led government to reintegrate at least some of the security and military forces of the former regime into a broad-based security force—a common conflict resolution practice.

Another point of the Weinberger-Powell Doctrine is the necessity for military operations to have all necessary resources to accomplish a mission before troops are committed. Rumsfeld's lean invasion force proved capable of defeating the conventional forces of the Saddam regime; however, there were not enough forces to secure the country. Rumsfeld had been warned by army chief of staff Eric Shinseki that Iraq would require two hundred to three hundred thousand troops as an occupation force (Engel 2003). Rumsfeld discounted the general's warnings and dismissed Shinseki. After Rumsfeld was himself dismissed, his successor initiated the troop surge to increase resources for the mission.

Critics of the administration assert that the invasion of Iraq was not undertaken to protect a vital national interest of the United States. However, the administration believed that it was initiating military action to protect the interests of the country. In the prelude to war, both houses of Congress voted overwhelmingly to authorize military action (the measure passed in the Senate on a vote of 77 to 23 and, in the House, 296 to 133). Public opinion polls demonstrated that 60–70 percent of the public supported military action. As a result of the initial overwhelming support of the effort, despite having adequate knowledge and implications of the challenges the nation would soon face in its efforts, the war should prompt a greater debate on presidential war powers and the oversight functions of Congress before military action is initiated.

IMPLICATIONS FOR DEFENSE POLICY

The main advantages of network-centric warfare also present challenges for military planners. Network-centric warfare allows reductions in the number of forces used in campaigns, but this decline in troop strength reduces capabilities. Writing in *Wired*, Noah Shachtman (2007) summarized the problem in the following fashion:

[N]etwork-centric warfare, with its emphasis on fewer, faster-moving troops, turned out to be just about the last thing the US military needed when it came time to rebuild Iraq and Afghanistan. A small, wired force leaves generals with too few nodes on the military network to secure the peace. There aren't enough troops to go out and find informants, build barricades, rebuild a sewage treatment plant, and patrol a marketplace.

Network-centric warfare greatly enhances the war-fighting capabilities of forces, but it does not necessarily increase their ability to secure the peace.

With this particularly important, yet seemingly ignored, strategic fault, network-centric warfare has been viewed as the panacea of U.S. defense policy for the known future largely because of the broad push of Rumsfeld's years as secretary of Defense. However, the strategy is rooted in a past that has traditionally focused on more conventional state-level warfare. It is becoming readily apparent that future U.S. military operations are more likely to be Military Operations Other Than War (MOOTW). One notable expansion of network-centric warfare is the Human Terrain Team (HTT) concept tested and applied in both Afghanistan and Iraq beginning in 2003. Under this project, anthropologists were embedded in army units in order to better understand the culture of the indigenous populations. Network-centric operations have to take on a community and culture element and thus reintegrate humanity into the equation.

Despite these implications, the 2006 *Quadrennial Defense Review* has maintained a largely state-centric view of warfare by keeping the "two overlapping regional conflicts" model as a standard and technology as a crutch for limiting actual U.S. troop commitment. With that stated, a strategic shift declared within the document places more emphasis on irregular operations, highlighting the increased threat of asymmetrical fourth-generation actors—a blurring of the line between national and substate actors. Thus, U.S. defense policy is torn between preparing for MOOTW, fourth-generation threats, and conventional state threats at a time when the government is becoming increasingly loath to raise defense budgets over the ongoing commitments in Afghanistan and Iraq. The fiscal 2008 peacetime military budget of $505 billion and requested fiscal 2009 peacetime military budget of $541 billion represent budgets not seen since the Cold War (Betts 2007). With increasing commitments abroad and higher costs of doing business, the budget does not leave much room for efforts to modernize the U.S. military for stability operations, despite the lessons learned in both Afghanistan and Iraq.

The Bush administration inherited a military without the tools to perform the tasks that have been asked of it; the administration did not quickly adapt to changing circumstances once boots were on the ground. Post–Cold War administrations have relied on technological innovation to make up for shortfalls in budgetary and political will in order to maintain the myth of a two-front strategic plan. While this has been a typical defense policy ploy as a way to make up for conventional shortfalls, the flawed logic that a quick military victory brings political success goes back even further.

With the Bush administration's dogmatic attachment to Rumsfeld and to technological solutions to traditional security problems, the weakness of the Rumsfeld military transformation came to light as quick "victories" failed to translate into quick democratic transformations. Despite this realization, the failure to adapt to changing circumstances and a changing political climate meant a failure to stay within the boundaries of the Weinberger-Powell Doctrine. Defense policy that incorporates the technological advantages that the U.S. holds with the tested precepts of the Weinberger-Powell Doctrine must be examined further, particularly

in terms of MOOTW and the modern stability operations that the United
States is most likely to encounter.

REFERENCES

"Afghanistan Foreign Troop Deaths in June Exceed Iraq." 2008. *CNN*, June 21. http://www
.cnn.com/2008/WORLD/asiapcf/06/21/afghanistan/index.html (Accessed September
2008).

Aspin, Les. 1992. "An Approach to Sizing American Conventional Forces for the Post-
Soviet Era: Four Illustrative Options." February 25. Washington, DC: House Armed
Services Committee.

Auten, Brian. 2008. *Carter's Conversion: The Hardening of U.S. Defense Policy*. Columbia:
University of Missouri Press.

Axe, David. 2008. "'Manned UAVs' for Afghanistan Surge?" *Wired*, August 18. http://blog
.wired.com/defense/2008/08/manned-uavs-for.html (Accessed September 2, 2008).

Beehner, Lionel, and Greg Bruno. 2008. *Backgrounder: What Are Iraq's Benchmarks?* March
11. New York: Council on Foreign Relations. http://www.cfr.org/publication/13333/
(Accessed September 3, 2008).

Bender, Bryan. 1998. "US Worried by Coalition 'Technology-Gap.'" *Jane's Defence Weekly*,
July 29, pp. 1–2.

Betts, Richard K. 2007. "A Disciplined Defense: How to Regain Strategic Solvency." *Foreign
Affairs* 86(6): 67–81.

Biddle, Stephen. 2002. *Afghanistan and the Future of Warfare: Implications for Army and
Defense Policy*. Carlisle Barracks, PA: Army War College.

Cebrowski, Arthur K., and John J. Garstka. 1998. "Network-Centric Warfare: Its Origin
and Future." *US Naval Institute Proceedings* 124(139): 28–35.

Clark, Wesley. 2001. *Waging Modern War: Bosnia, Kosovo and the Future of Conflict*. New
York: PublicAffairs.

"Dutch, Canadians Purchase Mini-UAVs for Use in Afghanistan." 2006. *Defense Industry
Daily*, May 4. http://www.defenseindustrydaily.com/dutch-canadians-purchase-miniuavs
-for-use-in-afghanistan-02217/ (Accessed September 3, 2008).

Eland, Ivan. 2001. *Putting "Defense" Back into U.S. Defense Policy: Rethinking U.S. Security
in the Post-Cold War World*. Westport, CT: Greenwood.

Engel, Matthew. 2003. "Scorned General's Tactics Proved Right." *Guardian*, March 29. http://
www.guardian.co.uk/world/2003/mar/29/iraq.usa (Accessed September 3, 2008).

Gellman, Barton, and Thomas Ricks. 2002. "U.S. Concludes Bin Laden Escaped at Tora
Bora Fight: Failure to Send Troops in Pursuit Termed Major Error." *Washington Post*,
April 17, p. 1.

Gordon, Michael. 2002. "Iraqis Seek to Oust Hussein with U.S. Military Training." *New
York Times*, January 31, p. A10.

Hoyos, Carola, and Gwen Robinson. 2001. "Multinational Peacekeeping Force Approved."
Financial Times, December 21, p. 70.

Institute for Strategic Studies. 1999. "After Kosovo: Implications for U.S. Coalition Warfare:
Executive Summary." Washington, DC: National Defense University. http://www.au.af
.mil/au/awc/awcgate/ndu/summary-after-kosovo.htm (Accessed September 3, 2008).

Lansford, Tom. 2002. *All for One: Terrorism, NATO and the United States*. Aldershot,
UK: Ashgate.

Larson, Eric, David T. Orletsky, and Kristin Leuschner. 2005. "Defense Planning in a Decade of Change." In *American Defense Policy*, ed. Paul J. Bolt, Damon V. Coletta, and Collins G. Shackelford Jr. Baltimore: Johns Hopkins University Press, 187–93.

Luddy, John. 2005. *The Challenge and Promise of Network-Centric Warfare*. Arlington, VA: Lexington Institute.

Moniz, Dave. 2002. "Afghanistan's Lessons Shaping New Military." *USA Today*, October 8, p. A13.

O'Hanlon, Michael E. 2004. "The Afghani War: A Flawed Masterpiece." In *The Use of Force: Military Power and International Politics*, 6th ed., ed. Robert J. Art and Kenneth N. Waltz. Lanham, MD: Rowman & Littlefield, 270–80.

Ricks, Thomas. 2002. "Military Sees Iraq Invasion Put on Hold." *Washington Post*, May 24, p. A1.

Shachtman, Noah. 2007. "How Technology Almost Lost the War: In Iraq, the Networks Are Social—Not Electronic." *Wired*, November 27. http://www.wired.com/politics/security/magazine/15-12/ff_futurewar (Accessed September 10, 2008).

Smucker, Philip. 2002 "How Bin Laden Got Away." *Christian Science Monitor*, March 4. http://www.csmonitor.com/2002/0304/p01s03-wosc.html (Accessed September 10, 2008).

Snow, Donald M. 2008. *National Security for a New Era: Globalization and Geopolitics After Iraq*, 3rd ed. New York: Pearson Longman.

Twining, David T. 1988. "The Weinberger Doctrine and the Use of Force in the Contemporary Era." In *The Recourse to War: An Appraisal of the "Weinberger Doctrine,"* ed. Alan Ned Sabrosky and Robert L. Sloane. Carlisle Barracks, PA: U.S. Army War College, 11–13.

U.S. Department of Defense. Office of Force Transformation. 2005. *The Implementation of Network-Centric Warfare*. Washington, DC: U.S. Government Printing Office.

PART FIVE

Judging George W. Bush

CHAPTER 15

Between Journalism and History

Evaluating George W. Bush's Presidency

WILLIAM A. GALSTON

EVALUATING AND RANKING PRESIDENTS is a popular parlor game among American historians and not a few political scientists. It seems straightforward enough, until one begins to think about the methodological problems it raises.

There is, first, the difficulty in distinguishing between the president's unchosen situation and what he brings to it; otherwise put, between the deal of the cards and the play of the hand. It is impossible to be a great president in times that do not call for greatness. Regardless of his personal merits, Calvin Coolidge could not have been a president of the first rank; the same was arguably the case for Bill Clinton. It is in the times that try men's souls—war, severe economic downturns, deep social conflict—that excellence or its absence becomes manifest.

Second is the problem of distinguishing the generic from the distinctive response to a given situation. If just about any president would have responded to the events of 9/11 by bringing down the Taliban government in Afghanistan, then it is a mistake to give the man who happened to be holding the office any particular credit for doing so. If many presidents would not have gone on to invade Iraq, then for good or ill, that decision becomes an important metric for judging George W. Bush's performance.

Third comes the problem of agency and responsibility. The fact that something happens—good or bad—on a president's watch does not mean that the president made it happen. Clear examples include developments driven by demography—for example, the relative stability of Social Security outlays during the past two presidencies, which has reduced budgetary pressures. Similarly, the past two presidents have benefited from rates of productivity growth far above that of the 1970s and 1980s, but neither can plausibly claim much responsibility for this favorable trend, which many economists attribute to the increasing integration of information technology into the workplace.

More ambiguous is the diffusion of responsibility inherent in a system of checks and balances, especially in circumstances of divided government. While the Clinton administration deserves substantial credit for initiating fiscal restraint and teeing up welfare reform, only partisans would deny that the post-1994 Republican Congress contributed significantly in these areas as well.

Presidents can be held accountable, however, for the way they deal with divided government. If the opposition party is determined to cripple the administration by denying the president any policy successes, the path of conciliation may well lead nowhere. But because the president typically holds the upper hand in placing items on the agenda, focusing public attention, and convening elected leaders, it is his responsibility to explore the possibility of agreement across deep differences. It may well be that there were no circumstances under which congressional Democrats would have entered into serious discussions with the Bush administration about Social Security reform. Nonetheless, President Bush was responsible for adopting, and then holding fast to, a proposal that he must have known Democrats would never accept.

Presidents exercise a fair amount of influence over the content of legislation, and it is reasonable to judge them on the basis of the bills they shape and sign. It is dicier to hold them responsible for the full range of legislative consequences. Put more technically, presidents have more control over the *outputs* of government than over its *outcomes*. Consider the 1996 welfare reform. Bill Clinton campaigned on a promise to "end welfare as we know it," and he signed the bill after vetoing two previous versions and obtaining some important changes in levels of support for mothers making the transition from welfare to work. In doing so, he thereby assumed a share of the credit, but also the responsibility, for this important shift in the U.S. social contract. The bill's outcome was better than many critics had predicted, largely because it took effect during a period of robust economic growth whose fruits were widely shared. Judgments differ about the amount of credit Clinton deserves for this context and, accordingly, about the extent to which we should attribute to him the relatively favorable effects of welfare reform.

Fourth is the question of time horizon, which might be termed the "Truman problem." When he left office in 1952, Harry Truman was wildly unpopular, receiving the lowest approval numbers ever recorded (including Richard Nixon at the depths of Watergate).[1] The unsatisfactory progress of the Korean War and corruption scandals had undermined public confidence in his administration, and most pundits regarded his tenure as a failed presidency. Two decades later, his star began to rise, and it has ascended steadily ever since. Today, many historians regard him as a near-great president. The immediate sources of his unpopularity have receded in importance, and his leading role as the architect of the institutions, alliances, and doctrines that contained and ultimately brought down Soviet communism stands out in higher relief. He also gets far more credit today for the courageous early steps he took to racially integrate the armed forces. At the time, the secessions of the left-leaning supporters of Henry Wallace and the segregation-backing Dixiecrats, seemed to have fatally narrowed the base of the Democratic Party. In fact, they laid the foundation for the Cold War liberalism that held the center of American politics for the next two decades.

The question of time horizon is inescapable when we confront, as we must, the normative question: Is an effective president necessarily a good president? Suppose that a president is an effective communicator, a good manager, highly skilled at getting his program enacted, and leaves office with high approval ratings, but even decades later, experts and citizens cannot agree whether his program promoted the well-being of the nation? In the last analysis, criteria for judging presidents cannot be entirely technical or value-neutral. What seems good to one epoch may appear questionable to the next, and standards of relative importance shift as well. If Truman's integration of the armed forces had not come at the beginning of a historic shift in race relations, it would not have been accorded the significance we now attach to it.

In the end, we may have no choice but to base normative evaluations of presidents on the settled judgments of the American people. While a handful of conservative theoreticians continue to do battle with the New

Deal, the overwhelming majority of the people have endorsed it as a core component of what modern governments (and presidents) should do. Ronald Reagan declared—and for the most part meant—that his quarrel was with Lyndon Johnson's Great Society and not with FDR, for whom he voted four times. And while Johnson's civil rights legislation was controversial for years after its enactment, virtually all Americans now regard it as an act of statesmanship that made our country better—a conclusion that rests not only on LBJ's intentions but also on the laws' long-term effects. These examples suggest that many evaluations of presidents represent the judgment of history and that evaluations of current or recent presidents should be offered tentatively and modestly, if at all.

Finally, there is Henny Youngman's question: Compared to what?[2] George W. Bush has publicly mused about the parallels between his presidency and Truman's, an analogy that consigns judgment to the farther future. Some detractors have seen a resemblance to Jimmy Carter, another president who was (in Richard Norton Smith's words) "tuned out" before he was "turned out" (quoted in Cannon and Cannon 2008, 293), but the similarity is confined to low approval numbers. Others have argued for a parallel between Bush and Lyndon Johnson, but this too seems forced. Like Bush, LBJ presided over a long, unpopular war; unlike Bush, Johnson had a long list of domestic accomplishments, topped by Medicare and landmark civil rights laws, to put on the other side of the scales. If Johnson were to be judged solely by his performance in domestic affairs, he would be ranked great or near-great, which few would say about Bush.

In the sections that follow, I will compare George W. Bush to his most recent two-term predecessors—Ronald Reagan, whose example he sought to follow, and Bill Clinton, whom he took as an object lesson in how not to conduct a presidency. While this approach is less than comprehensive, it roughly corresponds to the scope of sensible judgments that the available evidence and myopic perspective of this moment will permit us to reach.

GEORGE W. BUSH AND RONALD REAGAN

It is clearly plausible to compare Bush with his acknowledged model, Ronald Reagan. A conservative intellectual, Jeffrey Bell, puts it this way: "Broadly and from the beginning, Bush's issue profile has been closer to that of Reagan than has the profile of any other Republican president or nominee in the six presidential elections starting with 1988." Bell describes Reaganism as "traditionalism on social issues, supply-side tax rate cuts in economics, and an assertive foreign policy featuring American moral leadership on behalf of a more democratic world." While praising Bush for his fidelity to these themes, Bell criticizes what he sees as the president's lack of clarity and steadfastness in promoting them and regards Bush's tenure as a "failed presidency" (2008, 20).

Lou and Carl Cannon (2008), the authors of the most balanced appraisal thus far of the Bush presidency, take much the same tack. George W. Bush, they argue, is "Reagan's disciple" but fell far short of his mentor. The Cannons trace this shortfall to differences of temperament and experience. Ronald Reagan was a former Democrat and labor union leader, a skilled negotiator who typically left something to the other side, a manager willing to incorporate talented aides of defeated adversaries into his campaign and administration. He understood that when principles encounter reality, flexibility is required; witness his willingness to take back a portion of the 1981 tax cuts when they proved excessively costly.[3] Reagan was, in addition, a man willing to admit mistakes and cut his losses, a prudent commander in chief who committed American forces abroad cautiously and reluctantly. After beginning his presidency with a deep recession, he presided over a robust economic expansion. After early confrontations with both our allies and the Soviet Union, he embarked on negotiations with Gorbachev that set the USSR on the path to a peaceful demise. Between 1980 and 1984, Reagan succeeded in expanding the Republican coalition dramatically; he ended his presidency with high approval ratings; and he turned his office over to his less-than-riveting vice president, who won by a comfortable eight points. Michael Dukakis would have done George H.W. Bush no damage, and probably some good, if he had accused him of running for "Ronald Reagan's third term."

By contrast, the Cannons suggest, George W. Bush's shortcomings hampered his ability to implement his version of Reaganism. His divisive "base strategy" for reelection was at the opposite pole from Reagan's sunny, coalition-broadening 1984 campaign. To be sure, he got his way on tax cuts, Supreme Court appointments, and the Iraq War, but overall, the results did not meet expectations. Firmness is a virtue until it shades over into stubbornness; Bush's belief that strong convictions, held consistently, can change reality produced fiascos such as the costly attempt in 2005 to revamp Social Security. Until the Republican electoral defeat in 2006, Bush's negotiating style was to stake out a position and defend it, come what may. At home and abroad, he came only slowly and grudgingly to accept that parties on the other side of the table have interests and convictions that he must somehow take into account. For years, he and his senior aides employed a curious and revealing locution in speaking of foreign adversaries: Saddam, Syria, North Korea, Iran, and Hamas "know what we expect of them," as though endlessly restating our position would somehow bring them to heel.

Most important, by studying Reagan's withdrawal of the Marines from Lebanon after the deadly attack on their barracks as well as his refusal to use American troops to overthrow the Sandinistas in Nicaragua, the Cannons conclude that Reagan would not have sent our forces into Iraq.[4] In their account, Reagan's habit was to focus skeptical questions on the worse case and to weigh carefully the possible costs of ventures that seemed to promise quick and easy benefits. By contrast, George Bush seemed never to have considered the possibility that the costs of intervention—human, material, and moral—might prove far higher than the optimistic boosters around him were suggesting.

This is not to say that our venture in Iraq will end in failure, or that it will not produce favorable long-term consequences throughout the Middle East. It is to say that both impartial analysts and the American people are asking a question that the Bush administration seldom if ever considered, namely, whether the costs (including opportunity costs) are worth the gains. Since the spring of 2007, as the troop surge took hold, the percentage of Americans who believe that the situation on the ground in Iraq is improving rose substantially. Nevertheless, the proportion of Americans who believe that the war wasn't worth waging in the first place remained rock solid, at more than 60 percent. Unless this changes in coming decades, Bush's hopes of being judged a twenty-first century Harry Truman will not be realized.

GEORGE W. BUSH AND BILL CLINTON

Comparing George Bush to Ronald Reagan, his acknowledged ideal, is obvious and straightforward. By contrast, comparing him to Bill Clinton may appear perverse. In many respects, Bush campaigned as the anti-Clinton, pledging to restore honor and dignity to the White House. And he governed as the anti-Clinton as well, managing the White House crisply, focusing on a handful of top priorities, and holding fast to positions firmly (many would say stubbornly), even when the odds seemed daunting.

Still, Bush and Clinton are the only two presidents thus far to have governed after the end of the Cold War in circumstances of escalating global economic competition. In this context, comparing them is hardly inapt, and it seems fair to ask why Bill Clinton survived scandal and impeachment to leave office with a 60 percent approval rating, while George Bush left with a rating only half that high.

No doubt one factor is a war, undertaken on premises that turned out to be flawed, that has lasted longer and cost more than the American people were led to expect. Nor is there any question that the administration's inept response to Hurricane Katrina dealt the president's reputation a blow from which it has yet to recover. But the explanation goes further. President Clinton presided over fiscal, economic, and social trends that moved steadily in the right direction. President Bush was not as fortunate.

In what follows, I offer what some may regard as a hyper-empirical and pedantic comparison of the records of our two most recent presidents. This represents a deliberate effort to lean against both the inevitable partisan passions of the present and the distorting effects of temporal proximity.[5] This procedure, however, cannot distinguish sharply between outputs and outcomes, between the effect of what these two presidents did, on the one hand, and of the circumstances and trends within which they acted, on the other. I do not believe that we as yet possess the evidence, or the distance, needed to address this problem. Perhaps we never will; historians still debate the extent to which the policies of Herbert Hoover contributed to the severity of the Great Depression. But setting aside issues of causality and responsibility, we can at least get the facts straight as the basis for deeper judgments in the future.

Fiscal Policy

When Bill Clinton took office, he inherited a federal budget that amounted to 21.4 percent of GDP and a budget deficit of 3.9 percent. For the next eight years, federal spending grew only modestly, far less rapidly than the economy. As a result, the federal government shrank to only 18.4 percent of GDP by 2000 (down three full percentage points), and the deficit turned into a surplus of 2.4 percent, a swing of 6.3 points. To be sure, defense spending declined by 1.4 percent of GDP during this period, to a level that would have been unsustainably low even if the terrorist attacks of 9/11 had not occurred. Still, more than half the decline in the federal government's share of the economy is attributable to nondefense spending.

By contrast, government grew steadily during the Bush years. If Congress had passed the president's 2009 budget request without amendment, federal spending (excluding supplemental appropriations for the wars in Iraq and Afghanistan) would amount to 20.7 percent of GDP, an increase of 2.3 percent since the end of the Clinton administration, and the deficit would be 2.7 percent. (Taking into account war-related spending as well as lowered estimates of economic growth, both spending and the deficit as a share of GDP would be at roughly 1993 levels.) Much of the increased spending has come in defense and homeland security, although the number of men and women under arms is barely larger than it was at the end of the Clinton administration. The Bush administration also presided over increases in discretionary spending—notably agriculture, education, and human services—along with a major expansion of Medicare to cover prescription drugs.

It is true that Congress has had a hand in these developments. But it is also true that the budgets it has enacted were mostly in line with the president's wishes. During the first seven years of the administration, President Bush proposed discretionary spending totaling $9.63 trillion. Congress appropriated $9.72 trillion, less than one percent more than the president sought. This represented a continuation of congressional deference to the executive in fiscal matters. Despite the Sturm und Drang of divided government during the Clinton years, the record shows that after the president had proposed a total of $6.77 trillion in discretionary spending, Congress ended up appropriating $6.73 trillion, a difference of about half of one percent.

The Economy

Comparing the economic performance of the two most recent administrations presents many of the complications discussed earlier. President Clinton took over an economy in the early stages of recovery from the 1991–92 downturn. By contrast, President Bush inherited an economy in the early stages of recession, which was then hammered by the attacks of 9/11. Still, it seems fair to compare periods of recovery from trough to peak. From 1993 through 2000, GDP grew steadily, peaking at more than 4 percent in 1998, and the pace of job generation was brisk (more than twenty-two million). Not surprisingly, unemployment fell from an average of 6.9 percent in 1993 to only 4 percent in 2000. From 2003 through 2007, the economy grew more slowly than during the previous decade, at a rate never exceeding 3.2 percent, and jobs were generated at less than one-third the Clinton pace. Unemployment fell only slowly, from an average of 6 percent in 2003 to 4.6 percent in 2007. Late in 2008, the authoritative National Bureau of Economic Research determined that a recession had begun in December 2007. By the end of 2008, after nearly a year of unbroken monthly job losses, unemployment had risen to nearly 7 percent.

Not only was economic growth more robust in the 1990s, but also its fruits were more widely shared. Between 1993 and 2000, median family income (adjusted for inflation, rounded to nearest hundred) rose from $52,223 to $61,083, a gain of $8,860, about 17 percent. Between 2003 and 2007, by contrast, median family income grew by only $1,966 (roughly 3 percent), from $59,389 to $61,355. The first decade of the twenty-first century thus experienced the only postrecession recovery since World War II in which median incomes failed to exceed by a significant margin the peak attained at the end of the previous economic cycle. (Median household incomes fared even worse, peaking in 2007 below the level attained in 2000.) And while incomes grew at roughly the same pace for every income quintile during the 1990s, almost all the 2000s gains have flowed to the top quintile of earners.

Not surprisingly, these trends have translated into divergent effects on social indicators linked to economic growth and distribution. Between 1993 and 2000, the poverty rate fell from 15.1 to 11.3 percent. After rising to 12.5 percent during the economic downturn of 2001–2002, it has not budged since. Between 1993 and 2000, the share of Americans without health insurance fell by a percentage point; since 2003, it has actually risen by more than a percentage point, the first time on record that the uninsured rate has increased during a period of economic recovery and growth. Between 1993 and 2000, the rate of college completion among young adults rose strongly, from 23.7 to 29.1 percent. Since then, college completion has stagnated, exceeding the 2000 level only slightly in 2007.

Both administrations maintained, against considerable opposition, a commitment to an open international trade regime. The Clinton administration was able to win approval for NAFTA and the WTO despite the opposition of a majority of the Democratic Party, while the Bush administration managed to conclude a large number of bilateral trade deals. Nonetheless, the Bush administration was stymied in what are arguably its most significant trade initiatives—at home, to get approval for important bilateral trade pacts with nations such as Colombia and South Korea; internationally, to strike a bargain with large developing nations in the most recent trade negotiations. During neither administration did exports increase as rapidly as imports: after rising from $70 billion in 1993 to $380 billion in 2000, the current account deficit doubled to $753 billion in 2006 (a rise that preceded the recent oil price surge) before falling back somewhat in 2007.

Many factors have complicated the politics of trade during the 2000s, three chief among them. First, through discontent over the alleged negative effects of NAFTA, trade has become entangled in the poisonous debate over illegal immigration. Second, as dollars sent abroad have piled up in sovereign wealth funds, Congress has resisted attempts by China, the UAE, and other countries to purchase U.S. assets considered vital to our economic future or to homeland security. Third, the perceived impact of trade on U.S. manufacturing shifted between the Clinton and Bush administrations. During most of the 1990s, demand for our manufactured products rose roughly as fast as productivity, allowing employers to hold employment steady. Since then, the increase in demand has slowed even as manufacturing productivity surged. The consequence has been the loss of more than four million manufacturing jobs, devastating the economies of the industrial Midwest. Although most economists attribute this development to technology rather than trade, the people have a different view, creating a climate in which many lifelong free-traders have felt compelled to trim their sails. It would be unfair to hold President Bush wholly responsible for these negative perceptions of international trade. It is fair to say, however, that his administration did little to ensure that the gains from trade were more widely shared or to cushion American workers against the increased volatility and risks of the new global economy—a failure that allowed the already fragile coalition favoring new trade pacts to weaken still further.

Social Issues

I turn now to the two administrations' performance on domestic social issues. The Clinton years witnessed rapid and unexpected progress on several fronts. Teen pregnancy and birth rates declined sharply. In part as a result, the infant mortality rate, which is highest among the youngest mothers, declined by nearly 20 percent, and the percentage of children living in single-parent households, which had been rising for decades, stabilized at the 1993 level. The violent crime rate, which had surged through the late 1980s and early 1990s, fell by nearly one third between 1993 and 2000, while the property crime rate fell by about one quarter.

Despite vigorous efforts to focus on educational attainment rather than inputs, the Clinton administration was not able to achieve significant improvements in school achievement: scores did not budge on the National Assessment of Educational Progress (NAEP), the closest thing our country has to a national examination. The early returns from the Bush administration's trademark No Child Left Behind Act (its version of the Elementary and Secondary Education Act) are more encouraging: test scores are rising, especially in the elementary school years. It remains to be seen whether these gains can be extended to our middle and high schools, which present distinctive problems, particularly in poor and minority neighborhoods.

On other social fronts, the Bush administration had less to brag about. After more than a decade of unbroken declines, the teen pregnancy and birth rates stopped falling and then began to rise again. Trends linked to teen births also deteriorated: infant mortality stopped falling in 2001 and stagnated thereafter. Following the Clinton years, the decline in violent crime slowed, and the rate actually increased in both 2005 and 2006. Property crime continued to decline but at less than half the rate as during the Clinton administration. In contrast, rates of illicit drug and alcohol use among teens decreased substantially during the Bush years after increasing during the two Clinton terms.

Administration

Many observers of the Washington scene believe that the Bush administration was a tidier and more orderly place than was the Clinton White House but also less open to scrutiny and more closed to the press and public. While there may well be something to these perceptions, the facts (such as they are) paint a muddier picture. To be sure, meetings in the Clinton White House tended to start late and run long; the Bush White House was a model of punctuality. However, George Bush averaged twenty-six press conferences during the first seven years of his presidency, versus a not dissimilar twenty-four for Bill Clinton during his two terms. (Even if you exclude Clinton's final year, when he held only eight, his seven-year average was twenty-seven.) With the exception of the transition from his first to his second term, Bush's cabinet was very stable; but then again, so was Clinton's, with the same exception. Nor do staff turnover rates indicate a clear difference between these two very different presidents.

Nor, finally, do statistics on the administrations' legislative success diverge markedly. State of the Union addresses offer an annual summary of the president's agenda. Bill Clinton got about two-thirds of his 1993 proposals enacted into law, and a bit more than half of his 1994 proposals. After sweeping Republican victories in 1994, his agenda stalled in 1995, but by 1996 his success rate was back over 50 percent, a pace he maintained for the remainder of his presidency. George Bush got about 60 percent of his proposals enacted during his first three years but less than one third during the next three, even though his party maintained control of Congress. He actually did a bit better in 2007, even though Democrats had taken over both the House and the Senate.

This evidence-based comparison of the two most recent presidents' terms, while suggestive, does not speak for itself, because it raises all the methodological questions discussed in the opening section of this chapter. Disentangling the effects of demographic trends and political agency is never easy. For instance, it is hard to know how much Bill Clinton's efforts to combat teen pregnancy—through high-profile speeches as well as provisions of the welfare reform act—contributed to the rapid decline in that statistic during his administration. Nor is it easy to determine the impact of economic trends, such as the rising demand for skilled labor, as distinguished from tax and labor policies, on the distribution of wages or income. We know that Bill Clinton raised the top marginal tax rate and expanded the Earned Income Tax Credit, while George Bush's supply-side tax cuts pushed in the opposite direction. But it is a leap to attribute the broader scope of wage increases or the faster growth in median incomes during the Clinton administration to these legislative differences alone. The most we can suggest is that while both presidents were committed to economic growth, Bill Clinton seemed to care more than George Bush about sharing widely the fruits of growth. It will take a wider-angle historical lens to determine why the economy did so much better during the 1990s than in the following decade.

TWO 800-POUND GORILLAS AT THE BAR

The previous section began with the observation that Clinton and Bush are our only post–Cold War presidents. That said, it is also true that George W. Bush is our only post–9/11 president, and the long-term outcome of his struggle against militant jihadism and nations that support it will significantly shape his place in history. There is a continuum of possibilities. Suppose that a decade from now Iraq has a stable and reasonably decent government sustained by its own armed forces and police; the Taliban are a fading memory in Afghanistan; the United States and Pakistan have cooperated to eliminate al-Qaeda's safe haven; and Iran, held in check by a new alliance between traditional Sunni powers and Shia Iraq, has ended its support for organizations such as Hezbollah and Hamas. In this best-case scenario, our invasion of Iraq might be hailed as an act of visionary but misunderstood statesmanship, and the fact that it evoked so much dismay at home and abroad would be at most a footnote.

It is hard to assess the probability of this highly favorable outcome, however, and easy to imagine far worse ones. Our sustained troop commitment in Iraq has left our mission in Afghanistan undermanned, opening the door to a Taliban resurgence in the south and complicating efforts to interdict the flow of terrorists across the porous border between Afghanistan and Pakistan. It is not unimaginable that al-Qaeda and its sympathizers could establish new safe havens not far from the ones U.S. forces eliminated in the months after 9/11.

Similar cautions apply to the administration's efforts at reining in the other members of Bush's Axis of Evil. After turning his back on Bill Clinton's diplomacy with North Korea early in his presidency, George Bush finally consented to resume it—under the aegis of "six party" talks rather than face to face. While this approach has yielded an agreement and the partial decommissioning of Pyongyang's plutonium-producing reactor, it remains to be seen whether it will produce full denuclearization or, indeed, whether the North Korean government has decided definitively and in good faith to go down that path.

It is now clear that George Bush will bequeath the problem of Iran's nuclear program to his successor. We will never know whether it could have been otherwise. Reasonably well-authenticated reports suggest that the administration missed an opportunity to engage the Iranian government immediately after the invasion of Iraq, when our leverage was at a high point and the Iranians might have been willing to do business with us.[6] Today, our continuing involvement in Iraq makes military action against Iran less likely, and the Iranians know it. Recent reports suggest that the United States has actively discouraged Israeli action against Iran, in effect taking the last credible military threat off the table.

The logic of events may force the Obama administration to acknowledge what the Bush administration has not, namely, that although a nuclear Iran would be a grave threat, we lack the means to prevent the Iranians from obtaining nuclear weapons if they are determined to do so. This new reality might well trigger a nuclear arms race among Sunni powers such as Saudi Arabia and Egypt. One thing is clear: the world would be a more dangerous place if mutual assured destruction becomes the basis of nonaggression throughout the Middle East. It is impossible to say whether history would debit this development against George Bush's account or rather come to regard it as a tragic inevitability. Out of such imponderables are presidential reputations constructed.

There are aspects of national security policy, however, about which the jury has already returned a verdict. On the positive side, and contrary to the fears of many experts, the United States has not experienced another major terrorist incident since September 11, 2001. More than one threatening plot has been nipped in the bud, and improved sharing of information across agency boundaries has certainly helped make the country safer. While we may never know how much factors other than policy changes contributed to this result, it is clear that the administration's posture of heightened vigilance has made a real difference. Other clear positives include the administration's strong, well-funded effort to fight AIDS in Africa and the Millennium Challenge Account, an innovative effort to change the paradigm of foreign assistance by linking aid to specific performance measures.

On the negative side, the administration's effort to expand the president's Article II authority has been a damaging failure. Senior administration officials, especially Vice President Cheney, entered the White House with the conviction that the presidency had been dangerously weakened since Vietnam and that every opportunity should be seized to reclaim its powers from Congress (and to a lesser degree from the courts as well). But unlike other wartime leaders, such as Abraham Lincoln and Franklin Roosevelt, George Bush never succeeded in convincing other branches of government, or the American people, that he was justified in enhancing his powers. After a period of complaisance, Congress used its oversight powers to push back, and the Supreme Court asserted jurisdiction in areas from which the administration had sought to exclude it. Overall, future historians are unlikely to conclude that George Bush left the presidency stronger than he found it.

The other 800-pound gorilla is the financial and economic crisis that crashed like a tsunami over the United States and then the world in mid-September 2008. Historians will long debate causes and culpabilities. Dueling partisan interpretations emerged almost immediately, with Democrats charging the Bush administration with gutting financial regulatory institutions and Republicans blaming Democrats for defending Fannie Mae and Freddie Mac against the administration's moves to rein them in. There is something to be said for each side, as there is for other explanations, including the Federal Reserve Board's unduly prolonged period of monetary ease after September 11, 2001, and the excesses of President Bush's "compassionate conservative" effort to expand home ownership among working-class families (Becker et al. 2008).

What is not in dispute is that the Bush administration's response to the crisis lacked focus and consistency. The $700 billion Troubled Assets Relief Program (TARP), sold to a reluctant Congress as the way to get devalued mortgage-backed securities and derivatives off the balance sheets of endangered banks, morphed into a massive recapitalization of the banking system with few strings attached. The banks' subsequent failure to resume lending generated howls of protest, as did the administration's staunch refusal to use TARP funds to assist home owners in danger of defaulting on their mortgages.

Unlike Herbert Hoover, George W. Bush had only a few months to cope with an economic cataclysm before his successor took office. Still, it seems unlikely that history will regard his response as his finest hour. Indeed, it is possible that 2008 will turn out to be the year in which a three-decade cycle of American politics dominated by conservative economic assumptions—smaller government, lower taxes, looser regulation—came to an end and a new era of activism began.

CONCLUSION:
THE THREE PRESIDENCIES OF GEORGE W. BUSH?

An astute observer, Jonathan Rauch, has recently argued that the Bush years went through three phases, different enough to qualify as three presidencies. Early on, Bush tried to honor his campaign pledge to be a uniter rather than a divider, reaching across party lines to forge the No Child Left Behind education act and to sign campaign finance legislation that the base of his party heartily loathed. In the wake of 9/11, however, Republican political operatives saw and seized an opportunity to place national security issues in the service of a wholesale political realignment, ushering in a period of one-party government that came to an end only

with devastating Republican losses in November 2006. Since then, surprisingly, the president initiated yet another major course correction, "in
effect . . . behaving as if he were his own successor." The shift began with
major personnel changes and extended to new initiatives on issues ranging
from Iran and North Korea to global warming. Even on Iraq, the hard core
of partisan contestation, the president conceded to the Iraqi parliament
what he was never willing to give the U.S. Congress: a timetable for the
withdrawal of U.S. forces. As a result, rather than handing the incoming
president a mess, he will pass on roughly the same agenda of problems that
he inherited. Overall, Bush ascended from the bottom of the presidential
barrel to something approaching mediocrity; his two terms amount to a
detour rather than a disaster (Rauch 2008).

There is much to be said for this interpretation. The final two years of
the Bush presidency demonstrated more suppleness, at home and abroad,
than was previously on display. Despite his objections to billions in new
subsidies for local governments, President Bush signed a mortgage relief bill
that he might well have vetoed early in his administration, and he authorized more flexible approaches on a wide range of diplomatic issues. The
return of divided government gave George Bush new incentives to display
the unifying style he promised during his first presidential campaign. If the
president had pursued that course between 2002 and 2006, our history
would have been very different, and so would this chapter.

Granting this, the anodyne language of "opportunity costs" fails to
capture the Bush legacy, because time in politics is more than a neutral
metric. Opportunities lost may never be regained. As Heracleitus famously
remarked, we cannot step in the same river twice—to which I would add,
not even if that river is the Tigris. During the nearly seven years that the
Bush administration withdrew from active involvement in the Israeli-Palestinian controversy, the issues became even harder to resolve. It will be a
long time, if ever, before we regain the leverage over the Iranians we enjoyed
in mid-2003. Global warming was hard to address in 2000; it is harder
today. Our global reputation has suffered a grievous blow, and President
Obama will not be able to act as though our standing in the world did
not decline during the eight years that preceded him. And eight years of
inaction on our long-term fiscal problems, for which the administration

must bear substantial though not sole responsibility, have made them even harder to solve on a reasonable bipartisan basis.

It is difficult for this author, at least, to avoid the conclusion that George W. Bush will hand over to Barack Obama a wounded and uncertain America, a nation weaker economically, militarily, and diplomatically than the one he inherited.[7] Given the challenges of those eight years, it is possible to argue that no one could have done better—possible, but ultimately not plausible. The Oval Office pitilessly exposes each president's defects of intellect and character. In the case of George W. Bush, these defects turned out to be more substantial than even his detractors could imagine in 2000, and his country has paid the price.

NOTES

1. According to the Gallup survey, after his surprise victory over Thomas E. Dewey in 1948, Truman began his second term with an approval rating of 69 percent. In early 1952, around the time he was announcing that he would not run again, that figure had fallen to 22 percent. For the time series, see the Roper Public Opinion Archives, "Job Performance Ratings for President Truman" (2008).

2. So attributed to the well-known Borscht Belt comedian, whose routine included a politically incorrect joke: A man to his friend: "How's your wife?" The friend: "Compared to what?"

3. This is the overall thrust of *Reagan's Disciple*.

4. Kenneth Duberstein, Reagan's last chief of staff, quotes Reagan as saying, "Those sonsofbitches [the ultraconservatives] won't be happy until we have 25,000 troops in Managua, and I'm not going to do it" (Cannon and Cannon 2008, 165). For Iraq, see Cannon and Cannon (2008), 212–14.

5. All the statistics in this section are drawn from official U.S. government studies. I am deeply grateful to ace researchers Molly Reynolds and Matthew Corritore, without whom I could not have completed this comparison. For details, see the "Notes on Data Sources" below.

6. For one of the best reports, by someone who was there, see Leverett (2006).

7. For a comprehensive statement of the opposite view from a senior administration official, see Ed Gillespie, "Myths and Facts About the Real Bush Record" (2008). Gillespie served as the counselor to President Bush during the last years of the administration.

NOTES ON DATA SOURCES

GDP growth: "Gross Domestic Product, Percent Change from Preceding Period," Bureau of Economic Analysis, National Economic Accounts, http://www.bea.gov/national/xls/gdpchg.xls (in current dollars)

Inflation rate: "Consumer Price Index, All Urban Consumers—(CPI-U), U.S. city average, All items," Bureau of Labor Statistics, ftp://ftp.bls.gov/pub/special.requests/cpi/cpiai.txt (average to average; December to December also available)

Unemployment rate: "Employment Status of the Civilian Noninstitutional Population, 1942 to Date," Bureau of Labor Statistics, http://www.bls.gov/cps/cpsaat1.pdf

Productivity: "Fourth Quarter Revised Productivity and Costs Releases, 1993–2007," Bureau of Labor Statistics, http://www.bls.gov/schedule/archives/prod_nr.htm

Current account balance: "U.S. International Trade in Goods and Services, Exports, Imports, and Balances," Bureau of Economic Analysis, International Economic Accounts, http://www.bea.gov/newsreleases/international/trade/trad_time_series.xls

Median family income: "Table F-6. Regions—Families (All Races) by Median and Mean Income: 1953 to 2007," Historical Income Tables—Families, www.census.gov/hhes/www/income/histinc/f06AR.html

Median household income: "Table H-6. Regions—All Races by Median and Mean Income: 1975 to 2006," Historical Income Tables: Households, U.S. Census Bureau, http://www.census.gov/hhes/www/income/histinc/h06ar.html; "Income, Poverty, and Health Insurance Coverage in the United States: 2007," U.S. Census Bureau, August 2008

Budget

Federal spending as a percentage of GDP: "Revenues, Outlays, Deficits, Surpluses, and Debt Held by the Public, 1968 to 2007, as a Percentage of Gross Domestic Product," Congressional Budget Office, http://www.cbo.gov/budget/data/historical.shtml

Deficit as a percentage of GDP: "Revenues, Outlays, Deficits, Surpluses, and Debt Held by the Public, 1968 to 2007, as a Percentage of Gross Domestic Product," Congressional Budget Office, http://www.cbo.gov/budget/data/historical.shtml

Defense spending (aggregate and as percentage of GDP): "Outlays for Major Categories of Spending, 1968 to 2007, as a Percentage of Gross Domestic Product," and "Discretionary Outlays, 1968 to 2007, in Billions of Dollars," Congressional Budget Office, http://www.cbo.gov/budget/data/historical.shtml

Size of armed forces: "Military Personnel Statistics," Department of Defense, Statistical Information Analysis Division, http://siadapp.dmdc.osd.mil/personnel/MILITARY/Miltop.htm (as of September 30 of each year)

Personal financial situation: "Table 4: Current Financial Situation Compared to a Year Ago," Annual Tables of the Reuters/University of Michigan Surveys of Consumers (June of each year)

Success on legislative priorities: Based on *Congressional Quarterly*'s Presidential Support Data; CQ compiles a list of votes on which there was a clear presidential position. The figure here represents the proportion of votes in the House and Senate on which Congress sided with the president out of the total number of votes in the House and Senate on which the president took a position.

Poverty rate (percentage of population): "Table 2. Poverty Status of People by Family Relationship, Race, and Hispanic Origin: 1959 to 2006," Historical Poverty Tables: People, U.S. Census Bureau, http://www.census.gov/hhes/www/poverty/histpov/hstpov2.html

Uninsured/no health insurance rate (percentage of population): "Table HIA-1. Health Insurance Coverage Status and Type of Coverage by Sex, Race and Hispanic Origin: 1999 to 2006," Historical Health Insurance Tables, U.S. Census Bureau, http://www.census.gov/hhes/www/hlthins/historic/hihistt1.html; "Table HI-1. Health Insurance Coverage Status and Type of Coverage by Sex, Race and Hispanic Origin: 1987 to 2005," Historical Health Insurance Tables, U.S. Census Bureau, http://www.census.gov/hhes/www/hlthins/historic/hlthin05/hihistt1.html

High school dropout rate (percentage of total students, Grades 10–12): "Table A-4. Annual High School Dropout Rates of 15 to 24 Year Olds by Sex, Race, Grade, and Hispanic Origin: October 1967 to 2006," http://www.census.gov/population/socdemo/school/TableA-4.xls

Educational attainment: "Table 1. Educational Attainment of the Population 18 Years and Over, by Age, Sex, Race, and Hispanic Origin: 2007," http://www.census.gov/population/socdemo/education/cps2007/Table1-01.xls

NAEP scores: Accessed using the NAEP Data Explorer, http://nces.ed.gov/nationsreportcard/nde/

Percentage of children in single-parent households (percentage of total children under 18): "Living Arrangements of Children Under 18 Years Old: 1960 to Present," http://www.census.gov/population/socdemo/hh-fam/ch1.pdf

Infant mortality rate (per 1,000 live births): "Deaths: Preliminary Data for 2004," *National Vital Statistics Report,* Volume 54, Number 19, Centers for Disease Control, http://www.cdc.gov/nchs/data/nvsr/nvsr54/nvsr54_19.pdf; "Deaths: Preliminary Data for 2006," *National Vital Statistics Report,* Volume 56, Number 16, Centers for Disease Control, http://www.cdc.gov/nchs/data/nvsr/nvsr56/nvsr56_16.pdf; Marian F. MacDorman and T. J. Mathews, "Recent Trends in Infant Mortality in the United States," *NCHS Data Brief,* No. 9, October 2008

Teenage birth rate (ages 15–19, per 1,000): "Births: Preliminary Data for 2006," *National Vital Statistics Report,* Volume 56, Number 7, Centers for Disease Control, http://www.cdc.gov/nchs/data/nvsr/nvsr56/nvsr56_07.pdf

Abortion rate (per 1,000 women ages 15–44): "Table 2. Number, Ratio, and Rate of Legal Abortions and Source of Reporting for All Reporting Areas and for the 47 Areas That Reported in 1998-2003, by Year—United States, 1970-2004," Abortion Surveillance—United States, 2004, *Morbidity and Mortality Weekly Report,* Centers for Disease Control, November 23, 2007, http://www.cdc.gov/mmwr/PDF/ss/ss5609.pdf

Drug/alcohol statistics: "2007 Data From In-School Surveys of 8th-, 10th-, and 12th-Grade Students," Monitoring the Future, University of Michigan Institute for Social Research, http://www.monitoringthefuture.org/data/07data.html#2007data-drugs

Home ownership rate (percentage of population): "Table 12. Homeownership Rates by Area: 1960 to 2007," Historical Tables: Housing Vacancies and Homeownership, U.S. Census Bureau, http://www.census.gov/hhes/www/housing/hvs/annual07/ann07t12.html

SCHIP, WIC, child nutrition, food stamps (all: fiscal year outlays, billions): "Table 11-3. Outlays for Payments for Individuals by Category and Major Program, 1940–2013," Budget for Fiscal Year 2009, Historical Tables, http://www.gpoaccess.gov/usbudget/fy09/pdf/hist.pdf

TANF (fiscal year grants to states, billions): "Table 12-3. Total Outlays to Grants to State and Local Governments by Function, Agency, and Program, 1940–2009," Budget for Fiscal Year 2009, Historical Tables, http://www.gpoaccess.gov/usbudget/fy09/pdf/hist.pdf

Head Start (fiscal year appropriation, billions): "Head Start: Background and Issues," November 13, 2007, http://www.larson.house.gov/images/stories/PDF/Education/headstartbackgroundissues.pdf

Violent crime rate and property crime rate: Federal Bureau of Investigation, Uniform Crime Reports, http://www.fbi.gov/ucr/ucr.htm

Presidential approval ratings: Gallup Poll from UCSB Presidency Project, http://www.presidency.ucsb.edu/data/popularity.php (values represent the average of all polls during the year)

Presidential victories on votes in Congress: "Table 8–1. Presidential Victories on Votes in Congress," *Vital Statistics on Congress* (Brookings, 2008)

Number of bills vetoed and number of vetoes overridden: "President Clinton's Vetoes," Congressional Research Service, http://www.rules.house.gov/archives/98–147.pdf; "Vetoes by President George W. Bush," http://www.senate.gov/reference/Legislation/Vetoes/Bush GW.htm

Success rate of presidential appointments: *Vital Statistics on American Politics* (CQ Press, 2007)

Electoral outcomes of president's party in congressional elections: "Table 2–3. Net Party Gains in House and Senate Seats, General and Special Elections, 1946–2000," and "Table 2–4. Losses by the President's Party in Midterm Elections, 1862–2004," *Vital Statistics on Congress* (Brookings, 2008) (for presidential election years, the "president's party" is that of the sitting president)

Difference between president's budget proposal and final version passed: Author's calculation based on official presidential budget submissions, 1993–2007

Percentage of cabinet-level department heads retained from prior year: Calculations done based on listings in the *U.S. Government Manual*, various editions

Number of press conferences held: Calculations done based on archives available at http://www.presidency.ucsb.edu/news_conferences.php

Number of nationally televised addresses: Calculations done based on archives of "Addresses to the Nation," available at http://www.presidency.ucsb.edu/ws/

Public opinion reactions to State of the Union addresses: Change in Gallup approval rating based on poll most immediately before and poll most immediately after State of the Union; Gallup poll data available from UCSB Presidency Project, http://www.presidency .ucsb.edu/data/popularity.php

Staff turnover rates: Calculations done based on listings in the *U.S. Government Manual*, various editions

State of the Union address proposals adopted: Based on content analyses of State of the Union addresses, 1993–2007, and the *Congressional Quarterly Almanacs* for those years.

REFERENCES

Becker, Jo, Sheryl Gay Stolberg, and Stephen Labaton. 2008. "White House Philosophy Stoked Mortgage Bonfire." *New York Times*, December 21, p. 1.

Bell, Jeffrey. 2008. "The Politics of a Failed Presidency." *Weekly Standard*, March 17, pp. 20–32.

Cannon, Lou, and Carl Cannon. 2008. *Reagan's Disciple: George W. Bush's Troubled Quest for a Presidential Legacy*. New York: PublicAffairs.

Gillespie, Ed. 2008. "Myths and Facts About the Real Bush Record." www.realclearpolitics .com/articles/2008/12/myths_and_facts_about_the_real.html.

"Job Performance Ratings for President Truman." 2008. *Roper Center Public Opinion Archives*. http://webapps.ropercenter.uconn.edu/CFIDE/roper/presidential/webroot/ presidential_rating.

Leverett, Flynt L. 2006. "Leverett: Bush Administration 'Not Serious' About Dealing with Iran." Interview by Bernard Gwertzman, March 31. http://www.cfr.org/publication/10326.

Rauch, Jonathan. 2008. "Small Ball After All?" *National Journal*, September 20, pp. 22–28.

Afterword

Why Judging George W. Bush
Is Never as Easy as It Seems

JOHN J. DIIULIO JR.

WHEN IT COMES TO JUDGING presidents and presidencies, partisan or ideological diatribes are a dime a dozen, and not worth the dime. The same can be said about many assessments by ex–White House aides, whether they judge as legacy-minded loyalists out to justify their former boss's every decision, disaffected West Wing staff out to settle old scores, or self-important souls looking for quick book-selling bucks. But even for disinterested journalists and serious scholars, fairly and intelligently judging presidents and presidencies, past or present, is never as easy as it seems.

William Galston's concluding chapter to this splendid scholarly volume is aptly entitled "Between Journalism and History." As Galston counsels, judging any president's leadership requires distinguishing between the "deal of the cards and the play of the hand." The "Truman problem" is Galston's term for how President Harry S Truman was unpopular with the mass public and with many presidency-watchers when he left office but became ever more widely beloved and respected as a leader in the decades thereafter. I would only add that the difficulty associated with soberly and synoptically judging a president can persist not only for decades but for centuries.

Take the first "W." In 2007, I moderated a panel discussion at the National Constitution Center featuring three new books on George Washington's presidency. Each book focused mainly on Washington's beliefs and actions as president as they related to church-state issues and government support for religious organizations. And I have on my bookshelves a dozen other recent or new books judging the president and the presidency that ended in 1797. Maybe we can speak of the "Washington problem."

With respect to George W. Bush and his presidency, I have not always or perfectly practiced the academic circumspection I just preached. In 2001, I served as first director of Bush's White House Office of Faith-Based and Community Initiatives. As an assistant to the president, I was equal in rank, formally at least, to the dozen or so other Bush senior staff, including Karl Rove, Karen Hughes, and Condoleezza Rice. In a memo made public in December 2002, I characterized the Bush staff as "Mayberry Machiavellis" who served "a godly man and a moral leader." Leavened by the foregoing chapters, my perspective on judging Bush is best presented by reconstructing that characterization, reexamining it in light of the administration's post-2002 record, and addressing certain beliefs about Bush and his presidency that have since become widely associated with it.

"MAYBERRY MACHIAVELLIS" . . .

I am a pro-life, pro-poor Catholic Democrat and Philadelphia native. After graduating from my hometown Ivy League school, Penn, I did my Ph.D. in political science at Harvard and then taught public policy for thirteen years at Princeton. I also served as director of the Brookings Institution's Center for Public Management before returning to Penn as a faculty member in 1999. I came to the Bush White House in 2001 having known the new president's father a bit from work I had done on federal crime policy in the 1980s. I also knew his brother Jeb a little. And I had met Vice President Gore and knew many on his campaign staff through my work in the 1990s on government reform. In 1999, I was intending to help Gore's 2000 campaign—and I did. But I also got called to Austin to meet Texas governor George W. Bush. I rebuffed the first half dozen contacts, but in April 1999 a few friends finally prevailed on me to go and meet him. I liked Bush. In the meeting, he sort of keyed on me and my comments; about a dozen others were in attendance. I had not left the governor's mansion before Bush asked how much I bench-pressed (400 pounds) and dubbed (300-pound) me "Big John," adding playfully that "the big's not for tall," a joke he would repeat.

I helped on Bush's maiden campaign speech, "The Duty of Hope," receiving an exceptionally kind call from him on the July 1999 morning before he gave it. He thanked me for "adding so much balance" to the speech. In fact, I helped both the Gore campaign and the Bush campaign on faith-based issues and social policy. I was in Tennessee with Gore in May 1999 and helped a little on the address he delivered that month touting community-serving religious nonprofits. But I grew bothered and bored by each campaign's increasingly partisan prattle and backed off both save for answering occasional calls for help from high-placed friends.

Just before Bush came to Philadelphia for a June 2000 speech on government reform, he asked to meet with me. I agreed to help on the speech, and he delivered it at historic Carpenter's Hall. After the speech, C-SPAN caught a moment of our exit together with Pennsylvania governor Tom Ridge. I rode to a local hotel in a limo with Bush, then spent about an hour one-on-one with him, talking mainly about church-state issues and my hope that either he or Vice President Gore (the Gore reference made him flash a smile) would put "faith-based" permanently into the public policy vernacular, onto the federal agenda, and into action through at least one new program with new money, namely, a program to mentor the children of prisoners.

I was deeply impressed and moved by Bush's response. He loved the locution "people of faith mentoring children of promise." He winced as if in pain when I recited once again (we had discussed the idea during the April 1999 meeting) the grim statistics on how life often turns out for those low-income urban minority children who, as he humanized the social science, have "a mom or dad in jail." He displayed intellectual depth (yes, he did) in asking precisely the right questions about how a good, constitutionally kosher federal program for mentoring the children of prisoners might be structured, what it might cost, and so on. When Governor Ridge and former Indianapolis mayor Stephen Goldsmith entered and joined us for lunch, Bush concluded, "That's exactly how this ought to go" and gave me a hug around the neck. A photo taken a moment before captured the good feelings. He was no Democrat with a capital "D," but he struck me as a personable and good-humored democrat with a small "d."

Still, while I felt that Bush was sincere, I knew that "compassionate conservatism" was a campaign slogan, and that some top Bush advisors were cynical about "compassion" and worse than cynical toward "faith-based." The last two articles I published before joining the administration were a June 2000 essay in the conservative political magazine the *Weekly Standard*, asking critically, "What Is Compassionate Conservatism?" and a December 2000 essay in the same magazine, "Equal Protection Run Amok," hammering the Supreme Court for its *Bush v. Gore* decision. Clearly, I was not interested in courting a job with the new Republican president, much as I liked, admired, and had high hopes for him.

Among many other domestic policy differences and social policy reservations, I had deep concerns about what "faith-based" would mean in an administration that was naturally going to be tempted by the GOP's all-important religious conservative leaders and legions to fashion the policy in ways that trifled with settled constitutional church-state limits, undercut religious pluralism, belied bipartisanship, and substituted symbolic support for substantive action and civic results. But I never imagined that it would be my problem. When I was asked to take the "faith czar" job, I agreed subject to several conditions, all of which were accepted. I publicly declared that it was to be a six-month stint, just long enough to launch the office and get a five-agency grant-making performance audit done: I had been a leader on "faith factor" research, and I knew many people in Washington, but overseeing a quasi-academic public administration study was my only true comparative advantage for the job.

I ended up serving closer to eight months, resigning in July and announcing my resignation, effective September 15, the very day in August 2001 that the audit report, *Unlevel Playing Field*, was released at my own old left-leaning Washington think tank home, Brookings. As I describe in my 2007 book, *Godly Republic*, my White House tenure was rocky, not only in relation to certain among the president's evangelical Christian supporters (for instance, I upset them lots with a March 2001 speech delivered in Dallas before the National Association of Evangelicals) but also in relation to many a well-connected, inside-the-Beltway GOP libertarian and small-government conservative, for whose views I found it impossible, both in public and in private, to disguise my disdain.

Still, I was well liked and had good relations with virtually all my senior staff colleagues. The only criticism the president ever made to me directly and more than once was that I was not "getting on (his) dance card"—that is, coming in to see and brief him—enough. In July 2001, I was asked whether I would stay on if I could move the office operation to Philly. I respectfully declined, and also declined a trip to Crawford, Texas, to talk it through with the president. I knew that I would probably end up serving all four years if I put myself on that plane and spent that up-close-and-personal time with him. Bush handwrote me an incredibly warm and gracious two-page letter accepting my resignation. All my staff colleagues, despite the public and private heartburn I had on occasion given them, were kinder and gentler than I deserved in their public remarks on my leaving—though some private remarks were another story.

On my last scheduled working morning in the White House, I handed in my badge and such. I was hanging out in the West Wing (my own desk and office over in the old Executive Office Building had already been cleared out) and saying good-bye to some friends. I planned to stay until around noon and maybe catch a one-way 1:00 P.M. train back to Philly. I had a memo in my breast pocket outlining the progress made since July 2001 on a new "faith bill," a bill I had worked on with my old friend, Democratic senator Joseph Lieberman, and his staff. The president was in Florida that morning; but, as I learned from an office colleague over breakfast in the White House senior staff dining room (located right next to the Situation Room), the president would be back at 2:00 P.M. for a meeting with a religious group that had been scheduled by another senior staff colleague. Great, I thought. My improvised plan was to step in to see the president just before that meeting, take a minute for a word on the bill, maybe grab a final neck hug in the bargain, and catch the 3:00 P.M. train home instead. The morning was September 11, 2001.

What Galston labels the "800-pound gorilla at the bar"—the post–9/11 reality—changed things for the Bush presidency, including putting domestic and social policy on hold for months. Still, contrary to what some have asserted, it is not true that the pre–9/11 Bush White House was ever anchored by the "uniter, not divider" campaign pledge, or ever dedicated to bipartisan legislative habits like those associated with the No Child Left Behind (NCLB) bill. Indeed, key Hill Republicans received repeated high-level assurances to the contrary. Before 9/11, except on

NCLB, the Bush White House never really twisted arms or made deals or worked hard or spent scarce presidential political capital on compassion agenda items that House Republican leaders and their staffs loved to hate. Nor, however, is it true that Bush and his senior staff rolled over for every right-wing Republican request or trimmed every compassion agenda proposal to suit the Hill's ultraconservatives. Both before and after 9/11, on issues as diverse as embryonic stem-cell research and prescription drugs, or increased spending for programs to increase volunteerism and new policies and programs affecting mostly Latino immigrants, Bush and his West Wing staff were disliked and often openly disparaged by the Beltway's most partisan GOP legislators and ideological leaders. And, again excepting NCLB, the Democrats' partisan legislators and ideological leaders generally gave Bush little help or credit, even when his actual policy positions were not far from their own.

Nonetheless, in early 2002 I still harbored hopes for the faith-based initiative and other compassion agenda items that had been championed not only by the White House staff (who Shirley Anne Warshaw rightly situates as the in-house moderates) but also, and more importantly, by the president, who was, as I suggested above, a compassionate conservative at heart—a president who repeatedly told me and others going back to meetings in 1999 that he did not want or intend to play campaign-type politics with these items, to have his staff do so in his name, or to have "faith-based" and the rest of the compassion agenda turn out to be (in his Texas vernacular) "all hat, no cattle."

For that very reason, by mid-2002 I had become increasingly frustrated by how the administration seemed to be letting faith-based initiatives languish, by how it appeared to be hollowing other items on the president's compassion agenda, and by early signs that it might use Democrats' supposedly defeatist response to terrorism as a wedge issue in the 2002 midterm congressional elections and in the president's reelection bid.

In April 2002, wearing my old Brookings public administration hat, I went public with a critique concerning the White House's new homeland security office and refusal to have its director, former Pennsylvania governor Ridge, testify before Congress. I published the piece, entitled "Homeland Insecurity," in the *Weekly Standard*. That same month, I penned my first

letter to the president describing not only my concerns about the homeland security office but also outlining my concerns about how his bipartisan prayers for faith-based programs were being buried, and generalizing
about how his presidency, touted as the "CEO presidency" by some, was
straying ever farther from fulfilling his other social policy pledges. I zeroed
in on the well-intentioned but wrong-headed staff's tendency to elevate
political rhetoric over policy substance; to ignore inconvenient facts; to
avoid thinking through complex administrative and policy implementation chores; and to reduce important governance matters to political talking points and campaign-style "messages." Without naming any names, I
therein referenced the staff as behaving like "Mayberry Machiavellis."

I mailed the letter but got no reply. Even old friends in the West Wing
seemed suddenly curt or cold to my appeals to remember the president's
compassion promises. I then did what I had not done since August 2001;
namely, I began speaking about the administration to a few trusted friends in
journalism, responding to select reporters' requests to offer on-background
(or what I thought was on-background) commentary, and redrafted and
resent the April 2002 letter, retaining the Mayberry Machiavellis locution.
I know at least one version that I had had hand-carried into the West Wing
arrived, for in late 2002 former staff colleagues, including Harriet Miers,
called to tell me so. What I do not know even now, however, is whether
the president ever saw it.

The Mayberry Machiavellis phrase became public during a December
2002 media flap concerning a memo I had vouched months earlier to Ron
Suskind, a journalist whose 1998 book *Hope in the Unseen* I had glow-
ingly reviewed for the *Weekly Standard*. The book was about a low-income
inner-city youth whose Pentecostal mother and church community had
helped him to avoid trouble, succeed in school, and get accepted to Brown
University. I met the author by chance later that same year at the funeral of
a dear former Harvard student of mine. So, when he contacted me in 2002
to discuss a story about the Bush White House, I knew him as the author
of that great book and as a man who had paid his respects to my beloved
former student. Suskind had, he told me, already interviewed other senior
Bush staff, including Andrew Card, Karen Hughes, and Karl Rove. He was,
he said, hoping for a more critical perspective from an ex-insider. We talked

by phone and traded e-mails. I liked and respected him, but rather than field his persistent calls and other communications or have him continue to pop up and pop questions at public meetings where I was speaking, I figured I would bundle my responses to him in a single, all-purpose memo.

Dated October 24, 2002, the memo I vouched to Ron Suskind, better known since as the "DiIulio Letter"—three-thousand-plus words in all, including the Mayberry Machiavellis phrase—was actually based in large part on the letters that I had previously drafted and redrafted, sent and resent, to the president (I write fast, but not that fast). Dozens of Bush presidency-watchers have since cited it, none more kindly (kind to me at least) than *Boston Globe* correspondent Thomas Oliphant. In his 2007 book, *Utter Incompetents*, Oliphant writes that the memo's "devastatingly shrewd observations . . . stand years later as a definitive portrait of the Bush administration in operation—the perverted triumph of ideological politics and interest group politics at the expense of governance" (Oliphant 2007, 18).

My own assessment remains mixed and tends toward self-indictment. On the one hand, the memo is sloppy and streams consciousness in parts. It uses a few dramatic but not duly representative examples to illustrate criticisms. And, of course, it contains the smart-alecky Mayberry Machiavellis phrase. On the other hand, the letter is generally factual, circumspect, and balanced. Contrary to what some have asserted, it does not take critical aim by name at any White House official. Here are several key parts, pro and con:

In my view, President Bush is a highly admirable person of enormous personal decency . . . a godly man and a moral leader. He is much, much smarter than some people—including some of his supporters and advisors—seem to suppose. . . . There is still two years, maybe six, for them to do more and better. . . . And, needless to say, 9/11, and now the global war on terror and the new homeland and national security plans, must be weighed in the balance. But . . . even allowing for those huge contextual realities, they could stand to find ways of inserting more serious policy fiber into the West Wing diet . . .

They are almost to an individual nice people, and there are among them several extremely gifted persons who do indeed know—and care—a great deal about actual policy-making, administrative reform, and so forth. But they have been, for whatever reasons, organized in ways that make it hard for policy-minded staff, including colleagues [and] even secretaries of cabinet agencies, to get much West Wing traction, or even get a non-trivial hearing. . . . [What] they needed, I thought then and still do now, was more policy-relevant information, discussion, and deliberation. In eight months, I heard many, many staff discussions, but not three meaningful, substantive policy discussions . . .

Every modern presidency moves on the fly, but the lack of even basic policy knowledge, and the only casual interest in knowing more, was somewhat breathtaking. . . . Even quite junior staff would sometimes hear quite senior staff poohpooh any need to dig deeper for pertinent information on a given issue.

Likewise, every administration at some point comes to think of the White House as its own private tree house . . . [M]aybe because they were coming off Florida and the election controversy, maybe because they were so unusually tight-knit and "Texas," maybe because the chief of staff, Andy Card, was more a pure staff process than a staff leader or policy person, or maybe for other reasons I can't recognize—[the Bush administration] was far more inclined in that direction, and became progressively more so as the months pre–9/11 wore on.

This gave rise to what you might call the Mayberry Machiavellis—staff, junior and senior, who consistently talked and acted as if the height of political sophistication consisted in reducing every issue to its simplest, black-and-white terms for public consumption, then steering legislative initiatives or policy proposals as far right as possible. These folks have their predecessors in previous administrations, left and right, Democrat and Republican, but in the Bush administration they were particularly unfettered . . .

Some are inclined to blame the high political-to-policy ratios of this administration on Karl Rove . . . [but] often, [Rove] supplies such policy substance as the administration puts out. Fortunately, he is not just a largely self-taught, hyperpolitical guy, but also a very well informed guy when it comes to certain domestic issues. Whether, as some now assert, he has such sway in national security, homeland security, and foreign affairs, I cannot say . . .

The good news, however, is that the fundamentals are pretty good—the president's character and heart, the decent, well-meaning people on staff. . . . I believe that the best may well be yet to come from the Bush administration. But, in my view, they will not get there without some significant reforms to the policy-lite inter-personal and organizational dynamics of the place.

The president is a "moral leader" and "smarter" than people suppose. The staff members are mostly "nice people." And "the best may well be yet to come." All well and good, but the memo's finer or fairer points did not and do not excuse its broad-brushed implication that if not Karl Rove himself or alone, then other senior and junior staff in a West Wing largely powered, politically and intellectually, by him, were "Mayberry Machiavellis."

To make matters worse, in December 2002 and thereafter, many print and electronic stories selectively cited the three-thousand-plus word letter, liberally paraphrased it, or spliced in other quotes attributed to me and others—sometimes correctly, sometimes not; sometimes fairly, sometimes not; and sometimes impossible to recall or tell. What weighed heaviest on me was that I had still-serving, longtime friends in that White House, including speechwriters Michael Gerson and Pete Wehner, Domestic Policy Council chief John Bridgeland (the man who got the president's post–9/11 volunteer service initiative off to a flying start), and others, such as my dear young pal David Kuo over in the faith-based office. All would now be tarred with my broad-brushed criticisms and potentially scarred by others' spray-painted stories.

Before the October "DiIulio Letter" or any stories based, or ostensibly based, on it became public, I apologized in private notes and in phone calls. I apologized to the president, and to the White House staff members, senior and junior. In several private communications, I characterized my barbs as baseless and groundless. I asked forgiveness not only for what I had actually written and said but also for all the worst that others, fairly or not, were going to make from my now-public criticisms.

In public, I also issued several full and complete apologies, including one in which I matter-of-factly agreed with the White House press spokesman, Ari Fleisher, when he characterized certain of the criticisms exactly as I myself had characterized them, privately and previously, namely, as "baseless and groundless" (I had also used "harsh and hasty"). But even a senate term (six years) later, I still heard that I was being threatened with Siberia (or was it Wasilla?), that I was kowtowing while courting government grants (had none, sought none, got none, want none), fending off defamation lawsuits (we are all public figures), or being intimidated by sitting Bush staff, who so far as I knew and know, bore me no personal malice despite my criticisms and the media flap, and who in any case knew me, my temperament, and my background well enough to know better than to try, if they did. Although some cynical souls in Washington and its press corps seemed to think such a thing to be impossible, I was simply and sincerely sorry, the same in private and in public, for doing something that I believed was thoughtless, and I was willing to assume full responsibility (and that before my Catholic self-examination of conscience at Easter), not only for what I actually said or did that offended or hurt others but for what I unintentionally and indirectly empowered others to do to offend or hurt others.

That self-indictment included, and still includes, the charge of putting a seemingly authoritative, quasi-academic cloud over a president and a presidency then still in only its second year and still struggling to recast itself in relation to 9/11. It was a president and a presidency that had not, *at least not up to that point*, done enough that was lamentable (and duly documented as such) to deserve such characterization, least from a former senior staff member sounding like a Monday morning academic armchair quarterback entranced by his own centrist political will, intellectual wit, and moral self-righteousness. And least from one who in every single public and private communication had maintained, as stated in the memo, that "President Bush is a highly admirable person of enormous personal decency. He is a godly man and a moral leader. He is much, much smarter than some people—including some of his own supporters and advisors— seem to suppose."

. . . AFTER ALL?

It was not until August 2005 that questions like "Mayberry Machiavellis, after all?" and "Mayberry Machiavellis or not, was I right about Bush?" really began to cross my mind. In 2003 and 2004, revelations about the weapons of mass destruction (WMD) goose chase and the poorly planned occupation of Iraq, especially the surreal Coalition Provisional Authority (CPA) saga, troubled me as they did so many others. The CPA tale is a tragic case study in half-baked policy making, inept communications, and utter administrative incompetence. The WMD "intelligence" and its facile usages, the costly bungling by the CPA, and the post-2002 Cheney-Rumsfeld decision making on Iraq all produced an ungodly mess, which still had former secretary of state Colin Powell frustrated and fuming in 2006 when he testified before the Iraq Study Group.

Still, on Bush and Iraq, two questions loom. First, if it ever was "all politics" or "all campaign tactics" with Bush or his closest advisors, then why did the president nearly risk not being reelected and why did he remain steadfast long after all, including many a conservative and GOP stalwart, not to mention mass public opinion, had fled his position on Iraq? And second, if Bush and his advisors were all so misguided, inept, or worse on Iraq, then why did almost no one inside the administration and only a few in Congress see this clearly and say so plainly before things went from tolerably bad to bloody worse in pre-surge Iraq?

In judging Bush on Iraq, an early first stop must be famed *Washington Post* journalist Bob Woodward's four books on the subject. Or make that "four first stops," because Woodward's four books on Iraq give four different looks at judging Bush, commencing with swooning (*Bush at War*, 2002), becoming more skeptical (*Plan of Attack*, 2004), turning sour (*State of Denial*, 2006), and then surging (pun intended) to a highly critical but not quite so sour assessment (*The War Within*, 2008). Writing in 2008, Woodward avers that after years of bumbling and fumbling past basic facts about the conflict's nature and what was needed to curtail sectarian violence and stabilize the Iraqi government, Bush stumbled into the Tall Afar success and then stumbled into the surge. On net, Woodward's 2008 judgment on Bush's leadership on Iraq is negative:

[Bush] didn't want an open, full debate that aired possible concerns and considered alternatives. . . . There was no meeting to discuss whether to go to war. . . . The result has been impulsiveness and carelessness, and, perhaps most troubling, a delayed reaction to realities and advice that run counter to his gut. . . . By his own ambitious goals of 2001, Bush had fallen short [431–35].

But note that Woodward, considered since Watergate to be among the best journalists and last "real reporters" in Washington, arrived at that latest (and final?) judgment after writing over one thousand pages all told, and after starting with an assessment in 2002 that plainly and simply did not begin to foreshadow the interpretive twists and turns in his next six years of judging Bush on Iraq (and although Iraq is a huge and historic issue, it is not the only one with which future scholars judging Bush must grapple). A decade or more from Bush's final day in office, will the scholarly consensus on the Iraq invasion, war, and "mission accomplished" occupation seem as broadly and deeply critical as the incipient scholarly consensus was in 2008? Personally, I suspect that it will be less critical but not by much; however, no one can know for sure or deny that for all the damning things about administration decision making which are already documented, we are still much closer to journalism than to history in judging Bush on Iraq.

Iraq aside, through the 2004 reelection season and by mid-2005, I had a long, not-happy list concerning the administration's policy actions (or inactions) on numerous domestic and social policy and administrative reform matters, including but not limited to shortfalls on faith-based initiatives, cuts in Head Start spending, and rolling back federal support for children's health care; assertions about executive powers that would make James Madison weep, including signing statements by the hundreds, sweeping executive orders by the scores, and national law preemption claims that no states' rights advocate or federalism-loving conservative could abide; record deficit-spending and fly-by-the-pants fiscal policies enough to make even urban Democrats like me skittish; disciplining or displacing several low-level political appointees and career civil servants who failed to mouth some West Wing message or follow a political script; and more.

Still, it was not until the president and the White House responded to Hurricane Katrina in August 2005 and into September; it was not until I made the first in what has since become over a dozen trips to post-Katrina New Orleans; it was not until I witnessed the White House witnessing a great American city succumb to biblical-sized floods wrought by biblical-sized government sins, starting with decades-old federal government malfeasance (those lousy levees) and culminating in "Heck of a job, Brownie" following the president's flyover and preceding his "Do whatever it takes" speech at Jackson Place (St. Louis Cathedral in the background)—it was not until then that I felt, for the first time since my sincere private and public apologies and retractions in 2002, that maybe Bush's senior staff were, if not to an individual then in institutional character, much as I had outlined three years earlier. Or maybe worse?

Anne Khademian's Katrina account in this volume is excellent and judges Bush's response to Katrina to be a "failure of homeland security." That it certainly was; but to me, it was much more than that. As I now see it, the White House response to Katrina was the domestic bookend to the CPA saga and all the other defective pre-surge Iraq decision making. I have read all there is to read about the response to Katrina, including the White House's version and the many other federal, state, and local government reports. I have read or listened to accounts by people who were on the ground in New Orleans as it happened, and also by former senior Bush officials who were present when Bush's response to the hurricane was fashioned and defended.

In his 2007 book, *Heroic Conservatism*, the aforementioned former top Bush speechwriter Gerson is fairly candid in characterizing Bush's decision making on Katrina as a disaster. In Scott McClellan's 2008 book, *What Happened*, the former Bush press secretary leaves even less to the imagination:

Katrina was a defining turning point for Bush and his administration. It left an indelible stain on his presidency. The tardy efforts to help the people of the Gulf Coast did not convince Americans to forgive the initial ill-prepared response and the inadequate preparations and plans. . . . We spent the first week in a state of denial. . . . As we sought to protect the president and his reputation, instead of just accepting fault and moving aggressively to remedy the problem, we tried to deflect responsibility away from the White House and the federal government [290].

There is no way to prove that Katrina dealt a lasting blow to Bush's public approval. The relevant public opinion data suggest that it was only Independent voters who deserted Bush in significant numbers after it appeared that the White House had deserted New Orleans. That acknowledged, I can only observe that the stubbornly low public confidence in Bush, and ever wider public receptivity to Bush-bashing views, seem to me to have become a permanent fixture only after Katrina.

Of course, what we do not yet know is who in the White House was most decisive in the administration's failed first response to the disaster or its subsequent follies and fibs about the recovery process. Federal Emergency Management Agency (FEMA) director Michael Brown, and FEMA itself, made easy initial scapegoats, but Brown's boss, Homeland Security chief Michael Chertoff, was the primary decider. Further up the command chain from Chertoff, I wish that Shirley Anne Warshaw or some other scholar, journalist, or ex-insider could tell us what if any role Vice President Cheney and his staff played in the disaster's decision-making disaster. Does the Katrina case furnish more grist for Warshaw's "Cheneyization" and "co-presidency" mill, and if so, how, if at all, would that mitigate Bush's responsibility for what happened?

Whatever the answers may turn out to be, Katrina was a ruinous, and ruinously revealing, moment for Bush, his White House staff, and his entire administration, not to mention an outright failure to protect and serve American citizens by the thousands. Thank God for the U.S. Coast Guard, which performed admirably and heroically even as the federal government's other units from 1600 Pennsylvania on down performed in ways that justified the public disgust and disbelief that followed. I only wish that the White House had taken me up on my March 2007 challenge, penned in *Time* magazine, to move my former office to post-Katrina New Orleans in order to boost the region's human, physical, and financial recovery process. Some thought that I was joking; the real joke, however, is how the administration missed an opportunity to make partial amends for its first-response fiascoes and its recovery process derelictions.

JUDGING THE PRINCE

But even with and after Katrina; even after the double-proof (a.k.a. the 2006 and 2008 election results) that red dreams or blue nightmares about Bush ushering in a permanent Republican majority through a Rove-crafted strategy were never to be taken seriously; even with a historic global economic meltdown on Bush's final-year watch; and even with nearly three in four Americans disapproving the president's performance as he left office—is it obvious that "judging Bush" must mean agreeing, at least for now and in the main, with assessments like that offered in October 2008 by the unfailingly judicious *Economist* in the headline to its Lexington column: "Reaping the Whirlwind: George Bush's Presidency Is Ending in Disaster"?

No, not exactly. In August 2008, I found myself defending Bush in an open session at the Democratic National Convention in Denver (nobody else there seemed up for that task). I could easily list a dozen "Bush got right" things—for instance, the fact that President Barack Obama has changed but kept Bush's faith-based office and related initiatives; Bush's multi-billion-dollar, multi-year HIV/AIDS program in Africa; his initial stabs at more humane immigration policy packages; his Medicare administrative modernization reforms and prescription drug financing program; the resolute leadership he showed in the days right after 9/11, including his repeated calls for calm and his impassioned injunctions about respecting fellow citizens who happen to be Muslims; and more.

On the one side, we have today's journalistic and quasi-academic Bush critics declaring the forty-third president and the Bush presidency to be the "worst" or "among the worst" in American history. On the other side, we have the forty-third president himself, speaking in April 2007 before a friendly crowd at Virginia Polytechnic Institute and quipping, "If they're still writing about 1, 43 doesn't have to worry about it." A *New York Times* story about the speech carried this headline: "Bush, on Friendly Turf, Suggests History Will Be Kind to Him."

Standing between these two contemporary extremes, we have careful but early scholarly assessments like those in this volume, and perhaps the patience to wait until most Bush White House papers, records, and first-hand testimonies are public before coming to any hard-and-fast or final judgments. My own tentative judgment is that while history will be kinder to Bush's leadership and his presidency than most contemporaries have been, future fair-minded historians will find little or nothing in the as-yet unpublished record resulting in a revisionism that ranks Bush's leadership, staff, administration, or public policy and administration legacy highly.

I am, however, sure about one thing: the editors and authors of this volume have the focus and the book's title right. It is "Judging Bush," not "Judging Rove," or "Judging Rice," or even, with apologies to Shirley Anne Warshaw, "Judging Cheney." My "Mayberry Machiavellis" letters, both those to the president and the one that was made public, thus got it wrong by looking, as it were, at and to the prince's ministers rather than at and to the prince himself.

Although strained by the facts as I now think I know them, my respect and regard for Bush, as expressed in those letters, remains much what it was when I wrote them. But my disappointment in how his second term seemed to amplify rather than correct the policy and administrative defects that were apparent to me quite early on in his first term—the governance failures and their roots in how the White House and the executive branch were led, organized, and managed, and in how Bush surrounded himself mostly with senior advisors who never truly challenged his tendency toward intellectual lethargy or sincerely shared what he once called his special "charge to keep" in promoting civic unity and social compassion—remains palpable and deepens, not lightens, every time I return to New Orleans and see more painstaking human, physical, and financial recovery happening, little thanks to belated efforts by my former boss and all the president's men and women.

The in-house Machiavellis matter, but it is the prince, not the ministers, who ultimately makes or breaks what Princeton's Fred I. Greenstein terms "the presidential difference" (2004). As the foregoing chapters combine to suggest, judging any president requires knowing lots about his strategic, political, tactical, and moral "competence" while in office. Judging Bush, save preliminarily, requires knowing lots more on all these counts than any of us do as of this writing.

REFERENCES

Greenstein, Fred I. 2004. *The Presidential Difference*, 2nd ed. Princeton, NJ: Princeton University Press.
McClellan, Scott. 2008. *What Happened*. New York: PublicAffairs.
Oliphant, Thomas. 2007. *Utter Incompetents*. New York: St. Martin's Press.
Woodward, Bob. 2008. *The War Within*. New York: Simon & Schuster.

Index

ABC News—*Washington Post* polls, 91n12, 92nn19,27, 93n29
Aberbach, Joel D., 127
Abizaid, John, 248
abortion, 46, 54, 142; late-term abortions, 101; partial-birth abortions, 144, 146, 151–52
Abraham, Spencer, 45, 51
Abramoff, Jack, 87, 88
Abramowitz, Alan, 77
Abramowitz, Michael, 223
Abrams, Creighton B., 255
abstinence education, 46, 54, 80
Abu Ghraib, 52, 66, 67, 68, 77, 87, 227, 239, 240
Academic Achievement for All Act, 161
Achievement Alliance, 169
Ackerman, Gary, 107
Addington, David: relationship with Cheney, 44, 45, 52, 55, 70–71, 124, 125; and Terrorist Surveillance Program, 132n6
affirmative action, 142, 144
Afghanistan: Bagram Air Force Base, 66, 67, 68; Northern Alliance, 247, 259, 260, 262, 263; promotion of democracy in, 223; al-Qaeda in, 120—21, 258, 259, 260–61, 263, 286; reconstruction efforts in, 253, 267; role of NATO in, 236, 241, 263; Soviet war in, 257; Taliban in, 6, 34, 62, 68–69, 241, 243, 244, 247, 252, 253, 258, 259–60, 261, 263, 273, 285, 286
Afghanistan War, 6, 17, 234, 242; Afghan Model, 253, 257–63, 264; Bin Laden's escape from Tora Bora, 120–21, 260–61; and Cheney, 120; decision to invade, 37, 59, 120, 237, 243, 273; economic cost of, 104, 106, 180, 268,

280; evaluation of, 248, 273, 285–86; and France, 259; and Iran, 246–47; vs. Iraq War, 34–35, 252, 253, 263–64, 266, 273, 286; and Italy, 259; and NATO, 236; and Obama, 90; and Rice, 61, 237; and Rumsfeld, 258, 260, 262; and UK, 259; U.S. casualties in, 260
Agee, G. Steven, 143
Agresto, John, 18n14
Ahmadinejad, Mahmoud, 230
AIDS program in Africa, 106, 287, 309
AIG, 55, 182
Aldrich, John H., 17n9
Algeria, 240
Alito, Samuel, 104, 142–43, 144, 145, 152
Allbaugh, Joseph, 201, 202
Allen, Mike, 90
Allen, Scott A., 67
American Association of Retired Persons (AARP), 85
American Bar Association (ABA), 138–39
American Center for Law and Justice, 139
American Civil War, 225, 227, 268
American Federation of Teachers, 157, 160
American Petroleum Institute, 45
American Trial Lawyers Association, 150
Amos, James F., 240
Andrews, Edmund, 64
anthrax attacks, 31
Anti-Ballistic Missile Treaty, 236
Aquinas, Thomas, 217
Arafat, Yasir, 223, 242
Aron, Nan, 138–39
Aron, Raymond, 220
asbestos litigation reform, 148–49
Ashcroft, John, 51–52, 123, 141
Aspin, Les, 254

Council of Economic Advisors, 122
Council of La Raza, 169
Council on Environmental Quality, 45
Covarrubias, Jack, 17
Cox, Christopher, 48
CQ Weekly: "When the President has
  Won," 105
crime rate, 283, 284
criteria, evaluative: and crises, 3–4, 9;
  and divided government, 274; domestic policy, 5, 6–7; and economic
  conditions, 273–74; Felzenberg on,
  17n6; foreign policy, 5–6; political
  organization, 5, 12; political skills,
  5, 8–9; presidential character, 5, 9,
  11–12; presidential opportunity level,
  5, 9–11, 273–74, 294; relationship
  to time horizon, 275–76; Schlesinger
  on, 4–5; short-term success vs. long-
  term sustainability, 108, 130; and
  wicked problems, 206–7. *See also*
  competence
Crotty, William, 80, 81, 92n25
*C-SPAN Survey of Presidential Leader-
  ship*, 5
Customs and Border Protection, 196, 199

Daley, Suzanne, 236
Darfur, 220
Daschle, Tom, 148
Davis, Susan, 90, 106
Defense Science Board, 258
De Gaulle, Charles, 220
Delay, Tom, 88
Democrats: and authorization to use
  force against Iraq, 83; and civil rights
  groups, 168, 169; and Clinton, 13,
  282; Democratic Leadership Council, 91n8, 167; and Iraq war, 33,
  93n29, 97, 106, 265; multilateralists
  among, 215–16; National Convention of 2008, 309; and NCLB, 157,
  160, 162–63, 165, 167, 168, 169–70,
  172–73, 299; relations with George
  W. Bush, 4, 29–31, 37, 49, 96–97,
  101, 102, 103, 107, 109, 162–63,
  184, 187–88, 192, 274, 284, 287–88,

299; support by group for, 77, 90; and
  teachers unions, 157, 160, 168, 169,
  173; in Texas, 29–30. *See also* Con-
  gress, Democrats in
Democrats for Education Reform (DFER),
  169
Dempsey, Martin, 226
Department of Agriculture, 45
Department of Commerce, 51
Department of Defense, 51, 54–55, 62,
  90, 123, 248, 257–58, 265. *See also*
  Aspin, Les; Gates, Robert; Rumsfeld,
  Donald; U.S. military
Department of Education, 71, 160; and
  NCLB, 159, 162, 165, 166–67, 168,
  172; Office of Innovation and Improvement, 172; Republican hostility
  toward, 157, 161, 162
Department of Energy, 45–46, 51, 71
Department of Health and Human Services, 46, 149
Department of Homeland Security (DHS):
  and all-hazards approach, 199–200,
  204, 206, 207–8; creation of, 10,
  83, 101, 122, 199, 208, 209nn3,5,6,
  299–300; and Hurricane Katrina, 16,
  195, 196, 198–205, 308; mission definition, 198–201; National Infrastructure Simulation and Analysis Center,
  204; and war on terror, 199–201,
  204, 207–8
Department of Justice: firing of U.S. attorneys, 77, 86, 125–26, 127, 138,
  145–46; and interrogation policy,
  239–40; Office of Legal Counsel,
  43, 55, 68, 70–71, 123, 124; Office
  of Legal Policy (OLP), 137–38; and
  Plame identity, 84; political appointees
  in, 127–28. *See also* Ashcroft, John;
  Gonzales, Alberto
Department of Labor, 51
Department of State, 48, 51, 55, 60, 64,
  125. *See also* Powell, Colin
Department of the Interior, 45, 51
Department of the Treasury, 51
Detainee Treatment Act of 2005, 68
Detterman, Douglas K., 23

De Vries, Brian, 24
Dewey, Thomas E., 290n1
Diamond, John, 32, 33–34
DiIulio, John, 17, 43, 49, 52–53, 127,
    130; DiIulio Letter, 300–304, 309–10
Dinh, Viet, 137, 138
Dionne, E. J., Jr., 85
director of national intelligence (DNI),
    209n5
divided government, 274, 280–81
DNI (director of national intelligence),
    209n5
Doan, Douglas, 203
Dole, Bob, 78, 81, 161, 174n
domestic policy: and Congress, 5, 6–7,
    30; as evaluative criterion, 5, 6–7; vs.
    foreign policy, 6, 7, 13, 17n8, 31, 99,
    107; relationship to election victories,
    7; relationship to politics, 117–18
domestic policy of George W. Bush: bail-
    out policy, 96–97, 110, 111, 183, 288;
    campaign finance policy, 288; civil
    justice reform, 136, 146–52; creation
    of moral and civil society/compassion-
    ate conservatism, 53, 77, 79–81, 84,
    157, 161, 163, 288, 299, 300, 301,
    304, 310; creation of moral society,
    41, 46; Domestic Policy Council,
    52, 119–20, 121, 296–97; economic
    stimulus policy, 106, 108, 181; energy
    policy, 41, 45–46, 50, 51, 53, 56, 71,
    89, 104, 111, 124, 127; "fast track"
    trade authority, 101, 178, 287–88; re-
    garding federal regulation, 42, 45–46,
    51, 55, 110, 124, 127, 150–51, 152,
    184; fiscal policy, 280–81, 289–90,
    306; homeownership expansion, 288;
    immigration policy, 80, 103, 105,
    111, 309; Medicare reform, 6, 7, 85,
    87, 92n22, 97, 110, 163, 280; and
    permanent Republican majority, 80,
    130, 131, 157–58, 308; promotion of
    volunteerism, 52, 54, 56, 299, 303;
    Social Security reform, 7, 8, 50, 77,
    80, 86, 103, 105, 129, 130, 163, 177,
    274, 278; trade policy, 281–83. See
    also economic policy of George W.

Bush; education reform; faith-based
    initiatives; Hurricane Katrina; judicial
    appointments; tax policy
Donahue, Amy K., 205
Draper, Robert, 123
Draper, Roger, 64
Drew, Christopher, 127
Druckman, James N., 193n4
Duberstein, Kenneth, 290n4
Duelfer Report, 224
Dukakis, Michael, 277
Dumbrell, John, 32, 55
Durant, Robert F., 126
Durbin, Richard, 97

East Timor: UN peacekeeping in, 220
economic and financial crisis of 2008, 3,
    16, 89, 176–77, 180–84, 281, 287–
    88, 308; automobile companies, 183;
    Bush's bailout policies, 96–97, 110,
    111, 183, 288; and Cheney's pro-busi-
    ness agenda, 55; and Congress, 181,
    182–83; and home-ownership expan-
    sion, 178; and Paulson, 122, 131,
    180, 182, 184; role of Federal Reserve
    System in, 181, 182, 184, 288; stock
    market during, 182, 183; and sub-
    prime mortgages, 180–81, 288, 289
economic class, 184, 186–87, 189–92,
    281–82
economic growth, 179, 185, 191, 274,
    281–82, 285
Economic Growth and Tax Relief Recon-
    ciliation Act of 2001, 177
economic policy of George W. Bush, 157,
    176–93; bailout program, 96–97, 110,
    111, 182–84; budget deficits, 179–
    80; and economic inequality, 184,
    186–87, 191–92; economic stimulus
    efforts, 106, 108, 181; home-owner-
    ship expansion, 178; and mortgages,
    181–82, 288, 289; public perceptions
    of, 176, 177, 184–93; Troubled Assets
    Relief Program (TARP), 183, 288. See
    also tax policy
Economist: "Reaping the Whirlwind," 308
Eddy, Rebecca, 172

Hess, Frederick M., 16, 30, 160, 167–68,
170, 172
Hezbollah, 285
Hickock, Eugene, 163
Higher Education Act, 106
Hilgruber, Andreas, 217
Hispanics, 77, 79, 81, 85, 91n8, 112n6,
157, 299
Hitler, Adolf, 32, 217, 218, 219
Hochman, Dafna, 246
Hochschild, Jennifer, 31
Hoff, David J., 168
Holmes, Lisa M., 141
Homeland Security Act of 2001, 120
Hoover, Herbert: vs. George W. Bush, 176,
288; and Great Depression, 279, 288;
opportunity level of, 10
Horowitz, Steven, 204
Houston, Tamara, 204
Howard, Jack, 47, 108
Howell, William G., 170
Hoyos, Carola, 263
Hsu, Spencer, 103
Hubbard, Glenn, 122
Huber, Peter: *Liability*, 146
Huckabee, Mike, 90
Hughes, Karen, 43, 46, 52, 60, 119, 128,
129, 295, 300
Hughes, Siobhan, 124
Hulse, Carl, 128
Hult, Karen M., 16
Hurricane Andrew, 207
Hurricane Gustav, 196–97
Hurricane Hugo, 207
Hurricane Katrina: Bush administration
response to, 3, 4, 14, 16, 77, 87–88,
103, 118, 131, 198–208, 279, 306–8,
310; Coast Guard during, 207, 308;
and DHS, 16, 195, 196, 198–205,
308; Federal Coordinating Officer
(FCO), 197; FEMA during, 103, 195,
197–98, 201, 202, 204, 205–6, 306,
308; FPS during, 201–2, 207; vs.
Hurricane Gustav, 196–97; National
Guard during, 203–4; Principal Federal Official (PFO), 197; and privatization of emergency response, 201–2,

204; relationship to popularity of
George W. Bush, 4, 87–88, 279, 307,
308; strategic competence during,
207–8; tactical competence during,
198–207; Wal-Mart during, 203–4;
and wicked problems, 206
Hussein, Saddam, 59, 84, 218, 219, 220,
238, 247, 252, 278; capture of, 264;
during Gulf War, 224; vs. Hitler, 219;
trial of, 225; and WMD programs,
32–33, 56, 217, 234, 237

Ibrahim, Saad, 226
Ifill, Gwen, 236
Iglesias, David, 126
Ikenberry, G. J., 219
Immelman, Aubrey, 23, 26–27, 28
immigration, illegal, 282
income: distribution of, 184, 186–87, 282,
285; median income, 281–82; and
public opinion regarding Iraq War,
189–91
independents, political, 4, 92n17, 109,
161, 192, 307
India: democracy in, 223; economic conditions in, 229; nuclear cooperation
with U.S., 106, 244; relations with
China, 229; relations with Pakistan,
242, 243–44; relations with U.S., 106,
229, 242, 244
infant mortality rate, 283, 284
inflation, 179
Institute of Education Sciences, 172
integrative complexity (IC) score, 24–25,
38n4
Intelligence Reform and Terrorism Prevention Act, 209n5
International Committee of the Red Cross,
240
International Criminal Court (ICC),
235–36
Iran: and Afghanistan, 246–47; nuclear
program, 220, 229, 230–31, 246,
286–87; as part of axis of evil, 60,
247; policy regarding terrorism, 229;
relations with Egypt, 286; relations
with Iraq, 32, 36, 224, 229, 230, 285,

286; relations with Israel, 230, 286; relations with Saudi Arabia, 286; relations with United States, 60, 215, 216, 227, 229–31, 246–47, 249, 278, 286–87, 289

Iraq: Baathist regime, 32–33, 63–65, 230, 234; Basra, 226; border with Syria, 225; CIA intelligence regarding, 32–34, 38n7; Coalition Provisional Authority (CPA), 266, 304–5, 307; economic conditions in, 225; elections of 2005, 103–4; infrastructure of, 225; Israeli strike on Osirak reactor, 217; Kurds in, 33, 224, 263, 265; occupation of, 26–65, 35–37, 58, 63–65, 101, 105, 225, 227, 234, 237, 249, 253, 266, 267, 304–5, 306, 307; as part of axis of evil, 60; promotion of democracy in, 216, 222, 223, 225, 226, 230; al-Qaeda in, 226; reconstruction efforts in, 3, 105, 267; relations with Iran, 32, 36, 224, 229, 230, 285, 286; relations with Kuwait, 32, 33, 217, 219–20; Sadr City, 226; sectarian conflict in, 225, 237, 264–65; Shiites in, 224, 226, 230, 265, 285; status-of-forces agreement with U.S., 107; Sunnis in, 226, 265; Tal Afar, 305; UN sanctions on, 219, 224; withdrawal of U.S. troops from, 216, 226–27, 265, 289; WMD programs, 32–34, 35, 36, 56, 84, 97, 217, 224, 234, 237, 304–5. *See also* Hussein, Saddam

Iraq Liberation Act of 1998, 218

Iraq War, 11, 17, 25, 52, 77, 110, 131, 242, 252, 278; vs. Afghanistan War, 34–35, 252, 253, 263–64, 266, 273, 286; and Bush Doctrine, 215, 218–19; and Bush's psychological character, 22, 31; and Cheney, 32, 42, 54–55, 121, 123; vs. Civil War, 225, 268; Congressional authorization, 83, 101, 123, 266; debate leading up to, 218; decision to invade, 22, 27, 31–37, 38n5, 58, 59–61, 84, 118, 236–37, 243, 249; and Democrats, 33, 93n29,

97, 106; economic cost of, 106, 180, 224–25, 265, 268, 280; evaluation of, 13, 18n14, 21, 54–55, 157, 223–31, 234, 243, 246, 248, 265–67, 285–87, 304–6; and Feith, 32, 34, 54; vs. Gulf War, 222, 261, 263; vs. Korean War, 225; and moral competence, 72, 253–54; and National Security Strategy (NSS), 234–35, 237–38, 239; and NSC, 61; opposing forces in, 264; vs. Philippine insurrection of 1898–1902, 225; planning for, 14, 37; and Powell, 60–61, 84; public opinion regarding, 6, 89, 92nn19,20, 93n29, 102, 103–4, 129, 184, 186, 189–91, 192, 193n8, 265, 266–67, 278; relationship to Bush's popularity, 6, 9, 129, 170, 184, 186, 188–91, 192, 193n4, 216; and Rice, 60, 61, 123; and Rumsfeld, 32, 34, 36, 37, 54, 60, 241, 262; surge of June 2007, 88, 217, 225–26, 265, 266, 278, 305; tactical competence in, 217, 239–46, 253; U.S. casualties in, 92n19, 224, 225, 237, 265, 266; veterans of, 111; vs. Vietnam War, 13, 225, 252, 265; and Wolfowitz, 32, 54; vs. WWI, 225; vs. WWII, 225, 227

Irish Republican Army (IRA), 240, 248

Israel: during Gulf War, 224; relations with Iran, 230, 286; relations with Palestinians, 223, 224, 242–43, 289; relations with United States, 286; strike on Osirak reactor, 217

Italy: and Afghanistan War, 259

Jackson, Andrew: evaluation of, 17n5; opportunity level of, 10; personality of, 26; and political organization, 12

Jackson, David, 106

Jackson, Michael, 201

Jacobs, Lawrence R., 21, 83

Jacobson, Gary C., 4, 14, 79, 80, 81, 82, 84, 85, 86, 92n16, 92nn18,19, 189

Janis, Irving: on groupthink, 116

Japan: Pearl Harbor attack, 227; Taisho democracy, 222; after WWII, 221–22, 223, 227, 229

Jarrett, Jeffrey, 45
Jefferson, Thomas: evaluation of, 17n5; opportunity level of, 10; and political organization, 12
Jeffords, James, 30, 82, 91n14, 100, 141
Jervis, Robert, 22, 30, 31; *Perception and Misperception in International Politics*, 32
Jews, orthodox, 84
Job Creation and Worker Assistance Act of 2003, 83, 117
Jobs and Growth Tax Relief Reconciliation Act, 84–85
Johnson, Carrie, 126
Johnson, Chalmers, 110
Johnson, Clay, 45
Johnson, David, 126
Johnson, Lori, 11, 16
Johnson, Lyndon: vs. George W. Bush, 125, 159, 167, 252, 276; civil rights policy, 276; domestic policy, 6, 7, 13, 117, 159, 160, 167, 276; education policy, 160, 167; Medicare, 276; opportunity level of, 9; and political organization, 12; relations with Congress, 7, 98, 99; Vietnam War, 6
Johnston, David, 239
Jones, Bryan, 208
Jones, Charles O., 9
Jones, Jeffrey M., 89
Jones, Seth G., 248
J. P. Morgan Chase: and Bear Stearns, 181; and Washington Mutual, 182
Judicature, 152n
judicial appointments, 16, 101, 125, 136, 137–46, 278; Alito nomination, 104, 142–43, 144, 145, 152; Miers nomination, 28, 79, 104, 105, 142, 145, 146; moral competence regarding, 145–46; political competence regarding, 140–43; Republican vs. Democratic appointees in appellate circuits, 144; Roberts nomination, 104, 142; role of American Bar Association (ABA) in, 138–39; role of Federalist Society in, 139; role of Judicial Selection Committee (JSC) in, 137–38;

strategic competence regarding, 143–44; tactical competence regarding, 137–43
just war theory, 217, 228

Kahlenberg, Richard, 168
Kane, Paul, 106
Karzai, Hamid, 247, 266
Kassop, Nancy, 125
Katrina. *See* Hurricane Katrina
Kaufman, Robert G., 11, 13, 17, 17n4
Kavanaugh, Brett, 137–38, 140
Kay Commission, 224
Keegan, John, 225
Keller, William, 91n10
Kengor, Paul, 218
Kennedy, Anthony, 152
Kennedy, Edward, 30, 109, 122, 159
Kennedy, John F.: Bay of Pigs operation, 14; vs. George W. Bush, 125, 191; Cuban Missile Crisis, 14; economic policy, 191; foreign policy, 14, 254; military policy of, 254; tactical competence of, 14
Kernell, Samuel, 8
Kerry, John, 38n6, 85, 102, 167
Kettl, Donald F., 4, 34, 203, 206, 208
Khademian, Anne M., 14, 16, 201, 206, 208, 209n6, 307
Khalilzad, Zalmay, 63
Khan, A. Q.: nuclear smuggling ring of, 226
Khmer Rouge, 248
King, Anthony, 17n8
Kingdon, John W.: on focusing events, 99
Kirkpatrick, David, 138
Klein, Joe, 81
Klein, Joel, 169
Korb, Lawrence J., 11, 13, 17, 238
Korean War, 216–17, 219, 225, 227, 252, 275
Kosovo War, 220, 258, 260, 263
Kramer, Gerald H., 188
Kress, Sandy, 30
Kristof, Nicholas, 79
Kumar, Martha Joynt, 45, 129
Kuo, David J., 130, 303

national security policy; September
11th attacks
Warren, Rick, 90
Warshaw, Shirley Anne, 14, 15, 117, 299,
308, 309
Washington, George: vs. George W.
Bush, 294–95, 309; evaluation of, 3,
17nn1,5, 18n12, 294–95; policy to-
ward British prisoners, 62
Washington Mutual, 182
Washington Post, 123, 196
Waxman, Henry, 105
Wayne, Stephen J., 117
weapons of mass destruction (WMD): and
Bush Doctrine, 216, 219; and NSS of
2002, 244–46
Weart, Spencer, 221
Webber, Melvin M., 206
Weber, Edward, 206
Wehner, Peter, 43, 303
Weinberger, Caspar, 257–58, 263, 266,
268–69
Weisberg, Jacob, 22, 25, 27, 28, 31, 38n5;
The Bush Tragedy, 26
Weiss, Juleanna Glover, 45
Welch, William, 196
Wells Fargo: and Wachovia, 182
West, Bing, 226
West, Martin R., 170
White House staff, 115–32, 284; Budget
Review Board, 124; and Cheney, 42,
43, 46–49, 52–53, 54, 56, 123–25,
132n5; chief of staff's role, 117, 119,
120, 123; communications strategy,
115, 118, 128–30; Counsel's Office,
123, 124, 125–26, 137–38, 140;
decision-making processes, 115–16,
118–21, 130–31; Domestic Policy
Council, 52, 119–20, 121; email of,
86, 105; and full transparency, 46–49;
Homeland Security Council (HSC),
120, 122, 132n2; as Mayberry Machiavellis, 130, 295–304, 309, 310;
and multiple advocacy, 115–16; Office
of Faith-Based and Community Initiatives (OFBCI), 53, 122, 295, 303,
308, 309; Office of Homeland Secu-

rity (OHS), 122, 132nn2,3, 203; Office of Public Liaison, 129; Office of
Strategic Initiatives, 129; organization
of, 119–21; and permanent campaign,
118, 128, 132n8; policy development,
monitoring and implementation, 115,
117–18, 121–28; and political appointees, 126–28; and polling operations,
118; relationship to cabinet officers,
62; and relations with interest groups,
118; and war on terror, 120–21. See
also National Economic Council;
National Security Council; Office of
Management and Budget
Wildavsky, Aaron, 5, 17n8
Wilkerson, Lawrence, 47, 66–67
Williams, Armstrong, 87
Wilson, Joseph, 84
Wilson, Woodrow: vs. George W. Bush,
25, 216; evaluation of, 17n5; foreign
policy, 13, 221; integrative complex-
ity (IC) score of, 25; public appear-
ances by, 8
Winik, Jay, 25, 32
Winston, David, 161
Wise, Charles, 197, 202–3
Witt, James Lee, 207, 209n6
Wolff, Candida, 47, 106
Wolfowitz, Paul, 44, 46; and Iraq war, 32,
54, 237
Woodward, Bob, 27, 35, 60, 61, 237,
305–6; Bush at War, 305; Plan of At-
tack, 305; State of Denial, 305; The
War Within, 305
World Trade Organization (WTO), 282
World War I, 32, 221, 225
World War II, 221, 225, 227
Wright, Robin, 239
Wuertz, David, 204

Yoo, John, 107
Young, James Sterling, 12, 18n12
Youngman, Henny, 276, 290n2

Zakaria, Fareed, 223, 225
Zeller, Shawn, 102, 105, 112n2
Zuk, Gary, 139